Introduction to
Flight Test Engineering
Volume I

Third Edition

Don Ward

Thomas Strganac

Rob Niewoehner

KENDALL/HUNT PUBLISHING COMPANY
4050 Westmark Drive   Dubuque, Iowa 52002

CONTENTS

Contents

List of Figures

Chapter 4

Chapter 5

Chapter 9 (continued)

List of Tables

Symbols and Abbreviations

Chapter 1

AGARD	Advisory Group for Aerospace Research & Development (now RTA)
CD	Concept Definition
CDD	Capabilities Development Document
COI	Critical Operational Issues
CPD	Capabilities Production Document
CTP	Critical Technical Parameters
DAB	Defense Acquisition Board
DIA	Defense Intelligence Agency
DoD	Department of Defense
DT&E	Developmental Test and Evaluation
FOT&E	Follow-on Operational Test and Evaluation
ICD	Initial Capabilities Document
IOT&E	Initial Operational Test and Evaluation
IPT	Integrated Product Team
IT	Information Technology
JCIDS	Joint Capability Integration and Development System
JROCS	Joint Requirements Oversight Council
LFOT&E	Live Fire Operational Test and Evaluation
LRIP	Low Rate Initial Production
MDA	Milestone Decision Authority
MS X	Milestone X (A, B, or C)
NASA	National Aeronautics and Space Administration
OT&E	Operational Test and Evaluation
PM	Program Manager
RAC	Risk Assessment Code
SAE	Society of Automotive Engineers
T&E	Test and Evaluation
TEMP	Test and Evaluation Master Plan
UAV	Unmanned Aerial Vehicle
USD	Undersecretary of Defense

Chapter 2 (only those symbols not previously introduced are listed)

a	speed of sound	fps
a_0	standard day sea level speed of sound	fps
C	volume of instrument chamber	ft^3
C_L	lift coefficient	none
d	internal diameter of tubing or distance along the speed course line	ft
D	diameter of pitot-static tube	ft
g	gravitational acceleration	ft/sec^2
g_0	gravitational acceleration in ideal atmosphere	ft/sec^2
h	geopotential altitude	ft
h_a	absolute altitude	ft

Chapter 2 (continued)

h_a	absolute altitude	ft
h_c or h_{cal}	calibrated altitude	ft
$h_{cal_{altimeter}}$	calibrated altitude measured at the altimeter	ft
$h_{cal_{eyepiece}}$	calibrated altitude measured at the eyepiece	ft
$h_{cal_{ramp}}$	calibrated altitude measured on the parking ramp	ft
$h_{cal_{pacer}}$	calibrated altitude of the pacer aircraft	ft
h_{cal_t}	test day calibrated altitude	ft
h_g	geometric altitude	ft
h_i	geopotential altitude at the base of the i th layer or indicated altitude read from the altimeter	ft
$h_{i_{test}}$	indicated nominal altitude for the test point	ft
h_{ic}	instrument corrected altitude	ft
h_{ic_t}	test day instrument corrected altitude	ft
h_p	pressure altitude	ft
h_ρ	density altitude	ft
k_i	temperature lapse rate in the base of the i th layer	°R/ft
K	temperature recovery factor	none
L	length of tubing	ft
m	mass	slugs
M	Mach number	none
M_∞	freestream Mach number	none
n	load factor	none
p	pressure	psf
p_i	standard day pressure at the base of the ith layer	psf
p_s	sensed pressure	psf
p_T	total pressure	psf
p_0	standard day sea level pressure of the atmosphere	psf
p_∞	freestream static pressure	psf
p_{T_∞}	freestream total pressure	psf
q or $\bar{q}$	dynamic pressure	psf
q_{ic}	instrument corrected dynamic pressure	psf
q_{ic_t}	test day instrument corrected dynamic pressure	psf
q_c	sensed dynamic pressure	psf
R	universal gas constant	ft²/sec²°R
R_E	radius of the earth	ft
t_i	indicated temperature	°F
t_1	time at beginning of speed course run	sec
t_2	time at end of speed course run	sec
T	temperature	°R
T_i	temperature at the base of the ith layer or indicated temperature	°R
T_{ic}	instrument corrected temperature	°R
T_{std}	standard day temperature	°R
T_T	total temperature	°R

Chapter 2 (continued)

T_∞	freestream temperature	°R
V	volume	ft³
V or V_∞	true airspeed	knots or fps
V_{avg}	average true airspeed for speed course	knots or fps
V_{cal}	calibrated airspeed	knots or fps
$V_{cal_{pacer}}$	calibrated airspeed for the pacer aircraft	knots or fps
V_e	equivalent airspeed	knots or fps
V_g	ground speed	knots or fps
V_i	indicated airspeed	knots or fps
$V_{i_{test}}$	indicated nominal airspeed for the test point	knots or fps
V_{ic}	instrument corrected airspeed	knots or fps
V_{ic_t}	test day instrument corrected airspeed	knots or fps
x	distance from eyepiece to plane of sighting grid	in
	or a variable	various
y	height of airplane as measured on the sighting grid	in
	or a variable	various
z	distance from eyepiece to plane of tower flyby line	ft
Δh	height above the plane of the eyepiece	ft
$\Delta h_{cal_{altimeter}}$	calibrated altitude error measured at the altimeter	ft
$\Delta h_{cal_{eyepiece}}$	calibrated altitude error measured at the eyepiece	ft
$\Delta h_{cal_{pacer}}$	calibrated altitude error for the pacer aircraft	ft
Δh_{ic}	altimeter instrument error correction	ft
$\Delta h_{ic_{pacer}}$	altimeter instrument error correction for the pacer aircraft	ft
Δh_{ic_t}	test day altimeter instrument error correction	ft
$\Delta h_{ic_{test}}$	altimeter instrument error correction for the nominal test point	ft
Δh_{pc}	altimeter static position error correction	ft
$\Delta h_{pc_{pacer}}$	altimeter static position error correction for the pacer aircraft	ft
Δh_{pc_t}	test day altimeter static position error correction	ft
Δp_p	static position error	psf
ΔT_{ic}	temperature instrument error correction	knots or fps
ΔV_c	compressibility correction	knots or fps
ΔV_{ic}	airspeed instrument error correction	knots or fps
$\Delta V_{ic_{pacer}}$	airspeed instrument error correction for the pacer aircraft	knots or fps
$\Delta V_{i_{test}}$	instrument corrected airspeed for the nominal test point	knots or fps
ΔV_{pc}	airspeed static position error correction	knots or fps
$\Delta V_{pc_{pacer}}$	airspeed static position error correction for the pacer aircraft	knots or fps
α	angle of attack	°
γ	ideal ratio of specific heats for air (1.4)	none
δ	pressure ratio	none
λ	lag constant	psf²/sec
μ	viscosity	slugs/ft-sec

Chapter 2 (continued)

μ_0	standard day sea level viscosity	slugs/ft-sec
ρ	density of the atmosphere	slugs/ft^3
ρ_i	standard day density at the base of the ith layer	slugs/ft^3
ρ_{std}	standard day density	slugs/ft^3
$\rho_{tropopause}$	standard day density at the tropopause	slugs/ft^3
ρ_T	total density	slugs/ft^3
ρ_0	standard day sea level density of the atmosphere	slugs/ft^3
σ	density ratio	none
σ_{std}	standard day density ratio	none
$\sigma_{tropopause}$	standard day density ratio at the tropopause	none
θ	temperature ratio	none
θ_t	test day temperature ratio	none

Abbreviations and acronyms

AAR	Attitude Angle Recorder
AFFTC	Air Force Flight Test Center
Alt	Altimeter
APR	Absolute Pressure Recorder
ARDC	Air Research and Development Command
ASI	Airspeed Indicator
DPI	Differential Pressure Instrument
FAA	Federal Aviation Administration
GPS	Global Positioning System
GS	Ground Speed
ICAN	International Commission of Air Navigation
ICAO	International Civil Aviation Organization
INS	Inertial Navigation System
IPR	Impact Pressure Recorder
IT	Indicating Thermometer
LFS	Level Flight Speed
MSL	Mean Sea Level
NACA	National Advisory Committee for Aeronautics
RA	Recording Accelerometer
RT	Recording Thermometer
RPV	Remotely Piloted Vehicle
TAS	True Air Speed

Chapter 3 (only those symbols not previously introduced are listed)

AF	acceleration factor	none
b	span	ft
C_1	constant for induced drag expression	lbs
D	drag or	lbs
	engine characteristic length	ft
D_{std}	standard day drag	lbs
D_t	test day drag	lbs

Chapter 3 (continued)

E	total energy (kinetic plus potential)	ft-lbs
e	span efficiency factor	none
$\dot{h}$	time rate of change of pressure altitude	fps
k	ratio of specific heats	none
L	aerodynamic lift	lbs
M_{std}	standard day Mach number	none
M_t	test day Mach number	none
N	engine speed	rpm
n_{std}	standard day/weight load factor	none
n_t	test day/weight load factor	none
V_V	vertical component of true airspeed	knots, mph, or fps
P_s	specific excess power	fps
P_{s_t}	test day specific excess power	fps
R_c	radius of curvature	ft
R/C	rate of climb	fpm or fps
T_n	net thrust	lbs
$T_{n_{std}}$	standard day net thrust	lbs
T_{n_t}	test day net thrust	lbs
T_{∞_i}	indicated freestream temperature	°R
$T_{\infty_{ic}}$	instrument corrected freestream temperature	°R
$T_{\infty_{std}}$	standard day freestream temperature	°R
T_{∞_t}	test day freestream temperature	°R
THP_A	thrust horsepower available	hp
$THP_{A_{std}}$	standard day thrust horsepower available	hp
THP_{A_t}	test day thrust horsepower available	hp
THP_R	thrust horsepower required	hp
$THP_{R_{std}}$	standard day thrust horsepower required	hp
THP_{R_t}	test day thrust horsepower required	hp
V_H	horizontal component of true airspeed	knots, mph, or fps
V_{s_0}	power off stall speed, landing configuration	knots, mph, or fps
V_{s_1}	power off stall speed, clean configuration	knots, mph, or fps
V_V	vertical component of true airspeed	knots, mph, or fps
V_{W_i}	wind velocity at point i	knots, mph, or fps
V_{∞_t}	test day true airspeed	knots, mph, or fps
$\dot{V}_\infty$ or $\dot{V}$	time rate of change of true airspeed	fps/sec
W	weight	lbs
W_{avg}	average weight	lbs
W_{std}	standard (nominal) weight	lbs
W_t	test day weight	lbs
$h_{corrected}$	corrected (for weight change) indicated altitude	ft
h_e	energy height or specific energy height	ft
$\dot{h}_e$	time rate of change of energy height ($= P_s$)	fps/sec
$\dot{w}_f$	fuel flow rate	lbs/hr

Chapter 3 (continued)

ΔD_i	increment of induced drag	lbs
Δh	increment of altitude	ft
Δh_a	increment of absolute altitude	ft
Δh_e	increment of energy height or specific energy height	ft
Δh_i	increment of indicated altitude	ft
$\Delta P_{s_{wt}}$	specific excess power weight correction (induced drag)	fps
Δp_∞	increment of freestream static pressure	psf
ΔT_n	increment of net thrust	lbs
Δt	increment of time	sec
ΔW	increment of weight	lbs
ΔV_∞	increment of true airspeed	knots, mph, or fps
$\Delta \gamma$	increment of flight-path angle	°
δ_t	test day pressure ratio	none
δ_{std}	standard day pressure ratio	none
γ	flight-path angle	°
Φ_T	angle between the thrust line and the fuselage reference line	°
ρ_t	test day density	slugs/ft³

Chapter 4 (only those symbols not previously introduced are listed)

A or A_1	constant for first term in power equation	hp-ft-sec/lb
a	parameter for solving Buckingham Pi equations	none
B or B_1	constant for second term in power equation	hp-sec/lb-ft³
	or number of blades for a propeller	none
BHP_r	brake horsepower required	hp
BHP_t	test day brake horsepower available	hp
BHP_{std}	standard day brake horsepower available	hp
b	parameter for solving Buckingham Pi equations	none
C_D	drag coefficient	none
C_{D_i}	induced drag coefficient	none
C_{D_p}	parasite drag coefficient	none
C_{L_i}	propeller integrated design lift coefficient	none
C_m	aircraft pitching moment coefficient	none
C_P	power coefficient	none
C_Q	torque coefficient	none
C_{D_p}	parasite drag coefficient	none
c	propeller local chord	ft
	or parameter for solving Buckingham Pi equations	none
	or specific fuel consumption (SFC)	lbs/hr-hp
c_{ℓ_d}	blade section design lift coefficient	none
c_t	thrust specific fuel consumption (TSFC)	lbs/hr-lb
D	drag	lbs
	or propeller diameter	ft
E	endurance	hours

Chapter 4 (continued)

E_{max}	maximum endurance	hours
J	propeller advance ratio	none
$K_{n_{ic}}$	propeller torque meter scale factor	none
K_V	ratio of equivalent airspeed to equivalent airspeed for minimum power	none
L	fundamental unit for length	ft
MAP_t	test day manifold pressure	in Hg
MAP_{std}	standard day manifold pressure	in Hg
m	fundamental unit for mass (slugs = lb-sec^2/ft)	slugs
n	propeller rotational rate	revolutions/sec
	or number of fundamental variables	none
PIW	generalized power	none
p	number of fundamental units	none
Q	propeller torque	ft-lbs
Q_{ic}	instrument corrected propeller torque meter reading	ft-lbs
R	propeller radius	ft
R	range	nm
r	radius to a given airfoil section on a propeller	ft
r_h	propeller hub radius	ft
SR	solidity ratio	none
T_j	temperature in the j th engine component	°R
T_t	test day temperature	°R
t	fundamental unit for time	sec
$V_{E_{max}}$	true airspeed for maximum endurance	knots, mph, or fps
$V_{e_{mp}}$	equivalent airspeed for minimum power	knots, mph, or fps
VIW	generalized true airspeed	none
W_E	aircraft weight at the end of a cruise segment	lbs
W_0	aircraft weight at the beginning of a cruise segment	lbs
$\dot{w}_a$	weight flow rate of air through an engine	lbs/sec
X	net thrust from the jet exhaust for a turboprop	lbs
η_b	burner efficiency	none
η_c	compressor efficiency	none
η_i	inlet efficiency	none
η_n	propeller efficiency	none
η_P	propeller efficiency	none
η_t	turbine efficiency	none
π_i	i th nondimensional grouping from Buckingham Pi theorem	none

Chapter 5 (only those symbols not previously introduced are listed)

a	acceleration during takeoff or landing	ft/sec^2
$\bar{a}$	average acceleration during takeoff or landing	ft/sec^2
CFL	critical field length	ft
$C_{L_{max}}$	maximum lift coefficient	none

Chapter 5 (continued)

$C_{L_{tran}}$	lift coefficient during transition segment	none
BFL	balanced field length	ft
F	net accelerating force during takeoff roll	lbs
F_f	frictional force during takeoff roll	lbs
h_{tran}	vertical height at end of takeoff transition	ft
L_L	lift during landing	lbs
m	mass of the airplane of object studied	slugs
$\bar{P}_V$	average excess power during takeoff	hp
RA	runway available (runway length less allowance for lineup)	ft
R_c	radius of curvature for takeoff or landing trajectory	ft
s_a	horizontal distance to clear an obstacle of specified height (after liftoff for takeoff or before touchdown for landing)	ft
$s_{a_{se}}$	horizontal distance to clear an obstacle of specified height (during a single engine takeoff)	ft
s_{CL}	horizontal distance during acceleration to climb speed	ft
s_{DEC}	horizontal distance covered between engine failure and initiation of braking during an aborted takeoff	ft
s_{EF}	horizontal distance from brake release to engine failure	ft
s_{FA}	horizontal distance from obstacle clearance to landing flare	ft
s_G	horizontal distance from brake release to liftoff	ft
s_{G_L}	horizontal distance from touchdown to complete stop	ft
s_{G_2}	horizontal distance covered during takeoff rotation	ft
s_{LO}	horizontal distance from brake release to liftoff	ft
$s_{LO_{se}}$	horizontal distance from engine failure to liftoff	ft
s_{L_2}	horizontal distance covered during landing rotation	ft
s_{REF}	horizontal distance from brake release to attaining V_{REF}	ft
s_{STOP}	horizontal stopping distance after application of brakes	ft
s_{tran}	horizontal distance covered during takeoff (or landing) transition	ft
s_{CL}	horizontal distance during acceleration to climb speed	ft
T	thrust	lbs
T_L	thrust during landing	lbs
$\bar{T}_V$	average excess thrust during takeoff	lbs
t_r	time for rotation during takeoff or landing	sec
$\bar{V}$	true airspeed where average excess thrust occurs	fps
V_B	true airspeed at initiation of braking during an aborted takeoff	fps
V_{CEF} or V_1	critical engine failure speed	fps
V_{CL}	true airspeed during initial climb segment of takeoff	fps
V_{LO}	true airspeed at liftoff	fps
V_{LOF}	true airspeed at liftoff based on $1.2V_s$	fps
V_{REF}	refusal speed	fps
$V_{m_{ca}}$	air minimum control speed	fps
$V_{m_{cg}}$	ground minimum control speed	fps
V_{SSE}	safe single engine speed	fps
V_s	stall speed	fps

Chapter 5 (continued)

V_{TD}	touchdown speed	fps
V_{TOS}	takeoff safety speed	fps
V_W	wind speed during takeoff or landing	fps
$V_{2_{min}}$	minimum takeoff speed for FAR Part 25	fps
W_L	weight of aircraft during landing	fps
ΔC_L	increment of lift coefficient	none
Δn	increment of load factor	none
Φ	slope of runway	°
μ	coefficient of friction	none
μ_b	coefficient of friction for braking during landing roll	none
θ_{CL}	change in pitch angle during takeoff transition	°

Chapter 6 (only those symbols not previously introduced are listed)

A	constant coefficient in stick force equation	lbs
a	lever arm distance in gearing mechanism for control stick	ft
a_j	lift curve slope produced by deflection of the jth control surface	per ° or radian
a_e	lift curve slope produced by elevator deflection	per ° or radian
B	constant coefficient in stick force equation	lbs/psf
b	lever arm distance in gearing mechanism for control stick	ft
C_{h_e}	elevator hinge moment coefficient	none
C_{h_0}	hinge moment coefficient at zero lift and zero control surface deflection	none
$C_{h_{\alpha_j}}$	rate of change of hinge moment coefficient for the jth control surface with changes in local angle of attack	per ° or radian
$C_{h_{\delta_e}}$	rate of change of hinge moment coefficient with elevator deflection	per °
$C_{h_{\delta_j}}$	rate of change of hinge moment coefficient for the jth control surface with changes in surface deflection	per °
$C_{h_{\delta_{tab}}}$	rate of change of hinge moment coefficient for the jth control surface with changes in surface tab deflection	per °
C_L'	lift coefficient with the elevator free to float	none
C_{L_j}	trim lift coefficient produced by the jth control surface	none
$C_{L_{trim}}$	trim lift coefficient for the airplane	none
C_{L_α}	lift curve slope for the airplane	per radian
C_{L_α}'	lift curve slope for the airplane with elevator floating	per radian
$C_{L_{\alpha_j}}$	lift curve slope produced by the jth control surface	per radian
$C_{L_{\alpha_t}}$	lift curve slope for the horizontal tail	per radian
$C_{L_{\alpha_{wb}}}$	lift curve slope for the wing-body	per radian
$C_{L_{\delta_e}}$	change in lift coefficient with elevator deflection	per ° or radian
$C_{L_{\delta_j}}$	change in lift coefficient with deflection of the jth control surface	per ° or radian
C_{m_0}	zero lift pitching moment coefficient about cg	none

Chapter 6 (continued)

C_{m_0}' zero lift pitching moment coefficient about cg with the elevator free to float.. none

$C_{m_{0_{wb}}}$ zero lift pitching moment coefficient for the wing-body alone .. none

C_{m_α} change in pitching moment coefficient with change in α .. per radian

C_{m_α}' change in pitching moment coefficient with change in α with the elevator free to float... per radian

$C_{m_{\delta_e}}$ change in pitching moment coefficient with elevator deflection (elevator effectiveness) .... per ° or radian

c lever arm distance in gearing mechanism for control stick................ ft

$\bar{c}$ mean aerodynamic chord... ft or inches

c_e elevator chord .... ft

cg center of gravity.. acronym

d lever arm distance in gearing mechanism for control stick............... ft

e lever arm distance in gearing mechanism for control stick............... ft

F free elevator factor.. none

F_s stick force ....lbs

G gearing ratio (or gain) .... °/inch

H_e elevator hinge moment...ft-lbs

i_t horizontal tail incidence angle... ° or radians

L net aerodynamic rolling moment about the x axis ....ft-lbs

l_s control stick lever arm in gearing expression .... ft

l_t distance from aircraft cg to horizontal tail aerodynamic center....... ft

M net aerodynamic pitching moment about the y axis ....ft-lbs

N net aerodynamic yawing moment about the z axis.....................ft-lbs

$P \ or \ p$ x component of angular velocity...............................°/sec or rad/sec

$Q \ or \ q$ y component of angular velocity...............................°/sec or rad/sec

$\bar{q}$ dynamic pressure ....psf

$R \ or \ r$ z component of angular velocity ....°/sec or rad/sec

S wing planform area (reference area)..ft^2

SM stick-fixed static margin.. none

SM_{free} stick-free static margin... none

S_e elevator surface area...ft^2

S_t horizontal tail planform area ....ft^2

s control stick travel .... in

U x component of linear velocity of the aircraft center of gravity .....fps

V y component of linear velocity of the aircraft center of gravity .....fps

V_H horizontal tail volume coefficient.. none

V_H' horizontal tail volume coefficient with elevator free to float...... none

V_{H_n} horizontal tail volume coefficient with the cg located at the neutral point.. none

V_{H_n}' horizontal tail volume coefficient with the cg located at the neutral point with the elevator free to float .... none

$V_{V_{corrected}}$ vertical velocity corrected for engine thrust................................ none

Chapter 6 (continued)

W	z component of linear velocity of the aircraft center of gravity......fps	
W_j	weight of the jth control surface...lbs	
X	x component of the net aerodynamic force...lbs	
Y	y component of the net aerodynamic force...lbs	
Z	z component of the net aerodynamic force...lbs	
$x_{ac_{wb}}$	aerodynamic center of the wing-body..............................ft or inches	
x_{cg}	location of the center of gravity along the x axis ....ft or inches	
x_j	location of the jth control surface cg relative to the hinge line..ft or inches	
x_{np}	neutral point...ft or inches	
$x_{np}{'}$	neutral point with the elevator free to float.................ft or inches	
$x_{inertial}$	inertial x axis..ft or inches	
$y_{inertial}$	inertial y axis..ft or inches	
$z_{inertial}$	inertial z axis..ft or inches	
ΔC_L	change in lift coefficient..none	
ΔC_m	change in pitching moment coefficient ....none	
α'	aircraft angle of attack with the elevator free to float ...... ° or radians	
α_{trim}	trim angle of attack.. ° or radians	
α_{wb}	angle of attack of the wing-body.................................. ° or radians	
α_j	local angle of attack at the jth control surface .... ° or radians	
β	angle of sideslip .... ° or radians	
δ_a	aileron deflection .... °	
$\delta_{a_{left}}$	left aileron deflection.. °	
$\delta_{a_{right}}$	right aileron deflection.. °	
δ_e	elevator deflection .... °	
$\delta_{e_{trim}}$	elevator angle to trim... °	
δ_j	control surface deflection of the jth control surface .... °	
$\delta_{j_{free}}$	free floating angle of the jth control surface............................... °	
δ_r	rudder deflection .... °	
δ_{tab}	control surface tab deflection.. °	
$\delta_{tab_{trim}}$	control surface tab deflection to trim.. °	
γ_{PA}	flight-path angle in the power approach flight condition .... °	
ε	downwash angle.. °	
ε_0	downwash angle when wing-body lift is zero .... °	
Φ	Euler roll angle... °	
$\dot{\Phi}$	Euler roll rate...°/sec	
Θ	Euler pitch angle .... °	
$\dot{\Theta}$	Euler pitch rate..°/sec	
ω	angular velocity ....°/sec or rad/sec	
Ψ	Euler yaw angle .... °	
$\dot{\Psi}$	Euler yaw rate...°/sec	

Chapter 7 (only those symbols not previously introduced are listed)

b_e	span of the elevator	ft
C_{m_q}	pitch damping derivative	none
$C_{m_{q_t}}$	tail contribution to pitch damping derivative	none
C_N	normal force coefficient	none
K	correction coefficient accounting for wing-body contributions to the pitch damping derivative	none
L_{trim}	aircraft lift in the trim or wings-level equilibrium state	lbs
MM	stick-fixed maneuver margin	none
n_z	normal acceleration of the aircraft cg	none
n_0	load factor in equilibrium (trimmed) flight	none
q_0	body axis pitch rate in equilibrium (trimmed) flight	°/sec
$\bar{q}_t$	dynamic pressure at the horizontal tail	psf
x_{mp}	maneuver point	ft or inches
x_{mp}'	maneuver point with the elevator free to float	ft or inches
ΔC_{h_e}	change in elevator hinge moment coefficient	none
ΔF_s	change in stick force	lbs
Δq	change in pitch rate	rad/sec
$\Delta \alpha$	change in aircraft angle of attack	°
$\Delta \alpha_t$	change in angle of attack at the horizontal tail	°
$\Delta \alpha_w$	change in angle of attack at the wing	°
$\Delta \delta_e$	change in elevator deflection	°
α_{pu}	aircraft angle of attack during a wings-level pull-up	°
μ	relative mass parameter	none
θ	change in local angle of attack at the horizontal tail during a wings-level pull-up	°
τ	ratio of elevator lift effectiveness to stabilizer lift effectiveness	none
Ω	aircraft inertial turn rate	°/sec

Chapter 8 (only those symbols not previously introduced are listed)

a_r	side force curve slope produced by rudder deflection	per radian
$C_{h_{\alpha_F}}$	change in hinge moment due to change in local angle of attack	none
$C_{h_{\delta_r}}$	change in hinge moment due to rudder deflection	per °
$C_{L_{\alpha_a}}$	lift curve slope with ailerons deflected	per ° or radian
C_L	rolling moment coefficient	none
C_{L_β}	dihedral effect	none
C_{L_p}	roll damping derivative	none
C_{L_r}	rolling moment change due to yaw rate	none
$C_{L_{\delta_a}}$	aileron control effectiveness	per °
$C_{L_{\delta_r}}$	change in rolling moment coefficient due to rudder deflection	per °

Chapter 8 (continued)

$C_{L\delta_r}$ change in rolling moment coefficient due to rudder deflection .... per °

C_n yawing moment coefficient .... none

C_n yawing moment coefficient .... none

C_{np} change in yawing moment coefficient due to roll rate .... none

C_{nr} yaw damping derivative .... none

$C_{n\beta}$ directional (or weathercock) stability .... none

$C_{n\beta fixed}$ directional (or weathercock) stability with the rudder fixed ...... none

$C_{n\delta_a}$ adverse yaw .... per °

$C_{n\delta_r}$ rudder control effectiveness .... per °

C_Y side force coefficient .... none

C_{Y_F} vertical tail contribution to side force coefficient .... none

C_{Y_F}' vertical tail contribution to side force coefficient (rudder free) .... none

$C_{Y\beta}$ change side force coefficient due to sideslip .... none

$C_{Y\delta_a}$ side force coefficient due to aileron deflection .... per °

$C_{Y\delta_r}$ side force coefficient due to rudder deflection .... per °

$C_{Y\alpha_F}$ side force coefficient due to local angle of attack change .... per °

F_a aileron force .... lbs

1 distance from aircraft centerline to tip parachute force line .... ft

1_V distance from aircraft cg to vertical tail aerodynamic center .... ft

P indirect measurement of tip parachute force .... lbs

S_a aileron surface area .... ft²

T tip parachute force .... lbs

V_A design maneuver speed .... fps or mph or knots

V_F local true airspeed at the vertical tail (fin) .... fps

V_{FE} maximum flap extended speed .... fps or mph or knots

V_{LE} maximum landing gear extended speed .... fps or mph or knots

$V_{FC/MC}$ maximum speed for stability characteristics .... fps or mph or knots

Y_F side force contribution of the vertical tail (fin) .... lbs

y distance from aircraft centerline to wing center of pressure .... ft

z_V distance from aircraft x body axis to vertical tail center of pressure .... ft

ΔC_n increment of yawing moment coefficient .... none

$\Delta C_{n\beta}$ increment of directional (or weathercock) stability .... none

ΔN increment of yawing moment .... ft-lbs

ΔY_r increment of side force due to rudder deflection .... lbs

$\Delta \delta_a$ change in aileron deflection .... °

$\Delta \delta_r$ change in rudder deflection .... °

α_F angle of attack of the vertical tail .... °

$\delta_{r_{free}}$ rudder angle free to float .... °

σ sidewash angle .... °

List of Symbols

Chapter 9 (only those symbols not previously introduced are listed)

A	state matrix	various
B	control matrix	various
A_i	state matrix (not normalized)	various
B_i	control matrix (not normalized)	various
C_i	normalizing matrix (inverse is used to normalize A_i and B_i)	various
a_i	general coefficients for second order differential equation	various
C_{L0}	trim lift coefficient	none
C_{X_u}	nondimensional stability derivative	none
$C_{X_\square}$	nondimensional stability derivative	none
$C_{X_{\square e}}$	nondimensional control derivative	none
C_{Z_u}	nondimensional stability derivative	none
C_{Z_α}	nondimensional stability derivative	none
$C_{Z_{\dot\alpha}}$	nondimensional stability derivative	none
$C_{Z_{\delta e}}$	nondimensional control derivative	none
C_{m_u}	nondimensional stability derivative	none
C_{m_α}	nondimensional stability derivative	none
$C_{m_{\dot\alpha}}$	nondimensional stability derivative	none
$C_{m_{\delta e}}$	nondimensional control derivative	none
c	damping coefficient	lbs/fps
D	derivative operator with respect to $\hat{t}$	none
I_x	mass moment of inertia about x stability axis	slug-ft^2
I_{xz}	mass product of inertia about x and z stability axes	slug-ft^2
I_y	mass moment of inertia about y stability axis	slug-ft^2
I_z	mass moment of inertia about z stability axis	slug-ft^2
i_A	nondimensional mass moment of inertia about x stability axis	none
i_B	nondimensional mass moment of inertia about y stability axis	none
i_C	nondimensional mass moment of inertia about z stability axis	none
i_E	nondimensional product of inertia about x and z stability axes	none
K_{Dr}	Dutch roll mode residue	various
K_r	roll mode residue	various
K_s	spiral mode residue	various
k	spring constant	lbs/in
L_p	dimensional stability derivative	per sec
L_r	dimensional stability derivative	per sec
L_v	dimensional stability derivative	per ft-sec
$L_{\dot v}$	dimensional stability derivative	per ft
L_β	dimensional stability derivative	per rad-sec^2
L_{δ_a}	dimensional control derivative	per rad-sec^2
L_{δ_r}	dimensional control derivative	per rad-sec^2
l	characteristic length	ft
M_i	local maxima in response variable oscillation	various
M_q	dimensional stability derivative	per sec
M_u	dimensional stability derivative	per ft-sec

Chapter 9 (continued)

M_w	dimensional stability derivative	per ft-sec
$M_{\dot{w}}$	dimensional stability derivative	per ft
M_{δ_e}	dimensional control derivative	per rad-sec^2
M_i	local minima in response variable oscillation	various
N_p	dimensional stability derivative	per sec
N_r	dimensional stability derivative	per sec
N_v	dimensional stability derivative	per ft-sec
$N_{\dot{v}}$	dimensional stability derivative	per ft
N_β	dimensional stability derivative	per rad-sec^2
N_{δ_a}	dimensional control derivative	per rad-sec^2
N_{δ_r}	dimensional control derivative	per rad-sec^2
N_x^y	transfer function matrix (input y, output x)	none
P_0	angular velocity about the x stability axis in trim condition	rad/sec
p	perturbation in angular velocity about the x stability axis	rad/sec
p_0	initial peak value of roll rate response	°/sec or rad/sec
$\hat{p}$	nondimensional angular velocity about the x stability axis	rad/sec
$\dot{p}$	angular acceleration about the x stability axis	rad/sec^2
Q_0	angular velocity about the y stability axis in trim condition	rad/sec
q	perturbation in angular velocity about the y stability axis	rad/sec
$\hat{q}$	perturbation in angular velocity about the y stability axis	rad/sec
R_0	angular velocity about the x stability axis in trim condition	rad/sec
r	perturbation in angular velocity about the x stability axis	rad/sec
$\hat{r}$	perturbation in angular velocity about the x stability axis	rad/sec
s	Laplace operator	none
T	period of an oscillation	sec
t	time	sec
t^*	normalizing unit of time	sec
t_i	sample time points	sec
t_p	time-to-peak-amplitude	sec
t_r	rise time	sec
t_s	settling time	sec
t_2	time-to-double-amplitude	sec
$t_{1/2}$	time-to-half-amplitude	sec
$\hat{t}$	nondimensional time	none (airsecs)
U_0	x axis velocity component of aircraft cg at trim conditions	fps
u	linearized perturbation in x axis velocity of aircraft cg	fps
$\boldsymbol{u}$	control vector	various
v	linearized perturbation in y axis velocity of aircraft cg	fps
W_0	z axis velocity component of aircraft cg at trim conditions	fps
w	linearized perturbation in z axis velocity of aircraft cg	fps
X_q	dimensional stability derivative	ft per rad-sec
X_u	dimensional stability derivative	per sec
X_w	dimensional stability derivative	per sec

Chapter 9 (continued)

$X_{\dot{w}}$	dimensional stability derivative	ft per rad-sec
X_{δ_e}	dimensional control derivative	ft per rad-sec^2
x	state vector	various
Y_p	dimensional stability derivative	per rad
Y_r	dimensional stability derivative	per rad
Y_v	dimensional stability derivative	per sec
$Y_{\dot{v}}$	dimensional stability derivative	none
Y_β	dimensional stability derivative	ft per rad-sec^2
Y_{δ_a}	dimensional control derivative	per rad-sec
Y_{δ_r}	dimensional control derivative	per rad-sec
Z_q	dimensional stability derivative	ft per rad-sec
Z_u	dimensional stability derivative	per sec
Z_w	dimensional stability derivative	per sec
$Z_{\dot{w}}$	dimensional stability derivative	ft per rad-sec
Z_{δ_e}	dimensional control derivative	ft per rad-sec^2
Δx_i	increment in response variables	various
Δt_i	increment in time	sec
α	perturbation in angle of attack	°
β	perturbation in sideslip angle	°
Δ	characteristic matrix	various
δ_{a_0}	aileron deflection at the trim condition	°
δ_{e_0}	elevator deflection at the trim condition	°
δ_{r_0}	rudder deflection at the trim condition	°
ϕ	perturbation in bank angle or roll angle	°
λ	eigenvalue	various
λ_s	spiral mode eigenvalue	various
Θ_0	inertial pitch angle at trim conditions	°
θ	perturbation in inertial pitch angle	°
τ	time constant	sec
τ_{Dr}	Dutch roll mode time constant	sec
τ_r	roll mode time constant	sec
τ_s	spiral mode time constant	sec
ω_d	damped frequency	rad/sec
ω_n	undamped natural frequency	rad/sec
$\omega_{n_{Dr}}$	Dutch roll undamped natural frequency	rad/sec
$\omega_{n_{sp}}$	short period undamped natural frequency	rad/sec
ω_{n_p}	phugoid undamped natural frequency	rad/sec
ψ	perturbation in heading angle	°
ψ_{phase}	phase angle	° or rad
ζ	damping ratio	none
ζ_{Dr}	Dutch roll damping ratio	none
ζ_{sp}	short period damping ratio	none
ζ_p	phugoid damping ratio	none

The purpose of this book is to consolidate the fundamental principles used in classical performance and flying qualities flight testing of manned aircraft. It is intended for use as an introductory text for undergraduate students or as a self-teaching reference for an engineer newly engaged in flight tests. Worked examples are included in each chapter.

The first half of the book covers performance measurements. Chapter 1 is devoted to an overview of why flight tests are conducted and what the most important constraints are. Chapter 2 reviews the standard atmosphere and applies basic aerodynamic equations to the basic measurement system found in virtually every airplane, the pitot-static system. Techniques used to calibrate this system are described and illustrated. Chapter 3 reviews basic point performance equations and applies them to explain how to measure climb, descent, and turn performance. Both steady state and energy approximation expressions are used to lead into discussion of the sawtooth climb, the check climb, the level unaccelerated turn, and the level acceleration flight test methods. Chapter 4 briefly introduces propulsion systems, both for propeller-driven and jet-powered airplanes and summarizes useful relationships for determining range and endurance for such airplanes. Speed power flight tests commonly used to collect cruise performance data are introduced to close out this chapter. Chapter 5 rounds out the performance section of the book by outlining the equations used to estimate takeoff and landing performance and then describing measurements that must be taken to document appropriate measures of merit during these critical phases of flight.

The second half of the book deals with aircraft stability and control, concentrating on measurements that must be made to ascertain flying qualities. Chapter 6 covers the foundations of longitudinal static stability, concluding with a discussion of the flight test techniques often used to obtain such data. Chapter 7 does the same thing for maneuvering stability. Chapter 8 summarizes both the theoretical differences in the equations of motion and the flight test methods used to measure static lateral-directional stability. Chapter 9 is a concise summary of dynamic stability and control for both symmetric (longitudinal) motions and asymmetric (lateral-directional) ones. The importance of qualitative pilot ratings in describing aircraft flying qualities and their usefulness as a communications tool between the test pilot and the test engineer are stressed. The chapter concludes with a discussion of typical flight test techniques, including several practical ways of interpreting dynamic response data. Chapter 10 introduces post-stall flight tests, intending to interest the beginning flight test student in more advanced topics.

Gratitude is due to many people. First and foremost, for their unflagging support, I thank my family, especially my wife, Joyce. It is due to her patience with my early and late hours that the manuscript is finally finished. She also encouraged me throughout my twenty-seven years in the flight test profession, even though she undoubtedly often wondered why I was so obsessed. I thank her and dedicate this effort to her. All the students who have been exposed to my attempts to teach this subject at the United States Air Force Test Pilot School, at Texas A&M, at the University of Kansas, and at the United States Air Force Academy have contributed in no small way to this effort. Finally, thanks are due to all of the colleagues who reviewed these pages. Dr. Richard Howard of the Naval Postgraduate School deserves special mention for his contributions both as a PhD student who understood the practicality of the subject and as a peer who made insightful suggestions. The faculty of the Aerospace Engineering Department at Texas A&M University were wholly supportive, especially Dr. Walter Haisler, Dr. John Junkins, and Dr. Tom Pollock.

I hope this subject will provide as much pleasure and challenge to the reader as the writing of this book has brought to me.   Donald T. Ward
                                                                                                                        March 1993

Preface to the Second Edition

The second edition of **Introduction to Flight Test Engineering** has been expanded to include a new chapter (Chapter 10) outlining the background and techniques used to prepare for aeroelastic flight tests, a subject usually ignored in such an introductory volume. This addition is the major change in this edition. Of course, the other material has been slightly rearranged to accommodate this insertion and known errors in these other chapters have been corrected. Dr. Thomas W. Strganac, joins me in providing this new material. This new addition to the text is based largely on the teaching experience of both authors, notably on their short course, taught since 1991, titled "Hazardous Flight Tests". This course, sponsored by the Continuing Education Division of the University of Kansas, has provided much of the new material. We are very appreciative of the assistance provided by Mrs. Jan Roskam and her staff in this endeavor.   Donald T. Ward
                                                                                                                        July 1998

Of course, both of us are indebted to even more individuals than were mentioned in the original preface for their help in producing this text. I am indebted to those individuals who provided the many invaluable experiences afforded me during my 15 years as an engineer with NASA and 9 years on the faculty at Texas A&M University. The development and presentation of the "Hazardous Flight Test" short course with my co-author has been an extremely rewarding experience and collaboration. I dedicate my efforts as an engineer, researcher, and professor to my family. Sincere appreciation is given to my wife, Kathy, who has selflessly supported my pursuit of my professional interests. To my son, Christopher, who has begun to build his educational foundation in his desired profession (Paleontology) at the University of Texas, and to my daughter, Kasey, who continues to follow her love of life and horses, I hope the two of you will pursue your dreams with devotion.   Thomas W. Strganac
                                                                                                                        July 1998

Preface to the Third Edition, Volume I

The third edition of **Introduction to Flight Test Engineering** is being expanded to two volumes, with this first volume to be followed shortly with a second one addressing more advanced topics. This first volume is comprised of the same subject matter as the first nine chapters of the original book. The chapters on aeroelastic flight tests and post-stall flight tests have been moved to Volume 2. This reorganization of the material allowed us to insert additional information into Volume 1, notably a risk management section in Chapter 1 and section on instrumentation for each of the other chapters. Dr. (Capt.) Robert J. Niewoehner of the United States Naval Academy has joined Dr. Strganac and me in refreshing this book (and correcting more errors). Rob brings a wealth of practical experience from the naval aviation community and has taught these topics both at the Naval Academy and has joined us on several occasions in teaching short courses for the Continuing Education Division of the University of Kansas. Welcome, Rob.
                                                                                                                        Donald T. Ward
                                                                                                                        February 2006

Like Don, I am pleased to welcome Rob Niewoehner to our team; may you enjoy the fruits of your labor on this book as much as we have for over a decade. As we continue to present this material, I am impressed by the knowledge and curiosity of students who attend our short courses. We owe a big thank you to all of them for asking questions and forcing us to learn enough to answer them. Sincere appreciation is due all the ladies at University of Kansas who help us, prod us, and keep us on track to respond to our students. As always, my largest vote of thanks goes to my wife, Kathy. She continues to be my support in every thing I do. Kathy and our children, Christopher and Kasey, continue to be the joy of my life.

Thomas W. Strganac
February 2006

It has been a considerable pleasure for me to use Don Ward and Tom Strgnac's book for the past six years while teaching undergraduate flight test engineering. To be included as a partner both in the classroom and in print has been both an honor and delight. Flight test engineering constitutes the intersection of my professional life as a pilot, and my scholastic life as an engineer and educator. Educating future engineers and aviators is my daily concern, and there is no subject to which I would like them drawn as flight test engineering. I hope that my contribution to my colleagues' work faithfully represents their voice and interests. My professional tribute must be directed to Professor David F. Rogers, who patiently re-cast this fighter pilot into an engineering educator (and taught a Naval Aviator how to flare). While Dave endured only my poor landings, my wife, Natalie, has endured both my hours and my vocation. She and our sons are my delight.

Robert J. Niewoehner
February 2006

Chapter 1

PLANNING, DISCIPLINE, AND SAFETY

Flight testing piloted and unmanned aerospace vehicles is an interdisciplinary process fundamental to the development of new systems and to the advancement of aeronautical knowledge. Engineers from all branches of the engineering sciences are needed to successfully put a new system through a thorough and complete flight test program. The primary goal of such test programs is to support product development and upgrades. Typically, the flight test specialists act as part of a larger team to bring about safe, orderly, and cost-effective system evolution as part of the larger system development managed by a program manager assisted by systems engineers. In a very real sense, the flight test part of the effort is meant to reduce overall program risk and provide verification and validation of an integrated product team's efforts.

Aerospace engineers often lead efforts to develop aerospace systems because of their special familiarity with aerodynamics and the effects of vehicle configuration upon performance and dynamics. Electrical engineers are indispensable in developing appropriate instrumentation, in evaluating feedback control loops, and in evaluating electronic subsystems. Mechanical engineers provide special expertise in designing mechanical, hydraulic and pneumatic subsystems. Computer specialists are essential to a reasonable integration of the on-board computers and their seemingly unlimited capacity to control and display information for the crew or the ground operators. Flight testing is a complex process; it requires many different technical skills, as well as good judgment in managing the process. Therefore, the right place to start a discussion of flight test methods is with a brief philosophy of cost effective flight testing.

1.1   WHY FLIGHT TEST?

Flight test organizations have a reputation for costing too much and taking too much time, the cardinal sins for a program manager. If the test engineer finds a flaw in the design, the usual reply to the recommended fix is: *"We cannot afford such a drastic change!"* or *"Why did you not find the problem in the preliminary tests?"* The flight test team is also the first to hear from the disgruntled user: *"You gave me another piece of junk! Why did you let them send it to the field?"* The implications of these comments (and they are not altogether rhetorical) is that the flight test engineer must do his job well and he must communicate effectively with those who control the purse strings if the product is to be useful. Exactly what is the purpose of flight testing? The introduction to the AGARD Flight Test Manual[1] lists three fundamental reasons for flight testing of piloted aircraft:

◆ *To determine the actual characteristics of the machine (as contrasted to the computed or predicted characteristics)*

◆ *To provide developmental information*

◆ *To obtain research information*

These purposes hit at the classical reasons for doing flight test; they do not adequately recognize that modern aerospace systems are developed by teams of engineers and technicians; whether piloted or unmanned, they are complicated "systems of systems". Their utility may depend as much upon their interface with other air, space, or ground systems as the vehicle's own capabilities. Very few aerospace vehicles are designed by one engineer today. The military has insisted upon use of the "integrated product team" (IPT) approach for at least a decade now; recent policy revisions[2] emphasizes this approach:

> *The DoD acquisition, capability needs, and financial communities, and operational users shall maintain continuous and effective communications with each other by using Integrated Product Teams (IPTs). Teaming among warfighters, users, developers, acquirers, technologists, testers, budgeters, and sustainers shall begin during capability needs definition. MDAs and PMs are responsible for making decisions and leading execution of their programs, and are accountable for results.*

It is important that flight test personnel understand this concept and the role of flight test in it. From this perspective the value of data from flight test is to reduce uncertainty in the design process. Systems engineers think of flight test activities as one of the ways to verify that the design is built to the requirements and specifications and to validate that the end item gives useful and cost-effective capability to the user ("customer").

There is no reason to suggest that the testing of airplanes or UAVs or spacecraft differs substantially from these fundamental purposes, though the most appropriate technique is different for each classification of aerospace vehicles. For each of them "the proof of the pudding lies in the eating," and it is also still true that aerospace engineering is not an exact science. Some form of measurement must verify all of our theoretical and computed results. Consequently, flight testing is needed and is likely to be an integral part of the development of most if not all aerospace technology for the foreseeable future.

1.2   TYPES OF FLIGHT TESTS

Flight tests can be classified in many ways. Perhaps the most common classification is that associated with the stage of development of the project. The Department of Defense (DoD) and the systems engineering community also classify flight testing as to purpose. We now briefly introduce the terminology of flight test classifications.

1.2.1   Stage of Development

A better new system depends on new technology. In the aerospace community, new technology inevitably means basic research and much of this needed new information is empirically derived. Computational techniques are stretched to the limit to provide design information on unusual configurations. Wind tunnel tests are almost always needed to verify innovative ideas. This tool, used as early as the Wright Brothers, is invaluable in examining a large number of detailed changes when computational methods are not sufficiently advanced to produce believable results. But the wind tunnel also has limitations. Stability derivatives obtained from wind tunnel tests should be verified at full scale Reynolds numbers and Mach numbers. Dynamic derivatives calculated from wind tunnel data often do not match the same parameters extracted from flight data. Propulsion system characteristics must be verified in flight. Ultimately, full scale flight tests are required to provide the credibility designers need to create the latest technological advances.

Subsystem technology must also be proven in the flight environment to be credible. Radar, navigational systems, flight management systems, integrated displays, flight control systems, electro-optical target designator systems, defensive avionics systems, and communications systems are but a few of the subsystems that are sensitive to this environment. They are frequently flown as breadboard and/or advanced developmental models on test bed aircraft before they are installed as part of the vehicle they are designed to enhance and support. Again, flight test is essential to the orderly development of such subsystems.

As the cost of operating new aircraft and missiles goes up, the use of simulation expands. Commercial airline operations now do almost all of their training in new systems on sophisticated simulators. Military services depend on high fidelity full mission simulators for both training and for engineering support. Once again, though, credible simulation demands a credible data base to guarantee the fidelity of the mathematical models. If the data base is accurate, simulators are welcomed. If not, they are ignored. All too often simulator manufacturers have found, to their chagrin, that computed or wind tunnel estimates of the coefficients of the equations of motion were not the same as those experienced in flight. Flight tests usually pointed the way to changes that satisfied the users' demands. But all too often these flight tests were repetitions of tests done earlier and were therefore wasted precious time and money. As a result, many programs now include flight test data as a requirement to verify simulation models.

Prototypes of airplanes, helicopters, and missiles have frequently provided credible and valuable predictions for development efforts. Historically, military systems have heavily leaned on prototyping to insure that performance and handling qualities goals were met. Since the early 1970's, the YF-22 and YF-23, the YF-16 and YF-17, the YA-9 and YA-10, the AGM-109 and AGM-85, and the X-32 and X-35 efforts were all head-to-head flight test comparisons of competing prototypes. These projects are examples of the "fly-before-you-buy" concept of the DoD. Most major manufacturers of general aviation aircraft fly prototypes to check their design assumptions before committing to production. Examples of such general aviation prototypes include the Mooney M301, the Beech Starship, and the Piper Malibu. Prototype testing does not always lead to production and may instead lead to further development or even cancellation of a marginal design. Furthermore, prototype data may not be acceptable for certification purposes due to variances with production configurations.

For all aircraft, military or civilian, considerable development of a design is done on aircraft specifically built for certification (for civilian designs) or full scale development (for military) purposes. These aircraft are one step removed from their prototype cousins, but in some cases are later modified to the production configuration. All too often, especially for complex designs, such modifications are too expensive or too extensive to be practical and these developmental aircraft become museum pieces. These aircraft usually carry a considerable amount of instrumentation specified by the flight test team to provide the data and measurements the designers need. These full scale development programs are the best opportunity for the flight test team to contribute to the improvement of the design. Because the aircraft are specifically set aside for the certification or development process, and because of the instrumentation available, shortcomings can be discovered during this phase of flight testing. Furthermore, they can be more easily corrected during this relatively early stage of design evolution. But the burden of getting everything right with only one chance to make the correction falls to the flight test team during this period. If discrepancies are missed here, the operator is justified in questioning the professionalism of the flight testers involved.

On more complex systems, there is usually a further period of refinement after the production configuration is frozen. Changes required at this point are much more costly to introduce into the production line and consequently flight tests are usually the only

credible way to validate their value. This follow-on developmental testing (after a production decision) is particularly appropriate if the total aerospace system is heavily dependent upon a rapidly changing technology. The current generation of military aircraft
that take advantage of digital electronics in everything from cockpit displays to flight controls is a classic example. Commonly such improvements are introduced into the production line after some number of systems has been built. Follow-on development gives rise
to different models of the same aircraft or missile, often with very different capabilities
even though the external configuration of the machines may be quite similar. The latest
attempt to more quickly transition new technology to operational capability is called
"evolutionary acquisition". The DoD emphasis on this commercial technique (Boeing uses
this kind of development for the Boeing 787, for example) is reflected in the following
quote from their operating instruction[3]:

> ... Evolutionary acquisition is the preferred DoD strategy for rapid acquisition of ma-
> ture technology for the user. An evolutionary approach delivers capability in incre-
> ments, recognizing, up front, the need for future capability improvements. The objec-
> tive is to balance needs and available capability with resources, and to put capability
> into the hands of the user quickly. The success of the strategy depends on consistent
> and continuous definition of requirements, and the maturation of technologies that lead
> to disciplined development and production of systems that provide increasing capability
> towards a materiel concept.

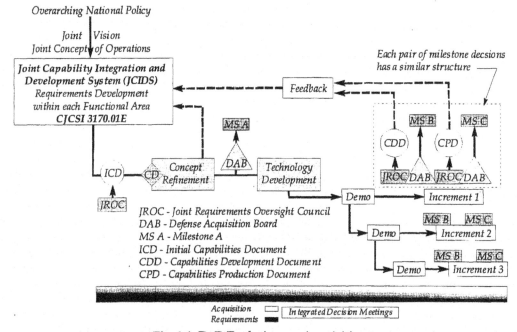

Fig. 1.1 DoD Evolutionary Acquisition
(Adapted from Defense Acquisition University charts[5,6])

1.2.2 Developmental Versus Operational Testing

The DoD has pushed for rigorous user-oriented flight testing, spurred by the 1970
Blue Ribbon Defense Panel that recommended stronger emphasis on operational suitability testing. The DoD established an independent operational test and evaluation (OT& E)

agency within each of the services, fostering a stronger integration of the eventual users of military systems into the development process. Van Pelt noted as early as 1981 that "the entire flight test portion of the acquisition cycle became a complex integration of tasks shared by the contractor, developing command, and using command."[4] The continued emphasis on IPTs and now on evolutionary acquisition makes it even more imperative that the flight test team understand their role in the overall acquisition process.

1.2.2.1 **Developmental Test and Evaluation**. Developmental Test and Evaluation (DT&E) is defined[6] as:

> *A technical test conducted to provide data on the achievability of critical system performance parameters. This testing is performed on components, subsystems, and system-level configurations of hardware and software.*

Flight test activity necessary to produce a system that meets its design goals clearly fits this definition. The current Defense Acquisition Guidebook[5] lists the following mandatory objectives for DT&E that the Program Manager (PM) must develop and fund:

♦ *Perform verification and validation in the systems engineering process;*

♦ *Develop an event-driven T&E Strategy, rather than a schedule-driven one, to ensure program success (required)[3];*

♦ *Identify technological capabilities and limitations of alternative concepts and design options under consideration to support cost-performance tradeoffs (required)[3]. The intent is to avoid locking onto one solution too early;*

♦ *Identify and describe design technical risks (required)[3]. The T&E Strategy should naturally flow from the systems engineering processes of requirements analysis, functional allocation, and design synthesis;*

♦ *Stress the system under test to at least the limits of the Operational Mode Summary/Mission Profile, and for some systems, beyond the normal operating limits to ensure the robustness of the design (required)[3]. This will ensure expected operational performance environments can be satisfied;*

♦ *Assess technical progress and maturity against Critical Technical Parameters (CTPs), including interoperability, documented in the TEMP (required). As part of an event-driven strategy, the use of success criteria is a suggested technique with which program managers can meet this requirement. Success criteria are intermediate goals or targets on the path to meeting the desired capabilities. There are two uses of success criteria. First, they can be used to assess technical progress and maturity against CTPs. Second, they can be used as metrics to assess successful completion of a major phase of developmental testing, such as a major phase of ground testing or of flight testing, and determine readiness to enter the next phase of testing, whether developmental or operational. In the case of operational testing, these success criteria are tantamount to OT&E entrance criteria (required)[3] for all operational tests. Technical parameters, such as levels of reliability growth or software maturity, increasing levels of weapons system accuracy, mission processing timelines, and the like, can be used as success criteria to assess technical progress. Alternatively, in the case of an event success criterion such as completion of the first set of missile test firings, the criteria can be a specified level of success, such as a percentage of successful missile firings from this group. Failure to meet this criterion might cause the program manager to decide on additional firings prior to transitioning to the next phase of testing. A program manager can use a combination of both types of success criteria and tailor them to best fit the program's T&E Strategy;*

♦ *Assess the safety of the system or item to ensure safe operation during OT&E, other troop-supported testing, operational usage, and to support success in meeting design safety criteria (required)[3]. The intent is to ensure that developmental systems are sufficiently free of hazards to prevent injury to the typical users participating in OT&E and fielding;*

♦ *Provide data and analytic support to the decision process to certify the system ready for OT&E (required)[3]. These data are provided in the DT&E report discussed below;*

♦ *Conduct information assurance testing on any system that collects, stores, transmits, and processes unclassified or classified information (required)[3];*

♦ *In the case of IT systems, including NSS, support the <u>DoD Information Technology Security Certification and Accreditation Process</u> and <u>Joint Interoperability Certification process</u> (required)[3];*

♦ *Discover, evaluate, and mitigate potentially adverse electromagnetic environmental effects (E3). (required)[3];*

♦ *Support joint interoperability assessments required to certify system-of-systems interoperability; (required)[3];*

♦ *In the case of financial management, enterprise resource planning, and mixed financial management systems, the developer shall conduct an independent assessment of compliance factors established by the Office of the USD(C) (required)[3];*

♦ *Prior to full-rate production, demonstrate the maturity of the production process through Production Qualification Testing of LRIP assets. The focus of this testing is on the contractor's ability to produce a quality product, since the design testing should already have finished. Depending on when this testing is conducted, the results might be usable as another data source for IOT&E readiness determinations; and*

♦ *Demonstrate performance against threats and their countermeasures as identified in the DIA-validated System Threat Assessment. Any impact on technical performance by these threats should be identified early in technical testing, rather than in operational testing where their presence might have more serious repercussions (required)[3].*

In addition to these mandatory objectives, the guiding instruction strongly recommends these additional activities to provide the most robust T&E foundation for programs:

♦ *Involve testers and evaluators, from within the program and outside, early in T&E planning activities to tap their expertise from similar experiences and begin identifying resource requirements needed for T&E budgeting activities;*

♦ *Ensure the T&E Strategy is aligned with and supports the approved acquisition strategy, so that adequate, risk-reducing T&E information is provided to support decision events;*

♦ *Utilize ground test activities, where appropriate, to include hardware-in-the-loop simulation, prior to conducting full-up, system-level testing, such as flight-testing, in realistic environments;*

♦ *The required assessment of technical progress should also include reliability, desired capabilities, and satisfaction of Critical Operational Issues (COIs) to mitigate technical and manufacturing risks;*

♦ *Increase likelihood of OT&E success by testing in the most realistic environment possible;*

♦ *Assess system-of-systems Command, Control, Communications, Computers, Intelligence, Surveillance, and Reconnaissance (C4ISR) prior to OT&E to ensure that interoperability under loaded conditions will represent stressed OT&E scenarios.*

1.2.2.2 **Operational Test and Evaluation**. It is not always clear just where DT&E ends and OT&E begins, especially since the two are often carried out concurrently during the initial stages of OT&E. While the IPT philosophy strongly encourages this kind of co-operation, there is no doubt about the distinctiveness of OT&E. OT&E determines[3]:

> *... the operational effectiveness and suitability of a system under realistic operational conditions, including combat; determine if thresholds in the approved CPD and critical operational issues have been satisfied; and assess impacts to combat operations.*

This kind of testing is now includes Initial Operational Test & Evaluation (IOT&E), Follow-on Operational Test & Evaluation (FOT&E), and Live Fire T&E (LFT&E). IOT&E[6] is:

> *...conducted on production or production representative articles to support a Full-Rate Production decision. It is conducted to provide a valid estimate of expected system operational effectiveness and suitability*

LFT&E[6] is:

> *... to evaluate the vulnerability and/or lethality aspects of conventional missiles, munitions, or weapon systems.*

The key words amidst all this jargon are "operational effectiveness and suitability". Testing under realistic operational conditions is essential: simulated enemy defenses for survivability, user maintenance whenever possible, and actual or simulated malfunctions. Operational testing is meant to provide credible information for decision makers prior to commitment to production of expensive weapons systems.

1.3   FACTORS TO BE CONSIDERED IN TEST PLANNING

Testing airborne vehicles is a complex and interrelated process. To do this job effectively requires careful and detailed planning. The best measures of effectiveness for a flight test team includes both time and dollar cost of the test program as well as completeness and accuracy of the data produced. Ultimately, the test manager will be graded on all these factors. The most significant cost for any program often occurs when safety considerations are slighted or even ignored. Therefore, safety must be one of the dominant concerns throughout the planning and conduct of any series of flight tests.

1.3.1   Safety

Flight testing always carries some element of risk. Risk elimination means never fly. That said, the human, financial, and programmatic cost of failure can, however, terminate a program or devastate a company/product's market reputation. Consequently, hazard awareness and risk management must pervade the planning process. Naturally, test safety begins with the design. But the test team also has the obligation to review and scrutinize every aspect of the testing for unseen dangers. What do you suppose might have happened to the NASA budget if a space shuttle orbiter had been lost on an early test flight? No one knows, of course, but at the very least the loss would have had grave consequences; the losses of Challenger and Columbia (much later in the program) led to demands for more attention to safety within NASA[7].

> *This report discusses the attributes of an organization that could more safely and reliably operate the inherently risky Space Shuttle, but does not provide a detailed organizational prescription. Among those attributes are: a robust and independent program technical authority that has complete control over specifications and requirements, and waivers to them; an independent safety assurance organization with line authority over all levels of safety oversight; and an organizational culture that reflects the best characteristics of a learning organization.*

With this motivation, let's look at some of the ways that careful test planning can minimize risks.

Disciplined T&E depends largely upon the quality of the preparation. Appropriate planning is the surest way the following guiding principles are applied:

♦ Testing must answer the critical questions, especially those of the sponsor. It is possible to devote considerable resources to an extensive test program which fails to answer fundamental questions.

♦ Testing must proceed efficiently.

♦ Testing must be carried out with minimum exposure to risk.

Our immediate concern is risk mitigation and management, but program pressures (typically cost and schedule) inevitably create tensions with risk mitigation; T&E risk will invariably be accepted to reduce test time and cost. Intelligent T&E risk management seeks to understand the risks and reduce them to levels that are acceptable.

While no single right way exists to manage the risk in engineering test processes, those organizations that manage risk well adopt fairly similar structures, which could be regarded as "best practices." The following summary is a distillation of procedures common to many flight test organizations (both government and industry). Details, if desired, can be found in each organization's specific safety instructions.[8,9,10]

The risk management process includes the following steps:

1) Hazard Definition
2) Cause Identification
3) Risk Assessment
4) Risk Mitigation
5) Residual Risk Assessment
6) Emergency Response

1.3.1.1 **Hazard Definition**. *Test Specific Hazards* are those that arise *as a direct consequence* of the test activity. There are many hazards that exist in the normal operation of a system, mitigated by design features and normal operational procedures. For example, every pneumatically wheeled vehicle risks blown tires, and the systems safety analysis during the design should address this eventuality. A roll bar on a SAE formula car provides a measure of safety against this potentiality. But these pneumatic tires are not a test specific hazard. A blown tire becomes a *test specific hazard* only when the test activity directly increases the probability of the event occurring. For example, a maximum braking test would elevate "blown tire" to a test specific hazard, because the nature of the test significantly elevates the likelihood of the hazard being experienced. Therefore it is the test team's responsibility to control those hazards uniquely introduced or aggravated by the testing, rather than revisiting the entire systems safety analysis presumably performed during the design. There is admittedly some ambiguity, as the test team also needs to provide safety margin for unknowns with respect to the design and its performance.

Risk management usually begins with a brain-storming session in which every imaginable test hazard is proposed. This exploratory step must include some ludicrous "what-if's" and compound failures that might initially breech the bounds of plausibility. This process cannot be left to an individual, and the leadership must demand that team members have complete liberty to propose even outlandish hazards. Upon the completion of brain-storming, consideration should first be given whether the hazards are indeed test unique. Routine hazards may be set aside at this point, along with those that are outlandish and inconceivable. However, hazards that might be judged implausible, yet conceivable, should be retained, as they may represent real danger. The danger is sometimes elevated specifically because test team participants are blind to the real nature of the hazard. The professional T&E communities have lengthy archives of unforeseen/unimagined hazards which resulted in death, injury, damage, or at "close calls" with catastrophy.

1.3.1.2 **Cause Identification**. Second, the likely causes of each hazard should be listed. Some hazards have a single cause, but most hazards have multiple potential causes. All causes must be listed.

TABLE 1.1 Risk Code Matrix

Likelihood of Occurrence	Code	Severity of Consequence	Code
Nearly certain – if the test is repeated multiple times over a lengthy test campaign, the specified event should occur at least once.	A	Catastrophic – death , serious injury, or destructin of an irreplaceable test asset.	I
Probable	B	Severe – injury involving lost work days, damage to test assets requiring major repair and loss of schedule	II
Possible	C	Moderate – injuries not involving lost work days, non-minor repair (multiple shifts)	III
Improbable	D	Minor – no personnel injury, easily repairable damage (less than 1 shift), cessation of testing that day	IV
Remote	E		

1.3.1.3 **Risk Assessment**. Once a list of test specific hazards is composed, each event's consequences are listed. These consequences may run the spectrum from death and destruction to interruption of the testing. Each hazard is then coded for its severity and its likelihood. The codes in Table 1.1 are representative of several T&E organizations. Definitions may vary from company to company, across or within industries, as may the number of levels and their resolution. Many organizations employ such risk assessment codes to provide some objectivity to the process and to ensure a common vocabulary. A risk assessment code is a matrix describing both the severity of a test specific hazard and the likelihood of its occurrence. Severity is commonly coded according to the following four severity levels of the consequents of an identified hazard, coded for our purposes with a Roman numeral (I-IV). The likelihood of occurrence is usually subjectively assigned within the T&E community, unlike the more rigorous values found in systems safety circles where manufacturers quantitatively calculate component and system reliability. The counsel of experienced test personnel with diverse backgrounds, provides legitimacy to this process.

A 2-dimensional matrix is thus formed, which captures the nature of the overall risk, ranging from Risk Assessment Code (RAC) I-A in the top left corner to RAC IV-E in the lower right. Fig. 1.2 depicts an example adapted from NASA's *Risk Management Procedures and Guidelines* (NPG 8000.4)[8].

	Likelihood Estimate				
Consequence Class	A	B	C	D	E
I	1	1	2	3	4
II	1	2	3	4	5
III	2	3	4	5	6
IV	3	4	5	6	7
High Risk					
Medium Risk					
Low Risk					

Fig. 1.2 Sample Risk Assessment Matrix

1.3.1.4 **Risk Mitigation**. Risk mitigation is the process by which risks are reduced, moving them down and right in the hazard matrix. (The vocabulary *mitigate* or *mitigation* may need definition. The Latin root means *to soften*; the English verb means *to reduce harshness, hostility or severity*, precisely describing our goal.) Reduction in the severity level usually requires specific hardware changes to the test equipment (perhaps the installation of safety equipment installed solely for the purpose of the test, or the modification of the design to permanently reduce the hazard severity). Procedural precautions alone seldom reduce hazard severity. Hazard likelihood, however, can be reduced by hardware, instrumentation, or procedurally. Again, brain-storming by a team of people is appropriate to devise mitigation measures to reduce the hazard level. Common risk mitigation techniques include:

1.3.1.4.1 *Hardware Mitigation* -- Modifications to hardware specifically to enhance the test safety:

 a. Safety equipment may be installed on a *test* article specifically to reduce *test* hazards. Such modifications are over and above the design features incorporated in order to enhance the safety of an in-service production article. Examples include protective equipment for participants, power cut-outs, etc.

 b. Instrumentation may make the tests safer; generally, the more the test team knows during the tests, the safer the activity. "Safety-of-test" parameters may be monitored in real time, or post-processed event to event during a build-up sequence (allowing a forecast of behavior on the next event). Note well that items identified in the test plan as "safety-of-test" become "no-go" items; if such a parameter is not operating and there is no backup, the test cannot be conducted.

1.3.1.4.2 Procedural Mitigation -- Procedures intended to reduce risk (typically the likelihood of occurence):

a. Scrutinized, detailed normal and emergency procedures alleviate many of the incidental risks of operating equipment. Not applying electrical power until closure of panels, and then removal of that power prior to any access is a good example of procedures of this type. RC modelers habitually conduct antenna pattern checks and loss-of-signal checks as part of their pre-flight preparations. Such activities must be codified and emphasized by leadership to guarantee discipline and professionalism in the test team.

b. Simulation and modelling is a huge discipline that spans a broad range of expense and effort: batch, man-in-the-loop, hardware-in-the-loop, part-task, full-task, component, systems level, environmental, and failure modes. Simulation can be used for engineering analysis, procedure development, test team training (test rehearsal or emergency procedure), and test planning. We will address this topic more completely in a chapter in Volume 2.

c. "Build-up/build-down" is a fundamental principle in flight testing in which performance in benign conditions is thoroughly understood prior moving on to more stressful conditions. Build-up/down can be in speed, weight, loading, aggressiveness/abruptness, altitude, or configuration. Build-up/down has the advantages of incrementally increasing the stress on the test system, and of familiarizing a human operator (where applicable). Trends can often be observed and anomalous behavior more easily detected or predicted. Appropriate instrumentation enhances the likelihood of detecting adverse trends. A cautious build-up/down improves the likelihood of detecting adverse behaviors, but is not always wholly reliable. Many systems exhibit nonlinear attributes which abruptly degrade system performance, giving little hint that 'cliffs' may be lurking.

1.3.1.5 Residual Risk Assessment. A single risk mitigation measure often does not adequately address any one causal factor or hazard; indeed the best hazard plans include diverse, overlapping measures. After mitigation measures are applied, the hazard is analyzed again for both severity and likelihood, and a Residual Risk code is assigned.

Since test hazards cannot be eliminated (except, perhaps, by test cancellation), T&E organizations must necessarily live with *accepted risk*. Accepted risks are those hazard codes for which tests are allowed to proceed. Organizations (and leadership) vary in where to draw the line through the risk matrix identifying blocks regarded as "acceptable." An organization's threshold invariably represents a stair-case running from lower left (inconsequential, and nearly certain) to upper right (catastrophic, but remote) . For example, some managers accept all severity codes of III and IV, plus those category I and II hazards whose probability is "Improbable" or "Remote." Other organizations allow for IIC, while prohibiting III-A, and ID. *The prerogative of drawing the line of acceptable risk does not reside with the test team, but with their executive leadership.* Indeed, professional T&E organizations convene review boards for tests exceeding certain thresholds of perceived risk. Senior engineers and managers, often deliberately chosen from outside the test team, critique the team's risk analysis and mitigation plans. These "murder boards" are vital for challenging the test team's assumptions; in truly high risk enterprises, their tone must border on adversarial. If not, program leadership may not adequately scrutinize the work of their test team, who often lack leadership's breadth of experience and understanding of risk that is unacceptable.

1.3.1.6 **Emergency Response**. Finally, to be complete, the Hazard Analysis should include some planning for a procedural response to a catastrophic event, should it occur despite the precautions. These responses are included in the "Emergency Procedures."

A warning from the past is in order. There is a real temptation to copy/paste an existing test hazard analysis of a prior program, thereby short-cutting the test hazard analysis process. There is genuine value in consulting the work of others lest either some hazard or viable mitigating measure be overlooked. However, uncritical acceptance of another's analysis risks missing vital differences and a unique hazard, or even one overlooked by others. Therefore, a prior analysis should be considered a baseline at best, or better yet, a check case after the initial brainstorming.

This approach to risk management is synthesized from exposure to the flight test practices of Navy, Air Force, NASA, and diverse civilian companies. It represents no one organizational philosophy, but resembles them all, the community of flight test professionals having collectively gravitated to this model over the past forty years. Details can be found in various organizations' instructions, many of which can be found on the web.

Safety in test flying has not always been paramount, but at today's prices (in dollar cost for hardware and in opportunity cost for highly visible programs) no one can afford to treat risks lightly. Planning and a healthy organizational attitude toward safety are extraordinarily important.

1.3.2 Cost

The cost of flight testing is staggering. It is therefore up to responsible engineers to consider the cost of each test to be done, to look for ways to reduce that cost, and to question the value of the data to be collected. *Why am I doing this test?* is always a good first question. Some of the items that drive the cost of a test are: ground support needed; required (not desired) instrumentation; and flying time required.

Ground and airborne support should be kept as simple as possible, consistent with the risks inherent in the tests, the complexity of the test, and the required information. It may be as simple as a mechanic to service the airplane and as complex as linked telemetry ranges to cover the complete flight profile. Question everything: *Is telemetry necessary? Do we need continuous radio communication? How much redundancy in measurements is enough? How many samples of data do we really need? Can we combine tests? Are chase aircraft really needed? Is real-time data reduction essential or nice to have? Is there a source of support available at better rates? What kind of flexibility is there in the range schedule?* Each of these questions leads to options and alternatives; all good test planners keep options.

Instrumentation is one of the most difficult (and often most costly) technical area for flight testers. Skimping on instrumentation can lead to poor data or even no data. You may have to repeat the test--late, of course--if you accept inadequate instrumentation. At the other extreme, complexity in the instrumentation package can buy more downtime than the program can stand.

Finally, every bit of time spent in the air must be used productively. Utilization of flying time is improved by combining tests; for example, collect data on the environmental control subsystem while flying low altitude performance tests. Aerial refueling, for airplanes equipped to refuel in flight, can multiply productivity of test time. Real-time data reduction, though it requires complex instrumentation and extensive ground support, can significantly speed up some tests and preclude repeating flights. Choose the time of day (or night) that not only suits test requirements, but that gives the most efficienct data collection. Allow time for maintenance crews to prepare aircraft and instrumentation fully; overscheduling flights can be counterproductive. Productive flying time is time when you collect useful data during flight testing; use it completely and wisely.

1.3.3   Schedule

Meeting a schedule is a fact of life for flight test, as it is in all other facets of engineering. For the company building civilian aircraft, missing a certification date often means lost sales and a poor marketing image. For the military customer, schedule slips can force a complete alteration in force structure--and, in the worst case, a return to Congress for approval of changes. Usually, the military contractor suffers contractual penalties when delays occur. Quite literally, time is money; plan wisely to meet the schedule.

If you are using government-owned ranges or support facilities that do not belong to your organization, a slip can put you off the schedule. Provision for rescheduling tests must be addressed in the master test plan. Be sure you know what scheduling flexibility is available and then conduct tests so as to never exercise that flexibility.

A major factor in meeting the test schedule is how many test vehicles are allocated to the flight test program. This factor can be particularly troublesome if the vehicles are expendable, as in tactical missiles or other unmanned vehicles. Reducing the number of prototypes or developmental aircraft is a favorite way of cutting the cost of a flight test program. It is up to the test manager to be sure his ability to meet the schedule is not removed along with the "excess" cost.

1.4   SUMMARY

One of the most important principles associated with IPT-style developments is involvement of all disciplines in the systems engineering process. For the test planning stage this concept cannot be overstated; listen to all interested parties. Though conferring with others takes time, it is usually time well-spent. Strive for continuity in the group which does this early planning; preferably, each member would stay on the test team and be accountable for his or her inputs throughout the test program. This overall plan must be put in writing and reviewed by each person; this step discourages second-guessing and is the test manager's best protection. Do not skimp on early test planning.

After the overall test plan has been hammered out, detailed planning for each test and each flight must continue. The engineer should maintain a careful matrix of required data and insure that the test crews understand exactly what is required on each flight. **Never** go beyond what has been planned on a particular flight. This cardinal rule prevents surprises and dictates that considerable thought be given to test cards. These cards should be complete, but readily understood. It is the responsibility of the flight test engineer in charge to be sure that these reminders are in good order. Test cards should call for more data than can be collected on the planned mission; never let your flight test crew run short of things to do. There should be alternative data requirements specified in case instrumentation malfunction or weather prevents collecting the planned primary data.

Flight testing is one of the most exciting and, at the same time, most challenging, of all engineering problems. Early and meticulous planning is mandatory to keep safety, cost, and schedule considerations in balance. Discipline is essential throughout the process to stick to the plan and to make judicious revisions to it. Good flight testers are team workers, recognizing that collective judgment sometimes outweighs the advantage of quick decisions by a single individual. Ultimately, flight test provides both objective and subjective measurements that prove or disprove the designer's dream.

REFERENCES

[1] Perkins, C. D., Dommasch, D. O., and Durbin, E. J. (Editors), **AGARD Flight Test Manual**, Pergamon Press, New York, 1959.

[2] "The Defense Acquisition System," DoDD 5000.1, Department of Defense USD (AT&L), Washington, DC, May 12, 2003.

[3] "Operation of the Defense Acquisition System," DoD Instruction 5000.2, Department of Defense USD (AT&L), Washington, DC, May 12, 2003.

[4] Van Pelt, L. G., "Flight Test Concept Evolution," AIAA Paper 81-2375, AIAA/SETP/SFTE/SAE/ITEA/IEEE 1st Flight Testing Conference, Las Vegas, NV, Nov. 11-13, 1981.

[5] http://akss.dau.mil/dag/Guidebook/Common_InterimGuidebook.asp, Chapter 9 Integrated Test and Evaluation, last modified Dec. 16, 2004.

[6] http://www.dau.mil/pubs/IDA/chart%20back.pdf, Integrated Defense Acquisition, Technology and Logistics Life Cycle Management Framework Chart, Defense Acquisition University, Fort Belvoir, VA, Version 5.2, Aug. 2005.

[7] Executive Summary, Columbia Accident Investigation Board Report, Vol. 1, Aug. 2003.

[8] *Risk Management Procedures and Guidelines*, NASA Procedures and Guidelines, (NPG 8000.4), Apr. 25, 2002 .

[9] Air Force Flight Test Center Instruction 99-1, *Test and Evaluation Test Plans*, Jan. 28, 2002.

[10] Air Force Flight Test Center Instruction 99-5, *Test and Evaluation Test and Control and Conduct*, May 10, 2002.

Chapter 2
PITOT-STATIC SYSTEM CALIBRATION

The atmosphere dramatically affects the performance and handling qualities of an aircraft. The atmosphere's variables change continuously so that no two flight tests produce the same results, requiring the data to be meticulously reduced to standard conditions. The performance and flying qualities of different vehicles can be equitably compared only on this basis. Thus, the flight test engineer expends considerable effort correcting his measurements for non-standard atmospheric conditions. This chapter addresses the characteristics of the standard atmosphere and the calibration of the airplane's air data system. The errors inherent in pressure-based measurement systems and corrections to the indications of altimeters and airspeed indicators are the subject matter of this chapter.

2.1 FOUNDATIONS

2.1.1 Historical Perspective
The measurement of altitude and airspeed in flight and appropriate calibration schemes have been important since the early days of aviation. Walter Diehl's early textbook[1] addressed the problem of airspeed calibration, but only after a number of engineers in both Europe and the United States had considered instrumenting airplanes to measure these basic flight parameters. Wieselsberger[2] and Proll[3] both made pressure measurements in flight, having as at least one purpose, recording the airspeed of the vehicle. Later, Brown[4,5] wrote of other devices (a multiple manometer and an air speed meter, for example) recorded on film and synchronized for flight test purposes, and culminating in measurement of the "true speed" in flight. These humble beginnings guide today's specialists to design and calibrate air data systems that feed flight management systems, weapons delivery systems, and navigational systems. A primitive technology has grown to underpin one of the most useful of all subsystems on an aerospace vehicle today.

2.1.2 Standard Atmosphere
Model atmospheres have existed for decades though the U. S. space program dictated refinements and validation of new atmospheric models time and again[6,7,8]. The International Commission of Air Navigation (ICAN) Standard Atmosphere[9] was used internationally for many years. In 1952 slight differences in the ICAN and NACA standard atmospheres were reconciled and the International Civil Aviation Organization (ICAO) Standard Atmosphere[10] became the international standard for member nations. In 1953 the ICAO formed a committee to extend the standard atmosphere to 300 kilometers, which was published in 1956. Further extensions were proposed in 1962 and again in 1975 as a result of the collection of more experimental data. In 1975 the International Organization for Standardization adopted a standard atmosphere which is virtually identical to the ICAO standard atmosphere up to 50 km, but also includes data up to 80 km. All of these standard atmospheres are quite similar, but the latter one is perhaps the most up-to-date. Many tabulations of these standard atmospheres have been published[11, 12]. We will not add to the size of this book by including such a tabulation. Instead, the student is encouraged as a homework exercise to write a computer program that calculates the properties of the standard atmosphere.

Before briefly reviewing the theory of the standard atmosphere it is essential to define certain terms and restate the assumptions used. There are a variety of altitude definitions used in the literature and there is considerable ambiguity in usage. In this book the following definitions will be used consistently. However, the careful student must confirm the meaning of various terms in other sources. **Geometric altitude**, h_g, is the tapeline vertical distance from mean sea level to the point in question. Sometimes this altitude is also called **true altitude**. **Pressure altitude**, h_p, is the geometric altitude in a standard atmosphere at which a given pressure is found[6]. A properly calibrated altimeter, set to 29.92 inches of mercury (in. Hg), indicates pressure altitude. The altimeter must be set to this value by the flight test crew during all tests so that data can be referenced to this standard pressure. **Density altitude**, h_ρ, is the geometric altitude in a standard atmosphere at which a given density occurs. Unlike pressure, density is measured indirectly; that is, it is calculated from measurements of pressure and temperature. Density altitude is of utmost concern in predicting available thrust or power from the propulsion system. **Absolute altitude**, h_a, is the distance measured from the center of the earth to the point in question. This altitude is of prime concern in orbital mechanics because the local gravitational acceleration, g, is a function of altitude.

$$g = g_0 \left[\frac{R_E}{h_a} \right]^2 = g_0 \left[\frac{R_E}{R_E + h_g} \right]^2 \tag{2.1}$$

where R_E is the radius of the earth.

Finally, **geopotential altitude**, h, is a fictitious altitude obtained from geometric altitude by assuming g is a constant from mean sea level up to any altitude.

$$dh = \frac{g}{g_0} dh_g, \text{ or integrating to get: } h = \left[\frac{R_E}{R_E + h_g} \right] h_g \tag{2.2}$$

Below 200,000 feet the error in assuming that $h = h_g$ introduces less than 1% error[7], justifying the assumption that h and h_g are equal for air-breathing airplanes.

The current standard atmosphere is based on the following assumptions meant to approximate atmospheric conditions at 40° North Latitude averaged over the year.

♦ Air behaves as a perfect gas obeying the equation of state:
$$p = \rho R T \tag{2.3}$$
where $R = 1716.55$ ft²/sec²°R; and T is the absolute temperature in °R. This assumption is valid up to a height of about 55 miles, where dissociation effects begin to play a major role.

♦ Temperature varies linearly within bands of altitude according to:
$$T = T_i + k_i (h - h_i) \tag{2.4}$$
where k_i is the lapse rate for the altitude band $h - h_i$; k_i, T_i, and h_i are given in Table 2.1 for altitudes up to 90 km (approximately 295,000 ft).

♦ Standard sea level conditions are:
$p_0 = 2116.22$ psf $= 760$ mm Hg $= 29.921$ in Hg $= 1.013250 \times 10^5$ N/m²
$T_0 = 518.67$ °R $= 288.15$ °K

♦ The gravitational constant is: $g_0 = 32.17405$ ft/sec² $= 9.80665$ m/sec²

♦ Relative humidity is taken to be zero (dry air).

The standard atmosphere, based on the above assumptions, builds upon eqns. (2.3), (2.4), and the hydrostatic equation which results from summing the pressure forces and the gravitational forces acting on a unit element of air as shown in Fig. 2.1. This summation gives: $p - (p + dp) - \rho g_0 dh = 0$. Assuming that g_0 is a constant over the altitude interval of interest allows us to integrate the resulting hydrostatic equation. This assumption also makes the altitude in eqn. (2.5) geopotential altitude.

$$dp = -\rho g_0 dh \qquad (2.5)$$

TABLE 2.1 Constants for the Standard Atmosphere

Index i	Lapse Rate k_i (°R/ft)	Base Temperature T_i (°R)	Base Geopotential Altitude h_i (ft)
0	-0.00356616	518.67	0.000
1	0.00000000	389.97	36,089.239
2	0.00054864	389.97	65,616.798
3	0.00153619	411.57	104,986.878
4	0.00000000	487.17	154,199.475
5	-0.00109728	487.17	170,603.675
6	-0.00219456	454.17	200,131.234
7	0.00000000	325.17	259,186.352

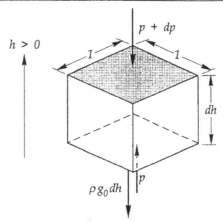

Fig. 2.1 Pressure Forces Acting on a Unit Element of Air

Combining eqns. (2.3) and (2.5): $\dfrac{dp}{p} = -g_0 \dfrac{dh}{RT}$

Recalling that $\dfrac{dT}{dh} = k_i$ and, if $k_i \neq 0$, $\dfrac{dp}{p} = -g_0 \dfrac{g_0 dT}{k_i RT}$

On the other hand, if $k_i = 0$ (the isothermal case), $\dfrac{dp}{p} = -\dfrac{g_0 dh}{RT}$

Integrating each of these expressions: first, with $k_i \neq 0$, gives $\ln \dfrac{p}{p_i} = -\dfrac{g_0}{k_i R} \ln \dfrac{T}{T_i}$. Then

with $k_i = 0$, the integration results in $\ln \dfrac{p}{p_i} = -\dfrac{g_0}{k_i RT_i}(h - h_i)$.

Substituting eqn. (2.4) into the first of these expressions yields:

$$\frac{p}{p_i} = \left[1 + \frac{k_i}{T_i}(h - h_i) \right]^{-\frac{g_0}{k_i R}}, \; k_i \neq 0 \tag{2.6a}$$

The second expression becomes:

$$\frac{p}{p_i} = e^{-\frac{g_0}{T_i R}(h - h_i)}, \; k_i = 0 \tag{2.6b}$$

Utilizing the equation of state, eqn. (2.3), density can be similarly expressed as a function of geopotential altitude.

$$\frac{\rho}{\rho_i} = \left[1 + \frac{k_i}{T_i}(h - h_i) \right]^{-\frac{g_0}{k_i R} - 1}, \; k_i \neq 0 \tag{2.7a}$$

$$\frac{\rho}{\rho_i} = e^{-\frac{g_0}{T_i R}(h - h_i) - 1}, \; k_i = 0 \tag{2.7b}$$

Equations 2.6 and 2.7 apply to any region in the standard atmosphere where we can assume a constant temperature lapse rate. In the troposphere, $i = 0$ and standard sea level conditions are relevant initial conditions. In the stratosphere, $i = 1$, $k_1 = 0$, and $T_1 = 389.97$ °R. Similarly, constants corresponding to $i = 2, 3, ..., 7$ represent the standard atmosphere in higher regions. So, a standard temperature variation, experimentally derived, used in eqns. (2.6) and (2.7), plus the equation of state, completely defines a standard atmosphere.

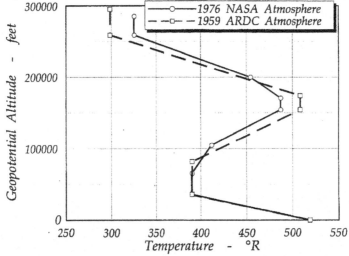

Fig. 2.2 Temperature Variations for Two Standard Atmospheres

Figure 2.2 compares temperature variation in the standard atmosphere we will use (1976 NASA Standard Atmosphere) with an earlier standard atmosphere. Standard atmospheres are frequently tabulated[10,11,12,13] in either dimensional or non-dimensional form in pressure, density, and temperature. These non-dimensional variables are defined by simply dividing each property by its standard, sea level value.

$$\delta = \frac{p}{p_0} \qquad \sigma = \frac{\rho}{\rho_0} \qquad \theta = \frac{T}{T_0} \qquad \delta = \sigma\theta \tag{2.8}$$

The last expression is simply the equation of state written in non-dimensional terms.

Example 2.1: Calculate δ, σ, and θ for standard day geopotential altitudes of 10,000 feet and 40,000 feet. At $h = 10,000$ feet, use eqn. (2.4) to directly calculate the temperature ratio.

$$\theta_{10K} = \frac{T}{T_0} = 1 + \frac{k_0\left(10,000 - 0\right)}{T_0} = 1 + \frac{(-0.00356616)(10,000)}{518.67}$$

$$\boxed{\theta_{10K} = 0.9312}$$

Equation (2.6a) gives δ_{10K}

$$\delta_{10K} = \frac{p}{p_0} = \theta_{10K}^{-\frac{g_0}{k_0 R}} = \theta_{10K}^{\frac{32.17405}{(-0.00356616)(1716.55)}} = \theta_{10K}^{-5.2559}$$

$$\boxed{\delta_{10K} = 0.6877}$$

Equation (2.7a) gives σ_{10K}

$$\sigma_{10K} = \frac{\rho}{\rho_0} = \theta_{10K}^{-\frac{g_0}{k_0}-1} = \theta_{10K}^{4.2559}$$

$$\boxed{\sigma_{10K} = 0.7385}$$

For $h = 40,000$ ft, use eqn. (2.4) again with $k_1 = 0$

$$\theta_{40K} = \theta_{tropopause} = \frac{389.97}{518.67}$$

$$\boxed{\theta_{40K} = 0.7519}$$

$$\delta_{tropopause} = \theta_{40K}^{5.2559} = (0.7519)^{5.2559}$$

$$\frac{p_{40K}}{p_{tropopause}} = 0.22336$$

$$\frac{p_{40K}}{p_{tropopause}} = e^{-\frac{g_0}{RT_1}(h-h_1)} = e^{-\frac{32.17405}{(1716.55)(389.97)}(40000-36089.239)} = 0.82864$$

$$\delta_{40K} = \frac{p_{40K}}{p_{tropopause}}\frac{p_{tropopause}}{p_0} = (0.82864)(0.22336)$$

$$\boxed{\delta_{40K} = 0.1851}$$

$$\frac{p_{tropopause}}{p_0} = \theta_{40K}^{-\frac{g_0}{k_0 R}-1} = \theta_{40K}^{4.2559} = 0.29707 \text{ and using } \frac{p_{40K}}{p_{tropopause}} = 0.82864 \text{ again}$$

$$\sigma_{40K} = \frac{p_{tropopause}}{p_0}\frac{p_{tropopause}}{p_0} = (0.29707)(0.82864)$$

$$\boxed{\sigma_{40K} = 0.2462}$$

2.1.3 Airspeed Theory

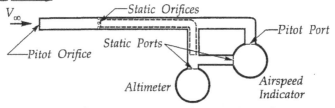

Fig. 2.3 Schematic Diagram of a Pitot-Static System

We must now develop the airspeed measurement equations. Both altitude and airspeed measuring systems are typically pressure sensing systems as depicted in Fig. 2.3. However, an airspeed indicator (ASI) measures differential pressure while an altimeter measures absolute pressure. Both use the same static pressure source, but an ASI measures the pressure difference between total pressure (sensed at the total head orifice) and static pressure. Writing Euler's equation for steady, streamline flow:

$$\frac{dp}{\rho} + VdV = 0$$

Integrating gives either the incompressible or the compressible Bernoulli equation:

$$p + \frac{\rho V^2}{2} = \text{constant (incompressible), or} \int \frac{dp}{\rho} + \frac{V^2}{2} = \text{constant (compressible)}$$

For an isentropic process, $\left(\frac{p}{\rho}\right)^\gamma = \left(\frac{p_T}{\rho_T}\right)^\gamma = \text{constant}$. A convenient form of the compressible Bernoulli equation results after solving for ρ and integrating:

$$\frac{\gamma p}{\rho(\gamma-1)} + \frac{V^2}{2} = \text{constant} \tag{2.9}$$

If eqn. (2.9) is applied to the flow into the total head orifice of the ASI where $V_\infty = 0$ and to the streamline flow past the static orifices in the Pitot-static system,

$$\frac{\gamma p}{\rho(\gamma-1)} + \frac{V^2}{2} = \frac{\gamma p_T}{\rho_T(\gamma-1)}$$

The differential pressure sensed by a conventional Pitot-static system, $q_c = p_T - p$, is described as the impact pressure and must be distinguished from the dynamic pressure, though it has a similar form as we shall see in eqn. (2.14):

$$q_c = p_T - p = p\left[\frac{p_T}{p} - 1\right]$$

Isentropically, $\frac{p_T}{p} = \left[1 + \frac{\gamma-1}{2}M^2\right]^{\frac{\gamma}{\gamma-1}}$, so

$$\frac{q_c}{p} = \left[1 + \frac{\gamma-1}{2}M^2\right]^{\frac{\gamma}{\gamma-1}} - 1 = \left[1 + \frac{\gamma-1}{2}\frac{V^2}{\gamma RT}\right]^{\frac{\gamma}{\gamma-1}} - 1 \tag{2.10}$$

Solving for V and multiplying both sides by $\sqrt{\sigma}$:

$$V\sqrt{\sigma} = \sqrt{\frac{2\gamma p}{(\gamma-1)\rho_0}\left[\left(\frac{q_c}{p} + 1\right)^{\frac{\gamma-1}{\gamma}} - 1\right]} \tag{2.11}$$

Equivalent airspeed is the name given to $V\sqrt{\sigma}$ and is a direct measure of the kinetic energy of a volume ($\mathbf{v}$) of moving fluid.

$$V\sqrt{\sigma} = V_e \tag{2.12}$$

$$\frac{kinetic\ energy}{volume} = \frac{mV^2}{2V} = \frac{\rho V^2}{2} = \frac{\rho_0 V_e^2}{2} = q$$

Equivalent airspeed appears in all force and moment equations and therefore commonly correlates directly to structural loads on the airframe. It has the practical benefit of being a unique function of dynamic pressure and consequently is the unit of choice for many flight test engineers (particularly those concerned with structural loads or flutter).

Careful examination of eqns. (2.10) or (2.11) reveals that calibrating a differential pressure gage (which the ASI is) in velocity units is not as easy as it first appears. Pressure and/or density are different at each pressure altitude and, even with V as the measure of velocity, that means a new scale would be needed for each pressure altitude. Such scaling is obviously impractical and in 1925 the U. S. Army and Navy agreed upon a scale based on standard day sea level conditions[14]. Virtually all airspeed indicators in the United States are based on this **calibrated airspeed** which is defined by:

$$V_{cal} = V\sqrt{\sigma}\,|_{\rho=\rho_0} \tag{2.13}$$

where $\sqrt{\sigma}$ is evaluated at standard day sea level pressure (but not necessarily standard day sea level temperature).

$$V_{cal} = \sqrt{\frac{2\gamma p_0}{(\gamma-1)\rho_0}\left[\left(\frac{q_c}{p_0}+1\right)^{\frac{\gamma-1}{\gamma}}-1\right]} \tag{2.14}$$

For incompressible flow, the difference between total and static pressure is **dynamic pressure**, q, which is a measure of the kinetic energy of a unit volume of air. It is not identical to q_c; the two parameters are equal only for incompressible flow. For incompressible flow, $V\sqrt{\sigma} = \sqrt{\frac{2q}{\rho_0}}$, if $V < 200$ mph and $h_p < 15000$ ft.

$$q = p_T - p = \frac{\rho_{V^2}}{2} \tag{2.15}$$

Relating the ASI reading and V_e requires the following correction.

$$\frac{V_e}{V_{cal}} = \sqrt{\frac{p}{p_0}\frac{\left[\left(\frac{q_c}{p}+1\right)^{\frac{\gamma-1}{\gamma}}-1\right]}{\left[\left(\frac{q_c}{p_0}+1\right)^{\frac{\gamma-1}{\gamma}}-1\right]}}$$

This ratio can been tabulated[15] for easy use or, more commonly, the difference between V_{cal} and V_e is plotted as a function of pressure altitude and calibrated airspeed (Fig. 2.4). This correction term has been called a "compressibility" correction; though as the preceding development shows, it is merely the result of a choice of airspeed indicator calibration constants and has nothing to do with compressibility itself.

$$\Delta V_c = V_e - V_{cal} \tag{2.16}$$

One final type of airspeed, **indicated airspeed**, must be defined for flight test data reduction. It is simply the dial reading from the specific differential pressure gage used. Each such gage used in experimental work should be calibrated periodically with a known differential pressure source against eqn. (2.13). A record of the deviations must be maintained for each ASI by serial number if precise data reduction is to be done. Altimeters should also be calibrated periodically in a similar manner.

Example 2.2: A high altitude remotely piloted vehicle (RPV) is flying at a pressure altitude of 40,000 feet where the temperature is -47°F. If the RPV's airspeed indicator is perfect, and it registers a calibrated airspeed of 200 KCAS, what is the true airspeed?

At 200 KCAS and $h_p = 40,000$ feet, Fig. 2.4 gives: $\Delta V_c = -9$ kts $= V_e - V_{cal}$

$V_e = V_{cal} + \Delta V_c = 200 - 9 = 191$ KEAS

To obtain TAS, $V_e = V\sqrt{\sigma}$ and $h_p = 40,000$ feet implies p in a standard atmosphere; ρ can be calculated from eqn. (2.3), knowing both p and T_0. Using the results from Example 2.1 for $\delta = 0.1851$ and then calculating ρ from the given data, $\theta = 0.7956$, $\sigma = \frac{\delta}{\theta} = 0.1473$. So, $V = \frac{191}{\sqrt{0.1473}} = 396$ knots ·

So far, our discussion has assumed no error in measurement of p_T and p, but there are a number of measurement uncertainties that must be considered.

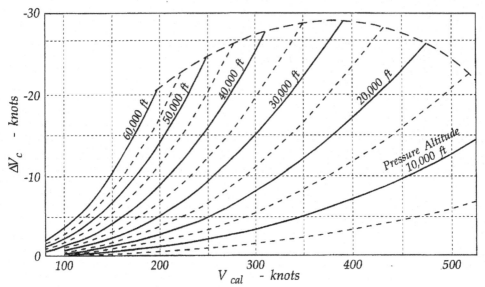

Fig. 2.4 Correction Factor (ΔV_c)

2.1.4 Pitot-Static Measurement Errors

The Pitot-static system suffers from all of the following errors:

◆ instrument error
◆ pressure lag error
◆ position error

Each of these errors will be defined and their relative importance will be discussed in this section.

2.1.4.1 **Instrument Error**. Instrument error is simply the deviation of the instrument indications from a known differential pressure standard. It results from imperfections in the gage itself and is typically measured in a calibration laboratory with the instrument disconnected from other parts of the Pitot-static system. A concise description of laboratory calibration procedures is given by Gracey[12]. Several factors contribute to instrument error: scale error, manufacturing deviations, magnetic fields, temperature fluctuations, coulomb and viscous friction, and the inertia of moving parts.

Several points must be kept in mind when calibrating airspeed indicators in the laboratory for instrument error. These differential pressure gages may be calibrated statically and dynamically. Typically, the static calibration is sufficient for most flight test measurements. Data should be taken in both directions so that hysteresis can be determined. If hysteresis loops are significant, the instrument should not be used for data collection. An instrument vibrator may reduce the effects of hysteresis, but care in design of the vibrator is essential to avoid electronic interference with data acquisition or with communications. Laboratory calibration data must be checked carefully for repeatability, and if it is not up to standard, the instrument should not be used for data collection. Wear will obviously change the calibration of an indicator over time. Consequently, a high rate of change in the calibration indicates wear reaching an unacceptable level.

Instrument corrections are usually given as the differences between instrument corrected values and gage readings. Notice that we now begin using $_{ic}$ as a subscript to imply readings that have been corrected using laboratory calibration data for a specific instrument. Also, an $_i$ subscript alone refers to the actual gage reading at a given condition. The corrections determined by such a ground calibration for each gage are:

$$\Delta V_{ic} = V_{ic} - V_i \tag{2.17}$$
$$\Delta h_{ic} = h_{ic} - h_i \tag{2.18}$$

These corrections can be either positive or negative depending on the particular instrument. A typical airspeed indicator and a correction curve is given in Fig. 2.5.

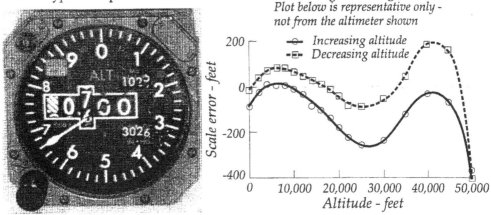

Fig. 2.5 Instrument Error Calibration Curve

2.1.4.2 Pressure Lag Error. Any pressure sensing system, including aircraft Pitot-static sensing systems, is subject to errors due to time delay in transmitting the pressure from the point of measurement to the sensor. In an airplane, this error is typically significant only when rates of change of pressure are high, such as in a rapid climb or descent. For a given rate of change of pressure, the lag error depends primarily on the length and diameter of the pressure tubing and the internal volume of the instruments. Obviously, a leak in the pressure lines also affects lag error. In all cases lag error is proportional to the pressure drop through the system lines from the pressure orifice to the pressure indicator.

The flow rate of the air in the system sets the lag error because of two types of time-dependent phenomena. First, acoustic lag occurs because the pressure changes are transmitted through the lines at the speed of sound. Since the speed of sound at low altitudes is typically on the order of 1000 fps, tubing lengths must be quite long before acoustic lag is significant. For most systems and flight envelopes, acoustic lag can be safely ignored. Second, and more important for practical flight test considerations, the air flowing in the lines produces a pressure drop. Following Gracey[12], the lag constant due to pressure drop with laminar flow in the tubing is:

$$\lambda = p\frac{\Delta p}{\Delta t} \quad \text{or, for laminar flow in the tubing:} \quad \lambda = \frac{128mLC}{pd^4 p} \tag{2.19}$$

where L = length of tubing, μ = viscosity of air, d = internal diameter of tubing, p = nominal pressure, and C = volume of instrument chamber.

Once λ is known for a given system and a specified flight condition, the pressure drop Δp can be estimated for a given rate of climb or descent, which we will specify as $\frac{\Delta p}{\Delta t}$.

Remember, eqn. (2.19) is valid only for laminar flow in the pressure lines and the limiting pressure drop for straight tubing is approximately:

$$\frac{\Delta p}{L} = \frac{p_0}{p} \left(\frac{\mu}{\mu_0} \right)^2 \left(\frac{0.0065}{d^3} \right) \qquad\qquad (2.20)$$

When lag error must be known with greater precision or when the laminar flow assumption is not warranted, the lag can be determined experimentally with procedures described by Huston[17].

Because the static portion of the system may have line lengths diffeerent than those for the Pitot portion, the pressure lag errors in the airspeed indicating system are not "balanced." The lag in the shorter line will be considerably less than the lag in longer line. This imbalance is dynamic since it depends on differing flow rates in each set of lines. It may be necessary to measure these errors experimentally as Wildhack[18] has suggested, but a more pragmatic approach suggested by Hamlin[14] is to merely add volume to the shorter line. The volume (or length of tubing) needed can be determined in a pressure chamber by changing the pressure at a rate commensurate with those encountered in representative maneuvers. Balancing the system in this fashion may cause significant errors for maneuvers other than those simulated by the balancing procedure. Reducing lag error is essentially a system design problem. The goal is to keep line lengths as short as possible since both acoustic lag and pressure drop lags depend on line length. Pressure drop, the dominant lag error in most installations, can also be minimized by increasing tube diameter or reducing instrument volume. Bends and connections in the pressure lines should also be minimized. Electronic pressure transducers are now small enough to help reduce line length (when mounted close to their sensing orifices) and to keep the system volumes low. Gracey[12] observes that lag error using this type of transducer in the Pitot and the static pressure lines is "...usually so small that it is of no concern."

2.1.4.3 **Position Error**. Position error in Pitot-static systems comes from two sources: 1) location of the static source in the pressure field of the aircraft and 2) the shape of the total pressure head or the incident flow direction.

Careful attention to design of the total pressure head will reduce the total pressure position error to a negligible value. Since the Pitot-static equations assume isentropic flow, the total pressure pickup cannot be located behind a propeller, in the wing wake, in the boundary layer, or in or behind a region of supersonic flow. (The effect of a shock wave produced by a properly shaped total pressure probe can be accounted for through the Rayleigh formula.[13]) Once a suitable location for the total pressure sensor is selected, the shape of the sensor surface and the flow direction determine the Pitot head position error. The shape must be suited to the application, but adequate design information is available, with Gracey's work a standard[10]. Carefully designed probes sense no significant total pressure error at flow inclinations of up to approximately 20° and Kiel-style Pitot probes measure total pressures up to 60°. For this reason, total pressure error may usually be ignored in Pitot-static calibrations. Helicopters are a major exception to this rule since the the entire aircraft is immersed in the rotor wash.

It is not generally possible, however, to eliminate static pressure position errors because the pressure field depends on Mach number, Reynolds number, angle of attack, and sideslip angle. With such an array of variables to be considered, rarely can a location for the static source be found so that the sensed pressure will be freestream static pressure throughout the flight envelope. The effects of flow inclination (α and β) can be minimized by manifolding two or more orifices on opposite sides of the aircraft or, on boom installations, by drilling static ports circumferentially. Figure 2.6 illustrates how locations can be chosen to minimize static pressure error for a subsonic airplane. Figure 2.7 like-wise illustrates guidelines for choosing static pressure locations for a Pitot-static boom mounted on the nose of a supersonic airplane.

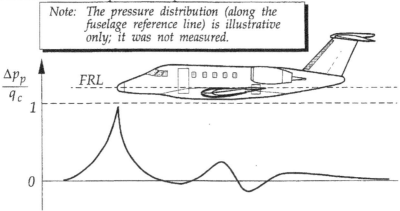

Note: The pressure distribution (along the fuselage reference line) is illustrative only; it was not measured.

Fig. 2.6 Locations for Static Pressure Orifices

Static position error can now be defined quantitatively.

$$\Delta p_p = p_s - p_\infty \tag{2.21}$$

where the $_s$ subscript indicates sensed pressure

Altitude and airspeed static position error corrections are both functions of Δp_p as de-fined below (the subscript $_{ic}$ denotes measurements corrected for instrument error):

$$\Delta h_{pc} = h_{cal} - h_{ic} \tag{2.22}$$
$$\Delta V_{pc} = V_{cal} - V_{ic} \tag{2.23}$$

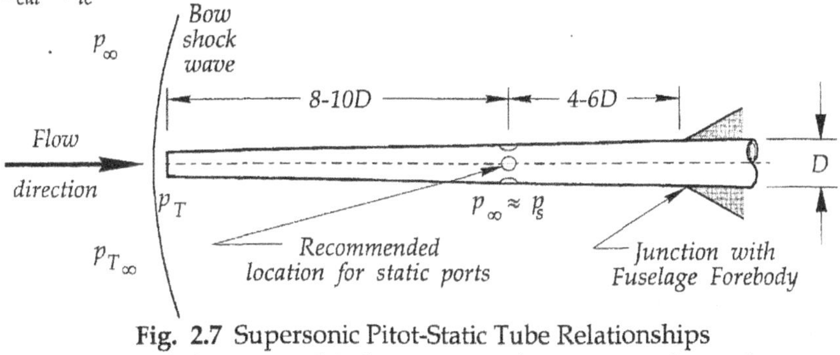

Fig. 2.7 Supersonic Pitot-Static Tube Relationships

Both the altimeter and the airspeed indicator sense the an approximate freestream static pressure, p_s, and Δh_{pc} and ΔV_{pc} are not independent variables. Our task in the remain-der of this section is to find an expression relating Δh_{pc} and ΔV_{pc}.

Starting with eqn. (2.5) in approximate incremental form, we first express the depend-ence of Δh_{pc} on Δp_p. (We also introduce yet another subscript 'std' to represent standard day conditions.) Let dp --> Δp_p ; that is, the Δp of interest is error in sensed static pres-sure and, correspondingly, dh --> - Δh_{pc}, the altimeter's static pressure error correction. Then, eqn. (2.5) becomes:

$$\Delta p_p = \rho_{std} g_0 \Delta h_{pc} \quad \text{or} \quad \Delta h_{pc} = \frac{\Delta p_p}{\rho_{std} g_0} \tag{2.24}$$

Then, $\dfrac{\Delta p_p}{\rho_{std}g_0} = \rho_{std}g_0 = \rho_0\sigma_{std}g_0 = 0.0764749\sigma_{std}$ (2.25)

But $\sigma_{std} = \dfrac{\rho_{std}}{\rho_0} = \dfrac{\rho_{std}}{\rho_i}\dfrac{\rho_i}{\rho_0} = \dfrac{\rho_i}{\rho_0}\left[1 + \dfrac{k_i}{T_i}(h-h_i)\right]^{-\frac{g_0}{k_iR}-1}$, $k_i \neq 0$, or

$\sigma_{std} = \dfrac{\rho_i}{\rho_0}e^{-\frac{g_0}{T_iR}(h-h_i)}$, $k_i = 0$

For $i = 0$, we substitute: $-\dfrac{g_0}{k_0R} = 5.25592$, $T_0 = 518.67\,°R$, $k_0 = -0.00356616\,°R/ft$

$\sigma_{std} = \left[1 - \dfrac{6.87559}{1000000}h\right]^{4.2559}$ (2.26)

For $i = 1$, $\sigma_{std} = \dfrac{\rho_{tropopause}}{\rho_0}\dfrac{\rho_{std}}{\rho_{tropopause}} = \sigma_{tropopause}e^{-\frac{g_0}{T_iR}(h-h_i)}$ (2.27)

$= 0.2979725e^{-(0.000048063797)(h-36089.239)}$

Fortunately, these equations for σ_{std} can be plotted and/or programmed for table lookup.

Approximate relationships between Δp_p and airspeed indications can also be obtained straightforwardly. Assuming no error in sensed total pressure, the indicated impact pressure is:

$q_{c_{ic}} = p_T - p_s.$
The impact pressure without static pressure error is:

$q_c = p_T - p_\infty$
Static pressure error is, therefore, just the difference between q_c and $q_{c_{ic}}$.

$\Delta p_p = p_s - p_\infty = q_c - q_{c_{ic}}.$
Rearranging eqn. (2.10)

$\dfrac{q_c}{p} = \left[1 + \dfrac{(\gamma-1)V^2}{2\gamma RT}\right]^{\frac{\gamma}{\gamma-1}} - 1$

This pressure ratio can be applied to any set of temperature and velocity measurements so long as the process is approximately isentropic. Specializing this expression to calibrated airspeed, which implies substituting p_0 for p and T_0 for T;

$\dfrac{q_c}{p_0} = \left[1 + \dfrac{(\gamma-1)V_{cal}^2}{2a_0^2}\right]^{\frac{\gamma}{\gamma-1}} - 1 = \left[1 + \dfrac{(\gamma-1)\left(V_{ic}+\Delta V_{pc}\right)^2}{2a_0^2}\right]^{\frac{\gamma}{\gamma-1}} - 1$ (2.28)

and, for instrument corrected airspeed V_{ic}, $q_{c_{ic}}$ replaces q_c

$\dfrac{q_{cic}}{p} = \left[1 + \dfrac{(\gamma-1)V_{ic}^2}{2a_0^2}\right]^{\frac{\gamma}{\gamma-1}} - 1$

Now, we can obtain an approximate expression relating Δp_p and ΔV_{pc} in the same way Herrington[9] does by using only the expression above and the definition $q_{c_{ic}} = p_T - p_s$. If p_T is measured with negligible error, then $dq_{c_{ic}} = -dp_s$. Differentiating and replacing $dq_{c_{ic}}$ with $-dp_s$ gives eqn. (2.29):

$$\frac{dp}{dV_{ic}} \approx \left[1+\frac{(\gamma-1)V_{ic}^2}{2a_0^2}\right]^{\frac{1}{\gamma-1}}$$ (2.29)

Approximating the differentials with finite differences: $\Delta p_p \approx dp_s$ and $\Delta V_{pc} \approx -dV_{ic}$,

$$\frac{\Delta p_p}{\Delta V_{pc}} \approx -\frac{\gamma p_0 V_{ic}}{a_0^2}\left[1+\frac{(\gamma-1)V_{ic}^2}{a_0^2}\right]^{\frac{1}{\gamma-1}}$$ (2.30)

This approximation is based on eqn. (2.10), which is a valid expression for an isentropic process (no shock waves). Equation (2.30) is valid only if $V_{ic} < a_0$. However, a similar approach, starting with the Rayleigh supersonic Pitot formula, gives an approximation when the Pitot tube does have an attached normal shock wave.

$$\frac{q_c}{p} = \left[\frac{(\gamma+1)V^2}{2a^2}\right]^{\frac{\gamma}{\gamma-1}} + \left[\frac{(\gamma+1)V^2}{1-\gamma+2\gamma\frac{V^2}{a^2}}\right]^{\frac{1}{\gamma-1}} - 1$$

Factoring out $1-\gamma$ from the $\left[\dfrac{(\gamma+1)V^2}{1-\gamma+2\gamma\dfrac{V^2}{a^2}}\right]^{\frac{1}{\gamma-1}}$ term, and rearranging gives

$$\frac{q_c}{p} = \left[\frac{(\gamma+1)V^2}{2a^2}\right]^{\frac{\gamma}{\gamma-1}} + \left[\frac{\gamma+1}{\gamma-1}\right]^{\frac{1}{\gamma-1}} + \left[\frac{2\gamma V^2}{(\gamma-1)a^2}\right]^{\frac{1}{\gamma-1}} - 1$$ (2.31)

Substituting $\gamma = 1.4$ for air:

$$\frac{q_c}{p} = \left(1.2^{3.5}\right)\left(6^{2.5}\right)\left[\frac{V}{a}\right]^7\left[7\frac{V^2}{a^2}-1\right]^{2.5} - 1 = 166.92158\left(\frac{V}{a}\right)^7\left[7\frac{V^2}{a^2}-1\right]^{2.5} - 1$$

If we now replace V with V_{ic}, p with p_0, and a with a_0, we can solve for the instrument corrected dynamic pressure read on the ASI by using the following equations:

$$\frac{q_{c_{ic}}}{p_0} = 166.92158\left[\frac{V_{ic}}{a_0}\right]^7\left[7\frac{V_{ic}^2}{a_0^2}-1\right]^{2.5} - 1$$

Still assuming no measurement error in p_T, and taking the derivative with respect to V_{ic},

$$\frac{dq_{c_{ic}}}{dV_{ic}} = (7)(166.92158)\left[\frac{V_{ic}}{a_0}\right]^6\frac{\left[2\frac{V_{ic}^2}{a_0^2}-1\right]}{\left[7\frac{V_{ic}^2}{a_0^2}-1\right]^{3.5}} = -\frac{dp_s}{dV_{ic}}$$

Using our finite difference approximations again, $\Delta p_p \approx dp_s$ and $\Delta V_{pc} \approx -dV_{ic}$,

$$\frac{\Delta p_p}{\Delta V_{pc}} \approx 52.85333 \left[\frac{V_{ic}}{a_0}\right]^6 \frac{\left[2\frac{V_{ic}^2}{a_0^2}-1\right]}{\left[7\frac{V_{ic}^2}{a_0^2}-1\right]^{3.5}} \qquad (2.32)$$

where $\dfrac{\Delta p_p}{\Delta V_{pc}}$ is in inches of Hg/knot. (Changing the constant to 2214.795 in eqn. (2.32)

gives $\dfrac{\Delta p_p}{\Delta V_{pc}}$ in psf/fps.)

The approximate expressions in eqns. (2.30) and (2.32) for $\dfrac{\Delta p_p}{\Delta V_{pc}}$ are valid only for fairly small errors in pressure measurement; Herrington[16] says that ΔV_{pc} must be less than 10 knots, which is usually quite adequate for well-designed Pitot-static systems. Since both Δh_{pc} and ΔV_{pc} are functions of the error in measuring static pressure, they must be related. Having determined one, we should be able to calculate the other. Dividing eqns. (2.30) or (2.32) by eqn. (2.25), for $\dfrac{V_{ic}}{a_0} < 1$ or $\dfrac{V_{ic}}{a_0} > 1$, respectively, and then using the appropriate form of σ_{std} from either eqn. (2.26) or (2.27),

$$\frac{\Delta h_{pc}}{\Delta V_{pc}} \approx 58.566 \left[\frac{V_{ic}}{s_{std}a_0}\right]\left[1+0.2\frac{V_{ic}^2}{a_0^2}\right]\frac{V_{ic}}{a_0} \ for \ \frac{V_{ic}}{a_0} < 1 \qquad (2.33)$$

where $\dfrac{\Delta h_{pc}}{\Delta V_{pc}}$ is in feet/knot.

Similarly, for $\dfrac{V_{ic}}{a_0} > 1$,

$$\frac{\Delta h_{pc}}{\Delta V_{pc}} \approx 48,880 \left[\frac{V_{ic}}{a_0}\right]^6 \frac{\left[2\frac{V_{ic}^2}{a_0^2}-1\right]}{\left[7\frac{V_{ic}^2}{a_0^2}-1\right]^{3.5}} \qquad (2.34)$$

Equations (2.33) and (2.34), plotted in Fig. 2.8, are valid approximations if $\Delta h_{pc} < 1,000$ feet and $\Delta V_{pc} < 10$ knots. For larger position error corrections, Herrington has developed and plotted more exact equations[16], good for $\Delta V_{pc} < 50$ knots. If increased range is needed for this correction, the interested reader should consult Herrington's handbook.

Example 2.3: An airplane is flying at 303 KIAS at an indicated pressure altitude of 29,750 feet. The outside air temperature is -25°F for these test conditions. The instrument corrections include $\Delta V_{ic} = -3$ knots, Δh_{pc} = 250 feet, and Δh_{ic} =75 feet. Calculate $\dfrac{\Delta h_{pc}}{\Delta V_{pc}}$, ΔV_{pc}, V_e, V_∞, and M_∞.

First, we will use our definitions to relate indicated and true airspeed

$V_\infty = V_{ic} + \Delta V_{pc} + \Delta V_c$, but $V_{ic} = V_i + \Delta V_{ic} = 303 - 3 = 300$ knots

Also, using $a_0 = 1116.4$ feet/sec = 661.489 knots, from eqn. (2.33),

$$\frac{\Delta h_{pc}}{\Delta V_{pc}} = \left(\frac{(58.566)(300)}{\sigma_{std}661.489}\right)\left(1+0.2\frac{300^2}{661.489^2}\right)^{2.5}$$

To obtain σ_{std}, we need the pressure altitude, which is:

$h = h_i + \Delta h_{ic} + \Delta h_{pc} = 29{,}750 + 75 + 250 = 30{,}075$ feet

Equation (2.28) gives σ_{std}: $\sigma_{std} = \left(1 - \dfrac{6.87559}{1{,}000{,}000}h\right)^{4.2559}$

$\sigma_{std} = \left(1 - \dfrac{6.87559}{1{,}000{,}000}30{,}075\right)^{4.2559} = 0.37310$, so

$\dfrac{\Delta h_{pc}}{\Delta V_{pc}} = 78.74 \dfrac{ft}{kt}$

$\Delta V_{pc} = \dfrac{250\ ft}{78.74\ ft/kt} = \qquad\qquad\qquad\qquad\qquad\qquad\qquad \Delta V_{pc} = 3.18\ knots$

From Fig. 2.4, $\Delta V_c = -15$ kts $= V_e - V_{cal}$, so $V_e = V_{cal} - 15$ kts $= 300 - 15$ $\qquad\qquad V_e = 285\ knots$

$V_\infty = \dfrac{V_e}{\sqrt{\sigma}} = \dfrac{285}{\sqrt{0.35314}}$ $\qquad\qquad\qquad\qquad\qquad V_\infty = 479.6\ knots = 810.0\ fps$

Notice that σ is calculated from the pressure at the known pressure altitude; it is not σ_{std} at that altitude as calculated above from eqn 2.28.

$M_\infty = \dfrac{V_\infty}{\sqrt{\gamma R T}} = \dfrac{810.0}{\sqrt{(1.4)(1716.55)(434.67)}}$ $\qquad\qquad\qquad M_\infty = 0.79$

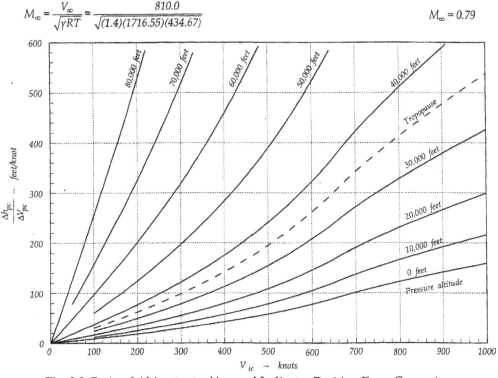

Fig. 2.8 Ratio of Altimeter to Airspeed Indicator Position Error Correction

2.2 POSITION ERROR CALIBRATION METHODS

From the preceding discussion, Pitot-static system calibration is primarily concerned with determining the static position error. Since the static source error leads to errors in both altitude and velocity position errors, multiple approaches exist. Direct measurement of the altitude position error by a freestream method yields the static source error and thence the velocity position error. Alternatively, direct measurement of the velocity position error can also lead to the static source position error and then to the altitude position error. Gracey[12] classifies position error calibration methods under four stategies:

◆ Freestream static pressure methods in which Δp_p is obtained from measurement of p_s and $p\infty$.

◆ True airspeed methods in which Δp_p is derived from values of V_∞ calculated from ground speed measurements or from anemometer readings.

◆ A temperature method in which Δp_p is determined from measured temperature and a pressure-temperature survey.

◆ Mach number methods in which Δp_p is obtained from Mach number.

Of these four calibration methods the first two are most common. They are especially well-suited for low speed and low altitude, although they include several techniques useful at high altitudes and airspeeds. Instrumentation needs are minimized with these two approaches. For brevity, we will describe only four calibration procedures, two that are freestream static pressure methods and two that are true airspeed techniques. For the reader whose needs go beyond this introductory material, Gracey lists fourteen calibration methods and summarizes relative accuracies (when data are available) and limitations. Table 2.2 is adapted from this table, emphasizing measurement errors associated with each method and adding the GPS/INS and the smoke trail methods to Gracey's list.

After describing the four selected techniques, the discussion will focus on the sensitivity of the position error correction to three major effects: gross weight changes, altitude variations, and Mach number deviations.

2.2.1 Freestream Static Pressure Methods

These methods depend on accurate experimental determination of the difference between measured static pressure and the actual freestream static at the test altitude. There are at least four ways to determine this differential pressure. First, Δp_p can be obtained from a reference pressure source moving with the aircraft but located outside the pressure field of the vehicle. The test aircraft may carry this reference pressure sensor onboard (trailing cone or trailing bomb) or the calibrated reference sensor may be carried in another airplane (pacer aircraft) flying formation with the test vehicle. Second, the reference value of p_∞ is obtained by interpolating the pressure gradient optically (tower flyby) for low altitude calibrations or with tracking radar for medium and high altitudes. In each of these cases, the reference barometer is either tower-mounted or flown through the test band with a radiosonde balloon. Third, p_∞ may be calculated by measuring p and T at the ground and assuming a temperature gradient up to the altitude where temperature is measured. Fourth, p_∞ at a given altitude can be obtained from measuring indicated pressure and temperature and noting the changes in height from an altitude where Δp_p is known. Ordinarily, for these freestream static methods where pressure differences are measured by aircraft instruments, the altimeter position error, Δh_{pc}, is the measured correction because h_{cal} is relatively easy to determine and the altimeter provides better resolution than the ASI. For example, at sea level and 150 knots, a ΔV_{pc} of 2 knots corresponds approximately to a Δh_{pc} of about 38 feet and to a Δh_{pc} of approximately 116 feet at 500 knots .

Let us now examine the tower flyby technique and the pacer aircraft technique and discuss in detail the data collection and data reduction procedures for each of them. We will also suggest some of the advantages and limitations of each approach.

Table 2.2 Air Data Calibration Methods for Use in Flight Test

Calibration Method	Altitude Range	Min Speed[2]	Max Speed[2]	Accuracy[1] %q_c (~1σ)	Precision[1] %q_c (~1σ)	Instruments[2]	Measurements
Tower flyby	Very low	Min LFS	Max LFS	±1.0 (M = 0.15) ±0.2 (M = 0.30)		Camera in tower	q_c, p Z_c, ΔZ
Speed course	Low	Min LFS	M = 0.2			ASI, Alt, IT, stop watch	q_c, p, T V_g, T
Pacer aircraft	Low/ high	Min LFS	Max LFS		±0.7 (M = 0.5) ±0.2 (M = 1.0)	ASI, Alt	q_c, p
GPS/INS	Low/ high	Min LFS	Max LFS			ASI, Alt	q_c, p
Trailing cone	Low/ high	Min LFS	M = 1.5		±0.2 (M = 0.7 to M = 0.88)	ASI, Alt, DPI	q_c, p, p
Smoke trail	High	Min LFS	Max LFS			ASI, Alt	q_c, p
Trailing bomb	Low/ high	Stall Speed	[3]M = 0.4 to 0.85	±2.0 (M = 0.1) ±0.2 (M = 0.35)		ASI, Alt, DPI	q_c, p, p
Tracking Radar	High	Min LFS	Max dive	±.2 (M = 0.5) ±0.1 (M = 0.88)		IPR, APR, radar	q_c, p Z
Recording Thermometer	High	Min LFS	Max dive	±4.5 (M = 0.8)		IPR, APR, RT	q_c, p, T
Accelerometer	High	Min LFS	[4]Max dive	±0.5 (M = 0.6 to 0.8)		IPR, APR, RT, RA, AAR	q_c, p, T a_x, a_z, θ

[1]Values quoted have been achieved; instrumentation and techniquesused may vary these values widely
[2]Abbreviations used:

AAR	attitude angle recorder		Alt	altimeter
APR	absolute pressure recorder		ASI	airspeed indicator
DPI	differential pressure instrument		IPR	impact pressure recorder
IT	indicating thermometer		RT	recording thermometer
RA	recording accelerometer			
LFS	level flight speed		V_g	ground speed

[3]Maximum speed at which unstable oscillations of bomb occurred in suspension cable
[4]Maneuvers must be carried out in vertical plane

2.2.1.1 **Tower Flyby Method**. In this technique, the calibrated altitude of the vehicle is determined by triangulation relative to a surveyed point on the ground for a typical tower flyby course (Fig. 2.9). The airplane is flown down the tower flyby line at an altitude approximately level with the eyepiece in the tower. The altitude and the airspeed both must be stabilized as the airplane passes abeam the tower. The height of the airplane in the sighting grid (y) and the pressure altitude in the tower are recorded for each pass. Then the calibrated altitude of the airplane's altimeter can be calculated by adding the pressure altitude of the tower to Δh, where $\Delta h = d \dfrac{y}{x}$.

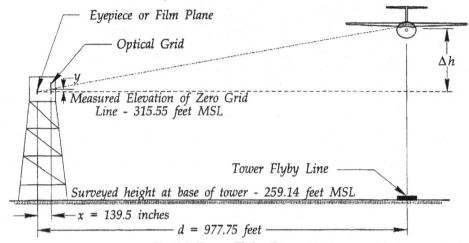

Fig. 2.9 Tower Flyby Geometry

Figure 2.10 illustrates how calibrated altitudes from the two ground blocks are used to obtain h_c at each test point. The data reduction for tower flyby information proceeds along the following lines. Determine the calibrated altitude of the test airplane's altimeter at each test point during the flight. The so-called "ground block" method, which assumes a constant change of calibrated altitude with time of day, is the most commonly used means of obtaining h_c for each test point. The flight test crew must obtain a preflight and postflight reading of the aircraft altimeter (set at 29.92 in Hg, of course) at a point of known elevation on the ramp. Then, $h_{cal_{ramp}} = h_{i_{ramp}} + \Delta h_{ic}$.

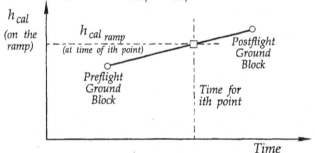

Fig. 2.10 Use of Ground Block Calibrated Altitudes

Using the interpolated value of calibrated altitude on the ramp, calculate calibrated altitude at the tower eyepiece. In Fig. 2.9 the eyepiece is 315.55 feet above mean sea level, the optical grid is 139.5 inches from the eyepiece, and grid lines are 1 inch apart. The bottom grid line is at eyepiece level. The flyby line is 977.75 feet in front of the eyepiece. The altimeter's height above ground for the particular test airplane must also be considered.

$$h_{cal_{eyepiece}} = h_{cal_{ramp}} + \Delta h_{cal_{eyepiece}} - \Delta h_{cal_{altimeter}}$$

The calibrated altitude of the test aircraft is then obtained from

$$h_{cal} = h_{cal_{eyepiece}} + \Delta h \tag{2.35}$$

where Δh is the correction for nonstandard temperature conditions.

Next, we must find the test day pressure-related parameters with instrument corrections. For this introductory course, we will consider only h_{ic}, V_{ic}, and $q_{c_{ic}}$, leaving M_{ic} to more detailed descriptions.

$h_{ic_t} = h_i + \Delta h_{ic}$ and $V_{ic_t} = V_i + \Delta V_{ic}$. As we saw in Section 2.1.3.3,

$$q_{c_{ic}} = \left[1 + 0.2 \frac{V_{ic}^2}{a_0^2} \right]^{3.5} - 1$$

Finally, we standardize Δh_{pc} and ΔV_{ic} to a reference altitude approximately equal to standard day elevation at the test site. The tower eyepiece elevation in Fig. 2.9 is 315.55 feet; therefore, we will correct each test day measurement to standard day at this elevation. No lag correction is necessary for steady state test data, so:

$\Delta h_{pc_t} = h_{cal_t} - h_{ic_t}$

To correct to standard day conditions at 315.55 feet, considering only small altitude and angle of attack changes:

$$\Delta h_{pc_{315}} = \Delta h_{pc_t} \frac{\theta_{315}}{\theta_t}$$

where $\theta = 1 - 0.00000687559 h_{cal}$

So, $\Delta h_{pc_{315}} = \Delta h_{pc_t}$ \hfill (2.36)

To correct V_{ic_t} to $V_{ic_{315}}$, assume that each test point was flown at 315 feet and the test day Mach number. Then, we observe that

$$\frac{q_{c_{ic_{std}}}}{p_{s_{std}}} = \frac{q_{c_{ic_t}}}{p_{s_t}} = \frac{q_{c_{ic_{std}}}}{p_0 \delta_{315}}.$$

For subsonic airspeeds, we solve this expression for $V_{ic_{315}}$:

$$V_{ic_{315}} = a_0 \sqrt{5 \left\{ \left[\frac{q_{c_{ic_{std}}}}{p_0 d_{315}} + 1 \right]^{0.2857142} - 1 \right\}} \hfill (2.37)$$

$\Delta V_{pc_{315}}$ can then be obtained from eqn. 2.33 or from Fig. 2.8, knowing $\Delta h_{pc_{315}}$.

This data reduction scheme has been simplified considerably by assuming small differences in altitude measurements and test day calibrated altitudes, small correction terms, and subsonic flight conditions. For other conditions ($M_{ic} > 1$, for example), different equations must be used. Do not apply these data reduction equations to data for which $\Delta h_{pc} > 1000$ feet or $\Delta V_{pc} > 10$ knots. Consult Herrington[16] and/or other flight test handbooks for complete details that are beyond the scope of this book.

The tower flyby procedure requires little instrumentation and is quite straightforward, though tedious. Photographic and/or theodolite equipment are often used to record the aircraft elevation at each measurement point, but hand-recorded optical data are also usable. Gracey[12] concluded from tests at NASA's Langley Research Center that Δp_p can be measured within $\pm$ 1% of q_c, even for very low speeds ($M = 0.15$ and 90 knots). The method is least accurate for such low speed points because angle of attack effects dominate. For higher speeds ($M = 0.3$ and 190 knots), accuracy within $\pm$ 0.2% of q_c was found. Altitude effects cannot be investigated using the tower flyby method and the speed range is limited because it is a low altitude procedure. Low speeds must include a margin above stall speed and maximum level flight speed at low altitude restricts the method.

2.2.1.2 **Pacer Aircraft Technique.** There are at least two variations of the pacer method, one in which the reference source is in an airplane flying formation with the test aircraft and one in which the test aircraft flies at various speeds past the reference airplane. The reference carrier simply maintains a constant speed and altitude. The latter method, though less demanding for the reference airplane, is not as accurate as the formation method because of the practical difficulties in determining small differences in the height of the two aircraft and in obtaining simultaneous readings. Lag errors are also more likely to affect data from the latter technique.

When calibration tests are flown in formation, the test aircraft may be either lead or wing man. It is important that the two aircraft fly at the same level, that their speeds are matched, and that they are far enough apart so that neither Pitot-static system is affected by the other pressure field. At least half a wing span in spacing is required between the two aircraft. The formation flying required to matched altitude and airspeed for each point suggests that lateral spacing should be little more than half a wing span. Level, in the case of dissimilar aircraft, means the two altimeters should be at the same height.

Data reduction for the pacer aircraft (formation) method is relatively simple. First, find h_{cal} and V_{cal} for the pacer's reference altimeter using its indicated readings, the laboratory corrections for its instruments, and the known static position error corrections.

$$h_{cal_{pacer}} = h_{i_{pacer}} + \Delta h_{ic_{pacer}} + \Delta h_{pc_{pacer}}$$
$$V_{cal_{pacer}} = V_{i_{pacer}} + \Delta V_{ic_{pacer}} + \Delta V_{pc_{pacer}}$$

It is assumed that the pacer aircraft system has a full and accurate set of calibrations. Next, obtain h_{ic_t} and V_{ic_t} for the test aircraft as was described for the tower flyby technique. Then, calculate Δh_{pc} and ΔV_{pc} for the test aircraft assuming that both aircraft were at the exactly the same test day calibrated altitude and airspeed at each test point.

$$\Delta h_{pc_t} = h_{cal_{pacer}} - h_{i_{test}} - \Delta h_{ic_{test}}$$

Correct Δh_{pc_t} to the nominal altitude for the test point just as we did the tower flyby data with eqn. (2.36).

$$\Delta V_{pc_t} = V_{cal_{pacer}} - V_{i_{test}} - \Delta V_{ic_{test}}$$

This approach gives ΔV_{pc} independent of the approximate conversion equations developed previously (eqns. 2.33 and 2.34) and offers a crude method of checking the total pressure error if any exists. (Caution: The measurement errors in the pacer method may be large enough to imply erroneously that the total pressure error is significant. Use this comparison only as an indication that further tests may be required. Remember, you are obtaining the correction by differencing two large numbers.)

The pacer aircraft method, particularly when the two aircraft that are closely matched can be flown together, is an accurate calibration method. Gracey[12] reports an accuracy in $\frac{\Delta p_p}{\Delta q_c}$ of ±0.7% at $M = 0.5$ and ±0.2% at $M = 1.0$ for this method. Also, altitude effects can be investigated within the envelope of the two vehicles and supersonic calibrations are feasible. Low speeds and transonic speeds may make stabilizing in formation difficult because of the handling qualities of the specific aircraft. Finally, this method allows collecting static position error data rapidly, though a pacer aircraft is costly to maintain and fly.

2.2.2 True Airspeed Methods

Static position errors can also be calculated by measuring true airspeed and determining V_{cal} from the measurements. The original attraction for such methods was the simple facility and instrumentation required; the speed course technique only requires a measured straight line distance and accurate stop watches. Widespread availability of the Global Positioning System (GPS), coupled with inertial navigation system (INS), is rapidly replacing this technique for calibrating Pitot-static systems today.

2.2.2.1 **Speed Course Technique**. The speed-course method uses the true airspeed approach. Obviously, the wind must be recorded at the time and altitude of the test; wind effects can be minimized by flying reciprocal headings if the wind is constant. Tests should be conducted when the wind speed is as near zero as possible to reduce such uncertainties. Calibrations are often carried out near sunrise or sunset for this reason.

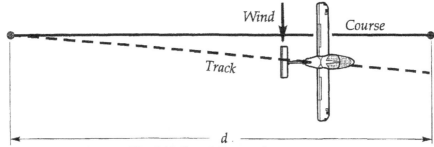

Fig. 2.11 Speed Course Geometry

Figure 2.11 is a sketch depicting the ground track of a speed course calibration test. The aircraft is aligned with a heading parallel to the desired course; no drift correction is used. The data needed from each pass are h_i, V_i, T_i, and time between the two points. If no other instrumentation is available, observers can note the time the airplane passes over each of the known points. However, GPS, INS, radar, or optical trackers will reduce the likelihood of human error in recording time accurately. The test should be planned so the timing interval is large compared to the error in marking the start and stop times. The most important parameter to be held constant is indicated airspeed and, if turbulence or poor pilot technique causes a variation of over ± 1 knot, the data point is suspect. Accurate ambient temperature at the test altitude is also necessary. This temperature becomes particularly important whenever medium altitude calibrations are attempted.

To reduce speed course data we must first find the average true airspeed.

$V_{avg} = \dfrac{1}{2}\left(\dfrac{d}{t_1} + \dfrac{d}{t_2}\right)$, where d is course length; t_1 and t_2 are times to traverse the course

Next, obtain the freestream temperature at the test altitude. If precise weather data collection equipment is available, one might obtain this information from the meteorologist. If the indicated temperature from the airplane is used, it must be corrected for the gage laboratory correction and the temperature recovery factor. Since the temperature gage reads the total temperature except for the kinetic term which requires a recovery factor because the flow is not perfectly adiabatic,

$\dfrac{T_T}{T_\infty} = 1 + K(\gamma - 1)\dfrac{V_\infty^2}{2\gamma RT} \approx \dfrac{T_{ic}}{T_\infty}$, where K is the temperature recovery factor.

Usually K is essentially constant throughout the flight envelope and for a good flight test measurement system it will be in the range of 0.95 to 1.0. However, with sloppy design or careless installation of the temperature probe, K may range as low as 0.7 and may be a function of airspeed. To summarize, ambient temperature is calculated from:

$T_\infty = (T_i + \Delta T_{ic} + 459.67) - K(\gamma - 1)\dfrac{V_\infty^2}{2gR}$, where T_i is in °F. Find the test day instrument cor-

rected altitude and airspeed; these values are based on average indicated gage readings. If large variations in either of these readings occur, the data are unusable.

$h_{ic_t} = h_{i_{avg}} + \Delta h_{ic}$ and $V_{ic_t} = V_{i_{avg}} + \Delta V_{ic}$

Then, obtain V_{cal} from the average true airspeed and the ambient temperature. Calculate the density ratio, using the perfect gas law and the measured temperature from the second step above, and substitute in the expression for equivalent airspeed.

$$V_e = V \sqrt{\sigma} = V_{cal} + \Delta V_c$$

Figure 2.4 offers a convenient means of graphically iterating to obtain V_{cal}. Calculate ΔV_{pc_t} and Δh_{pc_t} from $\Delta V_{pc_t} = V_{cal} - V_{ic_t}$ and Fig. 2.8. Finally, standardize Δh_{pc_t} and ΔV_{pc_t} to nominal altitude conditions exactly as was done for the tower flyby test data.

The speed course method is one of the least accurate techniques for obtaining the static position error correction. Gracey, taking a different approach to the reduction of the data than shown above, says that it is valid for a very limited airspeed range (speeds safely above the stall speed up to approximately 130 knots at sea level or about $M = 0.2$) and offers no estimate of the accuracy or precision[12]. On the other hand, the technique requires almost no instrumentation, apart from observers, a stopwatch or two, and an accurately known distance between two points on the ground. This simplicity does offer a simple way to calibrate the Pitot-static system but questions about accuracy will linger if the flight test team does not take meticulous care in flying and recording the data.

2.2.2.2 **GPS/INS Technique.** In the early 1970s Olson[19] suggested a flight profile and algorithm using precision radar tracking for airspeed calibrations. The flight paths involved flying three different headings separated by 120°, thus forming a "cloverleaf" (hence, the approach in Fig. 2.12). Olson, Lawford and Nipress, and Lewis[20,21,22] expanded the approach to include INS and GPS measurements instead of or in conjunction with radar tracking. Lewis showed that adequate accuracies and precision could be obtained with legs less than 120° apart. Recently, Niewoehner[26] has shown that flying four legs and using a nonlinear least squares algorithm has additional merit in terms of identifying and eliminating statistical variance in test events. This approach is quite attractive for many modern aircraft since these onboard sensors make the data collection self-contained. GPS units became quite commonplace and relatively inexpensive. Nowadays, every major test organization uses this approach to carry out most air data calibrations, though frequently in combination with other techniques.

Fig. 2.12 Cloverleaf Heading/Ground Speed Relationships

The technique was originally called the "cloverleaf" method because of the shape of the trajectory with the three passes differing in heading by 120°. An illustration of this original trajectory and a vector diagram suggested by Gray[23] (with considerable latitude in the shape of the trajectory) are shown in Fig. 2.12. Lewis[24] emphasizes that one of the best indications of accuracy for this technique is for the GPS-derived wind vector to remain constant throughout the maneuver. He illustrates with the data set in Table 2.3.

Table 2.3 Example Data for a GPS-Only Calibration[24]

Ground-speed$_1$		Ground-speed$_2$		Ground-speed$_3$		Windspeed		True Airspeed
Knots	Degrees	Knots	Degrees	Knots	Degrees	MPH	Degrees	MPH
116	236	131	135	153	46	18.9	219	134.2
131	135	153	46	134	316	19.4	221	133.7
153	46	134	316	116	236	18.7	223	134.3
154	316	116	236	131	135	18.1	221	133.6
					Average	18.8	221	134.0

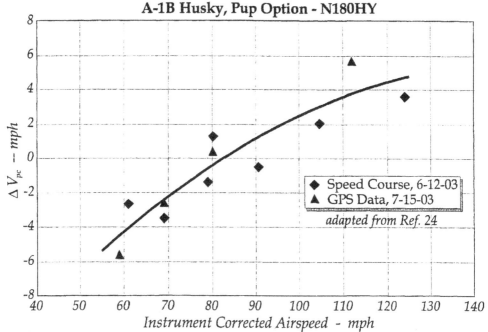

Fig. 2.13 Comparison of Speed-Course and GPS- Derived Calibrations[24]

Typical calibrations for a general aviation airplane are shown in Fig. 2.13. The comparison shows that GPS-derived data are at least comparable with speed-course information. These data were collected using a hand-held GPS unit and no other sensor.

Niewoehner used a similar GPS unit, again with no complementary measurements, and obtained error bands for each point (from the four legs flown and the nonlinear least squares data reduction scheme proposed). Comparison of these data with the manufacturer's calibration curve is shown in Fig. 2.14; quite clearly, smooth flight conditions produce much less uncertainty. It could even be argued that the manufacturer's published results may be slightly biased, though it would be necessary to fly other examples of the aircraft and collect a more statistically relevant set of data to establish this assertion.

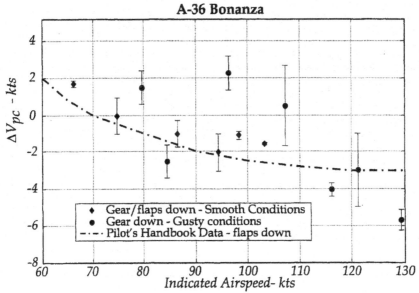

Fig. 2.14 Comparison of Pilot's Operating Handbook and GPS- Derived Calibrations[25]

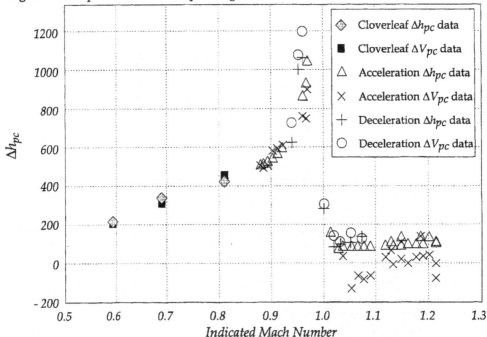

Fig. 2.15 Comparison of Acceleration/Decelerations with
a Pressure Survey and GP/INS- Derived Calibrations[26]

Olson makes a similar comparison with data obtained with an AFFTC pacer aircraft using a pressure survey with supersonic accelerations and decelerations along with GPS/INS-derived data[26], as shown in Fig. 2.15. Olson also gives complete details on the vector solutions of the wind triangle that lead to these results in this handbook along with details of how the accelerations and decelerations produce quality results in the transonic range. All of Olson's GPS/INS examples are based on either the "cloverleaf" maneuver or this pressure survey technique with accelerations and decelerations in the transonic and supersonic regime. However, Olson's data do not include standard deviations or error bars, to indicate those points that are more certain (taken in smooth conditions or with better airspeed control) as suggested by Niewoehner and Lewis.

These examples are a small sample of the growing body of knowledge for what is likely now the most popular technique for collecting Pitot-static calibration data. The general method has many advantages. The instrumentation is very inexpensive and readily available regardless of the program size or budget. No ground support or support aircraft are needed. The technique works at all altitudes and speeds. The four-leg method described by Lewis and Niewoehner provides an internal check of accuracy. While large, well-funded programs will likely continue to use multiple methods for calilbrations, it is just as likely that smaller flight test efforts will rely heavily on this method.

2.2.3 Factors Affecting Position Error Measurements

Dimensional analysis reveals that the static pressure field surrounding a moving body is a function of at least five variables, two dealing with the flow direction and three similarity parameters: angle of attack (α), sideslip angle (β), Mach number (M), Reynolds number (Re), and Prandtl number (Pn). If we neglect heat transfer effects, Pn is of no consequence; and if the static source is outside the boundary layer, Re effects will be negligible over large altitude bands. Finally, we assume that sideslip can be minimized for those maneuvers for which we insist that Pitot-static system measurements be reliable. Then,

$\dfrac{p_s}{p_\infty} = f(M, \alpha)$, where $f(M, \alpha)$ is an unspecified function of the two variables.

As C_L varies linearly with α for much of the flight regime, we may write $\dfrac{p_s}{p_\infty} = f(M, C_L)$.

But $C_L = \dfrac{2L}{\rho V^2 S} = \dfrac{2nW}{\left(\frac{p}{RT}\right)V^2 S} = \dfrac{2nW}{\left(\frac{S\gamma p_0 V^2}{\gamma RT}\right)} = \dfrac{2nW}{\delta M^2 \gamma p_0 S}$. So, the functional expression be-

comes: $\dfrac{p_s}{p_\infty} = f\left(M, \dfrac{nW}{\delta}\right)$ $\hspace{4cm}$ (2.38)

This expression shows the three major variables affecting sensed static pressure, p_s: Mach number, weight supported by the lifting surfaces, and altitude. Returning to standard usage, pressure difference is the prime variable of interest, so the functional relationship of eqn. (2.38) can also be written as:

$\dfrac{\Delta p_p}{q_{c_{ic}}} = f\left(M_{ic}, \dfrac{nW}{\delta_{ic}}\right)$ $\hspace{4cm}$ (2.39)

If M_{ic} is less than about 0.3, the flow field is essentially unaffected by compressibility effects. (Some references even suggest using a much higher limit for Mach number[13].) Then the pressure coefficient of eqn. (2.39) is a function of lift coefficient only. Also, for $M < 0.3$, altitude effects are generally negligible. Thus, eqn. (2.39) becomes

$\dfrac{\Delta p_p}{q_{c_{ic}}} = f\left(\dfrac{nW}{V_{ic}^2}\right)$ $\hspace{4cm}$ (2.40)

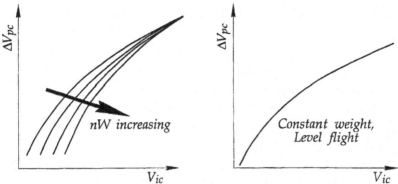

Fig. 2.16 Velocity Position Error Corrections for M < 0.3

At constant V_{ic}, this equation suggests Δp_p is a function of angle of attack only (which must change to accommodate changes in either load factor or weight while maintaining level flight). For aircraft where the weight change as fuel is used or payload is changed is a large fraction of the total weight, there is a family of curves for ΔV_{pc} (Figure 2.16a). But, if angle of attack changes are small, these curves collapse to a single curve (Fig. 2.16b).

However, Δh_{pc} is a function of altitude even if there are no angle of attack effects. Figure 2.17 depicts the changes in Δh_{pc} as a function of V_{ic} and altitude. The pressure difference is a function of altitude because the geometric altitude takes on a different value for every pressure level in the atmosphere.

In the transonic flight regime, especially near $M_\infty = 1$, it is very difficult to accurately measure static position errors. Certainly the complete functional, eqn. (2.39), is necessary. In fact, at high speeds the importance of changes in angle of attack diminishes because angle of attack changes little is small in any case. Mach number then becomes the dominant term. Figure 2.18 illustrates a complete variation of pressure coefficient with both low speed effects and the discontinuities in slope that occur in the transonic region. These discontinuities are the result of shock waves forming ahead of the static orifice. Figure 2.18 emphasizes the point that in this region the pressure coefficient is primarily a function of Mach number. Mach number is different for each V_{ic}, so ΔV_{pc} is a function of altitude in this region. Figure 2.19 illustrates this variation. Plotted versus V_{ic}, Δh_{pc} results in a family of curves displaced both vertically and horizontally for different altitudes, though if plotted versus M_{ic}, the horizontal displacement is removed.

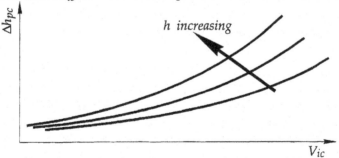

Fig. 2.17 Altitude Position Error Corrections for M < 0.3

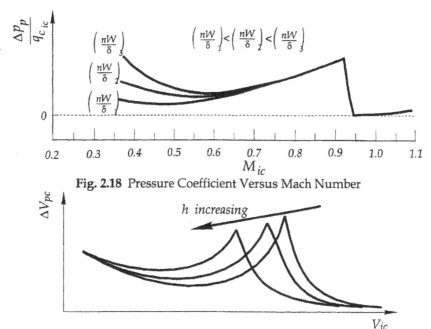

Fig. 2.18 Pressure Coefficient Versus Mach Number

Fig. 2.19 Airspeed Position Error Correction for Transonic Flight Conditions

2.3 INSTRUMENTATION

Instrumentation for conventional Pitot-static systems is largely pressure instrumentation. Calibration of Pitot-static measurements, therefore, revolves around pressure measurements satisfactory for the intended purpose. Production reference systems frequently lack adequate resolution for calibration purposes and a second flight test system, which also requires calibration, must be installed during this phase of testing. The largest errors come from static source location. So, care in choosing that location must be exercised. Furthermore, air data are now used by other subsystems, such as navigation, autopilots, or flight controls. The accuracies mandatory for these subsystems may drive air data system design, as well as the precision to which calibrations must be performed. With these considerations in mind, we break the instrumentation discussion into two major parts: (1) simpler Pitot-static systems essentially independent of other vehicle subsystems and (2) Pitot-static systems mandatory for operation of other major vehicle subsystems.

2.3.1 Instrumentation for Independent Pitot-Static Systems

Many Pitot-static systems are self-contained; they do not interact directly with the other subsystems on the airplane. If neither the production system or the flight test system (when one is utilized), do not directly supply inputs for the other subsystems, the calibration instrumentation is significantly simplified. Pressure transducers of sufficient quality are the basic measuring devices and must be sized to fit an appropriate range of altitudes (absolute pressures) and airspeeds (differential pressures) corresponding to the vehicle envelope. Common or sensitive altimeters and airspeed indicators are simply pressure gauges used to display this pressure information in a useful form to the flight crew. Flight test sensors usually simply convert measurements into analog or digital signals that are later converted into engineering units (pressures or feet or knots) for electronic display in the cockpit, in the control room, or for data reduction.

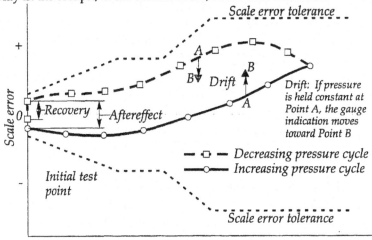

Fig. 2.20 Common Errors in a Pressure Altimeter

Measurements for calibration of independent systems aare often tied to the pressure sensors, and more often than not, to the pressure guages (altimeters and airspeed indicators) used. Gracey describes in detail (summarized in Fig. 2.20) the types of "errors" associated with altimeters approved by military standards and/or under FAA regulations. He also describes the procedure for "scale error" calibrations for each instrument, which is especially important for gauges to be used in Pitot-static calibrations.

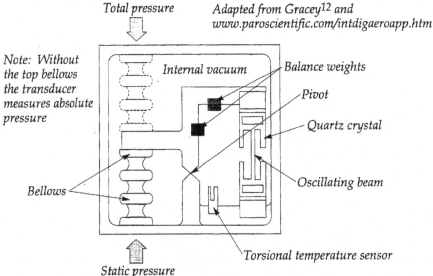

Fig. 2.21 Quartz Crystal Digital Pressure Transducer

2.3.2 Instrumentation for Interdependent Pitot-Static Systems

In modern aircraft and spacecraft Pitot-static information is collected, conditioned, and moved along a data bus for use by other subsystems. Architectures of this type provide straightforward data collection but they also increase the criticality of the calibration.

Most aircraft systems today use the most accurate of such pressure-measuring devices, what Gracey[12] calls pressure-transducers. They may be analog devices, but more commonly they are digital devices (or at least the analog outputs are digitized in signal conditioning downstream of the transducer itself). A quartz crystal element such as the one shown in Fig. 2.21 provides a resolution better than ± 0.0001% and typical transducer accuracies of ± 0.01% of full scale pressure range, according to the manufacturers. Such sensors are available in ranges from 3 psia to 40,000 psia and may be packaged with computational elements and software to output pressure measurements to other subsystems. Pure analog transducers used with analog to digital conversion electronics typically have accuracies of about ± 0.4% of the full scale pressure range. Of course, the ultimate accuracies and resolutions attainable in such interdependent pressure-sensing systems depends on many factors and is itself a complicated subsystem design problem.

2.4 SUMMARY

This chapter introduced Pitot-static system calibrations. Starting with the mathematical model of the standard atmosphere, a theoretical basis for these calibrations was laid. Three different methods of obtaining static position error were discussed, experience having shown that total pressure ports are highly accurate in most airplane applications.

No attempt is made in this introductory book to discuss all available methods of calibration, preferring to treat only the two classical approaches along with the GPS methods that are becoming the practice of choice. The reader who needs or desires detailed information on other methods of calculation will find a wealth of material in the references. While the engineer responsible for such calibrations is often accused of "measuring with a micrometer what is later to be cut with a hacksaw," careful Pitot-static calibrations are the foundation for accurate performance and stability and control flight test data. The calibration process cannot be shorted without paying the price later.

REFERENCES

[1] Diehl, W. S., **Engineering Aerodynamics** (Revised Edition), Ronald Press, 1936.

[2] Wieselsberger, G., "Manometer for Recording Air Speed," NACA Technical Memorandum 66, Feb. 1922.

[3] Proll, A., "Pressure Measurements During Flight," NACA Technical Memorandum 58, Nov. 1921.

[4] Brown, W. G., "The Synchronization of NACA Flight Records," NACA Technical Note 117, Langley Memorial Aeronautical Laboratory, Oct. 1922.

[5] Brown, W. G., "Measuring an Airplane's True Speed in Flight Testing," NACA Technical Note 135, Langley Memorial Aeronautical Laboratory, ???. 1923.

[6] Diehl, W. S., "Standard Atmosphere -- Tables and Data," NACA Technical Report 218, 1925.

[7] "Standard Atmosphere --Tables and Data for Altitudes to 65,800 Feet," NACA Report 1235, 1955.

[8] "U. S. Standard Atmosphere, 1962," U. S. Government Printing Office, Washington, 1962.

9   Minzner, R. A., Champion, K. S. W., and Pond, H. L., "The ARDC Model Atmosphere," AF CRC-TR-59-267, 1959.

10 "U. S. Standard Atmosphere Supplements, 1966," U. S. Government Printing Office, Washington, 1966.

11 DeAnda, A. G., "AFFTC Standard Airspeed Calibration Procedures," AFFTC-TIH-81-5, Air Force Flight Test Center, Edwards AFB, California, June 1981.

12 Gracey, W., "Measurement of Aircraft Speed and Altitude," NASA Reference Publication 1046, National Aeronautics and Space Administration, Langley Research Center, May 1980.

13 Anderson, J. D., Jr., **Introduction to Flight**, McGraw-Hill Book Company, New York, 1978.

14 Hamlin, B., **Flight Testing Conventional and Jet-Propelled Airplanes**, The Macmillan Company, New York, 1946.

15 Schoolfield, W. C., "A Simple Method of Applying the Compressibility Correction in the Determination of True Airspeed," **Journal of the Aeronautical Sciences**, Vol. 9, Oct. 1942, pp. 457-464.

16 Herrington, R. M., Shoemaker, P. E., Bartlett, E. P., and Dunlap, E. W., "Flight Test Engineering Handbook," AFFTC TR-6273 (AD 636392), Air Force Flight Test Center, Edwards AFB, California, May 1951 (Revised June 1964 and January 1966).

17 Huston, W. B., "Accuracy of Airspeed Measurements and Flight Calibration Procedures," NACA Report 919, 1948.

18 Wildhack, W. A., "Pressure Drop in Tubing in Aircraft Instrument Installations," NACA TN 593, 1937.

19 Olson, W. M., "True Airspeed Calibration Using Three Radar Passes," Performance and Flying Qualities Branch Memo, Air Force Flight Test Center, Edwards AFB, California, Aug. 1976.

20 Lawford, J. A. and Nipress, K. R., "Calibration of Air Data Systems and Flow Direction Sensors," AGARD AG-300, Vol. 1, Sept. 1983.

21 Olson, W. M., "PitotStatic Calibration Using a GPS Multi-Track Method," 29th Annual Symposium of the Society of Flight Test Engineers (SFTE), Reno, Nevada, Sept. 1998.

22 Lewis, G. V., "A Flight Test Technique Using GPS for Position Error Correction Testing," Cockpit, Society of Experimental Test Pilots, Lancaster, California, Jan.-Feb.-Mar. 1997.

23 Gray, D., "Using GPS to Accurately Establish True Airspeed (TAS)," National Test Pilot School, Mojave, California, June 1998.

24 Lewis, G. V., "Using GPS to Determine Pitot-Static Errors," National Test Pilot School, Mojave, California, Aug. 2003.

25 Niewoehner, R. ., "True Airspeed Determination and Nonlinear Least Squares Data Reduction," *Journal of Aircraft*, Vol. xx, pp. 123-125, American Institute of Aeronautics and Astronatutics, Washington, D. C., Nov. 2005.

26 Olson, W. M., "Aircraft Performance Flight Testing," FTC-TIH-99-01, Air Force Flight Test Center, Edwards AFB, California, 2000.

Chapter 3
CLIMB, DESCENT, AND TURN PERFORMANCE TESTS

Every airplane on every flight takes off, climbs, turns, descends, and lands. Thus, immediately after the pitot-static system is calibrated the test team can begin collecting performance data for these phases of flight. Since takeoff and landing performance is a more difficult measurement task, climb, descent, and turn performance will be tackled first.

The climb performance of an airplane is vital to the operator and directly reflects lift, drag, and thrust capabilities. Generally, measurements determine either a speed or Mach number profile that optimizes a performance parameter such as minimum time to altitude, minimum fuel to altitude, or minimum time to a total energy level. Furthermore, the resulting data can be manipulated to describe maneuver capability of the airplane or to evaluate tactical capability of the vehicle relative to an adversary.

Turning performance is an important characteristic for fighters or acrobatic craft but is hardly ever used for general aviation or commercial jets. It is more important for airplanes with an intended aggressive maneuvering combat role than for any other group of airplanes. The measurements can be made in a number of ways and with relatively simple sensors (like a stopwatch and the normal cockpit instruments). Therefore, it is useful, at least in a learning environment, to measure turn rates and radii even on airplanes for which turn performance is not a certification or contractual requirement.

This chapter treats straightforward performance measurements: climbs, descents, and turns. All of them are linked to the excess thrust or power available from the engine-airframe combination and are extremely important in assessing the utility of a design.

3.1 FOUNDATIONS

3.1.1 Historical Perspective

An airplane's best climb and descent performance of the airplane were immediately recognized as key descriptors of capability. Diehl[1], in his chapter on performance flight test data reduction, emphasized the importance of maintaining the "correct" airspeed in the climb. He pointed out that variations in the climb airspeed can easily reduce the climb rate by 5% or more and that the margin for error decreases rapidly as altitude increases. Diehl also suggested a method for reducing climb performance data to "standard" conditions (standard day). Hamlin[2], in perhaps the first book devoted solely to flight testing, also addressed the need to verify climb speed schedules. Later, Rutowski[3] set down and Boyd[4] advocated and demonstrated in flight an "energy maneuverability" approach that led to a unified technique to quantify airplane climb, acceleration, and turning performance. Boyd profoundly influenced fighter tactics, quickly finding their way into the textbooks of both Air Force and Navy test pilot schools and later into most modern textbooks[5,6,7,8] that discuss airplane performance.

3.1.2 Requirements and Governing Equations

Various documents define the required climb performance for a given aircraft. Table 3.1 is a Weight, Altitude, Temperature (WAT) chart from §27 of Advisory Circular 23-8B[9]. It illustrates one engine inoperative (OEI) climb certification requirements for Part 23 airplanes with a maximum takeoff weight (MTOW) > 6,000 pounds and all turbine-powered airplanes and suggests a matrix for planning climb performance flight tests. The matrix format of the WAT chart also applies to test planning for other flight test tasks.

Table 3.1 FAR 23 WAT Chart - Climb Requirements[9]

Regulation	23.67(a)(1)	23.67(a)(2)	23.67(b)(1)	23.67(b)(2)	23.67(c)(1)	23.67(c)(2)	23.67(c)(3)	23.67(c)(4)
Category	Normal, Utility, and Aerobatic				Commuter			
Engine Type and Airplane Weight	Recip 6000 lbs or less		Recips > 6000 lbs and Turbines					
V_{S0} (kts)	>61	≤61						
Power On Operative Engine	≤ MCP	≤MCP	MTOP	≤MCP	MTOP	MTOP	≤MCP	MTOP
Configuration	Flap and gear retracted	Flap and gear retracted	Take-off flap, gear retracted	Flap and gear retracted	Take-off flap, gear extended	Take-off flap, gear retracted	Flap and gear retracted	Approach flap*, gear retracted
Propeller Position on Inop Engine	Minimum drag	Minimum drag	Minimum drag	Minimum drag	Position it automatically and rapidly assumes	Position it automatically and rapidly assumes	Minimum drag	Minimum drag
Attitude					Wings level			
Climb Speed	≥1.2V_{S1}	≥1.2V_{S1}	Equal to that achieved at 50ft demonstrating 23.53	≥1.2V_{S1}	V_2	V_2	≥1.2V_{S1}	As in procedures but ≥1.5V_{S1}
Altitude (ft)	5000	5000	400	1500	Take-off surface	400	1500	400
Required Climb Gradient (%)	≥1.5	No minimum but must determine steady climb/descent gradient	Measurably positive	≥0.75	Measurably positive	≥2	≥1.2	≥2.1

* Approach position(s) in which V_{S1} does not exceed 110% of the V_{S1} for the related all-engines-operating landing positions

Notes: 1. This table is current as of January 17, 2006. ALWAYS consult the latest version of applicable regulations to be sure the certification regulations have not changed.

Military requirements, while similar to those described in Fig. 3.1, typically define specific mission profiles and associated performance requirements. In either case, the flight test team must verify or determine the optimum climb speed schedule as one of its first tasks for measuring the climb performance of the vehicle. Only then can either the minimum rate of climb or the minimum angle of climb or the minimum climb gradient be determined for a required configuration. However the requirement is stated, determination of climb (or descent) and turning performance is based on the familiar lift-weight and thrust-drag force balances, which we will now review briefly.

3.1.2.1 **Fundamental Relationships.** A free-body diagram of the basic forces acting on an airplane in a climb is sketched in Fig. 3.1. The forces perpendicular and parallel, respectively, to the flight path are:

$$L + T_n \sin(\alpha + \varphi_T) - W\cos\gamma = \frac{W}{g}\frac{V_\infty^2}{R_c} \tag{3.1}$$

$$T_n \cos(\alpha + \varphi_T) - D - W\sin\gamma = \frac{W}{g}\frac{dV_\infty}{dt} \tag{3.2}$$

where R_c = radius of curvature of the flight path.

The instantaneous velocity (or true airspeed) of the airplane's center of gravity is related to the time rate of change of the flight path angle γ, which is obtained by:

$$\lim_{\Delta t \to 0}\left(\frac{\Delta s}{\Delta t}\right) = \lim_{\Delta t \to 0}\left(\frac{R_c\Delta\gamma}{\Delta t}\right) = \frac{R_c d\gamma}{dt} = V_\infty$$

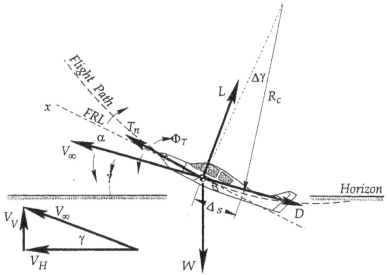

Fig. 3.1 Forces Acting on an Airplane in a Climb

Or, we can write: $\dot{\gamma} = \dfrac{V_\infty}{R_c}$, allowing eqn. 3.1 to be restated as

$$L - W\cos\gamma + T_n \sin(\alpha + \Phi_T) = \frac{W}{g} V_\infty \gamma \qquad (3.3)$$

If flight path curvature is slight ($R_c \to \infty$) and $\alpha + \Phi_T \approx 0$, eqns. 3.1 and 3.3 yield:

$$L = W\cos\gamma \qquad (3.4)$$

Eqn. 3.2 becomes: $T_n - D - \dfrac{W}{g}\dfrac{dV_\infty}{dt} = W\sin\gamma$. The angle of climb is then obtained from

$$\sin\gamma = \frac{T_n - D}{W} - \frac{dV_\infty}{gdt} \qquad (3.5)$$

Recalling that rate of climb is $\dfrac{dh}{dt} = V_\infty \sin\gamma$, we substitute to obtain:

$$\frac{dh}{dt} = \frac{(T_n - D)V_\infty}{W} - \frac{V_\infty}{g}\frac{dV_\infty}{dt} \qquad (3.6)$$

   3.1.2.2 Steady State Approximation. Equations 3.4, 3.5, and 3.6 are the governing equations for climb (or descent) performance. To further simplify the equation, it is often assumed that there is no acceleration along the flight path. Then, $\dfrac{dV_\infty}{dt} = 0$ and

$$\sin\gamma = \frac{T_n - D}{W} \qquad (3.7)$$

$$\frac{dh}{dt} = \frac{(T_n - D)V_\infty}{W} \qquad (3.8)$$

   Equations 3.7 and 3.8 are common approximations for low performance aircraft. If indicated airspeed is held constant and climb rate is low, the rate of change of true airspeed with altitude (and time) is small and this approximation is adequate. Or, if true airspeed is changing rapidly during the climb, rate of climb can be rewritten as

$$\frac{dh}{dt} = \frac{(T_n - D)V_\infty}{W} - \frac{V_\infty}{g}\frac{dV_\infty}{dh}\frac{dh}{dt} \quad \text{or rearranging} \quad \left(\frac{dh}{dt}\right)\left(1 + \frac{V_\infty}{g}\frac{dV_\infty}{dh}\right) = \frac{(T_n - D)V_\infty}{W}$$

$$\left(\frac{dh}{dt}\right) = \frac{(T_n - D)V_\infty}{W(1 + AF)} \tag{3.9}$$

where AF = acceleration factor = $\dfrac{V_\infty}{g}\dfrac{dV_\infty}{dh}$

3.1.2.3 **Accelerated Climb Equations**. More generally, the performance equations can be constructed by assuming that the angle $\alpha + \Phi_T$ is small and allowing both γ and V_∞ to be functions of time. Then the climb performance equations can be expressed concisely as a set of first-order nonlinear differential equations.

$$\dot{x} = \left\{\begin{array}{c} \dot{\gamma} \\ \dot{V}_\infty \\ \dot{h} \end{array}\right\} = \left\{\begin{array}{c} L + \dfrac{T_n(\alpha + \Phi_t)}{W} - \cos\gamma \\ g\dfrac{T_n - D}{W} - \sin\gamma \\ V_\infty \sin\gamma \end{array}\right\}$$

These equations can be extended to include other time-dependent variables such as $\dot{R} = V_\infty \cos\gamma$ or $\dot{W} = -\dot{w}_f$

where R = horizontal distance covered or ground range and $\dot{w}_f$ = fuel flow rate

This set of first order differential equations suggests the use of state variables, which opens the door to more powerful mathematical tools (like the calculus of variations) to optimize performance parameters. But our purposes are served in this chapter by simply using this formulation to lead into a discussion of Rutowski's energy approximation[3].

3.1.3 The Energy Approximation

If the airplane comprises a dynamical system having total energy made up of the sum of its kinetic energy and its potential energy, an equivalent set of climb performance equations can be written. Total energy is given by

$$E = \frac{1}{2}mV_\infty^2 + mgh$$

To more easily compare aircraft of different masses, it is customary divide by mg and rewrite total energy in terms of specific energy $\dfrac{E}{W}$ with units of distance or altitude:

$$h_e = h + \frac{V_\infty^2}{2g} \tag{3.10}$$

where h_e = specific energy or energy height

The time rate of change of specific energy, or specific excess power P_s, is

$$P_s = \dot{h}_e = \dot{h} + \dot{V}_\infty \frac{V_\infty}{g} \tag{3.11}$$

Recalling the V_∞ equation from Section 3.1.1.2, $\dot{V}_\infty = g\left(\frac{T_n - D}{W} - \sin\gamma\right)$

Multiplying by V_∞, we get: $V_\infty \dot{V}_\infty = V_\infty g\left(\dfrac{T_n - D}{W} - \sin\gamma\right)$. But, $\dot{h} = V_\infty \sin\gamma$, so

$$\frac{(T_n - D)V_\infty}{W} = \dot{h} + V_\infty \frac{\dot{V}_\infty}{g} = P_s \qquad (3.12)$$

Equation 3.12 merely confirms our earlier assertion that the energy approach to obtain specific excess power is equivalent to the force balance state equation relating V_∞ to T, D, W, and γ. Several books[4,5] elaborate on the utility of the energy approach, but it suffices for our purposes to point out that energy definitions allow computation of climb performance from thrust and drag measurements under accelerated flight conditions, not just constant true airspeed maneuvers. This result merely scratches the surface in demonstrating the uses of the energy approximation. Rutowski's approach leads naturally to performance optimization of not only climb and descent performance, but also of maneuvering flight. For example, consider a level, unaccelerated turn.

3.1.4 Forces in a Level, Unaccelerated Turn

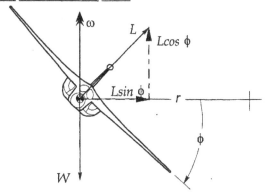

Fig. 3.2 Forces in a Level Turn

It can be inferred from the idealized force and moment diagram (Fig. 3.2) that the forces are in equilibrium (as long as you accept the notion of "centrifugal" forces being produced by a constant acceleration). This idealization describes a constant airspeed, constant altitude, and constant bank angle turn -- often called a stabilized turn or a level, unaccelerated turn. As we note from the force equilibrium, the load factor in such a turn is constant also. The force equations are almost trivial, but they do show the important variables to measure: $\cos\phi - W = 0$ or $L\cos\phi = W$, so

$$n = \frac{L}{W} = \frac{1}{\cos\phi} \qquad (3.13)$$

In this expression the definition of load factor n shows why a constant bank angle in a steady, level turn implies that n is a constant. Bank angle is a parameter to measure with an accurate vertical gyro or the load factor can be recorded if the test airplane is equipped with an accelerometer (g-meter). We will also see later that other parameters can be obtained from such relationships and that simple instrumentation suffices.

Another equation springs from the horizontal force "balance"; equating the component of lift acting in a horizontal direction to the "centrifugal force":

$$L \sin \phi = m \left(\frac{V^2}{r} \right) \tag{3.14}$$

where r is the radius of the turn (as suggested in Fig. 3.2) and V is the true airspeed. Using eqn. 3.13 with lift written in coefficient form and solving for turn radius:

$$r = \frac{2 \left(W/S \right)}{g \rho C_L \sin \phi} \tag{3.15}$$

Equation 3.15 shows that the turn radius: (1) varies directly with wing loading (W/S), (2) inversely with altitude (that is, increasing altitude increases r), and (3) inversely with lift coefficient. Minimum turn radius occurs, therefore, at low gross weights, low altitude, and maximum lift coefficient.

Other expressions useful in flight test relate to previously developed expressions. For example, rearranging eqn. 3.14 again to express load factor in other terms. Knowing that

$n = \dfrac{1}{\cos \phi}$ and using basic trigonometric definitions, gives $\sin \phi = \dfrac{\sqrt{n^2 - 1}}{n}$. Making this

substitution and solving for r gives:

$$r = \frac{V^2}{g \sqrt{n^2 - 1}} \tag{3.16}$$

Similarly, starting with the same expressions and recognizing that turn rate is simply angular velocity associated with the level turn and is therefore defined by V/r, we obtain an expression for the turn rate:

$$w = \frac{V}{r} = \frac{g \sqrt{n^2 - 1}}{V} \tag{3.17}$$

Radius of turn and rate of turn are purely functions of the true airspeed and load factor (or bank angle); they are not dependent upon any airplane attribute. Any two airplanes flying 150 knots in a level, unaccelerated turn with 30°degrees of bank angle have identical turn radii and turn rates. Measuring turn performance requires only a stop watch to time a specified heading change (usually 360°) and pitot-static measurements for · true airspeed. An accelerometer may also be used in lieu of measuring bank angle.

Having developed some simple equations to calculate stabilized turning performance, let us now turn to the kinds of turning performance that are of interest.

3.1.4.1 **Types of Turning Performance**. Equations in the preceding section should be related to operational considerations and modified to give better indications of the capability of a given aircraft. The unaccelerated level turn is closely related to sustained turning performance, but instantaneous turns are often of greater interest for combat maneuvering and are more closely related to specific excess power (especially when the aircraft is limited by thrust). The V-n diagram (Fig. 3.3) contains many of the elements important to both sustained and instantaneous turn performance. However, as we show later, more informative ways exist to present turning performance results. The point on the V-n diagram where the lift limit and structural limit coincide is the maneuver point . The true airspeed associated with that point is called the corner velocity; at this speed the airplane can turn with the smallest radius and the highest turn rate.

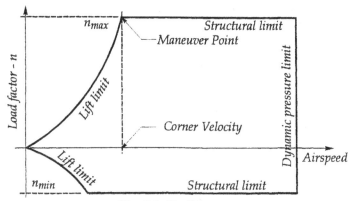

Fig. 3.3 V-n Diagram

As with climb performance, the excess power in combination with the aerodynamic and structural limits determines **sustained turn performance**. Sustained turns are those for which the maximum available thrust or thrust horsepower is sufficient to maintain a constant airspeed through a level turn.

Instantaneous turn performance allows for airspeed changes that may occur during the maneuver, and is frequently not a steady state maneuver. It is principally important in combat aircraft with weapons that can be employed with the nose pointing (perhaps only momentarily) at the adversary. It may be valuable in either getting off a first shot or in defeating an enemy's tracking solution, sacrificing energy (speed and altitude) to gain tactical advantage or neutralize a defensive situation.

The V-n diagram limits bound both instantaneous and sustained turn performance; they describe the aerodynamic and the structural limits for the airframe. The stall characteristics of the airfoil, the planform, and other configurational features of the airplane prescribe lift limits. The maneuvering loads limits typically set the upper and lower structural limits. In today's modern fighters, these limits are usually expressed in g's and may reach +9g and -3g, accelerations which approach the physiological limits of the human pilot. Said another way, the turning performance of modern fighter airplanes is often not an airframe limit; instead, the pilot may be unable to tolerate the achievable accelerations. G-induced-Loss-of-Consciousness (G-LOC) is an example of such a physiological limit.

3.1.4.2 **Limitations on Turning Performance**. Turning performance limitations can be classified under three general headings for any airplane.

3.1.4.2.1 *Thrust-Limited (or Power-Limited) Turning Performance*. To turn at constant altitude the airplane's lifting surfaces must produce lift over and above that required to maintain altitude with the wings level (Fig. 3.2). However, additional lift produces additional induced drag; the increased induced drag is proportional to the square of the load factor — so a 2-g turn quadruples the induced drag! This added drag must be balanced with additional thrust to maintain constant airspeed. For many aircraft, available thrust cannot overcome this additional drag, and the aircraft decelerates in the turn. The airplane is then thrust-limited in the turn.

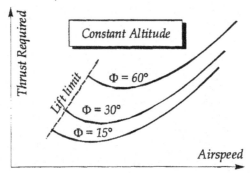

Fig. 3.4 Thrust Required at Various Bank Angles

As bank angle increases, thrust required increases rapidly (Fig. 3.4). Of course, there are many fighter aircraft today with very high thrust-to-weight ratios. Because of the high available thrust (or power in propeller-driven aircraft) these machines are less likely to encounter thrust limitations during turns, suggesting the aerodynamic (or lift) limits in Fig. 3.4, are more likely to limit turning performance.

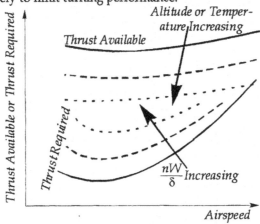

Fig. 3.5 Parameters Affecting Thrust-Limited Turning Performance

If conducting turning performance tests in a propeller-driven airplane, changes in induced drag must be considered. They change the power required curves rather than thrust required curves as shown in Fig. 3.4; but power required is simply $\frac{DV}{550}$.

The thrust-limited turn is often the primary focus of turn performance measurements and is closely tied to energy concepts. In fact the same test technique (the level acceleration) provides data for turning performance and is used to determine optimum climb performance. P_s is relevant to both types of performance and thrust-limited turning performance is affected by exactly the same factors that affect climb performance (Fig. 3.5). Anything that affects excess thrust changes turning performance. Corrections to turning performance measurements are based on similar considerations:

(1) Temperature effects on thrust   (3) Weight effects on induced drag
(2) Pressure altitude effects on thrust   (4) Pressure altitude effects on drag

3.1.4.2.2 *Lift-Limited Turning Performance.* The dashed line in Fig. 3.4 is set by the maximum lift coefficient the wing can generate; that is, the lift limit is indicated by this line, simply because the wing will stall if it is exceeded. Stall speed in a turn is directly proportional to the square root load factor and the stall speed in level flight; that is, $V_{s_\phi} = \sqrt{n}V_s$, where V_{s_ϕ} is the stall speed in a level turn at a constant bank angle. This result suggests that the dashed line in Fig. 3.4 increases as $\dfrac{1}{\sqrt{\cos\phi}}$.

This lift boundary for turning performance is of particular interest in acrobatic, tactical and trainer aircraft.. Sometimes specially designed tests are laid out to explore the lift boundary; the interest is primarily one of controllability, not turning performance. What levels of buffet are to be expected? Will they adversely affect the ability of the pilot to operationally maneuver and track an adversary for weapons delivery? Is there a strong likelihood that the airplane will go out of control with little or no warning? Though the lift limit does bound the performance as suggested in Figs. 3.3 and 3.4, these considerations are are better discussed under handling qualities testing.

3.1.4.2.3 *Load-Limited (Structural) Turning Performance.* The loads that the airframe is designed to carry are statically tested on the ground and monitored during early envelope clearance flights. These load limits are normally expressed in load factor (both positive and negative) as suggested in Fig. 3.3. These limits are typically specified in the contract and/or by the certification agency. Federal Aviation Regulations[10] in the United States spell out limits of +4.4/-2.2 g for utility category aircraft certified under FAR Part 23. These load limits are seldom achieved in flight and there is always a margin of safety applied by the designer to allow for unexpected turbulence in the atmosphere or inadvertently overstressing the aircraft.

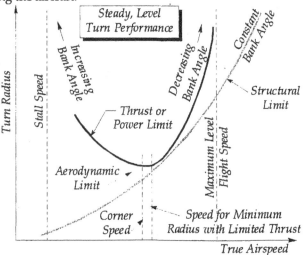

Fig. 3.6 Summary of Turning Performance Limitations

Figure 3.6 is yet another way to show and summarize different limitations on turning performance. At speeds less than the corner speed even aircraft that are not thrust-limited cannot reach the limit load factor. They are aerodynamically (lift) limited. At higher speeds the vehicle may be limited by either the strength of the structure or by the available excess thrust. For example, most general aviation airplanes are thrust-limited throughout much of their envelope.

3.1.5 Experimental Versus Analytical Performance Methods

Performance measurements have little meaning unless the data are reduced to some common basis of comparison, typically the standard atmosphere. Hence, performance reduction refers to the process by which test data taken under nonstandard day conditions are converted to standard day conditions. As Lush[11] puts it, "...reduction methods are necessary to rationalize the test results so that they may be used for valid prediction and comparison."

There are two broad categories of performance data reduction. Experimental methods are so named because they require no advance knowledge of the components of the dynamical system. For example, no knowledge of the airplane's power plant characteristics are needed using this method. Analytical methods do require *a priori* sources to complete the analysis and are somewhat more widely used. Analytical methods are further broken down into differential methods and performance analyses. Differential methods assume that linearization is appropriate for small corrections. These methods depend on a generalized characterization of airframe drag and engine behavior. The differential technique is not appropriate, however, when compressibility effects are significant. Performance analyses rely on advance information of engine behavior and are generally used when experimental methods are inconvenient or impractical.

One of the most perplexing problems in performance reduction is the number and type of variables to be considered, some of which are controllable while others are not. For example, engine parameters are usually controllable over the range of interest while outside air temperature is not. Tests are ordinarily planned to cover a suitable range of controllable variables, while those variables that cannot be controlled are "standardized". Choice of a standard weight, like 95% of akeoff weight, is typical of the latter case.

3.1.5.1 **Experimental Methods.** Dimensional analysis is a tool that allows us to reduce the number of variables by grouping them. Furthermore, if uncontrolled variables can be associated with controlled variables, experimental methods may be used to deduce standard day performance from nonstandard day test data. One use of this technique is in reducing performance data for turbojet airplanes. We will briefly introduce the subject for now and illustrate it in greater detail in Chapter 4. The success of dimensional analysis rests upon the assumption that all pertinent variables can be conceptually identified, though the mathematical form of the relationships may remain unknown. We could assume, for instance, that the climb rate of a turbojet-powered airplane depends explicitly on true airspeed, engine compressor speed, aircraft weight, outside air temperature, and pressure. If such a function exists, it can be represented by: $f_1(V_\infty, N, W, T_\infty, p_\infty) = 0$. (Notice that $_\infty$ has been used with T_∞ to differentiate it from T for thrust, as used previously. We will stick to this convention throughout the book.) If Buckingham's Pi Theorem is applied, the variables can be reduced to three: $f_2\left(\dfrac{V_\infty}{\sqrt{T_\infty}}, \dfrac{ND}{\sqrt{T_\infty}}, \dfrac{W}{p_\infty D^2}\right)$. In the first expression there are five independent variables and two of them, W and T_∞, are not easy to control or adjust during flight tests. Dimensional analysis reduces the number of independent variables by two, illustrating the reduction in number of independent variables realized by applying dimensional analysis.

Pragmatically, reducing the number of independent variables by only two often makes it difficult to use experimental methods. Usually, there are still too many variables affecting the performance reduction. However, insight into the physics usually permits us to identify the dominant dependencies and neglect those influences that are likely small. A good example of such a simplification is the level flight performance of a jet aircraft, discussed in detail in Chapter 4. If the test altitude is reasonably close to standard conditions, viscosity can usually be ignored as an independent variable in determining the level speed of the airplane.

3.1.5.2 **Analytical Methods**. Of the two "analytical" methods, the differential method is the easiest to use when background data are available. This type of performance data reduction is used with conventional reciprocating engine powered aircraft. The database for reciprocating engines is rather extensive and most of this class of airplanes do not approach any compressibility effects, making the differential method both convenient and accurate to use. The *a priori* knowledge necessary to use this method does not have to be extremely precise because the differential corrections for nonstandard conditions are usually small. Turboprop-powered aircraft are generally analyzed using this approach; jet thrust introduces more variables and reduces the accuracy of the corrections.

The second analytical method, performance analysis, is based on determination of drag and/or power curves (both required and available) over the altitude and airspeed envelope of the airplane. Again, one needs *a priori* information on the output of the propulsion system and propeller efficiencies, along with the effects of changes in temperature and forward speed on these parameters.

Choosing the appropriate performance reduction method is a difficult task. The most important considerations involved are the amount of data required (number and character of variables to be measured), the size of the flight envelope to be covered, and the availability and nature of generalized data on the airplane and its power plant. In virtually every instance, the choice is a compromise and it is often a combination of the various methods. Now, let us turn our attention from these general considerations to the data collection methods for climb and turning performance and to appropriate use of data reduction methods.

3.2 CLIMB PERFORMANCE AND TURN PERFORMANCE TEST METHODS

Climb performance tests fall into two broad categories: those designed to determine an optimum speed or Mach number schedule or those designed to measure the actual performance of the vehicle. For the first category of tests, the optimization may be carried out with any of the following purposes:

- ◆ minimum time to altitude
- ◆ minimum time to energy level
- ◆ minimum fuel to altitude
- ◆ minimum fuel to energy level
- ◆ maximum climb angle

The second category of climb tests are sometimes called "check" climbs or "performance" climbs since verify that a chosen profile meets specified optimization objectives. This validation should also ensure that cooling considerations, lack of forward visibility, poor handling qualities, or some other operational consideration does not dictate deviation from the optimized climb schedule. Both types of these tests will be introduced in this section, along with some of the techniques used. The reduction of climb data from such tests to standard day conditions will also be described briefly.

Turning performance is usually determined in one of two ways: (1) directly by performing turns at specified flight conditions or indirectly (2) from level acceleration tests. Fortunately, level acceleration tests can be used for more than one purpose (to establish climb schedules, to determine energy states, and to predict turning performance). Consequently, level accelerations and decelerations are very powerful techniques and can be quite efficient in collecting data useful for several purposes in a single test event.

3.2.1 Climb Schedule Determination

Optimization of a climb schedule is based on the airplane's lift, drag, and thrust relationships over an appropriate speed range, as discussed above. The measurement may be either direct or, more often, indirect. The two most common techniques, the sawtooth or partial climb test and the level acceleration test, will be described. Of these two test methods, the sawtooth climb is easier to understand and requires only rudimentary instrumentation. However, it is only useful for low climb rates. Level accelerations provide more data with less flying time and the data are useful for more than just determining a climb schedule. They are especially useful for high performance aircraft with high climb rates. The technique requires some means of automatically recording altitude and airspeed as a continuous function of time. Level accelerations are are problematic with gear or flaps extended for high thrust-to-weight airplanes, necessitating use of both methods.

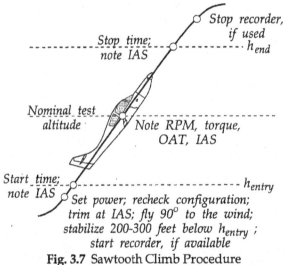

Fig. 3.7 Sawtooth Climb Procedure

3.2.1.1 **Sawtooth Climb Method**. The sawtooth climb, so named because of the shape of the altitude trace it produces, is used to determine the airspeed for maximum rate of climb at a nominal pressure altitude under test day conditions. A series of timed climbs is made over an altitude band bracketing the nominal pressure altitude chosen. Increments of altitude used for each airspeed point should be chosen so that timing can be carried out precisely; if a stopwatch is manually started and stopped as suggested in Fig. 3.7, the altitude increments should be chosen so that the elapsed time during the measurement is at least 1 minute. Indicated airspeed or Mach number must be maintained very precisely (± 1 knot is desirable) to obtain valid results without excessive scatter. The landing gear, flaps, cowl flaps (in other words, the configuration) as well as the desired power setting must be set before commencing the data run. Trim should only be adjusted between runs. While constant winds have no effect on the results, the pilot should attempt to make data runs perpendicular to the wind at test altitude in order to minimize the influence of wind gradients. He should also attempt to conduct each climb in approximately the same air mass if the test area permits. A range constant airspeeds should be flown to define the shape of the rate of climb curve. Typical time to climb data are shown in Fig. 3.8 (open circles). For each nominal altitude, a minimum and a maximum speed point (using the same configuration and power setting) should be flown first to anchor the ends of the curve. A running plot of the observed time to climb through the altitude band, as shown by the open circles in Fig. 3.8, often gives clues as to which of the data points should be repeated to better define the maximum rate of climb speed.

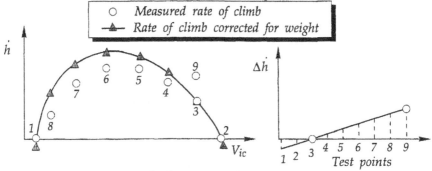

Fig. 3.8 Weight Correction of Sawtooth Climb Data

Dommasch[12] suggests that no corrections are necessary for nonstandard weight or for power changes due to nonstandard atmospheric conditions if sawtooth climb data are used solely to determine the maximum rate of climb speed schedule. Others correct for these conditions[7,8,9,11] and those due to wind gradients. These references provide detailed discussions of the data reduction techniques, but for our purposes we will describe only the simplest two of the possible ways to correct for changes in gross weight. Ways to minimize the effects of wind shear will also be briefly discussed.

The simplest way to correct sawtooth climb data for differences in gross weight during a set of climbs amounts to prorating the change in rate of climb over the time interval. A second climb is repeated at a selected airspeed. This repeated point should be flown near the end of the series to provide a comparison with a point flown at a heavier weight earlier in the series. Points 3 and 9 in Fig. 3.8 illustrate this repetition. It is assumed that rate of climb varies linearly with time due to the change in gross weight. The solid triangles in Fig. 3.8 illustrate how the measured times to climb (or rates of climb) might change with this form of correction. Alternatively, if the weight of the airplane is known for each data point, the rate of climb may be corrected by a simple ratio of weights: $\dot{h}_{corrected} = \dfrac{W_t}{W_{avg}} \dot{h}_i$.

Both of these approximations produce roughly the same results and both of them ignore an induced drag correction term. However, they are easy to use and provide results that are little different from more elaborate schemes.

Nonstandard temperature conditions may also require corrections to the power output of the propulsion system. If so, the effects of atmospheric variations on engine performance must be known in advance and outside air temperature measurements become necessary. The Empire Test Pilots' School (ETPS) Handbook[13] details British practice in making such corrections for reciprocating engine aircraft. Since these types of corrections depend entirely on the engine data available and are totally unique to each installation, we will discuss them no further.

Fig. 3.9 Effect of Vertical Wind Shear on Sensed Rate of Climb

Finally, sawtooth climb data may be affected by both changes in wind speed and direction. Shifts in wind direction are usually of little consequence since the altitude band traversed is usually small and directional variations affect only the measured pressures. They can usually be ignored. Vertical speed gradients cannot, however, be ignored. Referring to Fig. 3.9, at constant true airspeed the pitot-static system senses an increasing wind speed as a deceleration. The effect in the rate of climb equation is quite similar to the acceleration factor (eqn. 3.9), but, if the increment in velocity is taken as starting at the higher altitude, the sign changes on the correction term as shown below.

$$\frac{dh}{dt} = \frac{(T_n - D)V_\infty}{W\left(1 + \dfrac{V_\infty}{g}\dfrac{dV_\infty}{dh}\right)} \quad \text{corresponds to} \quad \frac{dh}{dt} = \frac{(T_n - D)V_\infty}{W\left(1 - \dfrac{V_\infty}{g}\dfrac{\Delta V_\infty}{\Delta h}\right)}$$

where $\Delta V_\infty = V_{w_{i+1}} - V_{w_i}$

If the vertical wind gradient $\dfrac{\Delta V_\infty}{\Delta h}$ is positive, rate of climb increases and, if the vertical wind gradient is negative, rate of climb decreases. But this knowledge is not easy to use. Determining wind gradients is very difficult and since they constantly change, correcting for them mathematically is impractical. The best way to handle wind effects on sawtooth climb data is by flying data runs close to perpendicular to the wind direction. One other possible technique is to repeat each data point (each V_{ic}) on reciprocal headings. Unfortunately, this approach also doubles test time required to complete determination of the climb schedule. In short, it is difficult to correct sawtooth climb data for vertical wind shears; shears problem should be avoided with good flight planning if possible.

Example 3.1: The following data were collected in flight on a twin-engine STOL transport during a series of sawtooth climb tests. The nominal (midpoint) test pressure altitude was 8,750 feet. Assume that the first six points were flown at constant weight and that the last six points were flown at a different (lighter) constant weight. Between the two sets of sawtooth points, a maximum speed of 120 KISAS was observed at the climb power setting used. Plot the two curves thus obtained and find the average curve between the two sets of faired data. Based on this average curve, what is the best rate of climb speed (KIAS) for this airplane at 8750 feet pressure altitude?

The plot on following page shows the resulting sawtooth curves with the peak rate of climb occurring at approximately 77 KIAS. Thus, these sawtooth tests suggest that, for maximum rate of climb, an indicated airspeed of 77 KIAS should be maintained as the airplane passes through 8,750 feet.

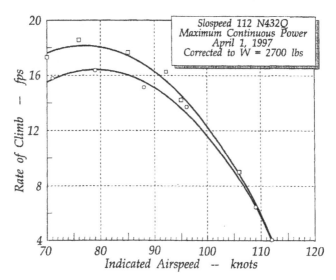

3.2.1.2 **Level Acceleration Method**. Equation 3.6 shows that the excess power avail-able from any airframe-powerplant combination can be measured by maintaining a con-stant altitude and recording the change in true airspeed with time. Motion picture film, video, magnetic tape, or telemetered signals can readily provide such time histories. Fur-thermore, acceleration data can also be used to define the maneuvering capability of the design, especially if the customer is interested in the energy maneuverability. Finally, the acceleration performance may itself be a figure of merit in the contractual specifications.

The level acceleration technique is a simple concept. The airplane is accelerated, using a fixed power setting and configuration, from near its minimum level flight speed to the maximum level flight speed, while maintaining constant pressure altitude. Of course, there are complications. First, the pilot does not usually have a calibrated altimeter and altitude measurements must be corrected for pitot-static errors. Since the pilot must keep these corrections as small as possible, knowledge of the static pressure error as a function of indicated airspeed is used to plan data runs. Because mechanical altimeters exhibit hysteresis, reversals in altimeter readings should be avoided. Therefore, an acceleration or deceleration run should be planned to hold a slight climb or descent (100-200 fpm maximum), whichever minimizes the altitude error after the static pressure error correc-tion is applied. The flight test team must obtain ground block readings with the altimeter set at 29.92 (all test data taken at a pressure altitude must be taken with this altimeter set-ting). Typically, the airplane is trimmed at some midpoint speed for the range of speeds to be covered and the trim setting is not changed. The pilot must exercise care in passing through this point to transition from back pressure to forward pressure smoothly and not allow an altimeter reversal. If the airplane is capable of a wide speed range, it is possible to piece together several different acceleration runs. If such a procedure is used, the test team may have to account for small changes in drag due changes in trim. A particularly sensitive part of the acceleration run occurs at speeds near Mach 1 when the pitot-static system is affected by shock waves. Ordinarily it is best to simply maintain the same rate of change of attitude (by using either visual references or guidance system commands derived from the airplane's inertial reference system) until the pitot-static system settles down in supersonic flight.

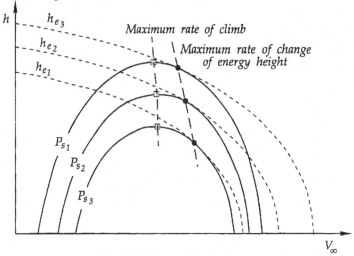

Fig. 3.10 Uses of P_s Contours

Level acceleration data can be used to optimize climb schedules in any one of the several ways suggested at the beginning of this section (Fig. 3.10). For the purposes of these introductory notes, we will only discuss the reduction of level acceleration data for either the maximum rate of climb schedule or the minimum time to an energy level. For either of these purposes, specific excess power P_s is the preferred measure of merit. As Fig. 3.10 shows, the maximum rate of climb can be estimated from constant altitude (horizontal) tangent lines to the various P_s contours and the maximum change in energy level can be estimated from contours of constant total energy height (the parabolic tangents in Fig. 3.10). This abbreviated discussion merely hints at the usefulness of specific excess power contour maps in terms of altitude and velocity parameters.

With regard to standard day corrections, P_s data from level accelerations can be treated as rate of climb. To be complete, the data reduction process should include corrections for nonstandard temperature effect on the thrust output of the propulsion system, both inertia and induced drag weight corrections, and wind gradient corrections. In many cases these corrections will not be significant and the test team must choose the ones to be made. In this section we will discuss the weight correction only, leaving the nonstandard temperature correction discussion to the check climb section. The wind gradient correction is identical to that of the sawtooth climb technique. The only means of taking such gradients into account is through careful flight planning and execution.

In considering the weight correction for sawtooth climbs, no mathematically rigorous analysis was used. Another approach is to express test day thrust as a function of the other variables and then see how weight affects them. As a part of this analysis, it will be convenient to refer all calculations to a standard weight for ease of comparison. The general expression for P_s on a given test day is

$$P_{s_t} = \frac{\left(T_{n_t} - D_t\right)V_{\infty_t}}{W_t}$$

Rearranging to express test day thrust as:

$$T_{n_t} = \frac{W_t}{V_{\infty_t}} P_{s_t} + D_t$$

The effects of weight on the acceleration due to thrust are given by differentiating with respect to weight.

$$\frac{dT_{n_t}}{dW_t} = \frac{W_t}{V_{\infty_t}} \frac{dP_{s_t}}{dW_t} + \frac{P_{s_t}}{V_{\infty_t}} + \frac{dD_t}{dW_t} = 0$$

Typically, thrust is affected little by changes in weight at constant power setting (usually military or maximum) as the airplane accelerates in level flight. Angle of attack also has little effect on thrust available for acceleration, so

$$\frac{dP_{s_t}}{dW_t} = -\frac{P_{s_t}}{V_{\infty_t}} - \frac{V_{\infty_t}}{W_t} \frac{dD_t}{dW_t} = 0 \qquad (3.18)$$

Defining the weight difference at any instant in the maneuver as $\Delta W = W_{std} - W_t$ and expressing all differentials in eqn. 3.18 as differences

$$\Delta P_s \approx -\left(\frac{P_s \Delta W}{W_t} + \frac{\Delta D_i V_{\infty_t}}{W_t} \right) \qquad (3.19)$$

Equation 3.19 assumes that the only change in drag is due to the weight not being nominal, altering the induced drag. This simplified differential correction method yields two primary correction terms, the first due to inertia of the vehicle and the second due to induced drag changes between test weight and standard weight. The induced drag term can be further expanded by writing D_i as:

$$D_i = C_1 (nW)^2 \frac{\cos^2 \gamma}{b^2 e M^2 \delta}, \quad \text{where } C_1 = \frac{2}{k \pi p_0}. \text{ Then } \Delta D_i \text{ becomes}$$

$$\Delta D_i = C_1 \left(\frac{\cos^2 \gamma}{b^2 e M^2} \right) \left[\left(\frac{(nW)^2}{\delta} \right)_{std} - \left(\frac{(nW)^2}{\delta} \right)_t \right] = \left(\frac{2\cos^2 \gamma}{k p_\infty b^2 e M^2} \right) \left(n_{std}^2 W_{std}^2 \frac{\delta_t}{\delta_{std}} - n_t^2 W_t^2 \right)$$

where k is the ratio of specific heats (typically, 1.4) and γ is the flight path angle. The P_s correction for nonstandard weights then follows:

$$\Delta P_{s_{wt}} = -P_{s_t} \frac{\Delta W}{W_t} + \left(\frac{2\cos^2 \gamma}{k p_\infty b^2 e M^2} \right) \left(n_t^2 W_t^2 - n_{std}^2 W_{std}^2 \frac{\delta_t}{\delta_{std}} \right) \frac{V_{\infty_t}}{W_t} \qquad (3.20)$$

Since $n_{std} = n_t = 1$ and $\cos \gamma = 1$ for the level accelerations, eqn. 3.20 can be written as

$$\Delta P_{s_{wt}} = -P_{s_t} \frac{\Delta W}{W_t} + \left(\frac{2 V_{\infty_t}}{k p_\infty b^2 e M^2 W_t} \right) \left(W_t^2 - W_{std}^2 \frac{\delta_t}{\delta_{std}} \right) \qquad (3.21)$$

Typical level acceleration data reductions include the following:
1. Correct indicated gage readings for instrument corrections for each individual gage and each data point to be reduced; that is, for every V_i, h_i, and T_{∞_i} calculate the corresponding V_{ic}, h_{ic}, and $T_{\infty_{ic}}$. Then, apply appropriate position error corrections to obtain calibrated values of each parameter.

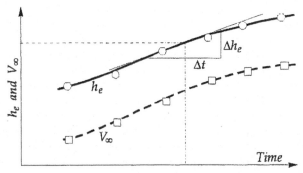

Fig. 3.11 Determining P_s Graphically

2. Calculate the test day true airspeed from calibrated airspeeds for each data point. Plot these points versus time as shown in Fig. 3.11 or arrange them in a time history array for step 5 in this process.

3. Calculate test day P_s from $P_s = \dot{h}_e = \dot{h} + \dfrac{V_\infty \dot{V}_\infty}{g}$ and plot these points on the same graph with the true airspeed time history as suggested in Fig. 3.11. Alternatively, arrange the h_e points in a time history array similar to the true airspeed array so that energy height can be numerically differentiated.

4. Estimate P_s for test day conditions by numerically differentiating the energy height time history for an approximate rate of change of h_e for each instant of time and the corresponding true airspeed. This process is best visualized as a graphical process, though the actual work can be carried out by manipulating the appropriate data arrays in a computer.

5. Correct P_{s_t} to standard day and standard weight conditions as suggested previously for rate of climb data.

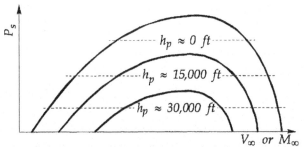

Fig. 3.12 Specific Excess Power versus Airspeed

6. Plot P_s versus V_∞ (or M_∞) for several altitudes. Notice that the resulting curves, as sketched in Fig. 3.12, are very similar in appearance to sawtooth climb curves for low performance airplanes. However, the shape of P_s curves for supersonic airplanes is quite different.

7. Crossplot P_s as a function of pressure altitude and velocity by taking lines of constant P_s across the constant altitude curves of Fig. 3.12. The resulting crossplot of constant P_s curves as a function of altitude and true airspeed, sketched previously in Fig. 3.5, is perhaps the most common way to depict level acceleration data. Recall that this format allows the determination of

both the maximum rate of climb schedule and the minimum time to energy height climb schedule.

Alternatively, plot both test day true altitude and test day true airspeed versus time and numerically differentiate both quantities. The sum of $\dfrac{dh}{dt}$ and $\dfrac{dV_\infty}{dt}$, using eqn. 3.11, also yields test day P_s. Whichever of the measured quantities is numerically differentiated, the test engineer should carefully smooth the data and remove fluctuations with a half-cycle less than 20 to 30 seconds. Potential to kinetic energy exchanges do not occur more rapidly than this rate and higher frequency disturbances are usually noise in the data, which the numerical differentiation has amplified.

Level accelerations return a considerable amount of useful data in a relatively short amount of test time. It is a very efficient flight test technique, providing optimized climb schedules for both subsonic and supersonic airplanes. The acceleration characteristics of a given airframe-powerplant combination are direct measurements. Finally, level accelerations conducted at different load factors also provide the airplane's maneuvering capability. Interested students should consult references 1,3, and 5 for details of this extension of the level acceleration method.

In high performance airplanes, level accelerations usually give more consistent and repeatable data than sawtooth climbs, both because of the use of the acceleration term and because vertical wind shear has little effect on level flight data. However, data handling is slightly more complex than it is for sawtooth climbs. Data must be recorded automatically and time stamped, requiring slightly more sophisticated instrumentation is required. Data reduction itself is rather more tedious and begs for automated processing. Neither of these objections is particularly troublesome with modern instrumentation and computer capabilities.

Time (sec)	TAS (fps)	Altitude (feet)	$\dot{h}$ (fps)	$\dot{V}$ fps^2	P_s (fps)
0.40	86.8	19970.7	3.50	3.50	12.904
0.80	88.2	19973.0	7.00	3.50	16.557
1.20	90.1	19978.0	20.00	2.50	26.982
1.60	91.5	19985.0	15.00	4.50	27.735
2.00	93.3	19991.0	15.00	4.50	27.986
2.40	95.6	19996.0	10.00	6.50	29.182
2.80	98.2	20000.0	10.00	6.50	29.708
3.20	100.9	20003.7	13.50	5.50	30.654
3.60	103.9	20007.0	10.00	7.00	32.453
4.00	107.6	20009.6	4.50	10.00	37.632
4.40	111.6	20011.7	5.50	10.50	41.578
4.80	115.6	20014.9	4.50	11.00	43.646
5.20	120.4	20016.7	3.00	12.50	49.291
5.60	126.4	20012.9	-15.00	16.00	47.062
6.00	132.5	20007.1	-13.00	14.50	46.061
6.40	137.6	20002.8	-11.00	12.50	41.974
6.80	142.1	19998.0	-10.00	10.00	33.855
7.20	144.7	19997.0	5.00	4.50	25.175
7.60	146.1	19999.1	0.50	4.50	20.871
8.00	147.4	19999.2	-2.00	3.50	13.997

Example 3.2: Level acceleration data for a fictitious small jet trainer are tabulated on the left. Data were collected at a pressure altitude of 20,000 feet and they have been partially reduced (that is, standard day true airspeed and pressure altitude have already been calculated from the test measurements). Calculate and plot the P_s curve for this airplane at 20,000 feet. Based on this curve, what is the true airspeed for best rate of climb? First, we estimate $\dot{h}$ and $\dot{V}$ from $\dfrac{\Delta h}{\Delta t} \approx \dot{h}$ and $\dfrac{\Delta V}{\Delta t} \approx \dot{V}$. The first two lines in the table give:

$$\dot{h} = \frac{19970.7 - 19970.0}{0.2} = 3.5 \text{ fps and}$$

$$\dot{V} = \frac{86.8 - 86.1.0}{0.2} = 3.5 \text{ fps}^2. \text{ Then,}$$

$$P_s = \dot{h} + \frac{V}{g}\dot{V} = 3.5 + \frac{(86.1 + 86.8)(3.5)}{(2)(32.17405)}$$

$$\boxed{P_s = 12.904 \text{ fps}}$$

We could have found the slopes of the curves with elaborate numerical schemes, but this straight-line average is adequate with closely spaced data points. The plot on the right, using a spline fit, shows an approximate maximum climb airspeed of 123 fps.

$$V_{max\ rate\ climb} \approx 123\ fps$$

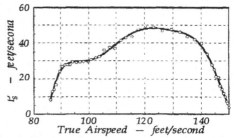

3.2.2 Performance Climbs

Once a climb schedule for a given purpose is determined, the schedule must be validated by actually flying the schedule and measuring performance. Time to climb, climb angle, fuel used during the climb, and distance traveled during the climb are measured along the optimized path to prove that contractual specifications or certification requirements were met by the design. Such easily measured quantities are not all the test team must evaluate in performance climbs, however. Qualitative operational factors, such as pilot field of view and handling qualities, are also important. Subsystems operation may also be affected by the climb schedule. Engine cooling, critical altitudes for supercharging, and other powerplant characteristics are typical of subsystem operational characteristics examined during the performance climb. Performance climbs are validate the climb speed schedule established by flight tests and verify vehicle subsystems performance.

3.2.2.1 **Performance Climb Procedures**. Figure 3.13 shows a typical performance climb data card and emphasizes data collection requirements. Flying a performance climb demands considerable concentration from the pilot; automatic data recording devices (video camera, photopanel, magnetic tape, or telemetry) are vital for sinle-pilot airplanes. In a relatively low performance configuration, data can be hand recorded but hand-recorded climb data is a backup procedure to be used when instrumentation fails.

Project Name

Pilot _____ FTE _____

Runway Temperature _____ Pressure Altitude _____ Wind _____

TAXI AND TAKEOFF		Fuel Allowance	_____	
Data Point	Time	Fuel Reading	Counter Number	Remarks
Engine Start				
Brake Release				
Start Climb				
CHECK CLIMB				
h_i	V_i	Time	Event Number	Remarks
2000	175			
4000	175			
6000	175			
---	----			

Fig. 3.13 Example Performance Climb Data Card

Climb entry is key to a successful performance climb. The desired power, configuration, and altitude (or rate of change of altitude) must be established and stabilized before data collection starts. The climb schedule itself must be religiously followed; if, for example, indicated airspeed is used as the primary cue for the pilot, it should be kept as close to desired as possible. A sensitive instrument (airspeed or Mach meter) permits quick detection of small changes in the controlling variable quickly. (Even a ± 0.5 knot variation calls for a response from the pilot). As with sawtooth climb tests and level accelerations, plan to minimize the effects of wind gradients. Since a change in altitude is involved, fly 90° to the average wind.

Each airplane and each configuration dictate different control techniques, but the pilot must be positive and make smooth changes at all times; load factor variations greater than ± 0.1g invalidate the climb. The pilot must anticipate abrupt changes in the profile, whether due to mechanical constraints in the propulsion system, limits on the airframe, or an unusual climb profile, and the flight test engineer must expect to correct the data for variations from the optimum. At high altitude and/or low airspeed (low dynamic pressure), deviations from the profile must also be expected. The pilot must be briefed on the allowable test tolerances and challenging profiles warrant rehearsal in ground simulators prior to incurring the cost of incorrectly flown test flights.

3.2.2.2 **Performance Climb Data Reduction**. Data reduction procedures for sawtooth climbs and level accelerations are subsets of corrections for the complete performance climb. Corrections for nonstandard atmospheric conditions and acceleration errors will complete our discussion of climb data reduction.

The correction for nonstandard atmospheric conditions accounts for the influence of test day temperatures on altitude and airspeed measurements, and available thrust from the powerplant. Figure 3.14 shows that as test day altitude increments (as measured by an altimeter set at 29.92 in. Hg.) are not the same as actual or tapeline altitude changes if temperature does not follow the assumed standard temperature profile. This temperature deviation may be due to either a nonstandard lapse rate or to a warmer (or cooler) surface temperature with a standard lapse rate. The latter condition is sketched in Fig. 3.14 and is the first correction normally made to rate of climb data. Indicated ambient pressure change Δp_∞ reflects a potential energy change of Δh_i, not the actual potential energy change Δh_a. To correct for this shortcoming in the measurement system, the hydrostatic equation (eqn. 2.5) can be written for each altitude increment.

$$\Delta h_i = \frac{\Delta p_\infty}{\rho_{std}\, g_0} \qquad \text{and} \qquad \Delta h_a = \frac{\Delta p_\infty}{\rho_t\, g_0}$$

Then, dividing Δh_i by Δh_a

$$\frac{\Delta h_i}{\Delta h_a} = \frac{\rho_t}{\rho_{std}} = \frac{p_t \big/ RT_{\infty_t}}{p_{std}\big/ RT_{\infty_{std}}} = \frac{T_{\infty_{std}}}{T_{\infty_t}}$$

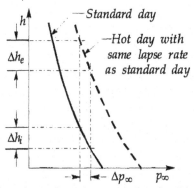

Fig. 3.14 Tapeline Altitude Correction for Rate of Climb

Finally, the tapeline altitude correction can be expressed as the limit of the altitude increment divided by the corresponding time increment. This correction is valid for small corrections only. By convention the subscript $_2$ indicates the tapeline altitude correction.

$$\left(\frac{dh}{dt}\right)_2 = \frac{dh}{dt}\frac{T_{\infty_{std}}}{T_{\infty_t}} \tag{3.22}$$

Example 3.3: During a check climb on a new jet trainer an indicated rate of climb of 1100 fpm was recorded at 9000 feet pressure altitude. The outside air temperature was 32° F at that test altitude. Calculate the tapeline altitude correction for this measured rate of climb under these conditions. To make the correction, we must have absolute temperatures at the test altitude on the test day and on a standard day.

$T_{\infty_t} = 459.69 + 32 = 491.69°R$ and $T_{\infty_{std}} = 486.61°R$ from standard atmosphere tables. Then, eqn. 3.22 gives:

$$\left(\frac{dh}{dt}\right)_2 = \frac{dh}{dt}\frac{T_{\infty_{std}}}{T_{\infty_t}} = 1100\frac{486.61}{491.69} \qquad \boxed{\left(\frac{dh}{dt}\right)_2 = 1008.635\ fpm}$$

The next correction is for changes in thrust output of the powerplant in nonstandard temperature variations. Thrust horsepower available can be written as $THP_A = T_n V_\infty$ and $THP_R = D V_\infty$
(Note: Net thrust is denoted by T_n in the following development. Do not confuse this symbol with any temperature. In the literature this conflict is sometimes avoided by denoting thrust with F_n.) With $_{std}$ and $_t$ denoting standard day or test day conditions, respectively, the ratios between standard day power and test day power are:

$$\frac{THP_{A_{std}}}{THP_{A_t}} = \frac{T_{n_{std}}V_{\infty_{std}}}{T_{n_t}V_{\infty_t}} = \frac{T_{n_{std}}}{T_{n_t}}\sqrt{\frac{T_{\infty_{std}}}{T_{\infty_t}}}$$

$$\frac{THP_{R_{std}}}{THP_{R_t}} = \frac{D_{std}V_{\infty_{std}}}{D_tV_{\infty_t}} = \sqrt{\frac{T_{\infty_{std}}}{T_{\infty_t}}}, \text{ since } M_t = M_{std} \text{ implies that } D_{std} = D_t$$

The key to this simple relationship is that Mach number for test day conditions is the same as for standard day conditions. Defining a new corrected rate of climb as:

$$\left(\frac{dh}{dt}\right)_3 = \frac{THP_{A_{std}} - THP_{R_{std}}}{W} \tag{3.23}$$

Let the increment of net thrust be: $\Delta T_n = T_{n_{std}} - T_{n_t}$ or $\frac{T_{n_{std}}}{T_{n_t}} = 1 + \frac{\Delta T_n}{T_{n_t}}$. Substituting in eqn.

3.23: $\left(\frac{dh}{dt}\right)_3 = \left(\frac{T_{n_{std}}}{T_{n_t}}THP_{A_t} - THP_{R_t}\right)\frac{1}{W}\sqrt{\frac{T_{\infty_{std}}}{T_{\infty_t}}} = \left(THP_{A_t} - THP_{R_t} + \frac{\Delta T_n}{T_{n_t}}THP_{A_t}\right)\frac{1}{W}\sqrt{\frac{T_{\infty_t}}{T_{\infty_{std}}}}$

If we make the tapeline altitude correction first and assume that it fully reflects test day power available and power required,

$\left(\dfrac{dh}{dt}\right)_2 = \dfrac{THP_{A_t} - THP_{R_t}}{W}$, which directly substitutes into the earlier correction term,

$$\left(\frac{dh}{dt}\right)_3 = \sqrt{\frac{T_{\infty_{std}}}{T_{\infty_t}}}\left[\left(\frac{dh}{dt}\right)_2 + \frac{THP_{A_t}\Delta T_n}{W T_{n_t}}\right] \tag{3.24}$$

The climb correction expressed in eqn. 3.24 now includes both the tapeline altitude correction and an allowance for the difference in engine thrust available and required on the test day rather than on a standard day. Notice, that this differential power correction requires measuring the difference between test day net thrust and standard day net thrust. Such a measurement is difficult for most airplanes, and we must usually rely on engine manufacturer's data rather than direct measurement. Consequently, controversy surrounds this climb correction.

Example 3.4: For the climb of Example 3.3, 100% of rated rpm of its nonafterburning engine was used. The calibrated test engine was instrumented with pressure taps and net thrust was calculated as 4627 lbs while climbing at a true airspeed of 375 fps. The engine manufacturer has tested the engine and shown that on a standard day at 9000 feet the engine should develop 4800 lbs of thrust. The initial weight of the airplane was 12780 lbs and 2100 lbs of fuel have been burned. Calculate the rate of climb correction for variation in thrust horsepower due to nonstandard temperature for this test point.

Again, $T_{\infty_{std}}$ and T_{∞_t} are needed. Using the values previously calculated, eqn. 3.24 gives:

$\left(\dfrac{dh}{dt}\right)_3 = \sqrt{\dfrac{486.61}{491.69}}\left[1088.635\,fpm + \dfrac{(4800 - 4627)(4627)(375\,fps)(60)}{(12780 - 2100)(4627)}\right]$. Notice that units must be consistent

between the two additive terms inside the [ ]. $\boxed{\left(\dfrac{dh}{dt}\right)_3 = 1445.6\,fpm}$

The third and last correction in this series of rate of climb corrections account for the effect of nonstandard temperature lapse rates on measured true airspeeds. Figure 3.15 illustrates the rationale for this correction, remembering that, even for constant indicated airspeeds, true airspeeds for each indicated pressure altitude will be affected by nonstandard temperature. This apparent acceleration appears whether the climb is made at constant airspeed or at constant Mach number.

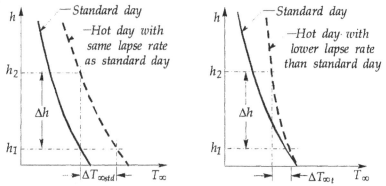

Fig. 3.15 Apparent Acceleration Correction

The acceleration factor introduced earlier corrects for the apparent acceleration due to nonstandard temperature lapse rate. Applying eqn. 3.9 to obtain the accelerated rate of climb for both standard day and test day conditions,

$$\left(\frac{dh}{dt}\right)_{std} = \frac{\left(T_{n_{std}} - D_{std}\right)V_{\infty_{std}}}{W\left(1 + \frac{V_{\infty_{std}}}{g}\frac{dV_{\infty_{std}}}{dh_{std}}\right)} \quad and \quad \left(\frac{dh}{dt}\right)_{t} = \frac{\left(T_{n_{t}} - D_{t}\right)V_{\infty_{t}}}{W\left(1 + \frac{V_{\infty_{t}}}{g}\frac{dV_{\infty_{t}}}{dh_{t}}\right)}$$

After dividing to obtain the ratio between these two rates of climb, apply the binomial theorem to each of the terms containing the acceleration factor and retain only first order terms since only small changes (differential corrections) will be considered. The result is

$$\frac{dh_{std}/dt}{dh_t/dt} = \left(1 - \frac{V_{\infty_{std}}}{g}\frac{\Delta V_{\infty_{std}}}{\Delta h_{std}}\right)\left(1 + \frac{V_{\infty_t}}{g}\frac{\Delta V_{\infty_t}}{\Delta h_t}\right) \approx \left(1 + \frac{V_{\infty_t}}{g}\frac{\Delta V_{\infty_t}}{\Delta h_t} - \frac{V_{\infty_{std}}}{g}\frac{\Delta V_{\infty_{std}}}{\Delta h_{std}} + H.O.T.\right)$$

If we also assume that $V_{\infty_{std}} \approx V_{\infty_t}$ and that $\Delta h_{std} \approx \Delta h_t$,

$$\left(\frac{dh}{dt}\right)_{std} = \left(\frac{dh}{dt}\right)_t \left(1 - \frac{V_{\infty_{std}}}{g\Delta h}\left(\Delta V_{\infty_{std}} - \Delta V_{\infty_t}\right)\right)$$

Continuing the serial numbering of rate corrections

$$\left(\frac{dh}{dt}\right)_4 = \left(\frac{dh}{dt}\right)_3 \left[1 - \frac{V_{\infty_{std}}}{g\Delta h}\left(\Delta V_{\infty_{std}} - \Delta V_{\infty_t}\right)\right]$$

$$(3.25)$$

Note that in eqn. 3.25 Δh and ΔV_∞ are small increments in altitude and true airspeed over which the measured climb rate is measured. These differences must be small for our approximations to be valid; so climb rate must be measured over a small altitude change and the corresponding airspeed changes must also be small.

Example 3.5: Continuing our performance climb corrections as introduced in Examples 3.3 and 3.4, the airplane's rate of climb is measured between 8500 feet and 9500 feet to obtain the measured rate of climb. At each of these altitudes, the outside air temperature was 32.7°F and 31.3°F, respectively, and a constant Mach number was maintained for this segment of the climb. For the same pressure altitude band, calculate the apparent acceleration correction to the rate of climb previously corrected with tapeline altitude corrections and for power available due to nonstandard test day conditions.

First, calculate ΔV_∞ for the Δh in question. The temperatures at each altitude are: $T_{\infty_{t_1}} = 459.69 + 32.7 = 492.39°R$ and $T_{\infty_{t_2}} = 459.69 + 31.3 = 490.99°R$. Also, the constant M_∞ (identical at both test and standard day conditions) comes from standard day conditions:

$$M_\infty = \frac{375}{\sqrt{(1.4)(1716.55)(486.61)}} = 0.3469.$$

For the test day lapse rate, the ΔV between the two measurement altitudes is:

$$\Delta V_{\infty_t} = M_\infty\sqrt{\gamma R}\left(\sqrt{T_{\infty_{t_2}}} - \sqrt{T_{\infty_{t_1}}}\right) = -5.3679 \ fps$$

For a standard lapse rate: $\Delta V_{\infty_t} = M_\infty\sqrt{\gamma R}\left(\sqrt{T_{\infty_{std_2}}} - \sqrt{T_{\infty_{std_1}}}\right) = -13.578 \ fps$

Substituting into eqn. 3.25,

$$\left(\frac{dh}{dt}\right)_4 = 1445.6\left(1 - \frac{375}{(32.17405)(1000)}\right)(-13.7578 + 5.3679)$$

$$\boxed{\left(\frac{dh}{dt}\right)_4 = 1587.0 \ fpm}$$

Example 3.5 illustrates how a nonstandard test day temperature lapse rate affects the correction of test day climb corrections to standard day conditions. The magnitude of the cumulative correction, $\left(\frac{dh}{dt}\right)_4$ demonstrates the importance and value of this effort.

3.2.2.3 **Summary of Rate of Climb Corrections**. Collecting all rate of climb corrections (including those developed earlier), the complete correction is:

$$\left(\frac{dh}{dt}\right)_{std} = \sqrt{\frac{T_{\infty_{std}}}{T_{\infty_t}}} \left[\left(\frac{dh}{dt}\right)_t + THP_{A_t} \frac{\Delta T_{n_t}}{WT_{n_t}} \right]$$

$$+ \left(\frac{-V_{\infty_t} \Delta V_w}{g \Delta h} \right) \sqrt{\frac{T_{\infty_{std}}}{T_{\infty_t}}} \left[\left(\frac{dh}{dt}\right)_t + THP_{A_t} \frac{\Delta T_{n_t}}{WT_{n_t}} \right]$$

$$+ \left[\frac{-V_{\infty_t}}{g \Delta h} \left(\Delta V_{\infty_{std}} - \Delta V_{\infty_t} \right) \right] \left(\frac{-V_{\infty_t} \Delta V_w}{g \Delta h} \right) \sqrt{\frac{T_{\infty_{std}}}{T_{\infty_t}}} \left[\left(\frac{dh}{dt}\right)_t + THP_{A_t} \frac{\Delta T_{n_t}}{WT_{n_t}} \right] \qquad (3.26)$$

3.2.3 Turn Performance Flight Test Techniques

3.2.3.1 **Level, Unaccelerated Turn Technique**. The simplest approach to measuring thrust-limited turning performance is to simply fly turns at constant altitude, constant power setting, and selected constant airspeeds. Typically, the powerplant is operating at a power setting at or near military or maximum power (since we are discussing thrust-limited turns. In such a stabilized level turn the bank angle and the load factor are also constant. The instrumentation required is just a stopwatch to time the total heading change. Frequently, a stabilized turn of 360° is used for convenience in this timing, though the turn could be through any desired heading change. To avoid significant timing errors due to human reaction times, it is usually best to turn for at least a minute, preferably two minutes. Turns should be made in both directions to check for any secondary effects on the turn performance. Care must be exercised by the pilot to guarantee that altitude and speed variations are kept small, usually less than ± 50 feet and ± 1 to 2 knots throughout the maneuver. It is far more important to maintain a constant airspeed throughout the timing period than it is to make the turn at exactly the target airspeed. Depending on the resolution of the available cockpit sensors, the pilot may use either the attitude indicator (or some more precise bank angle indicator) or the accelerometer to maintain constant load factor. At high load factors with the bank angle increasing beyond 60° for level flight, greater care must be exercised to stay within acceptable tolerances. If the turn continues beyond 360° and the pilot has precisely maintained altitude, he may encounter his own jet wash. Such an event can upset the stabilized turn, but usually is nothing more than a nuisance. The reliability of cockpit heading indications should be checked; if they are reliable in turns at all load factors, the heading indicator can provide starting and stopping points that are useful. Hand recorded data are usually adequate, but if other instrumentation (rate gyros, stable platforms, event markers, and the like) is available, it should be used and backed up with hand-recorded data. As with all tests, care must be taken to observe all aircraft structural and aerodynamic limits. At speeds above the predicted maneuvering speed (corner velocity) the pilot must insure he does not exceed the maximum allowable load factor. Another caution in this part of the performance envelope: remember to relax the load factor before rolling out of the maneuver; typically, the load factor limit in a rolling maneuver is considerably lower than in a symmetrically loaded condition.

3.2.3.2 **Level Acceleration Technique**. This technique for level acceleration data is identical to that described in section 3.2.1.2. The only change is in how the data are used to describe the performance of the airplane. It is important to carry the level acceleration out to maximum airspeed so that the point for zero excess thrust is established. The usefulness of the data to characterize turning performance depends on the thrust limitations. Said another way, P_s (again as discussed in section 3.2.1.2) is just as useful as a measure of merit for thrust-limited turning performance as it is for climb performance. Figure 3.16 illustrates one of the plots commonly produced from level acceleration data to depict the turn performance capability of a fighter aircraft. These plots, sometimes called "doghouse" plots because of their characteristic shape, often overlay the turn performance metrics and P_s contours.

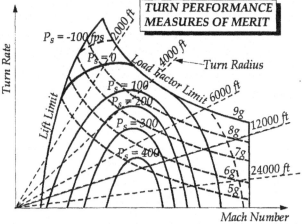

Fig. 3.16 Turning Performance Measures of Merit

By overlaying the P_s contours, whether the turn rates and radii for sustained and instantaneous turns can be determined. If the turn rate and Mach number are such that P_s is negative, the indicated turning performance is an instantaneous turning capability. The "doghouse" plot also are clearly depicts aerodynamic and structural limits.

3.3 INSTRUMENTATION
3.3.1 Instrumentation for Sawtooth Climbs
One attractive facet of this test technique is the very simple instrumentation needed to produce useful results. The tests require only production air data (altimeter and airspeed indicator), a stop watch, a kneeboard and an outside air temperature gauge (if temperature corrections are desired). Sensitive air data displays improve data credibility, as do instrument panel vibrators to reduce the effect of stiction in the movement of the pointers on these instruments. Engine parameters and configuration settings (gear and flap positions, trim positions, and cowl flap settings) should also be recorded. Finally, wind direction and velocity at test altitudes are needed to both orient the tests and apply the full set of corrections described in section 3.2.
3.3.2 Instrumentation for Performance Climbs
Since this test confirms the aggregate results from several sawtooth climbs, the same instrumentation suffices. Propulsion system sensors are usually needed this technique may reveal engine cooling deficiencies. Therefore, it is advisable to install temperature

sensors at strategic locations to identify hot spots. This information is generally manda-tory for FAA certifications as part of the substantiation package.

3.3.3 Instrumentation for Level Accelerations

Level accelerations must have automated recording of altitude and airspeed changes along with a correlated powerplant readings. Either an analog recording device or a digi-tal one can be used; video or film record of the cockpit air data displays have been used. However, though this type of recording might be simple and inexpensive to obtain, con-verting the information to rate information as suggested in Fig. 3.11 may be a labor-intensive and expensive process. Analog-to-digital (A/D) converters and digitized data are much more likely to be used today. The sample rate for these recording channels need not be very high; typically 2-5 samples/second is adequate. These measurements will be usually be smoothed (filtered) to remove the high frequency content of the time series measurements. If the level acceleration data are taken at elevated g (as for energy plots and some turning performance plots), the cockpit displays should include a sensi-tive accelerometer for the pilot. The accelerometer readings are also captured by the data system. The scale on this display ought to allow easy identification of changes no greater than 0.1g and for some purposes even smaller resolutions may be needed. This resolu-tion is much better than most production accelerometers provide, so sensitive ones are usually needed. It is also highly desirable to provide a means for marking the data with an event maraker so data can be more easily sorted and processed automatically after the files are written.

3.4 SUMMARY

This chapter has introduced common flight test methods used to optimize climb schedules, to validate climb schedules, and to measure turn performance. The methods are straightforward, though somewhat time-consuming, with the level acceleration tech-nique holding a definite advantage over sawtooth climbs and level, unaccelerated turns in efficiency of data collection. Climb tests are relatively easy to describe in theory, but de-mand careful attention to detail in data reduction to achieve the accuracies needed for cer-tification or specification compliance. Turn performance flight tests are related to climb and descent performance largely because they are usually limited by available excess thrust. This fact allows test data to be collected in level accelerations for use in character-izing both the optimized climb paths and the instantaneous and sustained turn perform-ance. Stabilized level turns with production instrumentation also provide considerable insight into the capability of the airplane and certainly provide opportunity for an intro-duction to the measurement of this important aspect of aircraft performance.

REFERENCES

1 Diehl,W. S., **Engineering Aerodynamics** (Revised Edition), Ronald Press, 1936.

2 Hamlin, B., **Flight Testing Conventional and Jet-Propelled Airplanes**, The Macmillan Company, New York, 1946.

3 Rutowski, E. S., "Energy Approach to the General Aircraft Performance Problem," **Journal of the Aeronautical Sciences**, Vol. 21, Mar. 1954, pp. 187-195.

4 Boyd, J. S., "Energy Problem,".

5 Nicolai, L. M., **Fundamentals of Aircraft Design**, METS, Inc., San Jose, California, 1975.

6 McCormick, B.., **Fundamentals of**, , 1975.

7 "Performance," Volume I, FTC-TIH-70-1001 (Revised December 1976), USAF Test Pilot School, Edwards AFB, California, 1976.

8 "Fixed Wing Performance, Theory and Flight Test Techniques," USNTPS-FTM_No. 104, Naval Air Test Center, Patuxent River, Maryland, Jul. 1977.

9 Advisory Circular AC 23-8B, "Flight Test Guide for Certification of Part 23 Airplanes," Federal Aviation Administration, Aug. 14, 2003. (Available at: http://www.airweb.faa.gov/Regulatory_and_Guidance_Library/rgAdvisoryCircular.nsf/0/469CD77D24955F4E86256DA60060C156?OpenDocument.)

10 FAR Part 23, "Airworthiness Standards: Normal, Utility, Acrobatic, and Commuter Category Airplanes," January 17, 2006, (Available at: http://www.airweb.faa.gov/Regulatory_and_Guidance_Library/rgAdvisoryCircular.nsf/0/469CD77D24955F4E86256DA60060C156?OpenDocument.)

11 Lush, K. J., "A Survey of Performance Reduction Methods," Chapter 3, Vol. I, **AGARD Flight Test Manual**, Pergamon Press, New York, 1959.

12 Dommasch, D. O., "Data Reduction and Performance Test Methods for Reciprocating Engine Aircraft," Chapter 6, Vol. 1, **AGARD Flight Test Manual**, Pergamon Press, New York, 1959.

13 "Performance, Book B-2," Empire Test Pilots' School, Royal Aircraft Establishment, Farnborough , England, 1966.

Chapter 4
CRUISE PERFORMANCE TESTS

The cruise performance of any vehicle is one of the most important matters to be determined by flight test. Estimates of cruise performance are made from the very beginning of the conceptual design. Range and endurance under specified mission profiles are contractual requirements that must be validated for any aerospace vehicle. Hence, the topic is one of prime concern to the flight test team.

The elemental aerodynamic variable in determining cruise performance is the drag produced by the airframe-engine combination for the particular configuration or configurations and the specified mission profile. Unfortunately, there is no direct way to measure drag in flight. Test engineers usually rely on approximate mathematical models for drag to start cruise performance analyses. Figure 4.1 is a block diagram representing types of drag and suggesting possible ways to simplify the mathematical model.

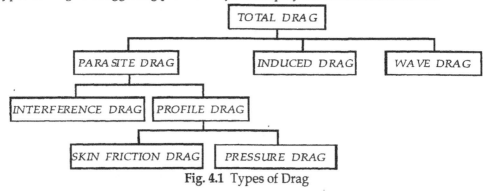

Fig. 4.1 Types of Drag

One of the simplest mathematical models for low speed airplanes is the subsonic drag polar given in eqn. 4.1.

$$C_D = C_{D_p} + \frac{C_L^2}{\pi e AR} \qquad (4.1)$$

where C_D is total drag coefficient and C_{D_p} is effective parasite drag coefficient. Equation 4.1 is valid only for airplanes in which compressibility drag rise is not a factor; in this book the parabolic drag polar is assumed to be a good approximation for airplanes powered by reciprocating engines.

4.1 FOUNDATIONS

Cruise performance is determined by both the available thrust (or power) from the powerplant and the thrust (or power) required by the airframe. Thus, it is necessary to correct the outputs from different propulsion systems to standard day conditions, much like the corrections required in climb performance data reduction. However, because of the fundamental differences between propeller-driven and jet-propelled airplanes, it will be convenient to discuss the performance reductions under separate sections. Different performance reduction methods are used for the two types of powerplants. Propeller-driven aircraft will be considered first since they tend to be lower performers and the data reduction procedures are simpler (though perhaps more tedious). Typically, propeller-driven airplanes are analyzed using an analytical performance reduction method that draws upon the extensive data bank supplied by reciprocating engine manufacturers.

Turboprop-powered aircraft usually are also analyzed with an analytical method, although a mixture of the analytical approach with differential techniques from the experimental performance method is often necessary to account for missing information on the powerplant. Turbojet and turbofan powered airplanes typically are analyzed with an experimental performance reduction method.

4.1.1 Propeller-Driven Aircraft

The analytical performance reduction method for propeller-driven aircraft performance relies heavily upon data collected by the engine manufacturer, usually brake horsepower data taken at sea level. For any airplane, $THP_r = \dfrac{DV_\infty}{550}$, with V_∞ in fps and D in pounds. With the usual definitions of dynamic pressure q, aspect ratio AR, Oswald's efficiency factor e, and assuming a parabolic drag polar with $L = W$:

$$THP_r = \frac{\rho_\infty V_\infty^2 C_{D_p} S V_\infty}{1100} + \frac{\rho_\infty V_\infty^2 C_L^2 S V_\infty}{1100\pi e AR} = \frac{\rho_\infty V_\infty^3 C_{D_p} S}{1100} + \frac{W^2}{275\rho_\infty S V_\infty \pi e AR}$$

Inflight measurement of thrust, especially from a reciprocating engine-propeller combination, is uncertain and requires expensive instrumentation. It is common practice to use measured brake horsepower data from the engine manufacturer. But propeller efficiency must be included in the horsepower relationship.

$\eta_p BHP_r = THP_r$

So, $BHP_r = \dfrac{\rho_\infty V_\infty^3 C_{D_p} S}{1100\eta_p} + \dfrac{W^2}{275\rho_\infty S V_\infty \pi e AR \eta_p}$

Setting $A = \dfrac{C_{D_p} S}{1100\eta_p}$ and $B = \dfrac{1}{275\pi e b^2 \eta_p}$, and multiplying by V_∞,

$$BHP_r V_\infty = \rho_\infty A V_\infty^4 + \frac{BW^2}{\rho_\infty} \tag{4.2}$$

This relationship, with weight and density identified as dependent variables, clearly shows the dependence of power required upon airplane weight and altitude, the two variables that must be standardized if performance data are to be comparable between different tests. However, the power requirements can be further generalized to allow all test data for a given configuration to fall on a single power required curve. In other words, this further generalization of the power equation will allow direct comparison of test data and easy interpolation of the generalized curve to points within the envelope where test data were not collected to verify the mathematical model. Such an approach allows minimum flight test data collection to validate the mathematical model. Choose a standard weight W_{std} for the configuration and use ρ_0 to define a generalized velocity parameter VIW and a generalized power parameter PIW.

$$VIW = \sqrt{\frac{2W_{std}}{\rho_0 C_L S}} \quad and \quad PIW = \frac{DVIW}{550} = \frac{1}{550}\sqrt{\frac{2W_{std}^3 C_D^2}{\rho_0 C_L^2 S}} \tag{4.3}$$

Since $L = W_{std} = \dfrac{1}{2}\rho_\infty V_\infty^2 S C_L$ and $D = \dfrac{W_{std} C_D}{C_L}$, and at a given altitude and C_L:

$V_\infty = \sqrt{\dfrac{2W}{\rho_\infty C_L S}}$ and $THP_r = \dfrac{1}{550}\sqrt{\dfrac{2W^3 C_D^2}{\rho_0 C_L^2 S}}$. If each term in eqns. 4.3 is multiplied by "one" in the appropriate form,

$$VIW = V_\infty \frac{\sqrt{\dfrac{2W_{std}}{\rho_0 C_L S}}}{\sqrt{\dfrac{2W}{\rho_\infty C_L S}}} = V_\infty \sqrt{\frac{\sigma W_{std}}{W}} \tag{4.4}$$

$$PIW = \frac{THP_r}{550} \frac{550\sqrt{\dfrac{2W_{std}^3 C_D^2}{\rho_0 C_L^2 S}}}{\sqrt{\dfrac{2W^3 C_D^2}{\rho_\infty C_L^2 S}}} = THP_r \sqrt{\sigma\left(\frac{W_{std}}{W}\right)^3} \tag{4.5}$$

Using eqn. 4.2, THP_r can be written as $THP_r = \eta_p\left(\rho_0 \sigma A V_\infty^3 + \dfrac{BW^2}{\rho_0 \sigma V_\infty}\right)$

Multiplying both sides by $\sqrt{\sigma\left(\dfrac{W_{std}}{W}\right)^3}$:

$$PIW = THP_r \sqrt{\sigma\left(\frac{W_{std}}{W}\right)^3} = \eta_p\left(\rho_0 \sigma A V_\infty^3 + \frac{BW^2}{\rho_0 \sigma V_\infty}\right)\sqrt{\sigma\left(\frac{W_{std}}{W}\right)^3}$$

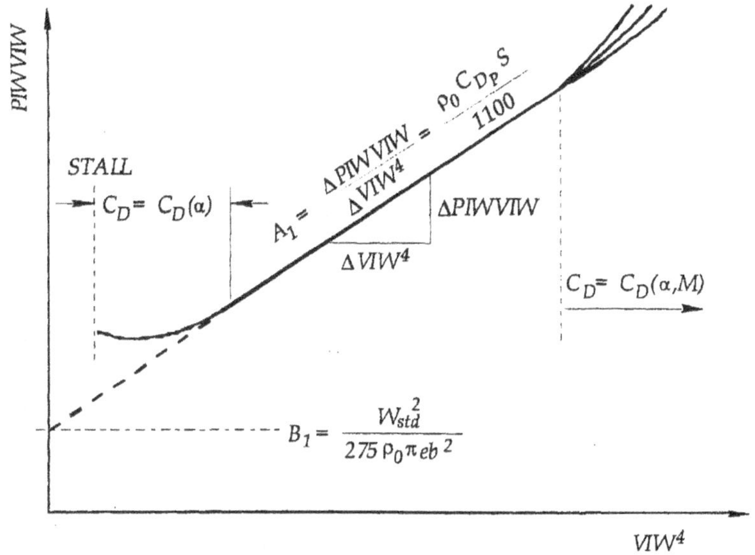

Fig. 4.2 Generalized Power Curve

Since ρ_0 and W_{std} are constants and η_p is approximately constant, we readily obtain

$$PIWVIW = A_1 VIW^4 + B_1 \tag{4.6}$$

where $A_1 = \dfrac{\rho_0 C_{D_p} S}{1100}$ and $B_1 = \dfrac{W_{std}^2}{275\rho_0\pi e b^2}$

A generalized power curve (Fig. 4.2) is a reasonable approximation for a parabolic drag curve and constant propeller efficiency except at either the high or the low speed ends. At low speed (high α) nonlinearities due to separated flow appear. At low C_L, compressibility effects are important and the curve often splits into multiple branches. So, eqn. 4.6 is a simplified, but useful, mathematical model of the cruise performance for a low speed, propeller-driven aircraft. The slope and intercept of this generalized curve readily give estimates of Oswald's efficiency factor and of the minimum drag coefficient.

$$e = \frac{W_{std}^2}{275 B_1 \rho_0 \pi b^2} \qquad (4.7)$$

$$\text{and} \quad C_{D_p} = \frac{1100 A_1}{\rho_0 S} \qquad (4.8)$$

Table 4.1 Cruise Data for a Propeller-Driven Airplane

TAS (kts)	TAS (fps)	BHP_r	THP_r	W_t (lbs)	VIW (fps)	PIW	VIW^4 ($\times 10^{-9}$)	$PIW(VIW)$
55	92.828	512	424.960	5512	80.64	334.86	0.0423	27002.57
60	101.267	442	366.860	5430	88.63	295.65	0.0617	26203.83
65	109.706	383	317.890	5376	96.50	260.06	0.0867	25094.84
70	118.144	343	284.690	5322	104.45	236.45	0.1190	24696.38
75	126.583	318	263.940	5288	112.27	221.34	0.1588	24848.28
80	135.022	286	237.380	5236	120.34	202.04	0.2097	24313.51
90	151.900	248	205.840	5198	135.88	177.12	0.3409	24066.47
100	168.778	225	186.750	5165	151.46	162.23	0.5262	24571.56
110	185.656	221	183.430	5111	167.48	161.88	0.7868	27112.15
120	202.533	225	186.750	5079	183.28	166.37	1.1285	30492.86
130	219.411	235	195.050	5021	199.70	176.78	1.5904	35303.81
140	236.289	252	209.160	4948	216.64	193.78	2.2028	41981.70
160	270.044	302	250.660	4875	249.44	237.47	3.8712	59233.66
180	303.800	375	311.250	4805	282.65	301.34	6.3829	85174.16
200	337.556	458	380.140	4722	316.81	377.78	10.0740	119683.50

Example 4.1: Table 4.1 shows data for a general aviation airplane with a propeller efficiency of 0.83. Data were collected at 6000 feet pressure altitude with an outside air temperature of 40°F. The airplane's "standard" weight is 5000 lbs. Wing area is 175 ft^2 and aspect ratio is 5.5. Calculate C_{D_p} and e by plotting a generalized power required curve and measuring the slope and the intercept of that curve.

First, density is calculated from $\rho = \frac{p}{RT}$, with $T = 40 + 459.69 = 499.69°R$; that is,

$$\rho = \frac{1696}{(1716.55)(499.69)} = 0.0019773 \text{ slugs/ft}^3. \text{ Then, } \sigma_t = \frac{0.0019773}{0.0023769} = 0.83188. \text{ With } V_\infty = 55 \text{ knots} = 92.828 \text{ fps,}$$

$$VIW = 98.828 \sqrt{\frac{(0.83188)(5000)}{5512}} = 80.638 \text{ fps. Also, } PIW = THP_r \sqrt{\sigma \left(\frac{W_{std}}{W_t}\right)^3} = \eta_p BHP_r \sqrt{\sigma \left(\frac{W_{std}}{W_t}\right)^3} \text{ or}$$

$$PIW = (0.83)(512)\sqrt{0.83188\left(\frac{5000}{5512}\right)^3} = 335 \text{ hp. Finally, carrying out the multiplications for } (PIW)(VIW)$$

and VIW^4 gives the last two columns in Table 4.1. The plot below shows the resulting generalized power curve. A linear curve was fitted to the last 8 data points in Table 4.1. The resulting straight line had a slope of 0.0000100502 and a PIW-VIW intercept of 19573.9. Utilizing eqns. 4.7 and 4.8, we estimate the required parameters:

$$e = \frac{5000^2}{(275)(962.5)(0.0023769)(19573.9)}$$

$$\boxed{e = 0.646}$$

$$C_{D_p} = \frac{(0.0000100502)(1100)}{(0.0023769)(175)}$$

$$\boxed{C_{D_p} = 0.0266}$$

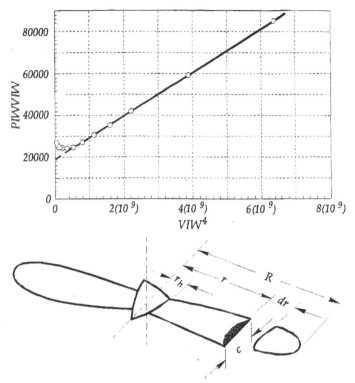

Fig. 4.3 Geometric Variables for a Propeller

4.1.1.1 **Propeller Efficiency**. Propeller efficiency is not easily measured in flight, although Bull and Bridges[1] have used specially designed instruments and a maximum likelihood mathematical modeling technique to measure it. Their approach shows considerable promise, but the method is not yet widely used. More commonly, propeller efficiency is estimated by either an analytical technique[2] or a semi-empirical method[3]. Each of these methods is straightforward, provided the appropriate inputs are known. To use them, one must know altitude, true airspeed, brake or shaft horsepower, and number of propeller blades, all readily obtainable configuration constants. Variables peculiar to propeller performance such as advance ratio, activity factor, solidity ratio, and integrated design lift coefficient must also be known or estimated. Advance ratio J is defined as the forward speed of the propeller divided by the rotational speed:

$$J = \frac{V_\infty}{nD} , \qquad \text{where } n \text{ is propeller rotational rate in revolutions/second}$$

Activity factor AF is a measure of the power absorbed by the propeller and is defined as

$$AF = \frac{100000}{16} \int_{x_h}^{1.0} \frac{c}{D} x^3 dx$$

(4.9)

where $x = \dfrac{r}{R}$, $D = 2R$, and $c = c(x)$ (Fig. 4.3.)

The non-dimensional hub radius, usually taken to be about 0.15, is x_h. The solidity ratio SR is simply the ratio of total blade area to the disk area swept by the rotating blades.

$$SR = \frac{Bc}{pR} \quad \text{where } B \text{ is the total number of blades.}$$

The integrated design lift coefficient is defined as

$$C_{L_i} = 4 \int_{x_h}^{1.0} c_{\ell_d} x^3 dx \tag{4.10}$$

where c_{ℓ_d} is the individual blade section design lift coefficient and is a function of x.

Optimizing a propeller for cruise performance means that C_{L_i} will be small (on the order of 0.35), while optimizing the propeller for high thrust at lower forward speeds (climb speeds, for example) will result in an integrated design lift coefficient of about 0.60.

It is convenient (for the same reasons that we use nondimensional coefficients like C_L, C_D, and C_m) for engineers to describe propeller performance using nondimensional coefficients. Three terms typically characterize an aircraft powerplant's output: power, thrust, and torque. The three important propulsive coefficients include:

- ◆ Power coefficient $\qquad\qquad C_P = 550 \dfrac{BHP}{\rho_\infty n^3 D^5} \tag{4.11}$

- ◆ Thrust coefficient $\qquad\qquad C_T = \dfrac{T_n}{\rho_\infty n^2 D^4} \tag{4.12}$

- ◆ Torque coefficient $\qquad\qquad C_Q = \dfrac{Q}{\rho_\infty n^2 D^4} \tag{4.13}$

Once these coefficients and the advance ratio are known (and often propeller manufacturer's empirical handbooks or experimental data sheets provide the most reliable estimates), propeller efficiency can be calculated from:

$$\eta_P = J \frac{C_T}{C_P} \tag{4.14}$$

Having indicated how propeller efficiency can be estimated, consider next how we estimate the power available from an engine.

4.1.1.2 **Power Available**. Earlier, we saw that propeller-driven aircraft analysis often uses engine manufacturer's data (charts similar to Fig. 4.4) to estimate the available output power; this approach is a widely accepted practice for reciprocating engines. However, it is possible to directly measure the output power to the propeller shaft with a torque meter installed specifically for this purpose. Production torque meters, which generally do not provide the accuracies needed for flight test, are routinely installed on airplanes powered by turboprop powerplants. To find BHP, you only need the torque meter reading, the rotational rate of the propeller shaft, and a calibration constant for the torque meter (usually found during ground tests using a dynamometer).

$$BHP = \frac{2pnQ}{550} \quad \text{or } BHP = K_{n_{ic}} Q_{ic}$$

Flight test quality torque meters are hard to install, require frequent calibration, and are expensive. Smaller engines cannot accommodate commercially available torque meters and many project budgets cannot afford their cost. So, engine characteristic curves, obtained from ground test stands, provide estimates of available engine power.

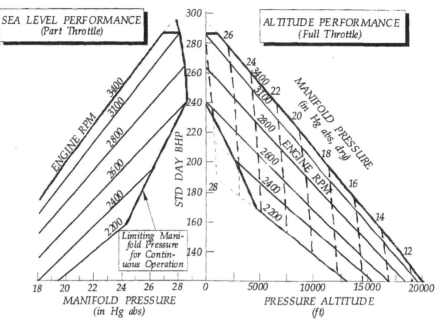

Fig. 4.4 Engine Power Chart for Normally Aspirated Engines

Since the manufacturer's data sheets (similar to Figs. 4.4 and 4.5) are usually based on ground tests, the flight test analyst must estimate engine output data for a given test condition from charts like those shown. Remember that measurements are usually taken at or near sea level for such charts. The altitude estimates are usually calculated by the powerplant engineers. For reciprocating engines these data are usually quite accurate and their ready availability makes them attractive for use. Also, they are usually based on standard day conditions; corrections must be made for nonstandard conditions. The flight test engineer must carefully study the engine data sheets for his powerplant to be sure that all nonstandard conditions have been considered. Once again, a few terms must be defined to make this process easier.

For a reciprocating engine the **critical altitude** is the altitude at which the throttle must be fully opened to develop rated power at rated RPM. The British give this altitude a more descriptive name, **full-throttle height**. Thus, the critical altitude is the altitude at which the power begins to decrease regardless of the position of the throttle. Whenever an engine reaches a structural limit because of cylinder pressures or if the manufacturer seeks longer life, or for any other practical operational reason, rated power may be produced at part throttle up to the critical altitude. Such "de-rating" is, in fact, more common than having not having any operating limits. Figure 4.6 illustrates this idea for the case when the power output of the engine is limited by the pressure allowed in the cylinders.

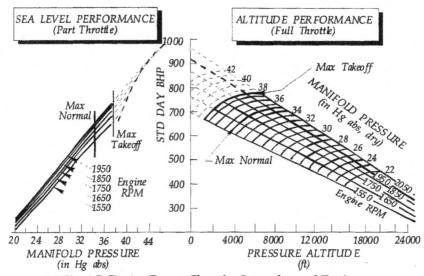

Fig. 4.5 Engine Power Chart for Supercharged Engines

A reciprocating engine that takes in ambient air and does not compress it prior to the combustion process is **normally aspirated**. If a geared compressor is attached to the crankshaft accessory drive, the pressure of the air used in the combustion process may be raised to produce more power. Such engines are called **ground-boosted** engines. Both normally aspirated and ground-boosted engines may have sea level as a critical altitude.

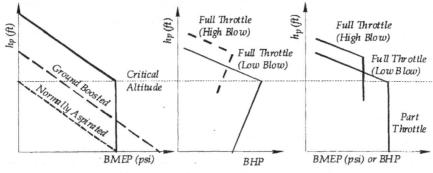

Fig. 4.6 Critical Altitudes for Reciprocating Engines

Turbosuperchargers are the most common form of supercharging in modern reciprocating engines and engine limits may be set by BMEP, BHP, turbine RPM, or turbine temperatures. Of course, multi-stage supercharging results in more than one critical altitude (Fig. 4.6 illustrates these definitions).

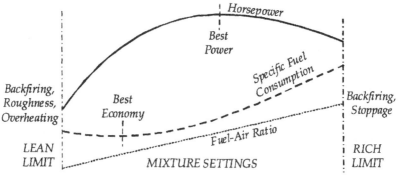

Fig. 4.7 Effect of Mixture Setting

Fuel-air mixture setting also strongly affects available brake horsepower. Figure 4.7 shows how deviation from the desired fuel-air ratio affects reciprocating engine performance. The mixture may significantly affect the results of cruise performance tests and therefore requires careful adjustment. Full rich is the most repeatable setting, but cruise tests at full rich are not representative of the airplane's best cruise performance. The most common approach is to use a sensitive cylinder head temperature gauge and follow the engine manufacturer's recommendations for leaning the engine.

4.1.1.3 **Corrections** to **BHP Available**. For part throttle operation with no mechanical limitations, corrections to power available (primarily those dealing with temperature) from a reciprocating engine are usually given on engine charts (Fig. 4.8).

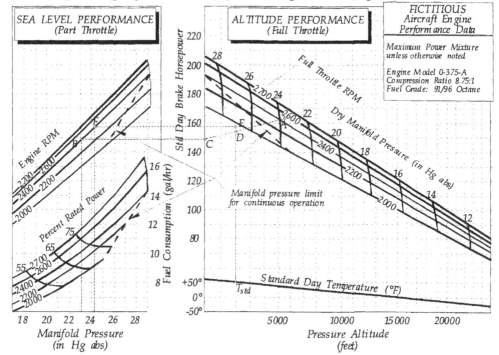

Fig. 4.8 Engine Operating Charts

To estimate actual test day horsepower from manifold pressure, engine rpm, altitude, and inlet temperature on such typical charts, the following procedure is recommended. The outlined procedure helps explain how and why flight tests are necessary to verify installed engine characteristics from manufacturer's data. Keep in mind that these charts are usually based on test data taken near sea level; altitude performance is calculated from that information. A typical estimate of test day power available is obtained by:

1. Locate point A on the full throttle altitude curve for a given dry manifold pressure-full throttle rpm curve.
2. Find the corresponding point B on the sea level performance curve for the manifold pressure and rpm used in step 1.
3. Project the horsepower for point B to the ordinate on the altitude performance scale (point C) and connect points A and C with a straight line.
4. At the test day pressure altitude and standard day temperature (nomogram at the bottom of the altitude performance chart in Fig. 4.8) project upward to the straight line found in step 3 to locate point D.
5. Modify the horsepower at point D using the following expression to estimate actual (nonstandard) power output available under test conditions.

$$BHP_{std} = BHP_t \sqrt{\frac{T_{std}}{T_t}} \quad or \quad MAP_{std} = MAP_t \sqrt{\frac{T_{std}}{T_t}}$$

Full throttle operations often involve other limits or constraints that require corrections including:

◆ Nonstandard intake temperature (carburetor or supercharger inlet)
◆ Nonstandard exhaust back pressure
◆ Nonstandard BHP
◆ Nonstandard turbine RPM

For a given engine and installation, consult the manufacturer's data base for limits that apply to the specific configuration under test. Any limit that may differ because test atmospheric conditions are not standard day conditions is a subject for careful study.

Having treated the propeller-driven aircraft, we turn now to jet-powered airplanes for which experimental methods are more appropriate.

4.1.2 Jet-Powered Aircraft

Experimental performance reduction methods are commonly used for jet-powered aircraft because their lift-drag relationship is complicated by their dependence on Mach number. Wave drag, shown in dashed lines in Fig. 4.1, must be included for these higher performance airplanes. The simple parabolic drag polar is usually not an adequate model, except for a few specific flight conditions. Performance measurements for jet airplanes, therefore, are somewhat more complicated by the number of variables that must be considered. Dimensional analysis, based on Buckingham's Pi theorem, reduces the number of parameters that must be covered in the test program. Even so, performance analysis is usually specialized to take into account instrumentation installed, time and money available, and/or accuracy demanded by the tests to be conducted. The latter consideration leads to different sets of nondimensional variables for different purposes. This section introduces the fundamentals with a typical set of variables used for cruise performance and exemplifying application to any other particular problem.

4.1.2.1 **Buckingham's Pi Theorem**. Buckingham's Pi Theorem can be stated as:

> If a physical problem is characterized by n variables having p fundamental units, then the functional relationship between the variables can be expressed in $n - p$ dimensionless numbers.

For the typical flight mechanics problem (like the turbojet performance problem), the fundamental units are mass, length, and time, abbreviated m, L, and t. Then, assuming that there only n variables that significantly affect performance, Buckingham's Pi Theorem asserts that the total number of parameters necessary to characterize the performance is reduced from n to $n - 3$, if one measures performance in appropriate dimensionless variables rather than the n physical variables. For flight test, reducing the total number of variables reduces test time and expense. The steps in this process include:

◆ Select p variables from the physical variables. These variables should include all the fundamental units so the following algebra can be completed.
◆ Form $n - p$ dimensionless equations by combining each of the variables from step 1 in turn with each of the others.

This procedure is illustrated with an example in the next paragraph. But, the process depends on the original assumption; that is, if one or more significant physical variable is omitted from the set p in step 1, its effect will be omitted from the answers.

Consider now the output of a jet engine. The important measurements might be taken as net thrust T_n, weight flow rate of air $\dot{w}_a$, weight flow rate of fuel $\dot{w}_f$, and characteristic temperatures T_j. (T_j might be turbine inlet temperature, exhaust gas temperature, or a host of other temperatures depending on the specific engine under consideration.) These measurements may be functions of true airspeed V_∞, ambient temperature T_∞, ambient static pressure p_0, a physical dimension of the engine like the diameter of the compressor rotor D, a characteristic rpm N of the rotating parts like the compressor rotor, air viscosity μ, and various engine component efficiencies like inlet efficiency η_i, compressor efficiency η_c, burner efficiency η_b, turbine efficiency η_t, and nozzle efficiency η_n. The list of variables might be simplified by assuming that each of the component efficiencies is also a function of V_∞, T_∞, p_∞, N, and D. Further, viscosity can be eliminated as an independent variable if it can be described adequately as a function of p_∞ and T_∞. Notice that this assumption is tantamount to saying that Reynolds number effects are not important. If Reynolds number effects do significantly affect the engine performance, the model will not account for them.

Example 4.2: Applying Buckingham's Pi Theorem to the functional relationships described above, that is, $T_n = T_n(V_\infty, T_\infty, p_\infty, N, D)$. Select the variables T_n, N, and D and operate on the dimensions of V_∞, T_∞, and p_∞ to group T_n, N, and D as dimensionless constants π_1, π_2, π_3.

First, we select $\pi_1 = T_n^a N^b D^c V_\square$ and apply Buckingham's Theorem:

$$L^0 m^0 t^0 = \left(\frac{mL}{t^2}\right)^a \left(\frac{1}{t}\right)^b \left(\frac{L}{1}\right)^c \left(\frac{L}{t}\right).$$

Solving for equal exponents on both sides of this equation

L:	0	$=$	$a + c + 1$	a	$= 0$
m:	0	$=$	a	b	$= -1$
t:	0	$=$	$-2a - b - 1$	c	$= -1$

Therefore, $\pi_1 = \dfrac{V_\infty}{ND}$ (4.15)

Similarly, the other two nondimensional groupings can be found by solving the dimensional equations for T_n, N, and D with temperature first and then with pressure. Next, $\pi_2 = T_n{}^a N^b D^c T_\infty$, which gives:

$$L^0 m^0 t^0 = \left(\frac{mL}{t^2}\right)^a \left(\frac{1}{t}\right)^b \left(\frac{L}{1}\right)^c \left(\frac{L}{t}\right)^2 .$$

L:	0	=	$a + c + 2$	a	=	0
m:	0	=	a	b	=	-2
t:	0	=	$-2a - b - 2$	c	=	-2

So, $\pi_2 = \dfrac{T_\infty}{(ND)^2}$ \hfill (4.16)

Finally, $\pi_3 = T_n{}^a N^b D^c p$, which gives $L^0 m^0 t^0 = \left(\frac{mL}{t^2}\right)^a \left(\frac{1}{t}\right)^b \left(\frac{L}{1}\right)^c \left(\frac{m}{Lt^2}\right) .$

L:	0	=	$a + c - 1$	a	=	-1
m:	0	=	$a + 1$	b	=	0
t:	0	=	$-2a - b - 2$	c	=	2

Finally, $\pi_3 = \dfrac{p_\infty D^2}{T_n}$. \hfill (4.17)

Continuing to specialize the example to jet engine performance, any of the functional relationships suggested by eqns. 4.15, 4.16, or 4.17 can be written in reciprocal form. For example,

$$\pi_3 = f_1(\pi_1, \pi_2) \text{ implies } \pi_3 = \frac{p_\infty D^2}{T_n} = f_1\left\{\left[\frac{V_\infty}{nD}\right]\left[\frac{T_\infty}{(ND)^2}\right]\right\} \text{ or } \frac{T_n}{p_\infty D^2} = f_2\left\{\left(\frac{V_\infty}{nD}\right)\left(\frac{ND}{\sqrt{T_\infty}}\right)\right\}$$

Noting that ND has units of length over time, and that $\sqrt{T_\infty}$ is proportional to sonic velocity with velocity units, the nondimensional groups can be altered to the following form without affecting the results of the dimensional analysis.

$$\frac{T_n}{p_\infty D^2} = f_3\left\{\left(\frac{V_\infty}{\sqrt{T_\infty}}\right)\left(\frac{ND}{\sqrt{T_\infty}}\right)\right\} = f_4\left\{M_\infty, \left(\frac{ND}{\sqrt{T_\infty}}\right)\right\}$$

If the engine has fixed geometry so that the characteristic length D is not a variable, the functional relation can be further simplified. While reordering the constants for engine geometry in the functional relationship, it is also convenient to reference the net thrust and temperature to standard day sea level conditions, rather than to ambient conditions alone. Making these adjustments in the constants results in

$$\frac{T_n}{\delta} = f_5\left(M_\infty, \frac{N}{\sqrt{\theta}}\right) \hfill (4.18)$$

You may still question the usefulness of nondimensional parameters. Figures 4.9 and 4.10 depict representative sets of variables that describe jet engine performance. Figure 4.9 illustrates engine performance for a single altitude and a single true airspeed. (Static thrust, rather than net thrust, is shown; but that fact is not important to understanding the utility of nondimensionalization.) Figure 4.10 shows what happens when just one of these parameters is charted for just two altitudes and three throttle settings. Six curves result for net thrust alone. Obviously, merely presenting the data becomes a cumbersome task. Collecting flight test data at each of the needed altitudes and at a complete set of engine rpm settings is simply not feasible. And, even if such a data collection effort were completed, the resulting data base would be quite unwieldy.

Nondimensional parameters are ideally generalize data from several different altitudes, throttle settings, and atmospheric conditions into a single curve. The principle is exactly the same as that used in generalizing the power curve for propeller-driven airplanes in section 4.1.1. But, no generalization is perfect; single curves rarely result. Instead, fairly closely related families of curves usually result. Figure 4.11 illustrates how

Mach number effects (and other parameters that were ignored in the original assumptions) generate a family of generalized net thrust curves for $\frac{T_n}{\delta}$ versus $\frac{N}{\sqrt{\theta}}$.

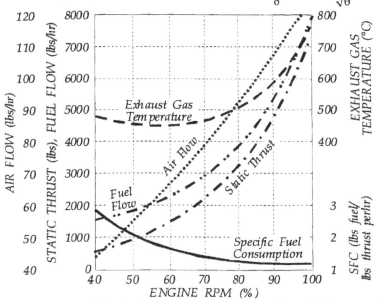

Fig. 4.9 Dimensional Engine Performance: Constant Altitude, Constant TAS

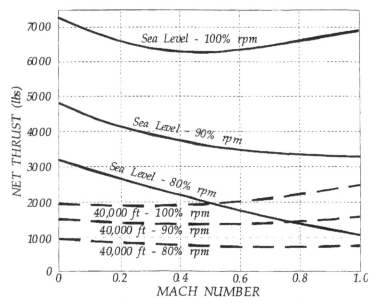

Fig. 4.10 Net Thrust Versus Altitude and Engine RPM

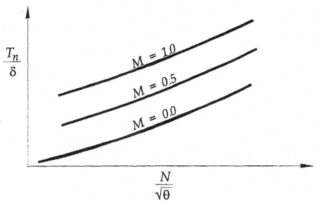

Fig. 4.11 Generalized Net Thrust

Part of the reason that these plots do not generalize perfectly lies in the assumptions used to develop the nondimensional relationships. Reynolds number effects were ignored by ignoring viscosity. But, if the component efficiencies depend strongly on Reynolds number, the generalization we seek does not occur. A family of curves results, rather than a single curve, just as Fig. 4.12 illustrates. Figures 4.12 and 4.13 suggest that mass flow rates and fuel flow rates do not generalize as well as thrust. Other variables (and Reynolds number is clearly one of them) could be included in the nondimensionalization procedure. However, this simplified model serves our purpose of introducing the Buckingham Pi Theorem and its usefulness in flight test planning.

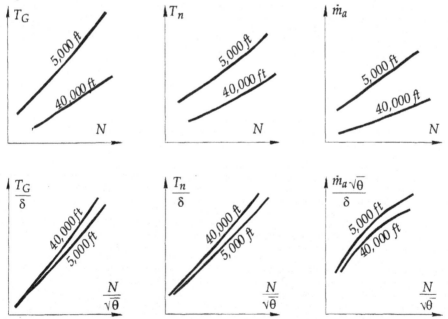

Fig. 4.12 Generalized Thrust and Mass Flow Rate

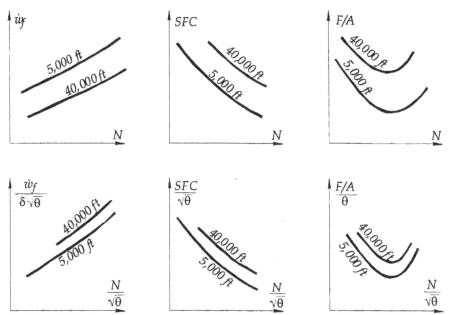

Fig. 4.13 Generalized Fuel Flow Rate and Specific Fuel Consumption

Developments similar to the one illustrated in Example 4.2 result in nondimensional groups as shown in Table 4.2. The Buckingham Pi approach leads to nondimensional parameters corresponding to each of the performance measures of merit, fully characterizing engine performance. Furthermore, they allow test day performance data to be corrected easily to standard conditions, a feature also important to the test engineer.

Table 4.2 Nondimensional Jet Engine Performance Parameters

Dimensional Parameter	Dimensions	Nondimensional Groups
Net Thrust	$\dfrac{mL}{t^2}$	$\dfrac{T_n}{\delta} = f\left(\dfrac{N}{\sqrt{\theta}}, M_\infty\right)$
Fuel Flow	$\dfrac{mL}{t^3}$	$\dfrac{\dot{w}_f}{\delta\sqrt{\theta}} = f\left(\dfrac{N}{\sqrt{\theta}}, M_\infty\right)$
Air Flow	$\dfrac{m}{t}$	$\dfrac{\dot{m}_a}{\delta} = f\left(\dfrac{N}{\sqrt{\theta}}, M_\infty\right)$
Temperature	$\dfrac{L^2}{t^2}$	$\dfrac{T_j}{\theta} = f\left(\dfrac{N}{\sqrt{\theta}}, M_\infty\right)$
SFC	none	$\dfrac{\dot{w}_f}{T_n} = f\left(\dfrac{N}{\sqrt{\theta}}, M_\infty\right)$

Dommasch[5] lists and derives a more complete set of nondimensional parameters. Grouping sets of physical variables systematically, as the Buckingham Pi theorem allows us to do, is extremely helpful in planning flight tests for cruise performance. While most useful for jet airplanes, many of the concepts also apply to propeller-driven aircraft.

4.1.2.2 **Combining Engine and Airframe Parameters**. To utilize the power of dimensional analysis and to reduce the size of the test matrix for an experimental performance reduction, we express airframe parameters as well as engine parameters in nondimensional terms. This nondimensionalization is straightforward when aerodynamic forces are in functional form. Lift can be written

$$L = \frac{2W}{\rho_\infty V_\infty^2 S} = \frac{2WRT_\infty}{p_\infty V_\infty^2 S} = \frac{2W}{\gamma p_\infty M_\infty^2 S} = \frac{2W/\delta}{\gamma p_0 M_\infty^2 S} \quad \text{or} \quad C_L = F_1\left(M_\infty, \frac{W}{\delta}\right) \tag{4.19}$$

Similarly, $C_D = F_2\left(M_\infty, \dfrac{W}{\delta}\right)$ (4.20)

In steady, unaccelerated flight net thrust is equal to drag and eqns. 4.20 and 4.18 can be equated: $f_5\left(M_\infty, \dfrac{W}{\delta}\right) = F_2\left(M_\infty, \dfrac{W}{\delta}\right)$. This expression is "solved" for any of the three variables in terms of the other two. Choosing Mach number as an independent variable,

$$M_\infty = F_3\left(\frac{W}{\delta}, \frac{N}{\sqrt{\theta}}\right) \tag{4.21}$$

the task has been simplified to controlling two variables $\left(M_\infty \text{ and } \dfrac{N}{\sqrt{\theta}}\right)$ and holding $\dfrac{W}{\delta}$ constant by adjusting altitude. Thus, dimensional analysis makes experimental performance data reduction tractable for jet-powered airplanes. We have also avoided measuring thrust directly. Instead, performance is obtained indirectly from more easily measured variables like engine RPM, Mach number, weight, atmospheric pressure, and atmospheric temperature. These measured variables are readily evaluated. One difficulty in this indirect approach is that engine RPM may not be a constant measure of engine thrust over the entire life of the engine. Mechanical wear will take its toll. There is also variation from engine to engine in the relationship between RPM and thrust. If these differences are relatively small, the performance of a fixed geometry turbojet engine can be validated experimentally using the nondimensional parameters shown in Fig. 4.14.

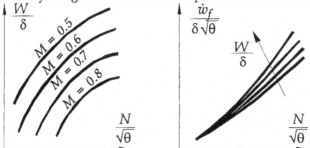

Fig. 4.14 Typical Performance Map for a Fixed Geometry Engine

For variable geometry engines the functional relationship of eqn. 4.17 needs at least one more parameter. It is usually best to map variable geometry engine performance in terms of one nondimensional thrust parameter. The same suggestion holds for dual rotor engines because the additional performance variable also complicates performance relationships. The use of nondimensional variables simplifies the task of experimentally measuring the performance of a jet-powered airplane. Without this simplification, validating performance would be an even more tedious process.

4.1.3 Endurance

The total time that an airplane can loiter on a specified amount of fuel is simply a function of how much fuel is carried and how fast is it consumed. The principle difference in the endurance equation between propeller-driven airplanes and jet-powered airplanes is in how fuel consumption is expressed.

4.1.3.1 Propeller-Driven Aircraft. Fuel flow rate is the basic parameter of interest for endurance. Typically, during cruise tests, the entire weight change is due to fuel consumed. Consequently, $\dot{w}_f = -\dfrac{dW}{dt}$. For a propeller-driven airplane, specific fuel consumption is expressed as pounds of fuel burned per horsepower produced at the propeller shaft: $c = \dfrac{\dot{w}_f}{BHP_r} = SFC$. Rearranging this relationship and integrating

$$E = \int_0^E dt = -\int_{W_0}^{W_E} \frac{dW}{\dot{w}_f} = \int_{W_E}^{W_0} \frac{DW}{cBHP_r}$$

where W_0 = aircraft weight at start of cruise segment
W_E = aircraft weight at end of cruise segment
E = endurance for a given fuel load, W_E - W_0

(Note: E is often defined simply as the maximum time the airplane can fly with a full fuel load. In this book, that time is denoted by E_{max}.)

But $BHP_r = \dfrac{DV_\infty}{\eta_p}$, so

$$E = \int_{W_E}^{W_0} \frac{\eta_p dW}{cDV_\infty} = \int_{W_E}^{W_0} \frac{\eta_p W dW}{cWDV_\infty} = \int_{W_E}^{W_0} \frac{\eta_p}{c} \frac{L}{D} \frac{dW}{WV_\infty}$$

True airspeed can also be written as $V_\infty = \sqrt{\dfrac{2W}{\rho_\infty S C_L}}$ for level flight. Then

$$E = \int_{W_E}^{W_0} \frac{\eta_p}{c} \sqrt{\frac{\rho_\infty S}{2}} \frac{C_L^{1.5}}{C_D} \frac{dW}{W^{1.5}} \tag{4.22}$$

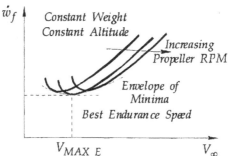

Fig. 4.15 Envelope of Fuel Flow Curves

The quantities to be measured include primarily fuel flow rate and weight of the airplane (eqn. 4.22). The aerodynamic term $\dfrac{C_L^{1.5}}{C_D}$ implies that maximum endurance occurs at a specific angle of attack. Speed for maximum endurance can be obtained by plotting a family of constant altitude and constant weight fuel flow curves for increasing propeller RPM (Fig. 4.15). For small changes in weight, changes in $\frac{\eta_P}{c}$ are often negligible. If so and if the drag curve is parabolic, the true airspeed for maximum endurance can be estimated from the commonly used Breguet approximation[3]: $V_{E_{max}} = V_{(C_L^{1.5}/C_D)_{max}}$. Recall that, under these simplifying assumptions, $3C_{D_\pi} = C_{D_i}$.

Propeller-driven aircraft endurance is readily measured by accurately recording fuel flow rates. Altitude has a small effect, but care must be taken to ensure that the mixture settings are consistent between comparable data runs. Fuel flow rate of the fuel should be measured as a weight per unit time (not volume per unit time), since the specific gravity of aviation gasoline varies significantly with temperature, an uncontrollable variable. Configuration, including power settings, must be painstakingly established to avoid excessive scatter in cruise data. Cowl flaps, for example, are an easy detail to overlook, yet they are produce measureable differences in drag.

4.1.3.2 **Jet-Powered Aircraft**. Measuring endurance for a jet airplane is very similar to measuring it for propeller-driven airplanes. The integral equation for endurance is unchanged. However, specific fuel consumption for the jet engine is expressed as a thrust specific fuel consumption.

$TSFC = c_t = \dfrac{\dot{w}_f}{T_n}$ where c_t is in pounds fuel per unit time per pound thrust. The endurance equation is then written

$$E = \int_{W_E}^{W_0} \frac{dW}{\dot{w}_f} = \int_{W_E}^{W_0} \frac{dW}{c_t T_n} = \int_{W_E}^{W_0} \frac{1}{c_t} \frac{L}{D} \frac{dW}{W} = \int_{W_E}^{W_0} \frac{1}{c_t} \frac{C_L}{C_D} \frac{dW}{W} \qquad (4.23)$$

Notice that airframe aerodynamics again appear in the L/D ratio. For simplifying assumptions similar those used earlier (constant c_t, parabolic drag polar), maximum endurance (E_{max}) occurs at the velocity for maximum L/D where $C_{D_p} = C_{D_i}$.

4.1.4 Range

Range is the distance an aircraft can fly on a given amount of fuel. Range is likewise affected by how the specific fuel consumption is expressed for the type of powerplant. The distance term in the definition for range performance can be either air distance or the distance covered over the ground. In the first case, the range is called air range and no wind effects are considered.

4.1.4.1 **Propeller-Driven Aircraft**. The integral expression for range in calm air (which is valid for general drag polars and for variations in η_p and c) comes from the definition of true airspeed for steady, straight cruising flight. Using this definition and the relationships described in section 4.1.3 to relate fuel flow rate, specific fuel consumption, thrust horsepower, and aerodynamic forces,

$$R = \int_0^t V_\infty dt = -\int_{W_0}^{W_E} V_\infty \frac{dW}{\dot{w}_f} = \int_{W_E}^{W_0} V_\infty \frac{\eta_P}{cTHP_r} \frac{W}{W} dW = \int_{W_E}^{W_0} V_\infty \frac{\eta_P}{cDV_\infty} \frac{L}{W} dW = \int_{W_E}^{W_0} \frac{\eta_P}{c} \frac{C_L}{C_D} \frac{dW}{W} \qquad (4.24)$$

where R = range for a given fuel load, $W_E - W_0$. Maximize the integrand or at least $\dfrac{\eta_P}{c} \dfrac{C_L}{C_D}$

for R_{max}. Assuming constant η_P and a parabolic drag curve, gives R_{max} with $C_{D_p} = C_{D_i}$.

4.1.4.2. **Jet-Powered Aircraft**. The range expression for jet-powered airplanes is affected in the same way as endurance is by the definition of specific fuel consumption.

$$R = \int_0^t V_\infty dt = -\int_{W_0}^{W_E} V_\infty \frac{dW}{\dot{w}_f} = \int_{W_E}^{W_0} V_\infty \frac{1}{c_t T_n} \frac{W}{W} dW = \int_{W_E}^{W_0} V_\infty \frac{1}{c_t} \frac{L}{D} \frac{dW}{W}, \quad \text{but} \quad V_\infty = \sqrt{\frac{2W}{\rho_\infty S C_L}}$$

$$R = \int_{W_E}^{W_0} \frac{\sqrt{\frac{2}{\rho_\infty S}}}{c_t} \frac{\sqrt{C_L}}{C_D} \frac{dW}{\sqrt{W}} \tag{4.25}$$

Maximizing the integrand of eqn. 4.25 must include consideration of both an altitude effect and an aerodynamic term, even with c_t constant. The density term reveals why jet-powered vehicles fly at high altitude for their best range performance. An upper limit on the altitude for best range is not apparent from this euation because it masks engine component efficiencies of the engine which are affected by altitude. When these efficiency effects are small, c_t will dominate the integrand. If the usual simplifying assumptions are made, the aerodynamic term is maximized when $C_{D_p} = 3C_{D_i}$.

4.2 CRUISE PERFORMANCE TEST METHODS

Cruise performance tests evaluate an airplane's endurance and range. Endurance is the time an airplane can spend in the air for a given fuel load and range is total distance (usually measured in air miles) that can be flown on a given fuel load. Fuel consumption and drag determine the achievable cruise performance. Variations of the speed-power test provide the most common flight test techniques for measuring range and endurance. Some customers may require a demonstration profile to verify the actual performance, but speed-power data are usually used to calculate range over specified mission profiles.

Speed-power tests require flying cruise leg segments for a range of airspeeds that cover both speed for maximum endurance and maximum range. Either pressure altitude or the nondimensional parameter $\frac{W}{\delta}$ is held constant for each data point. The appropriate engine parameters like RPM, manifold pressure, and/or mixture setting, are stabilized prior to starting the data run. The engine parameters, atmospheric conditions, and fuel flow rate are recorded. Each of these variables must be measured accurately to obtain useful results. Apart from the sensors for the engine variables and temperature, instrumentation requirements for this test are minimal. All data are steady state and can easily be recorded by hand. Timing can be done with a stopwatch.

4.2.1 Speed-Power Test Method for Propeller-Driven Airplanes

Cruise data are usually taken at constant pressure altitude for propeller-driven airplanes. Speed-power points cover the operating envelope of the airplane with concentration on those areas where powerplant limitations affect performance. Full throttle constraints are checked at a number of altitudes if cylinder pressures limit throttle opening. Maximum speed is checked at a number of altitudes. Measured data include BHP at full throttle, V_∞, THP_r as a function of V_∞, maximum manifold pressure as a function of altitude, and fuel flow rates throughout the envelope. Reduction to standard day conditions is best done with generalized power required versus velocity expressions unless the polar drag curve cannot be assumed. These tests yield both range and endurance data, as well as engine handling information (cooling procedures, mixture setting procedures).

4.2.2   Speed-Power Test Method for Jet-Powered Airplanes

For jet-powered airplanes speed-power tests are used to collect cruise data, holding $\frac{W}{\delta}$ constant. Tests are designed to measure fuel flow rates, drag characteristics, and range and endurance for all weights, speeds, power settings, and relavant configurations and loadings. Covering this complete envelope demands that the data collection be carefully planned and that maximum use of nondimensional groups be made. Otherwise, the experimental performance reduction method is not feasible.

Preflight preparation for constant $\frac{W}{\delta}$ speed-power tests includes preparation of either charts or tabulated data. The test team member who prepares these test cards must include the effects of altitude position error, instrument error, instantaneous weight of the airplane, and airspeed calibration errors. The following procedure may be used to obtain a chart that can be used in flight to and maintain constant $\frac{W}{\delta}$ for each data run.

(1)   Calculate pressure ratios for a range of altitudes at least 2000 feet on either side of this altitude. A range of altitudes is necessary because the weight of the airplane changes as fuel is consumed during the test.

(2)   Select the standard reference weight. Ordinarily, this weight should be the average weight for the test segment. Alternatively, $\left(\frac{W}{\delta}\right)_{ref}$ itself may be specified (as in Example 4.3). Calculate the reference value of $\frac{W}{\delta}$.

(3)   Using this $\frac{W}{\delta}$ and $W_i = \left(\frac{W}{\delta}\right)_{ref} \delta_i$, $i = 1,2,3,...n$; calculate weights corresponding to each of the altitudes above and below the nominal altitude selected in step 1. This constant $\frac{W}{\delta}$ line is the lower curve in Fig. 4.16.

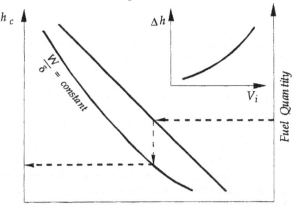

Fig. 4.16 Determining Altitude to Fly

(4) Next, construct a line relating cockpit fuel readings to changes in airplane weight. The scale on the right side (Fig. 4.16) illustrates this step for the case where total fuel used is available. This straight line may cross the constant $\frac{W}{\delta}$ line and it may have the scales inverted if fuel is displayed to the test crew as fuel remaining rather than fuel used. Thus, for any fuel reading, the test pilot or flight test engineer can read across from the fuel quantity scale and down to find the calibrated altitude to fly.

(5) Finally, to make this chart useful in flight, Δh_{ic} and Δh_{pc} corrections for the subject airplane must be included. The inset in the upper right corner of Fig. 4.16 illustrates this correction. Notice that $\Delta h = \Delta h_{ic} + \Delta h_{pc}$; it is a lumped correction for the altimeter for each indicated airspeed. This correction must be applied to obtain the target h_i for the test crew to fly during any constant $\frac{W}{\delta}$ cruise performance data run.

Example 4.3: The cruise performance of a small business jet is tested at a nominal pressure altitude of 25,000 feet at a reference $\frac{W}{\delta}$ of 55,000 pounds. The weight of the airplane with full fuel is 24500 pounds. The altimeter correction charts for the pilot's altimeter are shown below as functions of indicated airspeed. Construct a chart similar to Fig. 4.16 to be used to fly a set of constant $\frac{W}{\delta}$ cruise performance tests over an indicated airspeed range of 250 to 350 knots. The fuel used out of an available 10000 pounds is estimated to be 3800 pounds at the start of the cruise segment tests; the fuel flow rate should average approximately 1000 lb/hr during the cruise points. Assume constant fuel temperature and that each point will require approximately 6 minutes of flying time to stabilize and to collect the required data.

First, we must obtain δ for altitudes between 23000 and 25000 feet to give the test crew flexibility in flying the runs. We must allow for the likelihood that the aircraft will not arrive at the test conditions with exactly the nominal weight; fuel consumption will vary with air traffic control delays, management of the flight profile, and atmospheric conditions--none of which can be fully controlled by the test crew. These values to maintain constant $\frac{W}{\delta}$ = 55,000 pounds are tabulated in the table below.

h_c	δ_i	W_i
27000	0.3398	18689
26000	0.3552	19536
25000	0.3711	20410
24000	0.3876	21318
23000	0.4047	22258

With these values we can plot a curve of h_c versus W. On the right side of this plot we append a scale that corresponds the fuel used for each aircraft weight. (One could also use fuel remaining, though such a scale is rather uncommon.) With either form of fuel reading, a straight line of fuel used or fuel remaining versus weight is drawn.

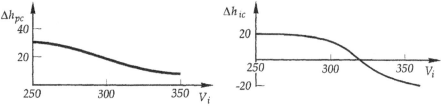

Fig. 4.17 Pitot-Static and Instrument Corrections for Example 4.3

To be useful in flight, h_c must be converted to h_i. One approach is to add a small Δh_{pc} and Δh_{ic}, as suggested in the inset in Fig. 4.16. Δh is a sum of two corrections; $h_c = h_i + \Delta h_{pc} + \Delta h_{ic} = h_i + \Delta h$ or $\Delta h = \Delta h_{pc} + \Delta h_{ic}$. The sample corrections illustrated in Fig. 4.17 lead to a usable Δh inset.

The final results are shown in Fig. 4.18.

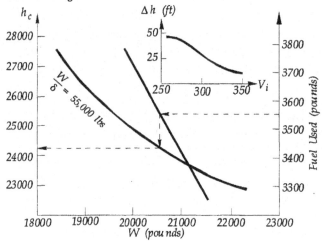

Fig. 4.18 Speed-Power Flight Test Card Corrections for Example 4.3

The following suggestions may speed up inflight collection of speed-power data and reduce data scatter. Jet airplanes generally decelerate quicker than they accelerate, especially with speed brakes; so, it is usually best to climb to just above the desired altitude for the first data point. The maximum speed for a set of altitude runs is a good starting point. Excess potential energy makes it easy to accelerate to desired speed. Subsequent data points can then be flown at decreasing speeds. Each point must be completely stabilized or else repeated. Altitude should not vary more than ±20 feet nor airspeed more than ±1 knot. Start timing after all engine variables stabilize and fly at least 3 minutes in the stabilized condition. Stabilizing at low airspeeds and high altitudes may be difficult; hold airspeed constant and adjust power to hold rate of climb or descent at 50 fpm or less. A longer data run, perhaps 5 minutes, should be used at these low speed points. BHP_r can be corrected for small variations in potential energy using

$$BHP_r = BHP_i + \frac{Wh}{33000\eta_P} \qquad (4.27)$$

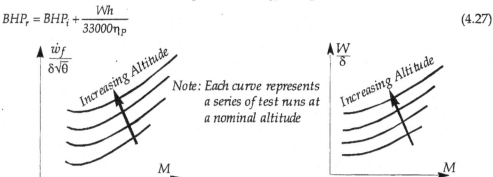

Fig. 4.19 Specific Endurance and $\dfrac{W}{\delta}$ versus Mach Number

Figures 4.19 through 4.21 illustrate how speed-power data for a jet airplane can be reduced to range and endurance information. The nondimensional specific endurance parameter $\frac{\dot{w}_f}{\delta\sqrt{\theta}}$ and $\frac{W}{\delta}$ are plotted versus Mach number and altitude (Fig. 4.19).

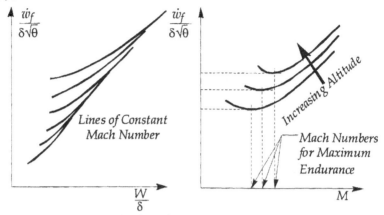

Fig. 4.20 Specific Endurance Crossplots

Since both families of curves are functions of M_∞, they can be transposed to a crossplot of $\frac{\dot{w}_f}{\delta\sqrt{\theta}}$ versus $\frac{W}{\delta}$ by picking off values of specific endurance and $\frac{W}{\delta}$ for any desired altitude and M_∞. The resulting curves are sketched in Fig. 4.20. The asymptote to these curves gives $\frac{\dot{w}_f}{\delta\sqrt{\theta}}$ achievable at a given $\frac{W}{\delta}$ for any selected M_∞. Obviously, the length of time that the jet airplane can fly on a given amount of fuel increases significantly as either weight (and fuel load) or altitude, that is, $\frac{1}{\delta}$, increases.

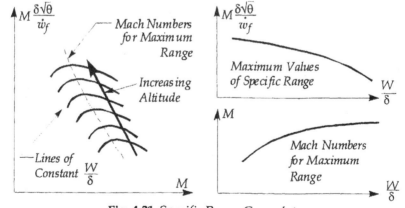

Fig. 4.21 Specific Range Crossplots

If we apply this technique to $\dfrac{\dot{w}_f}{\delta\sqrt{\theta}}$ plotted versus Mach number with the family of

curves now spread over $\dfrac{W}{\delta}$, maximum endurance and the Mach number for maximum

endurance can be graphically determined. The final result is sketched in Fig. 4.21.

A similar graphical approach for the specific range parameter $M\dfrac{\delta\sqrt{\theta}}{\dot{w}_f}$ typically re-

sults in a family of curves for constant $\dfrac{W}{\delta}$ (Fig. 4.21). The dashed line connects the peak

values of specific range for each $\dfrac{W}{\delta}$ and allows construction of the other two curves,

which graphically depict the Mach number for maximum specific range for any $\dfrac{W}{\delta}$ and

the maximum specific range available for the weight and altitude.

4.3 INSTRUMENTATION

4.3.1 Instrumentation Required for Cruise Performance

Cruise performance instrumentation is fairly straightforward and it is relatively simple to acquire data to confirm performance predictions and substantiate the Pilot's Handbook or FAA Approved Flight Manual (AFM). Again, carefully calibrated air data instruments and an outside air temperature gauge are needed. Production engine instruments like an RPM indicator for either the propeller or the turbine speed and production fuel flow gauges are often used to determine the powerplant side of the equation . Production torquemeters on turboprop aircraft are a common indication of power level set, though these instruments rarely exhibit suitable accuracy. The validity of cruise performance measurements probably depends more heavily on powerplant instrumentation than any other set of test parameters. Moreover, specialized performance measurements intended to verify research theory or computational estimates often dictate specialized instrumentation suites.

4.3.1.1 **Power/Thrust Measurements to Verify Design Characteristics**. Accurate flowmeters are very useful in producing reliable and repeatable cruise performance data. The literature largely focuses on three types of flow meters: (1) turbine, (2) variable orifice, and (3) angular momentum (true mass) flowmeters[10]. The latter type provides better accuracy (typically ±0.5% of full scale is achievable) and these devices do not require separate measurement of temperature or density. They measure mass flow rate directly, unlike the turbine flowmeters which report volumetric flow rate. The angular momentum devices do exhibit rather poor transient response because the flow rate is only sampled twice per revolution of the measurement assembly. The output from such a device does have the advantage of being a digital signal but it is typically sampled about every 300 milliseconds versus about every 10 milliseconds for turbine flowmeters. These three types of flowmeters usually impose a pressure drop of 1-4 psi in the flow stream to which they are added, with the orifice flowmeter having the worst pressure drop of the three.

A newer ultrasonic flowmeter, though not yet used widely in flight test, offers the promise of nonintrusive measurement, no moving parts, and immunity to effects of attitude and acceleration. The two types of ultrasonic devices, those based on the Doppler effect and those that depend on transit-time measurements of sound travel, both ultimately measure the fluid velocity. They are also susceptible to temperature gradients in the fluid and to changes in path length. Nonetheless, these devices also usually include an acoustic impedance element to measure density and thus correct the volumetric flow velocity to a mass flow rate.

Fig. 4.22 Typical Torquemeter

Torque meters, as previously discussed in Section 4.1.1.2, are not often used in flight test. The device illustrated in Fig. 4.22 is designed for industrial use and must be modified for installation on a propeller shaft. Two types of torquemeters have been adapted for flight test use, those using slip rings to transmit strain gauge signals to the data acquisition system and wireless devices. The specific device shown in Fig. 4.22 uses wireless (RF) to negate the need for slip rings, but that also means the receiving antenna must be mounted appropriately along with the supporting electronics. Typical diameters of the flanges for such an installation are 6-10 inches and the overall length is 3.5 to 8 inches. Obviously, fitting such a measurement device into an aircraft engine test installation often requires modification of the cowling and affects the cooling scheme. For tightly cowled, air-cooled engines these changes can significantly impact the overall drag of the powerplant installation.

Direct measurement of thrust for turbojet aircraft also requires specialized instrumentation and lacks accuracy and repeatability unless considerable care is taken in choosing and calibrating the instrumentation suite. A common approach (apart from using manufacturer's data) is instrumenting the engine with pressure rakes and using an analytical methods (gas-generator methods or similar computational codes) to estimate thrust. A fixed axial ring of pressure taps (similar to the one shown in Fig. 4.23) and a swinging rake mounted to traverse the nozzle exit plane have been used. Pressure rakes in the high temperature sections of the engine are subject to a severe temperature and vibration environment and are difficult to maintain. Alternatively, Connor and Sims[11] describe in detail how strain gauge instrumentation on the engine mounts was used to directly measure thrust on the F-15 Active test bed aircraft. A fairly complete introduction to this rather complicated measurements problem is available from the Engineering Sciences Data Unit publication[12]. A cursory reading of the literature on this subject should convince the flight test engineer that inflight thrust measurement must be addressed carefully if results are to be useful to end users and/or in verification of a design.

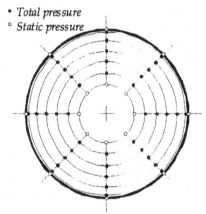

- *Total pressure*
- *Static pressure*

Fig. 4.23 Pressure Rake for Compressor Engine Inlet
(adapted from notes of W. G. Schweikhard[13])

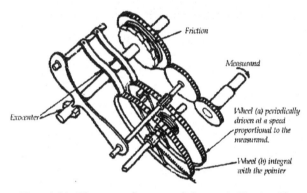

Fig. 4.24 Chronotachometer Schematic Design[14]

4.3.1.2 **Measurement of Engine Speed**. Finally, cruise performance verification tests must measure power settings. For reciprocating engines, these measurements usually take the form of both manifold pressure readings and propeller RPM measurements, along with mixture settings and cowl flap settings for engine cooling. Details of such measurements are spelled in the slightly dated, but still quite useful, AGARD document by Vedrunes[14]. This document describes three commonly used (in 1973) devices that measure engine speed: (1) chronotachometers (Fig. 4.24) , (2) tachogenerators, and (3) magnetic sensors. Vedrunes points out that chronotachometers are the simplest of the three categories and are quite suitable for use in small general aviation airplanes. They do not need external power. Tachogenerators provide an electrical output signal and also do not require external power, but they can be rather bulky. Both of these approaches usually have limitations associated with use of a flexible mechanical shaft to transmit the rotary motion of the measurand. Magnetic sensors are typically both smaller and lighter than tachogenerators and give comparable ranges and accuracies. Vedrunes also notes that he expects to "...witness a competition between optical fibers and photocells..." in the future. If we add to that expectation the growth of non-contact laser tachometers that are now available, one could assume that he was prophetic. Several manufacturers now offer such devices with accuracies listed as ±0.01% or less for shaft speeds up to 99,999 rpm with weights under 10 ounces. Such devices may require adaptation to be mounted in optimum locations and to provide suitable electronic output signals, but basic handheld packages can be obtained for less than $300. In short, modern electronics, laser technology, and electro-optics has reduced the measurement of engine speed largely to a problem of selecting a device and packaging it wisely.

4.3.2 Instrumentation for Flight Test Research

Measuring thrust, power, or drag in research projects follows much the same pattern as has been described for inflight thrust or power measurement, though requirements often dictates more sophisticated sensors and data systems. Typically, instrumentation is custom-designed for such efforts and includes much more extensive measurments of pressures, air flow, fuel flow, forces on engine mounts, and acceleration along the flight path. Bull and Bridges[1] describe one such special instrumentation challenge when they set out to measure propeller efficiency and drag on a propeller-driven airplane. Their description is a good example of developing a specific instrumentation suite for a specific measurement challenge.

4.4 SUMMARY

This chapter has introduced the theory underpinning the speed-power flight test method, which is used to measure the level flight cruise performance of both propeller-driven and jet-powered airplanes. Methods for performance reduction for these two types of airplanes were discussed and it was shown how analytical methods apply to propeller-driven vehicles. Dimensional analysis was used to develop the experimental method for jet-propelled aircraft. The utility of nondimensional variables was illustrated and connected to range and endurance, the primary physical variables of interest.

REFERENCES

1 Bull, G. and Bridges, P. D., "A Method for Flight-Test Determination of Propulsive Efficiency and Drag," **Journal of Aircraft**, Vol. 22, Mar. 1985, pp. 200-207.

2 Cooper, J. D., "The 'Linearized Inflow' Propeller Strip Analysis," WADC TR 56-615 (AD 118078), Wright Air Development Center, Wright-Patterson AFB, Ohio, February 1957.

3 Lan, C. E., and Roskam, J., **Airplane Aerodynamics and Performance**, Roskam Aviation and Engineering Corporation, Ottawa, Kansas, 1980.

4 Kuethe, A. M. and Chow, C. Y., **Foundations of Aerodynamics: Bases of Aerodynamic Design**, John Wiley & Sons, New York, 1976.

5 Dommasch, D. O., "Performance of Turbojet Engines," Chapter 4, Volume 1, **AGARD Flight Test Manual**, Pergamon Press, New York, 1959.

6 "Performance Flight Test Techniques," Volume III, FTC-TIH-70-1001 (Revised August 1975), USAF Test Pilot School, Edwards AFB, California, 1975.

7 "Fixed Wing Performance, Theory and Flight Test Techniques", USNTPS-FTM-No. 104, Naval Air Test Center, Patuxent River, Maryland, July 1977.

8 "Performance, Book B", Empire Test Pilots' School, Royal Aircraft Establishment, Farnborough, England, 1966.

9 Lush, K. J. and Moakes, J. K., "Performance Reduction Methods for Turbo-Propeller Aircraft," Chapter 5, Volume 1, **AGARD Flight Test Manual**, Pergamon Press, New York, 1959.

Chapter 5
TAKEOFF AND LANDING FLIGHT TESTS

Every successful flight begins with a takeoff and ends with a landing. An airplane's suitability for many missions may be determined by its performance in this dynamic environment. Since takeoff and landing (TO&L) performance involves accelerations and decelerations, we must concern ourselves with measurement of dynamic conditions, both in flight and on the ground. So, we usually break up takeoff and landing measurements into a ground phase and an air phase. Furthermore, few maneuvers are more difficult to perform consistently. Pilot technique can easily mask important trends in the data. This human variability makes it virtually impossible to exactly compare different data sets and puts the onus on flight test personnel to standardize procedures and techniques as much as possible. Even so, statistical tools are needed to correlate individual measurements and to compare the data to requirements. Average values of distances for number of takeoffs and/or landings are typically used to decide whether or not goals have been met. The large number of variables that affect TO&L performance further complicates these tests. Moreover, many of them are completely uncontrollable. For example, runway surface condition can only be changed with full fidelity by waiting for or by going to natural weather conditions (ice, snow, slush, rain, crosswind, etc.) to occur. But it is clearly impractical to delay a flight test program for months waiting for such conditions. So, we usually coat the runway with foam or other substances to simulate reduced friction. Finally, not only are TO&L tests difficult to perform repeatably, they are some of the most dangerous tests conducted in certifying an airplane. They require the flight test crew to establish flight envelope limits while on or very close to the ground with the airplane in its least controllable configuration. After all, most operational accidents occur during terminal tasks! So, while takeoff and landing tests are very important and can be crucial to a developmental effort, they are also one of the most demanding of all test demonstrations. They deserve the utmost in care and attention to detail.

5.1 FOUNDATIONS

5.1.1 Definitions and Terminology

The TO&L vocabulary is rather extensive and at times very confusing, especially since the various requirements documents are not wholly consistent. We start with clarifying the relevant definitions.

5.1.1.1 **Takeoff and Landing**. Dekker and Lean[1] define **takeoff** and **landing** as:

Takeoff is the process by which an airplane is brought from standstill to a safe flight condition.

Landing is the process by which an airplane is safely brought from a safe flight condition to a standstill.

For takeoff, this "safe flight condition" is clarified further to mean the point in the climb where the airplane first reaches a specified obstacle clearance height above the point of departure from the ground (liftoff) at an instantaneous true airspeed usually labeled V_2 or V_{CL}. For landing, the height at which the landing starts is a specified level above the runway, chosen to simulate obstacle clearance. The type of maneuver flown, especially how the transition is made from ground roll to climb path (or vice versa for the landing), is extremely important. We will discuss this transition shortly, but first we need to define the two basic phases of takeoffs and landings: the ground phase and the air phase (Fig. 5.1).

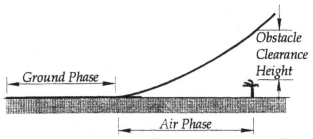

Fig. 5.1 Takeoff and Landing Phases

5.1.1.2 **Ground Phase**. The ground phase of the takeoff maneuver begins at brake release and ends when the airplane lifts off the takeoff surface (with minimum margin of speed above stall speed and/or above the minimum control speed). It is also customary to include a short allowance in the ground run estimate for the distance traveled while the airplane is rotated to the takeoff attitude, commonly 3 to 4 seconds[2,5]. While no attempt is usually made to measure this distance separate from the total ground run distance, we will discuss it separately as part of the design and analysis process since its estimation is important to predicting takeoff distances accurately. Test measurements must be made to ascertain ground run distance, lift off airspeed, and velocity and/or acceleration profiles during the ground phase. Ground run distance, s_G, is the primary metric. This parameter is frequently a certification measure of merit and is estimated during the design process[2]. The standard day takeoff distances need to be determined within ±5%. The accuracy of such measurements is affected by so many uncontrollable factors that it should be treated as a random variable. Dekker and Lean point out that at least 5 measurements in a given configuration with a nominal scatter of 4% in the measured ground roll provides a high (95%) confidence level of being within 5% of the true distance[1]. Six test runs provide ±2.5% accuracy with 4% scatter; so, good practice calls for planning at least 6 takeoffs in . each configuration. Additional runs reduce the precision required for each measurement to still achieve the desired 5% accuracy.

As a minimum, the ground speed at which the airplane lifts off, surface headwind, ambient temperature, and ambient pressure must be captured during the ground phase -- as well as s_G. Determining the exact point at which the airplane lifts off has always been troublesome. Event markers, triggered by extension of the landing gear struts, are perhaps the most accurate means of defining the lift off location. Such devices can fire a marker onto the runway itself or they can trigger a flash of light that can be recorded photographically as part of the data. Such a trigger can also be used to photograph or videotape the airspeed indicator at lift off. Alternatively, a continuous record of the airspeed readings can be made with event trigger used to note the point of lift off. This latter approach, after appropriate data reduction, can provide a measured velocity profile. Another approach is to record an analog signal that is proportional to the indicated airspeed reading (a differential pressure, of course) and then convert this pressure signal to standard day true airspeed. Of course, this analog signal is usually sampled at appropriate intervals to reduce the data reduction workload.

A different approach to takeoff measurements has become popular since modeling of aircraft performance has become so important for high fidelity simulations. Very accurate acceleration profiles can be obtained with high data rate inertial navigation systems (INS), providing the complete takeoff profile[3]. Accelerations are integrated once to obtain the velocity profile and integrated again to obtain position. A variation on this technique is to measure the position coordinates by a very accurate means (laser tracker, video tracker, or other optical device) and then to differentiate the position measurements to obtain velocity and acceleration profiles. This latter approach requires continuous coverage of the entire takeoff maneuver, dictating the use of multiple cameras and merging of data files from these cameras. Either of these two techniques gives a complete time history including air distance (Fig. 5.2) and ground distance.

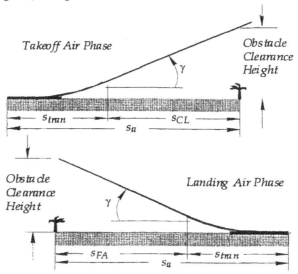

Fig. 5.2 Takeoff and Landing Air Phases

5.1.1.3 **Air Phase**. The takeoff air phase poses an even more complicated measurement problem than the ground phase. As suggested in Fig. 5.1, the **air phase** begins at liftoff and ends when the airplane passes obstacle clearance height and accelerates above VCL. For landing the **air phase** begins at the obstacle clearance height with either a constant rate of descent or a constant approach angle established; it ends when the airplane first touches the runway.

In both takeoffs and landings, the air distance can be further broken down into a transition segment and into steady climb or descent segments. Figure 5.2 schematically illustrates these segments. For takeoffs, the transition is merely the accelerating trajectory between liftoff and the initial climb speed, sometimes called the takeoff flare. For high performance aircraft or for a low obstacle clearance height (FAR part 25 specifies 35 feet as the obstacle clearance height, for example.), a steady initial climb speed is not attained until after obstacle clearance height is achieved. In that case, only the transition trajectory is included in the air distance. For landings, the transition includes the approach path from obstacle clearance height down through the landing flare to touchdown. The flare maneuvers, shown as acceleration and deceleration segments in Fig. 5.2, are often approximated with some simple curve like a circular arc. In any event, air distance is difficult to predict and difficult to measure directly. This phase of TO&L trajectories is quite sensitive to pilot technique.

5.1.1.4 **Available Runway**.

> The **runway available (RA)** is the actual runway length less a prescribed allowances (usually 200 feet) for lineup distance.

5.1.1.5 **Critical Field Length and Balanced Field Length**. These two terms are closely related and often misunderstood. The former is more often applied to military aircraft and the latter is usually associated with commercial aviation requirements.

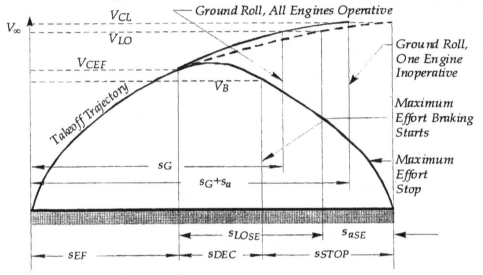

Fig. 5.3 Balanced Field Length Components

> **Balanced field length (BFL)** is the sum of the distance required to accelerate to V_{CEF} and the distance required to either continue the takeoff over 35 feet with one engine inoperative or to brake to a stop.[2]

Thus, BFL satisfies both a takeoff requirement and the civil accelerate-stop requirements. FAR Part 25 also stipulates a field length greater than either the accelerate-and-go distance or 115% of the all-engines-operating distance to a height of 35 feet. Fig. 5.3 illustrates the components of a BFL computation. This definition of BFL leads to the conclusion that V_{CEF} must be determined so that $s_{DEC} + s_{STOP} = s_{LO_{SE}} + s_{a_{SE}}$.

> **Critical field length (CFL)** is the total length of runway required to accelerate on all engines to critical engine failure speed (V_{CEF}), experience an engine failure, and then either continue the takeoff with remaining engines or stop.[4]

CFL is calculated as part of preflight planning for multiengine aircraft and must be less than runway available for a safe takeoff.

5.1.1.6 Critical Engine Failure Speed. As suggested in definitions of CFL and BFL:

> Critical Engine Failure Speed (V_{CEF}) is the speed to which a multiengine airplane can be accelerated, lose an engine, and then either continue the takeoff with the remaining engines, or stop.

Both possibilities require the same total runway distance.

Figure 5.4 illustrates critical engine failure speed trajectories for multiengine airplanes. (Note: V_{CEF} is also called V_1 in some documents[1,4] and critical speed, V_{CRIT}, in others[2].) Strictly speaking, V_{CEF} does not apply to single engine airplanes, but the principle applies, as we notice in the definition of refusal speed.

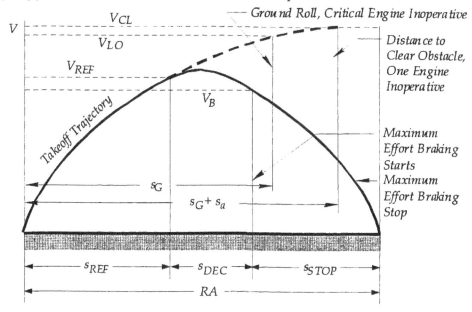

Fig. 5.4 Velocity Profiles for RA = CFL

5.1.1.7 Refusal Speed and Refusal Distance.

> Refusal speed (V_{REF}) is the maximum speed that an aircraft can obtain under normal acceleration conditions and then stop in the available runway.

V_{REF} and V_{CEF} are quite similar; $V_{CEF} = V_{REF}$ for multiengine airplanes. In other words, V_{REF} applies to both single engine and to multiengine aircraft. In this regard multiengine airplanes have an advantage over single engine craft; they can takeoff if an engine fails above V_{REF}. But neither type can stop in the available runway if a takeoff is aborted above V_{REF}. For this reason, during flight tests to determine V_{REF}, the pilot's reaction time to recognize an engine failure must be included (simulated) in the test. Usually, a 2-3 second delay is sufficient.

> Refusal distance is the takeoff ground run required to attain V_{REF}.

5.1.1.8 Ground and Air Minimum Control Speeds. Controllability of a multiengine airplane after the loss of an outboard engine is a major concern, especially during takeoff when the necessity to establish a safe rate of climb dictates that the engines be operated at high thrust or power levels. Rudder authority and the yawing moment due to asymmetric thrust determine whether or not a takeoff may be safely continued after the loss of an engine. If the failure occurs on the ground, nose or tail wheel steering may also be critical.

> The minimum speed at which a multiengine airplane, while on the ground, can lose an outboard engine and maintain directional control is the **ground minimum control speed**, $V_{m_{cg}}$.

For V_{CEF} to have meaning, it must be less than $V_{m_{cg}}$.

> The **air minimum control speed**, $V_{m_{ca}}$, is the minimum airspeed (out of ground effect) at which the critical engine can fail and lateral-directional control can be maintained, without saturating the rudder or ailerons, and with no more than 5° of bank into the operating engine.

Tests to determine $V_{m_{ca}}$ are among the most hazardous performed during any test program and have historically led to tragic loss of life. Their criticality and the subtleties of various data reduction and extrapolation methods have led to independent treatment in a dedicated chapter in Volume 2 of this series of books.

5.1.1.9 Safe Single Engine Speeds. During takeoffs or landings with one engine inoperative, a multiengine airplane must be operated with some margin of safety. Some literature calls this speed the takeoff safety speed, V_{TOS}, but the most common terminology in the United States is safe single engine speed, V_{SSE}.

> Safe single engine speed (V_{SSE}) is the airspeed below which a multiengine aircraft must not be operated after leaving ground effect with one engine inoperative.

V_{SSE} must exceed both V_s and $V_{m_{ca}}$ by a safe margin, as well as the speed required to achieve a safe rate of climb. While V_{SSE} is most important during takeoff, prudence dictates that the airspeed not be reduced below V_{SSE} during a single engine landing until the landing is assured.

5.1.2 Performance Equations

Because of the large number of factors that affect TO&L performance, it is practically impossible to model it perfectly. Major influences include:

- Gross weight
- Thrust available
- Ambient temperature
- Pressure altitude
- Wind direction and velocity
- Slope of the runway
- Coefficient of friction

To make any rational analysis of performance measurements, we will have to make several simplifying assumptions.

5.1.2.1 Ground Run Equations. First, let us consider the distance while the airplane is strictly rolling on the ground during either a takeoff or a landing. The takeoff or landing flares are not a part of this analysis; the distance covered during rotation during takeoff will be approximated separately. Hence, we will call this distance s_{G_1} for the takeoff, differentiating it from s_G (the total ground run distance to liftoff). The forces acting on an airplane during this first portion of the ground run of a takeoff or the last portion of a landing are sketched in Fig. 5.5. The contributing aerodynamic forces are defined in the usual sense: L and D, as shown, are conventional, as are T and W. The frictional force F_f

is rather difficult to ascertain, but it is usually defined in terms of a friction coefficient μ and the net normal force. That is, $F_f = L - W$. Lan and Roskam[2] give typical values for μ as shown in Table 5.1. Of course, the slope of the runway also produces a small component of W ($W \sin \Phi \approx W\Phi$) acting parallel to the takeoff surface, along with a small reduction in normal force. This latter component is usually neglected, since Φ is typically a very small angle (usually less than 3°). The runway gradient, or slope, is positive if the takeoff is uphill. So the net force accelerating the airplane parallel to the surface of the runway is

$$F = ma = T - D - \mu(W - L) - W\Phi \tag{5.1}$$

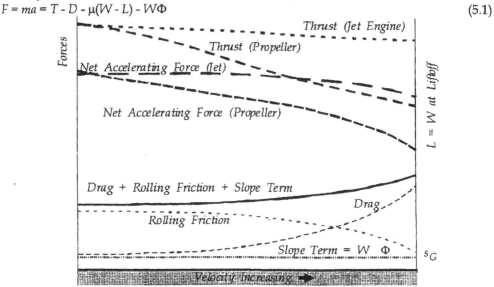

Fig. 5.5 Forces During Ground Run

TABLE 5.1 Values for Runway Surface Friction Coefficients

Type of Surface	Range for μ
Concrete	0.02-0.030
Hard turf or short grass	0.05
Long grass	0.10
Soft ground	0.10-0.30

We also want to consider wind effects: let $\pm V_w$ = wind speed. Here, "+" implies a tail wind and "-" a head wind. So, at any point in the takeoff ground roll the ground speed is

$$\frac{ds_G}{dt} = V \pm V_w \tag{5.2}$$

Of course, the acceleration is $a = \dfrac{dV}{dt}$, which we rearrange to $dt = \dfrac{dV}{a}$, and

$$ds_G = (V \pm V_w)\frac{dV}{a} \tag{5.3}$$

Integrating eqn. 5.3 yields an exact expression for takeoff ground run distance, provided we know a, V, and V_w throughout the takeoff roll and we can accurately determine the true airspeed at liftoff.

$$s_G = \int \frac{(V \pm V_w)\,dV}{a} \qquad (5.4)$$

Of course, we can not generally express each of these parameters analytically, but they can be measured by several means. If we solve the basic force equation (eqn. 5.1) for the acceleration and substitute it into eqn. 5.4,

$$s_G = \int \frac{W(V \pm V_w)\,dV}{g\left[T - D - \mu(W - L) - W\Phi\right]} \qquad (5.5)$$

Equation 5.5 is the basic equation for ground roll distance for either takeoffs or landings; it will be used in modified form for both purposes. We will use a second set of subscripts ("$_L$") to denote landing conditions. Notice that in eqn. 5.5 we have adhered to our sign convention that $\Phi > 0$ for uphill takeoffs. Remember that the acceleration during the ground roll after landing is negative and that the thrust term can be either positive or negative, depending on whether or not the test vehicle has thrust reversing or not. Though we have not included it, another similar term must be added if the airplane uses a deceleration device, like a drag parachute or a speed brake, to reduce the ground roll. We choose to lump this added drag with the aerodynamic drag. Even more important, the braking friction coefficient (μ_b) is quite different than it was for takeoff because the brakes are applied at some point during this segment of the landing. Typically, rolling friction coefficients vary considerably. Notice that μ_b is a strong function of runway surface conditions (wet or icy surfaces) and whether or not the tires are skidding or not (Fig. 5.6). Modern aircraft often have antiskid brake units to avoid tire slippage during heavy braking. It is usually not feasible to test for these stopping distances under actual runway surface conditions like those shown in Fig. 5.6. It becomes the flight test engineer's job to identify and plan for simulating such conditions. Often this task is one of the more difficult ones faced by the flight test engineer. The approach that is now most common is to develop a mathematical model and then carry out a limited number of tests to validate this model. Naturally, one of the more difficult facets of this kind of testing is measuring actual braking coefficients for other than dry runway surfaces. Sometimes, aerodynamic braking is so powerful that the recommended procedure is to maintain a high pitch attitude, applying brakes only after the nose wheel is lowered to the runway.

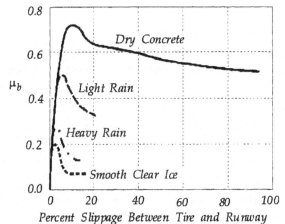

Percent Slippage Between Tire and Runway

Fig. 5.6 Coefficients of Friction during Landing Ground Run

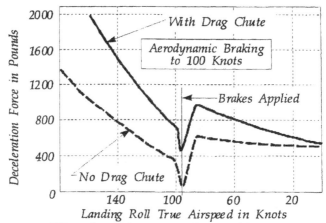

Fig. 5.7 Effect of Aerodynamic Braking and/or Drag Chute

Figure 5.7 illustrates this procedure and depicts potential drag chute effectiveness. While the landing ground roll distance equation is of the same form as the takeoff equation, the values of the terms may be significantly different; there are terms present that are not in the takeoff equation. These differences are indicated by the changed symbols and the apparent reversed order of integration (which accounts for the deceleration) in the following expression:

$$s_{G_L} \approx \int_{V_{TD}}^{0} \frac{W_L(V \pm V_w)dV}{g\left[T_L - D_L - \mu_b(W_L - L_L) - W_L\Phi\right]} \tag{5.6}$$

The T_L, μ_b, and the D_L in this equation are the landing roll expressions for the corresponding quantities in eqn. 5.5; the subscripts are merely used to remind you that these parameters are considerably different from those in the takeoff roll expression.

Example 5.1: An airplane with a wing area of 230 square feet weighs 9900 pounds and the speed brakes are opened for landing. In this configuration it has a drag equation: $C_D = 0.144 + 0.055C_L^2$. The speed brakes remain extended down to approximately 75 ktas. Idle thrust of the engine at sea level, standard day conditions is constant at 700 pounds with the airspeed at or below final approach speed. Touchdown on the main wheels occurs at 100 knots. If the average rolling coefficient of friction on dry concrete is 0.03 and the average braking coefficient of friction is 0.5, estimate the total landing distance from touchdown to a complete stop. Assume no wind. The nose wheel is lowered (instantaneously) to the runway at 75 knots, but the test pilot maintains a constant angle of attack after touchdown until he lowers the nose, giving $C_L \approx 1.25$ during this phase of the landing. As soon as the nose wheel is on the runway, the wheel brakes are applied and braking begins. With the airplane in this three-point attitude, $C_L \approx 0.1$.

V (ktas)	V (fps)	Lift ($C_L \approx 1.25$)	ΔD	Integrand	Σ	$\Sigma\Delta s_L$ (feet)
100	168.889	9745.88	1792.75	-47.36	--	--
95	160.444	8795.65	1617.96	-51.91	-49.36	419.1
90	152.000	7894.16	1452.13	-57.58	-104.37	881.42
85	143.556	7041.40	1295.26	-64.86	-165.59	1398.4
80	135.111	6237.36	1147.36	-74.61	-235.33	1987.2
75	126.667	5482.06	1008.42	-88.39	-316.83	2675.4

This problem breaks down into two parts: (1) from main wheel touchdown until the nose wheel is on the runway and braking begins and (2) from nose wheel touchdown until the airplane comes to rest. The first phase is dominated by aerodynamic braking. Wheel brakes provide most of the deceleration during the second part of the rollout. Equation 5.5 applies to the first phase and eqn. 5.6 to the second. At main wheel touchdown $L \approx W$. As the airplane brakes aerodynamically, eqn. 5.5 shows that the friction term becomes a more important part of the retarding force. But the principal deceleration still comes from aerodynamic drag. The aerodynamic drag decreases as V decreases, even though C_L is held constant. Tabulating these lift and drag changes at discrete speeds during the landing roll, in the table above we numerically approximate the integration of eqn. 5.5. The table summarizes the results of this numerical integration and estimates the ground roll prior to commencement of braking at 2675 feet.

V (ktas)	V (fps)	Lift ($C_L \approx 0.1$)	ΔL	Integrand	Σ	$\Sigma \Delta s_L$ (feet)
75	126.667	438.56	633.94	-8.36	--	--
70	118.222	382.04	552.24.	-7.89	-8.12	68.6
65	109.778	329.41	476.16	-7.41	-15.77	133.2
60	101.333	280.68	405.72	-.6.91	-22.92	193.6
55	92.889	235.85	340.92	-6.39	-29.57	249.7
50	84.444	194.92	281.75	-5.86	-35.70	301.4
45	76.000	157.88	228.22	-5.32	-41.28	348.6
40	67.556	124.75	180.32	-4.76	-46.32	391.2
35	59.111	95.51	138.06	-4.19	-50.80	429.0
30	50.667	70.17	101.43	-3.61	-54.70	461.9
20	33.778	31.19	45.08	-2.43	-60.74	512.9
10	16.889	7.80	11.27	-0.61	-65.31	551.5
0	0.000	0.00	0.00	0.00	-65.62	554.1

So, our approximation for the total landing roll is the sum of the two increments: $\boxed{s_{G_L} = 3230 \text{ feet}}$

The second phase of the ground roll is calculated using the same procedure, except that the terms in eqn. 5.6 are changed to the appropriate values for C_L and to μ_b (0.1 and 0.5, respectively) for this phase of the rollout. This calculation is illustrated in the preceding table and shows that the ground roll distance after the nose wheel is lowered is only 554 feet.

5.1.2.2 Rotation Distance.
As was pointed out earlier, most takeoff and landing distance predictions should include an allowance for the distance covered during the takeoff flare or the rotation down from touchdown attitude to the attitude where all wheels are on the ground and brakes are applied. We will call this distance either s_{G_2} (for takeoff) or s_{L_2} (for landing). Typically, the estimate is made by simply assuming a reasonable average time to complete the pitch rotation. The time chosen will be different for each airplane considered, but 3 to 4 seconds is a reasonable approximation for many types. The distance is assumed to be traversed at a constant speed, either V_{LOF} or V_{TD} (again, for liftoff or landing, respectively).

$$s_{G_2} = t_r V_{LOF} \quad \text{or} \quad s_{L_2} = t_r V_{TD} \tag{5.7}$$

where t_r is the approximate average time used to carry out the takeoff or landing flare.

5.1.2.3 Transition Distance.
Part of the air distance estimate is based on rather arbitrary assumptions. After liftoff the aircraft must transition from an essentially level acceleration along the runway surface to either a constant airspeed climb or a constant angle climb. For certification and for design purposes, the latter is usually taken to attain clearance height above any obstacles in the flight path near the ground. Later, another transition to a constant airspeed or a constant Mach number climb path is likely performed once clear of any ground-based obstacles. During the landing approach, a flare is used to transition from the ideal constant glide path angle descent to touchdown. This paragraph addresses the horizontal distance traveled while making this transition. To simplify the estimate (very approximate), we assume this transition path is a circular arc. To maintain a circular path, the velocity is constant and the acceleration is $\dfrac{V^2}{R_c}$, where R_c is the radius

of the circular transition path. Flying such a circular trajectory requires additional lift from the lifting surfaces, which can be measured as an increment in load factor given by:

$$\Delta n = \frac{V^2}{gR_c} = \frac{\Delta C_L \rho V^2 S}{2W} \tag{5.8}$$

The velocity in eqn. 5.8 (and in eqn 5.9 below) can be either V_{LOF} or V_{TD} depending on whether we are dealing with a takeoff rotation or a landing flare. We can rearrange eqn. 5.8 to calculate R_c.

$$R_c = \frac{V^2}{g\Delta n} = \frac{2W}{g\,\Delta C_L \rho V^2 S} \tag{5.9}$$

Another variation uses the R_c found from the total lift coefficient during transition ($C_{L_{tran}}$).

$$L = \frac{WV^2 C_{L_{tran}}}{V_s^2 C_{L_{max}}} = W + \frac{WV^2}{gR_c} \quad \text{where } V_s \text{ is the stall speed for the appropriate con-}$$

figuration and $C_{L_{max}}$ is the corresponding maximum lift coefficient (Fig. 5.8). Then

$$R_c = \frac{V^2}{g\left(\dfrac{V^2 C_{L_{tran}}}{V_s^2 C_{L_{max}}} - 1\right)} \tag{5.10}$$

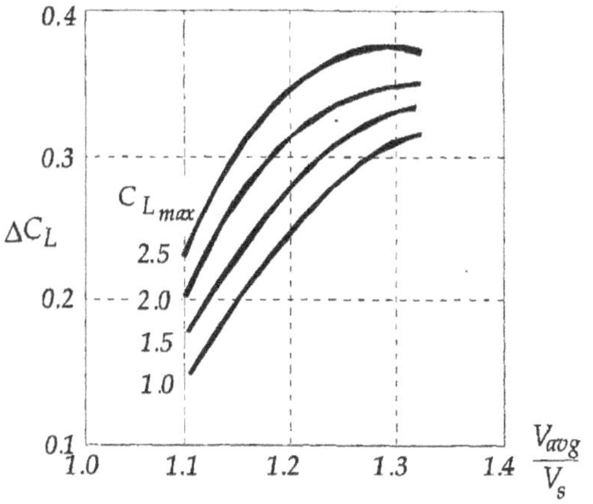

Fig. 5.8 Empirical Values of ΔC_L used in Equation 5.9

The estimate improves if the velocity in the calculation of R_c is accurate. One approach is to use an average speed during the takeoff transition or the landing flare. This speed is the average of V_{LO} and the speed during initial climb for a takeoff transition or of V_{TD} and the final approach speed for a landing flare. Lan and Roskam[2] note that Williams includes the effects of ΔC_L's in the manner. Figure 5.8 is an adaptation of their data.

Knowing the radius of the circular arc, the transition distance (Fig. 5.9) is a matter of trigonometry. The horizontal distance covered during either transition is:

$$s_{tran} = R_c |\sin\theta_{CL}| \tag{5.11}$$

The absolute value accounts for negative flight path angles during a landing approach.

5.1.2.4 **Climbout Distance.** The last part of the air distance phase of the takeoff or landing performance estimation is the distance covered during the initial climb before the standard obstacle distance is cleared or during the final approach after the obstacle is cleared but before the landing flare begins. If the altitude at the end of the takeoff transition is greater than the obstacle clearance height or if the landing flare begins above the obstacle clearance height, then this distance has no meaning and is not included in the air distance. Therefore, we must also find the height at the end of the takeoff transition (or the height at the beginning of the landing flare), h_{tran} (Fig. 5.9).

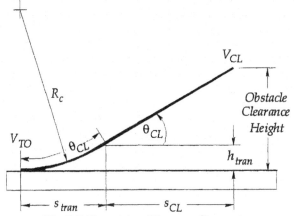

Fig. 5.9 Transition Distance Geometry

$$h_{tran} = R_c\left(1-\left|cos\,\theta_{CL}\right|\right) = \frac{s_{tran}}{\left|sin\,\theta_{CL}\right|}\left(1-\left|cos\,\theta_{CL}\right|\right) \qquad (5.12)$$

If h_{tran} > obstacle clearance height, then we are through with estimating the required distances. If h_{tran} < obstacle clearance height, we again refer to the geometry sketch (Fig. 5.9) and observe that for an obstacle clearance height of 50 feet:

$$s_{CL} = \frac{50 - h_{tran}}{\left|tan\,\theta_{CL}\right|} \qquad (5.13)$$

Example 5.2: Consider the airplane of Example 5.1. It has a stall speed of 92 knots and it lifts off at $1.2V_s$. Estimate the transition distance and the climbout distance to the climb path. Assume that the transition path is a circular arc and $\dfrac{C_{L_{tran}}}{C_{L_{max}}} = 0.8$ during transition to the climb path. Also, assume that $V = V_{LOF}$ and that this speed is constant during this part of the takeoff. Of course, $C_{L_{max}}$ occurs at V_s. The thrust during this transition phase is constant at 7000 pounds.

Then, $C_{L_{max}} \dfrac{2W}{\rho S V_s^2} = \dfrac{2(9000)}{0.00023769(92\times1.688889)^2(230)} = 1.5$. With this value of $C_{L_{max}}$ and also using $V =$

$V_{LOF} = 1.2V_s$ during the transition, we obtain, either from eqn. 5.9 or from Fig. 5.9, $\Delta C_L = 0.2757$. Calculating R_c from the other form of eqn 5.9:

$$R_c = \frac{2W}{\rho\Delta C_L Sg} = \frac{2(9000)}{0.00023769(0.2757)(230)(32.17405)} = 4079 \ feet.$$

As the note on Fig. 5.8 emphasizes, this value of the flight path radius is based on an assumption that the piloting technique is aggressive; the rotation is called a "maximum effort" rotation. Equation 5.9, on the other hand does not require this assumption; if we calculate R_c without a maximum effort rotation,

$$R_c = \frac{1.2(92\times1.688889)^2}{\left[1.2C_D=0.12+0.04C_L^2(0.8)-1\right]-32.17405} = 7109 \ feet.$$

Notice that there is a wide range in the results (a change of about 75%) depending on whether or not the "maximum effort" assumption is used. This oversimplified calculation underscores just how sensitive takeoff and landing performance estimates are to piloting technique.

Climb angle is set by the excess thrust available during the transition period; that is, $\sin\theta_{CL} = \dfrac{T_n - D}{W}$, with each of the variables evaluated during the transition phase. In the takeoff configuration the speed brakes are retracted and the flaps are at their takeoff setting. So, $C_D = 0.12 + 0.04C_L^2$. Since the maximum usable $C_L = 1.5 \times 0.8$, $C_D = 0.12 + 0.04(1.44)^2 = 0.1776$. Thus, the average drag during transition is about 1688 pounds. With these intermediate estimates available, $\sin\theta_{CL} = \dfrac{7000 - 1688}{9900}$. This expression gives, θ_{CL} = 34.5°. Now, we can finally estimate the transition distance, using a "maximum effort" flare to minimize R_c; that is, $s_{tran} = R_c = \sin\theta_{CL}$.

$$\boxed{s_{tran} = 2310\ feet}$$

$h_{tran} = R_c(1 - \cos\theta_{CL}) = (4079\ ft)(1 - \cos 34.5°) = 717\ feet$. Since $h_{tran} > 50\ feet$,

$$\boxed{s_{CL} = 0\ feet}$$

Airplanes with high thrust-to-weight ratios often reach or exceed obstacle clearance height before completing the takeoff flare. Lower performance airplanes will require calculation of s_{CL} using eqn. 5.13.

5.1.2.5 **Summary** of **Equations**. Having developed the component expressions making up total takeoff or landing distance, we simply sum the component parts to complete our estimate and our discussion of the takeoff and landing performance analysis.

$$s_{TO} = s_G + s_{G_2} + s_{tran} + s_{CL} \qquad\qquad (5.14)$$
$$s_{LND} = s_L + s_{G_2} + s_{L_{tran}} + s_{FA} \qquad\qquad (5.15)$$

5.1.3 **Parametric Analysis of Takeoff Performance**

Shevell[3] advocates a different approach to takeoff performance that is simple and allows straightforward comparison of competing designs. With judicious assumptions, he generalizes takeoff performance for most commercial airliners so that takeoff and field lengths can be estimated from a few charts. The underlying premise of this parametric approach is that "...takeoff performance is basically an acceleration to the required speed plus a climb segment to a 35-ft height (civil turbine-powered transports) or a 50-ft height (piston-powered, general aviation, or military aircraft)." Required runway length is defined as the distance from the start of the takeoff point to the point where these obstacle heights are reached.

5.1.3.1 **Key Parametric Assumptions**. In laying out this parametric approach, Shevell makes the following basic assumptions:

◆ Even though acceleration is not constant (as we have seen in preceding sections, it depends on thrust and drag and both are functions of speed), the effective average excess thrust $(T - D)$ occurs at $\bar{V} = \dfrac{V_{LOF}}{\sqrt{2}}$.

◆ Drag is small compared to thrust during the takeoff run.

5.1.3.2 **Basic Parametric Equation**. Considering only the first assumption above and denoting the acceleration at $\bar{V}$ as $\bar{a}$, we can approximate ground run distance:

$$s_G \approx \frac{V_{LOF}^2}{\bar{a}} \qquad\qquad (5.16)$$

FAR Part 25.107[4] mandates that the minimum takeoff speed $(V_{2_{min}})$ cannot be less than $1.2V_s$ for two-engine and three-engine turboprop and reciprocating engine-powered airplanes and for all large turbojet transports that do not have provisions for significantly reducing the one-engine inoperative power-on stall speed. So, we choose this nominal value and let $V_{LOF} = 1.2V_s = 1.2\sqrt{\dfrac{2W}{\rho S C_{L_{max}}}}$. Then eqn. 5.16 becomes:

$$s_G \approx 1.44 \frac{W^2}{\rho S C_{L_{max}} (T_n - D) V} \tag{5.17}$$

The constant in eqn 5.17 depends solely on $\frac{V_{LOF}}{V_s}$. Under certain constraints, this value can be reduced to 1.15. Then, the constant in eqn 5.17 becomes 1.3225 in stead of 1.44. In general, the distance for accelerating a body is directly proportional to the square of the speed and inversely proportional to the average acceleration. But V itself depends directly on wing loading W/S, inversely on $C_{L_{max}}$, and inversely on ρ. Acceleration, under the restriction of the second assumption on the previous page, is directly proportional to T/W. Lumping all these terms together and expressing s_G in functional form to allow for different constants and to correct for nonstandard density conditions:

$$s_G = f\left(\frac{W^2}{\sigma S C_{L_{max}} \overline{T}_V} \right) \tag{5.18}$$

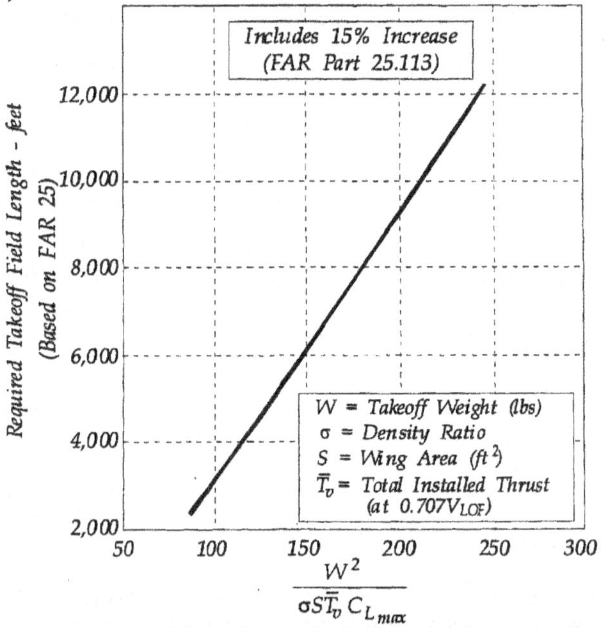

Fig. 5.10 Distance to 35-Foot Obstacle Height for Large Jet Transports
(All Engines Operating)

Equation 5.18 is a generalized takeoff performance approximation similar to the generalized performance curves introduced for turbojet-powered aircraft in Chapter 4. Shevell asserts, moreover, "...that if we plot takeoff distance for each airplane against the parameter $s_G = f\left(\frac{W^2}{\sigma S C_{L_{max}} \overline{T}_V} \right)$, the points will form a single curve." The scatter is small for similar airplanes and a single fairing gives a good approximation to the takeoff distance. Since the ground run is usually greater than the air distance plus the transition distance (by as much as 4 to 1), the total distance to the obstacle clearance height can also be approximated by an expression like eqn. 5.18. Figure 5.10 (adapted from Shevell's data) approximates required runway lengths under FAR Part 25. It was obtained by plotting a large number of takeoffs for different turbojet and turbofan-powered commercial transports and fairing a single curve through the points. This curve applies only to takeoff field lengths with all engines operating. FAR Part 25.113 requires a field length of 115% of the measured obstacle clearance distance; the faired curve includes this safety margin.

Fig. 5.11 is constructed from measured takeoff field lengths, based on FAR Part 25 requirements, for the same aircraft as Fig. 5.10 but with one engine inoperative. The 115% margin for uncertainty required by the certification regulation is applied in this chart.

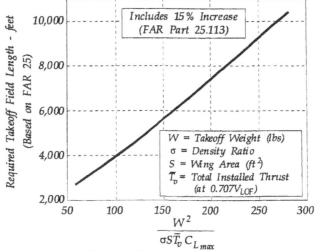

Fig. 5.11 Distance to 35-Foot Obstacle Height for Large Jet Transports
(One Engine Inoperative)

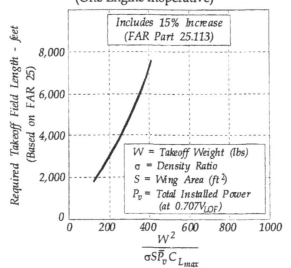

Fig. 5.12 Distance to 50-Foot Obstacle Height for Four-Engine Propeller Transports
(One Engine Inoperative)

For large commercial transports powered by reciprocating engines, the takeoff field lengths required can be approximated from similar parametric charts (Fig. 5.12). However, the acceleration is directly proportional to average installed horsepower, rather than average installed thrust (notice that both terms are installed values, not thrust or power available from engine manufacturer's charts). Equation 5.18 is modified to:

$$s_G = f\left(\frac{W^2}{\sigma S C_{L_{max}} \bar{\bar{P}}_V}\right) \tag{5.19}$$

The obstacle height in the regulations is 50 feet for propeller-driven airplanes, rather than the 35 feet used for commercial jet transports. Required field length, under the assumptions listed at the beginning of this section, collapses to a single curve.

Turboprop takeoff performance may be estimated from charts like Fig. 5.12 if total installed power is known or from curves like Figs. 5.10 and 5.11 if the total installed thrust is known. The form of the expressions is the same; only the experimental measurements (which change the slope and curvature of the generalized curve) differ. Typically, this approximation is more difficult to apply to such hybrid powerplants.

Shevell strongly underscores the value of such a parametric estimation process. He says, "...the parametric method can be used to check the reasonableness of detailed calculations of takeoff (performance)." This basic awareness is essential to a flight test engineer engaged in planning a series of takeoff and landing tests. From such reasonable approximations come those elusive qualities called "intuition" and "engineering judgment". They are acquired skills, not innate intelligence!

5.2 FLIGHT TEST METHODS

The nature of takeoff and landing measurements leaves much to the judgment of the individual flight test team; there is no well-defined "standard" for making these measurements as there is for pitot-static calibrations, climb performance, or cruise performance. This statement does not imply that the requirements documents for military full scale developments or for certification under FARs are imprecise or vague. Rather, these documents are often so specific that the test team must tailor a takeoff and landing test to the individual test program. So, this section is more general and offers only guidelines. Fortunately, the theory and "analytical" equations presented in section 5.1 are pragmatic; so, tailoring to specific requirements in a flight test program is usually straightforward.

5.2.1 Requirements for Takeoff and Landing Flight Tests

Takeoff and landing tests are made to provide data for the operator during these critical phases of flight. Apart from special tests conducted with a specific research goal in mind (for example, changes in stability derivatives in ground effect), both military and civil requirements are heavily slanted toward collecting information that goes into the AFM. These flight tests are a combination of performance and handling qualities assessments. As such, they involve measurement of performance parameters of interest. But they also usually involve some degree of subjective evaluation as to how the airplane's stability and controllability affect the pilot's ability to precisely maneuver the airplane during these terminal phases of flight. Partly because of the dual nature of such evaluations, certification requirements and military specifications spell out a very complicated matrix of test conditions. This matrix includes not only normal operating conditions, but also a large number of abnormal or emergency procedures in order to "demonstrate" standard or specification compliance. Ordinarily, this phrasing necessitates a flight test demonstration. Specifically, Part 23.21 states:

(a) *Each requirement of this subpart must be met at each appropriate combination of weight and center of gravity within the range of loading conditions for which certification is requested. This must be shown --*

(1) *By tests upon an airplane of the type for which certification is requested, or by calculations based on, and equal in accuracy to, the results of testing; and*

(2) *By systematic investigation of each probable combination of weight and center of gravity inferred from combinations investigated.*

(b) *The following general tolerances are allowed during flight testing. However, greater tolerances may be allowed in particular tests:*

Item	Tolerance
Weight	+5%, -10%
Critical items affected by weight	+5%, -1%
Center of gravity	+7% of total travel

While each of the subparts of FAR Part 23 listed below is applicable for takeoff and landing demonstrations and should be carefully studied by the test team, those subparts marked with an asterisk pertain directly to these flight tests. Most of the other compliance requirements can be extracted from tests that these subsections dictate. Since this book introduces the subject and does not attempt to comprehensively cover all aspects, the discussion is limited to these most important subparts.

Part 23.33	Propeller speed and pitch limits	Part 23.177	Directional and lateral stability
Part 23.49	Stalling Speed	Part 23.179	Instrumented stick force maneuvers
Part 23.51	Takeoff*	Part 23.181	Dynamic longitudinal stability
Part 23.75	Landing*	Part 23.201	Wings level stall
Part 23.143	Controllability and maneuverability: general	Part 23.207	Stall warning
		Part 23.231	Ground and water handling characteristics: Longitudinal stability and control*
Part 23.145	Longitudinal control		
Part 23.147	Directional and lateral control		
Part 23.149	Minimum control speed	Part 23.233	Ground and water handling characteristics: Directional Stability and control*
Part 23.153	Control during landings*		
Part 23.155	Elevator control force in Maneuvers	Part 23.235	Ground and water handling characteristics: Taxiing conditions
Part 23.157	Rate of roll		
Part 23.161	Trim	Part 23.239	Ground and water handling characteristics: Spray conditions
Part 23.171	Stability: general		
Part 23.173	Static longitudinal stability	Part 23.251	Vibration and buffeting
Part 23.175	Demonstration of longitudinal stability		

5.2.1.1 **Use of Mathematical Models and Simulation**. One of the more significant modern trends in evaluating TO&L performance is a shift from overall measurements (which are rather imprecise mainly due to variations in piloting technique) to measurement of segments of these maneuvers and use of modeling or mathematical simulation to tie segments together. The primary objective of most TO&L measurements is to determine and demonstrate for the operator how to achieve reasonable takeoff and landing distances and safe speeds for everyday operations. Flight tests are typically used to verify individual portions of the mathematical model rather than attempting to measure the performance on complete maneuvers. These "patched" maneuvers (or maneuver segments) can be compared and standardized more easily than can measurements from complete takeoffs or landings. Both military and civilian flight test specifications permit either approach. Complete takeoffs and landings, with careful attention to consistent piloting techniques, are still demonstrated. But the modeling approach allows thoughtful choice of valid maneuvers and better control of test variables.

In practice the test team should plan to collect data on almost every takeoff and/or landing until a data base is established for normal procedures. Even though repeatability in technique is emphasized, there will be wide variation in results. But, individual segments where nearly identical rotation rates and usable airspeeds are matched can be collected from multiple runs and statistically evaluated for consistency before the complete maneuvers are flown for validation of the modeled takeoff or landing. Such mathematical simulations are particularly useful in establishing takeoff acceleration profiles and in predicting landing rollout under slippery runway conditions. The segmented approach allows the test engineer to use portions of a maneuver to establish performance, even though the entire maneuver may have flaws in it that make the overall distances and velocities invalid. Segmented testing is more efficient; it allows almost every maneuver to contribute to the data base, thereby building statistical relevance.

However, complete maneuvers must also be done as final validation of the takeoff or landing model. As FAR 23[6] puts it: "... actual takeoffs using the AFM (recommended technique) should be conducted to verify that the actual distance to the 50-foot height does not exceed the calculated takeoff distance to the 50-foot height." Complete takeoffs and landings, with attention to consistent piloting techniques, must be demonstrated.

5.2.1.2 **Position and Velocity Measurement Techniques**. The instrumentation used to measure distances and velocities varies widely in precision, in complexity, and in versatility. The most useful measurement tools allow simultaneous capture of both horizontal and vertical position and velocity during either the takeoff or the landing.

Tracking devices – laser, radar, optical, or video – constitute the most widely used equipment for measuring ground roll distances. The flight test engineer is responsible for choosing the type of tracker and for guaranteeing (1) that its precision is adequate to satisfy the certifying agency, (2) that any special transponders or illuminating devices operate reliably, and (3) that the required data reduction effort is compatible with program budget and schedules. With regard to (2), the test engineer should be alert for any "undesirable side effects" from the transponder or illuminator. A laser tracker often needs a reflective surface painted on the airplane and the laser beam is intended to point at this surface only. The flight test engineer has to satisfy safety review authorities that a misdirected laser beam cannot harm (even temporarily) the pilot and/or the airplane and its systems. A radar tracker may also need a radar reflector or a transponder to return accurate spatial information; the test engineer must be sure that such an electronic device does not interfere with other aircraft or test instrumentation subsystems. Optical devices need clearly discernible levels of contrast so that data reduction does not become unwieldy. The same is true of video imaging systems, which do lend themselves to at least partially automated data reduction.[7]

At least for the ground roll portions of takeoff and landing trajectories, distances can also be measured by integrating accelerations and then velocities from inertial navigation systems (INS) if the airplane is so equipped. Cheney and Pham[8] describe how such an approach [along with instrument landing system (ILS) and radio altimeter measurements] was used to validate and certify Category III autoland performance for the MD-80 and the MD-87 commercial airliners. This indirect form of distance measurement is accurate provided (1) the INS is not strongly affected by acceleration errors during takeoff and (2) the events in question (liftoff, touchdown, and passage through obstacle clearance height can be precisely defined on the data records. This latter point means that the test planner must thoroughly evaluate techniques to define these events. Sometimes the flight test engineer may have to design additional equipment or improvise procedures to define the events critical to his measurement data. Landing gear microswitches and photoelectric beams are two such specialized devices that have been used for this purpose. Often the preparation for takeoff and landing tests must include qualification and proof testing of any specialized instrumentation before useful data can be collected. The wise flight test planner includes time in his schedule for such proof tests.

Spatial measurements against an accurate time base are a satisfactory way to estimate velocities only if atmospheric conditions are recorded at the same time, in order to correct to standard conditions and for comparison against simulation models. The meteorological conditions strongly affect thrust, braking and aerodynamic performance. Consequently, most major test ranges have runways that are heavily instrumented with atmospheric sensors. As a minimum, TO&L flight test data used for certification or proof of performance require the following atmospheric instruments: [6]

(1) *an altimeter or a sensitive barometer set to 29.92 inches of mercury to measure altitude;*

(2) *one or more anemometers that measure wind velocity and direction at the takeoff or landing surface (It is also useful is some means of measuring wind velocity and direction up through the obstacle height is available.);*

(3) *an accurate thermometer to provide free air temperature, again at the takeoff or landing surface; and*

(4) *when appropriate (as when tests are conducted in high temperature, high humidity conditions), relative humidity at the takeoff or landing surface.*

The atmospheric information is only a portion of the data set required to document TO&L trajectories. Aircraft position, velocity, and acceleration (or deceleration) history must be measured accurately to document aircraft TO&L performance. The instrumentation options for making these measurements are discussed more fully in Section 5.3.

5.2.2 Typical Part 23 Test Groups

5.2.2.1 Takeoff Tests. In laying out a series of takeoff tests, most data are collected coincident with other testing; after all, every successful flight must begin with a takeoff and end with a landing. However, every test plan should include a matrix (perhaps derived from a table like Table 5.2) of test conditions that covers specific TO&L test maneuvers. The test engineer can then simply annotate the appropriate data as it is collected, analyzed, and validated. For a typical light twin to be certified under FAR Part 23, the takeoff test matrix must also be expanded into detailed test cards for individual flights.

5.2.2.2 Landing Tests. Landing tests are also outlined to help organize the test matrix during the test planning phase. The primary difference between them and takeoff tests lies in the demonstration of adequate longitudinal control authority for the landing flare maneuver. Table 5.3 summarizes a typical grouping of such tests for a small twin-engine airplane. The detailed test planning involves laying out detailed test cards that cover all items in this matrix. The test planner must also anticipate considerable variation in the landing data, since the performance during this maneuver is quite uncertain due to a number of factors including: (1) atmospheric turbulence commonly affects landing, (2) pilot technique varies widely for making a "good" landing, and (3) ground effect changes the handling qualities for each airplane and pilot combination. Hence, quality results require a statistically significant number of landings carried out by a representative sample of pilots.

Table 5.2 Takeoff Conditions for a Light Twin Certification

Test Description	Conditions	Primary Purpose	References
Determination of V_r	Normal takeoff	Select techniques	Part 23.51, AC-23-8B
Demonstrate takeoff performance[2], including ground roll, flare distance, distance to clear obstacle, speed at obstacle height	At nominal weights[3], cg locations[4], flap settings, and atmospheric variables[5]	Proof of compliance, data for AFM	Part 23.51, AC-23-8B
Demonstrate minimum control speeds[7]	Specified weights[3], cg locations[4], sideslip conditions, and bank angles	Proof of compliance, data for AFM	Part 23.51, AC-23-8B
Demonstrate required roll responsiveness in the takeoff configuration[8]	At nominal weights[3], cg locations[4], and atmospheric variables[5]	Proof of compliance, data for AFM	Part 23.51, AC-23-8B Part 23.157

Notes: 1. Stall speeds must be determined before this matrix is begun.
2. Emphasis is on achieving a speed so that all maneuvers can be performed safely in the event of a power failure in reasonably turbulent conditions.
3. Takeoff distance tests are conducted at maximum weight and at a range of cg locations.
4. Takeoff distance demonstrations are performed at the most critical cg location (usually the most forward cg).
5. Humidity is measured and accounted for (Part 23.45) and wind velocity and direction is measured adjacent to the takeoff surface. Wind velocities should be as low as possible, not to exceed $1.2V_{s_1}$ or 10 knots.
6. The airplane is presumed to have desired maneuvering capability at obstacle clearance height if the speed attained at this point is the higher of $1.1V_{mc}$, $1.3V_{s_1}$, or some speed > $1.3V_{s_1}$ down to $V_x + 4$ knots (for multiengine airplanes). Since V_{mc} has no meaning for single airplanes, the first speed requirement at obstacle height does not apply.
7. Minimum control speed tests, obviously apply only to multiengine airplanes and are not takeoff tests in the strictest sense. The test team must determine the "critical" engine and must investigate all flap settings recommended for use. Dynamic or static V_{mc}, whichever is greater, will be included in the AFM.
8. Demonstrations should be accomplished by rolling the airplane in both directions.

Table 5.3 Landing Tests for a Light Twin Certification

Test Description	Conditions	Primary Purpose	References
Determination of Approach and landing speeds[1]	Landing at all proposed flap settings, cg locations[4], and power	Select techniques	Part 23.75, AC-23-8B
Demonstrate landing performance[2], including ground roll, flare distance, distance to clear obstacle, speed at obstacle height	At nominal weights[3], cg locations[4], flap settings, and atmospheric variables[5]	Proof of compliance, data for AFM	Part 23.75, AC-23-8B
Demonstrate longitudinal control during landing[6]	Specified weights[3], cg locations[4]	Proof of compliance, data for AFM	Part 23.153, AC-23-8B
Demonstrate required roll responsiveness in the landing configuration[7]	At nominal weights[3], cg locations[4], and atmospheric variables[5]	Proof of compliance, data for AFM	Part 23.157, AC-23-8B

Notes: 1. Stall speeds must be determined before this matrix is begun.

2. Emphasis is on achieving a steady speed at the obstacle height with the power set so the airplane passes through this reference point in stabilized conditions. A smooth flare to touchdown should be made. Normal pilot reaction times should be used for power reduction, brake application, and actuating other deceleration devices. At least six landings on the same wheels, tires, and brakes should be demonstrated to ensure serviceability.

3. Landing distance tests are conducted at maximum allowable landing weight and at a range of lesser weights expected in normal service.

4. Landing tests are performed at the "critical" (usually the most forward) cg location and the most aft cg location certified, as well as a range of other cg locations expected in normal service.

5. Humidity is measured and accounted for (Part 23.45) and wind velocity and direction is measured adjacent to the takeoff surface. Wind velocities should be as low as possible, not to exceed $1.2V_{s_1}$ or 10 knots.

6. The primary purpose of this demonstration is to ensure that airplanes over 6000 pounds gross weight have sufficient flare capability to overcome any excessive sink rate that may develop at a speed 5 knots lower than recommended normal approach speed and to ensure that control forces are not excessive. If the airplane is to be certified at approach speeds < $1.3V_{s_1}$, compliance with Part 23.153 must be demonstrated at the selected approach speed.

7. Demonstrations should be accomplished by rolling in both directions.

5.3 INSTRUMENTATION

Instrumentation for collecting precise TO&L data have largely been ground-based equipment in the past.[9,10,11] Cinethodolites, radar trackers, laser trackers (with laser ranging in many cases) are typically still found at most well-equipped test facilities in both the United States and in Europe. Using these facilities can be expensive and can generate schedule delays if the customer does not have high priority with the host organization. Currently there are two trends that look promising to make such measurements more independent; indeed there are a few companies now offering "turn-key" operations that provide measurements that satisfy at least some of the certification agencies for such "time-space-position-information" (TSPI) to the required accuracies. These approaches are almost always based on merging high-accuracy global positioning system (GPS) measurements with information from other systems (inertial navigation systems [INS] or laser trackers, for example). Remembering that TO&L trajectories are typically two-dimensional, let us briefly outline each of these TSPI schemes and how they are applied to such measurements. As will be noted, several of these methods applies to three-dimensional TSPI as well as to TO&L measurements.

5.3.1 Proven Measurement Devices

5.3.1.1 **Cinetheodolites.** A cinetheodolite is a "camera" (originally a high speed motion picture camera, though digital video cameras are probably more common today; hence, "kinetheodolite" is probably more descriptive terminology[10]) which records the azimuth and elevation to a target at frame rates suitable to accuracy requirements. It is a line of sight device and depends upon an operator (or an automated control loop in more sophisticated and expensive systems) to maintain the position of the target near the center of the frame which is typically aligned with the optical axis. Manual operation demands that each operator (one for azimuth and one for elevation) use a hand wheel and scope to track the target; these kinds of devices can be relatively inexpensive in initial cost, but the need for two operators and manual processing of the data can easily negate this cost advantage. De Benque d'Agut, Riebeek, and Poo[10] describe the components of an Askania cinetheodolite more completely, along with the typical preparations needed to collect data with this equipment. A typical frame of cinethodolite film[11] is shown in Fig. 5.13. The displacements from ($\Delta\gamma$ and $\Delta\sigma$) from the optical centerline are simply operator (or automatic control system) errors. These errors dictate tedious reduction of the data; often with operator intervention to be sure corrections are properly made. Cinetheodolite sites must be surveyed (more about that requirement in the next section on tracking radars) and index (or bias) errors expressing the difference between the correct angles to a known target and the angles read from the cinetheodolite film or video.

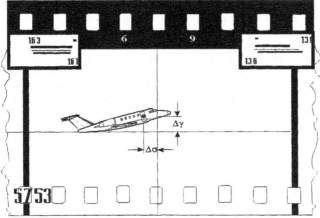

Fig. 5.13 Representation of a Cinetheodolite Frame
(adapted from Harrass[11], Figure 13.4)

Advantages usually given for cinetheodolite systems are:
- ◆ Errors in the data can be at or below 0.01°, given reasonable tracking mechanism accelerations and definitive target reference points.
- ◆ Overall cost of cinetheodolite systems can be lower than other tracking schemes.
- ◆ Targets on the ground or near the horizon or at higher elevations can be tracked. This capability, coupled with achievable precision, keeps cinetheodolite methods high on the list for takeoff and landing measurements.
- ◆ The visual images from a cinetheodolite provide additional information. For example, separation of stores or payload drops show up in the imagery.
- ◆ While two sites are needed for three-dimensional data, adding on a laser ranging device can give acceptable results with a single cinetheodolite.

Disadvantages associated with cinetheodolite systems include:
- ◆ Visual tracking conditions are essential; for many geographic areas with poor visibility, this limitation often leads to acquisition ranges of less than 10 kilometers. To assist in acquiring the target cinetheodolites are often slaved to other tracking devices. Strobe lights can help with tracking in low visibility, twilight, or night.
- ◆ Trying to track targets near the zenith of the trajectory can give angular velocities that cannot be readily followed with the tracking scheme (especially manual ones).
- ◆ Processing cinetheodolite measurements is usually a tedious task with significant manpower costs. Careful selection of reference points can help, though data are often dependent on attitude and aspect of the trajectory to the optical

axis of the device. Recording the azimuth, elevation, and range information in digital form can appreciably reduce the time spent in reducing the data sets. Displacement of the target from the optical axis still must largely be corrected by operators or analysts. Numerical differentiation (a process that always leads to loss of information) is necessary to obtain velocity and accelerations for TO&L trajectories. Application of error analysis algorithms[10] is also pertinent to the processing and must be carefully done.

♦ Careful site surveys and accurate tracker positioning are necessary to achieve quoted accuracies, with setup at mobile sites typically taking half a day.

5.3.1.2 **Tracking Radar.** Radar provides three-dimensional measurements (azimuth, elevation, and slant range). Position returns are based on the instantaneous center of the radar cross section (for a skin paint) or, more appropriately, on the location of transponders mounted on the target vehicle. Typically the radar beam acquires a signal by slaving to an "identification-friend-or-foe" (IFF) transponder code, using closed-loop control that "locks on" when the range gate is nearly coincident to the target. This closed-loop control of the tracking antenna (in azimuth, elevation, and slant range) utilizes error signals of three possible types: (1) conical scan, (2) sequential lobing, or (3) monopulse. The first two types of error signals must receive a continuous train of pulses to generate a useable signal. Monopulse radars generate an error signal from each echo return; range information is obtained by precisely measuring travel time between the transmission and the receipt of pulses of radar energy. Accuracies in range on the order of 2-3 meters with a 1 σ deviation in the measurements are common, so long as carefully planned and frequently calibrated radar sites are used. Angular errors of 0.02-0.03°, again with 1 σ deviation in the measurements achievable, though these measurements are strongly affected by refraction errors of the radar wave propagating through the atmosphere. Hurrass[11] gives considerably more detailed tracking radar characteristics in the AGARD monograph. He also gives a refraction correction along with short descriptions of least squares and Kalman filter algorithms frequently used with radar trackers.

The advantages[9,10,11] usually noted for tracking radars include:

♦ A single tracking site provides three-dimensional data.
♦ Slant ranges over 50,000 meters are achievable and slant range error is small (~2-10 meters) . This error is almost independent of the slant range measured.
♦ Tracking is possible even in clouds or in fog.
♦ Data collection, storage, and processing are relatively easy to automate.
♦ Tracking is possible even in clouds or fog.

Disadvantages for tracking radars are:

♦ Angular errors are small only for expensive equipment and the calibrations to produce good elevation angles can be problematic.
♦ Ground targets and targets low on the horizon are often lost in ground clutter.
♦ Radar tracking sites must be carefully surveyed and are not typically mobile. (This disadvantage has been largely mitigated with accurate GPS equipment for now used for surveying in most cases.)
♦ A target cannot be easily tracked when more than one target is in formation or close together, especially if they are of comparable size.
♦ The reference point for skin tracking is random partly due to changing aircraft attitudes and aspect with the tracking site. The use of transponders often re-

duces this effect quite satisfactorily, but installation/location of these transponders on the target must be carefully chosen for the intended maneuvers. Weber[9] elaborates on this point for both cinethodolites and tracking radars, describing the error fields of both types of tracking devices. Multiple transponder antennae (top and bottom of the vehicle, for example) are often used, but the system must then keep up with which transponder is reflecting the transmitted signal.

♦ Tracking radar may cost more than small flight test efforts can afford.

5.3.1.3 **Distance Measuring Schemes.** There are two categories of tracking equipment that measure distances only (distance-measuring equipment or DME). The first is based on travel time for radio signals between the interrogator (transmitter) and a transponder. Both phase differencing and time differencing are used to produce the distance-only measurements. At least three units are necessary (more units for redundant measurements are desirable), usually with a single transponder mounted on the target aircraft and interrogators on the ground. Motorola's Mini Ranger system uses this configuration. Some applications reverse this siting and carry a single interrogator on the target vehicle and transponders on the ground. Boeing used the latter scheme during verification of the B-1B navigational system. [14] This system, dubbed the Microwave Airplane Position System (MAPS), in an early 1980's configuration with up to 19 ground transponders gives standard deviations of less than 0.3 meters in all three coordinate directions at altitudes above 50 meters. Standard deviation of velocity measurements is around 0.5 meters/second. Degradation of accuracy at the lower altitudes has been improved enough to conduct autoland tests for certification purposes. The MAPS system provides high accuracy measurements at ranges up to 10 kilometers, a good fit for TO&L requirements. The geometry of the ground-based devices relative to the tracked vehicle (this kind of degradation of position accuracy is known as geometric dilution of precision or GDOP) strongly affects the accuracy of the measurements. The locations of all ground units must be accurately known. Nearly all systems of this type use a Kalman filter in the data reduction process to efficiently combine multiple measurements.

Advantages[9,10,11] with DME-only systems include:

♦ Very accurate trajectory and velocity data for ranges up to about 10 kilometers are available in near real-time to facilitate on-line data processing.

♦ Distance-measuring units are quite portable; they can be easily sited at any test range, given their small size and weight.

♦ These systems are useable in any weather conditions.

Disadvantages for DME-only schemes are:

♦ Range is usually limited to about 10 kilometers.

♦ Equipment (though small and light weight) must be installed on the target.

♦ Positions of at least three (usually more) ground stations must be known before taking measurements.

♦ Relative geometry (and/or redundancy) of the ground units and the trajectories to be measured must be planned to avoid GDOP.

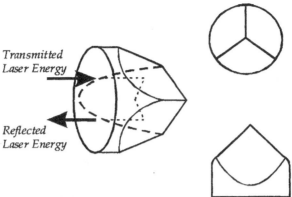

Fig. 5.14 Concept of a Corner Reflector
(adapted from De Benque d'Agut, et al[10], Figure 26)

5.3.1.4 **Laser** **Trackers.** Laser trackers, like radar trackers, depend on transmitted energy pulses and reflected signals, again providing azimuth, elevation, and slant range with a single device. Most laser trackers operate in the infrared frequency range. Retro reflectors or an assembly of corner reflectors (Fig. 5.14[10] illustrates the principle) insure that the useable low power pulses are reflected for any orientation of the aircraft. Transmitted power is usually kept low for tracking lasers to eliminate or at least mitigate eye safety concerns. Typically, transmitted power is 10 milliwatts to about 25 watts[10], though some laser trackers operate above 100 watts and, therefore, need automated programs to guarantee eye safety for operators and crew of the target aircraft.

Typical beam widths for the transmitted coherent laser beam are about ±0.1° so an acquisition element is used to "lock on" for automated tracking. Video schemes as well as tracking radar subsystems have been integrated with laser trackers for this acquisition task. Laser trackers provide excellent accuracy for most TO&L measurements (angular errors within ±0.01° and slant ranges inside ±1 meter are reported. Typical uses of laser trackers include: (1) TO&L TSPI measurements, (2) instrument landing system accuracy verifications, and (3) confirmation of navigational system precision (ILS VOR-TACAN, terrain following systems, and GPS).

Typical advantages[9,10,11] usually listed for laser tracker are:
- ♦ Accuracies attainable are quite high; the measurements are suitable for almost all TSPI purposes up to about 30 kilometers in range.
- ♦ Trajectory data measurements are processed immediately to facilitate automated data processing and to allow immediate quality checking of test events.
- ♦ Unlike tracking radars, accuracy is maintained down to the ground.
- ♦ One site can produce position in three coordinates.
- ♦ Accurate calibrations are straightforward with fixed retro reflectors in known locations.

Laser trackers have the following disadvantages:
- ♦ Tracking can only be done with good visibility.
- ♦ Safety issues proliferate with laser power.
- ♦ Some kind of laser reflector is required on the aircraft.

5.3.2   Other Measurement Schemes

5.3.2.1   Inertial Navigation Systems (INS).   INS units, especially those integrated with other measurement sensors, are common on high performance aircraft, but are rarely found on personal airplanes due to cost. Such a package typically outputs velocity, position, and attitude. Horizontal position accuracy is low (on the order of 20 meters), so velocity outputs are often used to calculate horizontal positions. The measured vertical acceleration can be used to compute altitude, though careful error handling is necessary to avoid unbounded altitude error. Redundant external measurements are essential to keep INS errors acceptably low. Many different precision position measurements have been used to correct inertial sensors – surveyed positions and heights, video measurements, GPS inputs, tracking radar, laser trackers, and radar altimeters. Consequently, the accuracy of INS measurement depends heavily on the accuracy of these redundant corrections and the length of time between updates.

Advantages[9,10,11] cited for INS sensors include:

♦ Position, velocity, and attitude angles are determined to a high accuracy; extensive use of Kalman filters adds to the usefulness of these measurements.
♦ INS data are nearly continuous in time; high frequency motions of the aircraft are measured accurately.

Inertial measurements have the following disadvantages:

♦ Both the weight and price of a high accuracy INS can be prohibitive for smaller, low performance aircraft.
♦ Careful alignment of the INS unit is necessary to produce quality data.
♦ Some post-processing of the data is necessary to achieve high accuracies; real time monitoring of the test event is a bit crude from such sensors.

5.3.2.2   Global Positioning System (GPS).   GPS appears to be one of the most attractive position measuring tools, providing excellent accuracy at low cost. GPS position is calculated from range measurements between a constellation of orbiting satellites and a unit in the target vehicle. GPS velocity is calculated from the Doppler shifts from the visible satellites. Time accuracy is critical, dictating that both the satellite and the GPS receiver have components to maintain the time information from which range information is derived. Three measurements are needed to determine position and a fourth is used to determine the user's clock error. Typically, GPS units use eight satellites for position measurements. The GPS specification allows a system accuracy of about 20 meters and velocity accuracy of less than 1 knot. These accuracies can be further refined by the use of Differential GPS (DGPS). With DGPS position accuracies better than 1 meter are now claimed. The FAA has indicated that GPS is useful for some of the most demanding certification tests. To quote the management summary: "These tests revealed that the Ashtech Z-12 was more accurate than the laser tracker that was being used as a truth source." [13]

Advantages[9,10,11] attributed to GPS are:

♦ Position al accuracy is good enough for nearly every TSPI purpose.
♦ GPS units are relatively inexpensive, even high accuracy systems are less expensive than most other measurement schemes.
♦ No operators are needed on the ground to operate the system.
♦ Real time data are readily available for decision-makers.

GPS use for flight test measurements has only one listed disadvantage:

♦ Availability depends on the U.S. Department of Defense. Though GPS is the only operational satellite navigation system at the time of this writing (2006), competing systems are being developed. The European Space Agency intends to have Galileo operational by 2008; the first satellite hardware was launched in late December 2005 from Baikonur in Russia. Galileo is entirely under civilian control and cooperates with GPS equipment as well.

5.3.3 Integrated Measurement Schemes

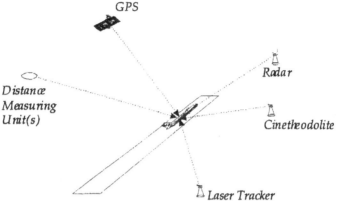

Fig. 5.15 Integrated System Concept

The most accurate systems integrate a number of sensors to provide the necessary data (Fig. 5.15). Such systems have been in use at major test agencies for some time and considerable detail on the design and operational characteristics of the DLR Avionics Flight Evaluation System (AFES) are given by Hurrass.[11] The high accuracies of such multisensor integrated schemes are expensive; they are often found only at major test facilities and require well-equipped test vehicles, significant investment in multiple ground sites, and several people to operate them. As the discussion of time synchronization in the section on GPS equipment suggested, time synchronization of these multiple sensors is key to obtaining the high accuracy data from integrated TSPI systems. But low cost integrated systems, relying heavily on GPS measurements, are now advertised as: "...a low cost single receiver GPS package ... capable of achieving centimeter to decimeter accuracy in both horizontal and vertical position...".[14]

5.4 SUMMARY

This chapter introduces methods of estimating takeoff and landing distances and speeds critical to attainment of this performance, reviewing both piecewise estimation techniques and parametric computations. Test methods for these flight tests are not as clearly defined or as precise as other performance measurements; pilot technique plays an important role. Although it is easy to gather large amounts of takeoff and landing data, repeatable complete maneuvers are difficult to obtain. Selecting consistent segments from several similar maneuvers and using them to verify mathematical TO&L models for a given configuration are often more practical. This approach is an example of how simulation augments experimental measurements and makes flight testing more efficient. General test groups for a small general airplane (FAR Part 23) are suggested that outline detailed test matrices for certification compliance demonstrations. Position, velocity, and time measurements are overviewed, emphasizing advantages and disadvantages of several common approaches.

REFERENCES

1 Dekker, F. E. D. and Lean, D., "Takeoff and Landing Performance: Chapter 8, Volume 1," **AGARD Flight Test Manual**, Pergamon Press, New York, 1959.

2 Lan, C. E. and Roskam, J., **Airplane Aerodynamics and Performance**, Roskam Aviation and Engineering Corporation; Ottawa, Kansas, 1980.

3 Shevell, R. S., **Fundamentals of Flight**, Prentice Hall, Englewood Cliffs, New Jersey, 1983.

4 Federal Aviation Regulation, FAR 25, Federal Aviation Administration, Government Printing Office, Washington, Mar. 30, 1967.

5 Federal Aviation Regulation, FAR 23, Federal Aviation Administration, Government Printing Office, Washington, Mar. 30, 1967.

6 Flight Test Guide for Certification of Small Airplanes, Advisory Circular 23-8B, Federal Aviation Administration, Government Printing Office, Washington, Nov. 14, 1983.

7 Dorsett, K., Robson, R., Pollard, S., and Albright, R., and Ward, D. T., "Takeoff and Landing Measurements with a Video Imaging Technique," Unpublished report, Texas A&M University, 1988.

8 Cheney, H. K. and Pham, C. T., "A New Method to Confirm Category II Autoland Performance," AIAA Paper 88-2126, Aug. 1988.

9 Weber, O., "Ground-Based Equipment," Chapter 11, **AGARDograph No. 160, Basic Principles of Flight Test Instrumentation Engineering, Volume 1, Issue 1**, (Edited by A. Pool and D. Bosman), Advisory Group for Aerospace Research & Development, Paris, France, 1973.

10 De Benque d'Agut, P., Riebeek, H., and Pool, A., "Trajectory Measurements for Take-Off and Landing Tests and Other Short-Range Applications," **AGARDograph No. 160, Basic Principles of Flight Test Instrumentation Engineering, Volume 16**, (Edited by A. Pool and D. Bosman), Advisory Group for Aerospace Research, Paris, France, 1973.

11 Hurrass, K., "Measuring Flightpath Trajectories," Chapter 13, **AGARDograph No. 160, Basic Principles of Flight Test Instrumentation Engineering, Volume 1, Issue 2**, (Edited by R. Borek and A. Pool), Advisory Group for Aerospace Research & Development, Neuilly Sur Seine, France, March 1994.

12 Lui-Kwan, G. and Atkinson, D. E., "Instrumentation System for Real Time Navigation Performance Assessment," AIAA Paper 1986-9731, AIAA/CASI/DGLR/IES/ITEA/ SETP/SFTE Third Flight Testing Conference, Las Vegas, Nevada, April 2-4, 1986.

13 Youngdahl, G., "Flight Tests of Ashtech GPS Receiver for Use as Time Space Position Information System (TSPI) to Verify Specific Performance Standards," FAA Technical Center, Airborne Systems Technology Branch, ACD-330, Atlantic City, New Jersey, 1996. (Cited by: http://www.volpe.dot.gov/acoustics/dgpsinfo.html)

14 http://www.bakerav.com/.

Chapter 6
LONGITUDINAL STABILITY TESTS

Longitudinal stability is usually the first subject introduced when one begins a study of the stability and controllability of airplanes. For relatively mild maneuvers and perturbations, this subject is a convenient introductory topic since only one moment equation is involved and the complications of coupled motions can be avoided. The development of flight test methods has generally followed the same pattern. It is also convenient to start the discussion with the fundamental definitions and assumptions for static stability before going on to the dynamics of the problem.

To evaluate the relative merit of any airplane's flying qualities, it is essential that all parties accept a yardstick. For years the flight test community struggled with standards (and on occasion still does!), but in time both the civil regulatory bodies and the military produced requirements documents that spell out what is expected in any class of aircraft. Van Pelt[1] gives some of this history to go with his examples[2,3] of such requirements. The student should recognize that these requirements change frequently and may be modified by specific contractual documents. Each flight test team must carefully examine the specifications, regulations, and contractual documents applicable to the design being evaluated before they design the test matrix needed to adequately explore its flying qualities.

6.1 FOUNDATIONS

To lay the groundwork for longitudinal stability test methods, we first briefly review the meaning of static and dynamic stability and the basic equations that govern such motions. To evaluate airplane stability, the test team must be keenly aware that flying qualities are important primarily as they affect the pilot. Therefore, we consider the pilot's reaction to an engineering modification the most important concern.

6.1.1 Definitions

Equilibrium must be clearly defined as the foundation for any concept of stability. Equilibrium for any body requires constant linear momentum and constant angular momentum. Thus, a rigid body of constant mass must either be at rest or in unaccelerated motion to be in an equilibrium state. For an airplane, both the forces and the moments about the center of gravity must be balanced.

> An airplane is in equilibrium (or is trimmed) when the sum of the external forces is zero and the sum of the moments about the center of gravity is zero.

While "equilibrium" is the common terminology of controls and dynamics, aeronautically, we typically call this state the "trim condition".

Aircraft *static* longitudinal stability is typically defined in terms of its initial tendency to return to equilibrium after a disturbance. Dynamic longitudinal stability, on the other hand, considers behavior about the pitch axis as a function of time after a perturbation. Disturbances can take many forms, but the one most often of interest is an angle of attack change, due to either turbulence or a control input. (Many older texts use C_L rather than α as the independent variable; however, as Etkin[4] points out, there are cogent reasons for using C_{m_α} as the measure of static longitudinal stability.) Perturbations in true airspeed often are also important to flying qualities investigations but they are a concern secondary to disturbances in α.

> An airplane is said to be **statically stable** in pitch if a disturbance in angle of attack produces an initial pitching moment that tends to restore the airplane to its trim angle of attack.

This definition primarily appeals to the engineer; the pilot senses static longitudinal stability quite differently. He perceives static longitudinal stability through the forces necessary to move the elevator and the displacement of the control stick or column. He sees positive static stability as an aft stick movement or a pull force on the stick as airspeed is reduced from the trim airspeed, countering the nose-down moment caused by the pitch stability. Similarly, a push force or a forward movement of the stick is expected as speed increases (α is reduced) from the trim condition. Both the control movement and the control forces indicate to the pilot whether or not the airplane is statically stable. The fact that there are two ways to sense static longitudinal stability suggests two different types of stability are of concern. Each is important for different reasons.

First, **stick-fixed stability** is a measure of the free response of the airplane being tested. The stick or control wheel is held stationary by the pilot so that the control surfaces will not move with changes in the aerodynamic forces on the surfaces.

> **Stick-fixed static longitudinal stability** is positive when the pilot's longitudinal controller must be deflected aft to trim the airplane at an α greater than α_{trim}.

The converse, of course, must be true for $\alpha < \alpha_{trim}$. For conventional tail-aft airplanes, this definition means that the elevator must move trailing edge up (TEU) when the speed is reduced below the trim speed and trailing edge down (TED) when the speed is increased above the trim speed. Stick-fixed static longitudinal stability is fundamentally important for all other kinds of stability, and it applies to airplanes with both reversible and irreversible flight control systems.

When the elevator is allowed to float freely (zero stick force applied by the pilot), a different form of static longitudinal stability can be evaluated. The pilot's force that must be applied to trim the airplane is a key issue and becomes a primary measure of this form of stability.

> **Stick-free static longitudinal stability** is positive when the force applied to the pilot's longitudinal controller is an aft (pull) force for α greater than α_{trim}.

With these basic concepts reviewed, we now turn our attention to quantifying them. But to do so, we must first establish sign conventions for our analysis.

6.1.1.1 <u>Sign Conventions</u>. Figure 6.1 shows the sign conventions used in the literature and in this book. The positive coordinate directions x, y, z and the right-hand rule define positive force, angular velocity, and moment vectors as illustrated. Two sign conventions for control surface deflections are shown. Since most stability and control textbooks use the "standard" convention (Fig. 6a) for control surface deflections, we use it in this book most of the time. The flight test convention (Fig. 6b) is easier to remember, but it is not always compatible with available data. In the former convention the observer is assumed to be sighting along the positive z axis and using the right hand rule to define positive angular deflections of the rudder; that is, left rudder deflection is positive. Positive elevator deflection is obtained by sighting along the positive y direction and again applying the right hand rule. This approach gives a positive deflection of the elevator surface when it is moved TED. Aileron movement is defined to positive when the right aileron is moved TEU. Similarly, if a "rolling tail" is used for lateral control, TEU for the right half of the stabilizer is positive. On the other hand, the flight test community typically considers a control surface movement to be positive when the deflection produces a positive moment increment about the axis. The sign convention for trim tabs is similar to that for the control surfaces, except the axis of rotation for applying the right-hand rule is the hinge line of the trim tab. (See Roskam[9] and Etkin[4] for a more complete discussion.)

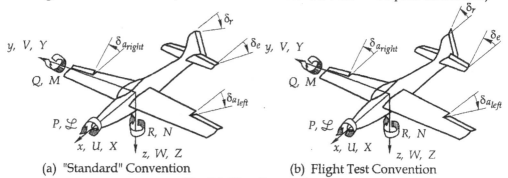

(a) "Standard" Convention   (b) Flight Test Convention

Fig. 6.1 Sign Conventions

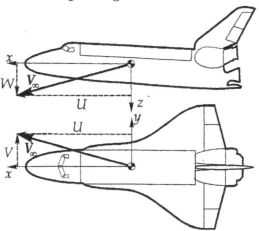

Fig. 6.2 Definitions of α and β

6.1.1.2 **Angle of Attack and Sideslip**. To analyze longitudinal handling qualities of an airplane with respect to disturbances in angle of attack (α), α must be precisely defined. Figure 6.2 defines α and β (sideslip angle, used later to describe lateral-directional handling qualities). Looking at longitudinal stability first, we note that α is defined by vector components of true airspeed lying entirely within the vehicle's plane of symmetry.

$$\alpha \equiv tan^{-1}\frac{W}{U} \tag{6.1}$$

Similarly, even though this definition is not used until Chapter 8,

$$\beta \equiv sin^{-1}\frac{V}{V_\infty}, \text{ where } V_\infty = \sqrt{U^2+V^2+W^2} \tag{6.2}$$

The sign convention for positive sideslip is easily remembered from the pilot's vernacular: "wind-in-the-right-ear produces positive sideslip".

6.1.1.3 **Inertial Orientation**. Euler attitude angles are often used to specify the orientation of the body-fixed stability axes relative to an inertial coordinate system located at the center of the earth. These inertial angles must be measured in a specified order to fit the usual aircraft conventions: 1) a yaw rotation (Ψ) about the inertial Z axis, commonly expressed as a change in magnetic heading; 2) a pitch rotation (Θ) about the y body axis (positive sense is nose up) after the first rotation; and 3) a roll rotation (Φ) about the x body axis (positive sense is right wing down) after the first two rotations. These inertial attitude angles are shown in Fig. 6.3.

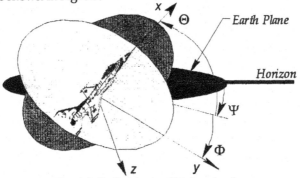

Fig. 6.3 Definitions of Euler Angles

The Euler attitude angles, Ψ, Θ, and Φ are not vectors, nor can they be thought of as vector components since the order of rotation spells out the final position. However, the angular velocity of the aircraft is a vector and can be expressed in either inertial components $\begin{bmatrix} \dot{\Phi} & \dot{\Theta} & \dot{\Psi} \end{bmatrix}^T$ or body axis components $\begin{bmatrix} p & q & r \end{bmatrix}^T$.

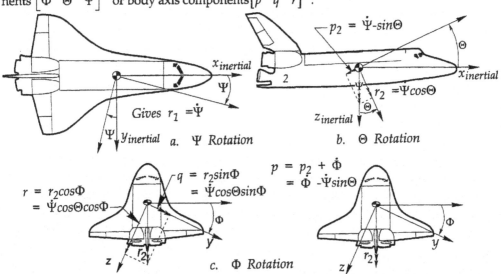

Fig. 6.4 Body Axis and Inertial Angular Velocity Components

6.1.1.4 Angular Velocity Transformations. Figure 6.4 depicts projections of $\dot{\Psi}$ on each of the body axis coordinate directions. First, $\dot{\Psi}$ is a rotation about the positive z-axis. If there is no pitch or roll rotation, $r_1 = \dot{\Psi}$. If the aircraft is then pitched nose up, as shown in Fig. 6.4b, $r_2 = \dot{\Psi} \cos \Theta$. If the airplane is banked through an angle Φ, $r = \dot{\Psi} \cos \Theta \cos \Phi$. Similarly, after three rotations, $p = -\dot{\Psi} \sin \Theta$ and $q = \dot{\Psi} \cos \Theta \sin \Phi$. Next, resolving $\dot{\Theta}$. in the same way, $q = \dot{\Theta} \cos \Phi$ and $r = -\dot{\Theta} \sin \Phi$. Resolving the roll rate ($\dot{\Phi}$) into body axis components, $p = \dot{\Phi}$. Collecting the individual vector components, and writing the resulting linear equations in matrix form:

$$\omega = \begin{Bmatrix} p \\ q \\ r \end{Bmatrix} = \begin{bmatrix} 1 & 0 & -\sin\Theta \\ 0 & \cos\Phi & \cos\Theta\sin\Phi \\ 0 & -\sin\Phi & \cos\Theta\cos\Phi \end{bmatrix} \begin{Bmatrix} \dot{\Phi} \\ \dot{\Theta} \\ \dot{\Psi} \end{Bmatrix} \tag{6.3}$$

Inverting the matrix to solve for the Euler angular velocities:

$$\omega = \begin{Bmatrix} \dot{\Phi} \\ \dot{\Theta} \\ \dot{\Psi} \end{Bmatrix} = \begin{bmatrix} 1 & \sin\Theta\tan\Phi & \tan\Theta\cos\Phi \\ 0 & \cos\Phi & -\sin\Theta \\ 0 & \sec\Theta\sin\Phi & \sec\Theta\cos\Phi \end{bmatrix} \begin{Bmatrix} p \\ q \\ r \end{Bmatrix} \tag{6.4}$$

6.1.1.5 **Reversible and Irreversible Control Systems**. Mechanical attributes of the control system strongly influence pilots' perceptions of handling qualities and stability. Reversible controls are those for which the pilot biomechanically provides the hinge moment required to deflect the aerodynamic control surfaces. Those forces are typically transmitted from the cockpit to the surface via cables, or push-rods. These systems are "reversible" because the forces travel bi-directionally, and the deflection of the stick or yoke is typically proportional to surface deflection. Irreversible controls are those for which the surface hinge moments are provided by some other source (typically hydraulic). Fly-by-wire systems are also irreversible, but so are those fully mechanical systems which employ hydraulic actuators to deflect the aerodynamic surfaces. Pilot stick forces are artificially provided by springs, bob-weights and dampers, and the stick/yoke deflection may or may not be proportional to the surface deflection. In either case, the flight test engineer must thoroughly understand the control system and its components.

6.1.2 Straight Flight Paths

Logically, the next terms to define are those used to quantitatively specify static longitudinal stability. From a flight test point of view, the discussion always starts with an engineering concept and proceeds to the pragmatism of the pilot's perception of static longitudinal stability.

6.1.2.1 **Neutral Point Concepts**. The stick-fixed and stick-free neutral points are terms used to relate center of gravity (cg) location to the level of stability for a configuration. Quantitative equations for both neutral points will be developed later, but to fix the concept, consider the following definition.

> The **stick-fixed neutral point** is that cg position for which the pitching moment is independent of α with the longitudinal control surfaces held stationary.

Much of the flight test literature[1,5,6] defines neutral point using C_L as the independent variable. As suggested earlier, neutral points defined in this way and associated with zero values of $\dfrac{dC_m}{dC_L}$ are not always directly related to stability with respect to angle of attack disturbances. Both C_m and C_L are functions of Mach number, Reynolds number, thrust coefficient, and dynamic pressure. Even with the longitudinal control surface and the cg position held fixed, both the derivatives of interest depend on the parameters listed in addition to α. Consequently, setting $\dfrac{dC_m}{dC_L} = 0$ to obtain the neutral point is only valid if the other variations are unimportant for disturbances in angle of attack. For low speed airplanes this assumption is valid. The neutral point is that cg position for which $C_{m_\alpha} = 0$, with the partial derivative implying that only variations in α are considered.

The floating characteristics of the longitudinal control surfaces also affect the stick-free neutral point definition. (Of course, "stick-free" conditions may be ignored for irreversible control systems since the control surfaces do not float with aerodynamic loads.)

> The stick-free neutral point is that cg position for which C_m is independent of α with the longitudinal control surfaces unrestrained.

Comparing these definitions to the aerodynamic center, the neutral point is conceptually equivalent to the aerodynamic center of the entire airplane. Recall that the total pitching moment coefficient for the airplane can be written as:

$$C_m = C_{m_0} + C_{m_\alpha}\alpha$$

where $C_{m_0} \equiv$ pitching moment coefficient about the cg with zero lift. C_{m_0} can also be written as:

$$C_{m_0} = C_{m_{0_{wb}}} + V_H C_{L_{\alpha_t}}\left(i_t + \varepsilon_0\right)$$

where $C_{m_{0_{wb}}} \equiv$ pitching moment coefficient for the wing-body combination (no horizontal tail) at zero wing-body lift

$\qquad V_H \quad \equiv$ horizontal tail volume coefficient, $\dfrac{S_t \ell_t}{S\overline{c}}$

$\qquad C_{L_{\alpha_t}} \quad \equiv$ tail lift curve slope $\dfrac{\partial C_L}{\partial \alpha_t}$ evaluated at trim conditions

$\qquad i_t \quad \equiv$ tail-setting or incidence angle

$\qquad \varepsilon_0 \quad \equiv$ downwash angle when wing-body lift is 0

Etkin has shown that

$$C_m = C_{m_{0_{wb}}} + C_{L_{\alpha_{wb}}}\alpha_{wb}\left[\left(\frac{x_{cg}}{\overline{c}} - \frac{x_{ac_{wb}}}{\overline{c}}\right) - V_H \frac{C_{L_{\alpha_t}}}{C_{L_{\alpha_{wb}}}}\left(1 - \frac{\partial \varepsilon}{\partial \alpha}\right)\right] + C_{L_{\alpha_t}}\left(i_t + \varepsilon_0\right)$$

where $\quad x_{cg} \quad \equiv$ cg position

$\qquad\qquad \overline{c} \quad \equiv$ mean aerodynamic chord

$\qquad\qquad x_{ac_{wb}} \equiv$ aerodynamic center or neutral point of the wing-body alone

Differentiating with respect to α (while also assuming $\alpha \approx \alpha_{wb}$)

$$C_{m\alpha} = C_{L_{\alpha_{wb}}}\left[\left(\frac{x_{cg}}{\overline{c}} - \frac{x_{ac_{wb}}}{\overline{c}}\right) - V_H \frac{C_{L_{\alpha_t}}}{C_{L_{\alpha_{wb}}}}\left(1 - \frac{\partial \varepsilon}{\partial \alpha}\right)\right]$$

Setting $C_{m_\alpha} = 0$ and solving for x_{cg} gives the stick-fixed neutral point:

$$\boxed{\frac{x_{np}}{\overline{c}} = \frac{x_{ac_{wb}}}{\overline{c}} + V_{H_n}\frac{C_{L_{\alpha_t}}}{C_{L_{\alpha_{wb}}}}\left(1 - \frac{\partial \varepsilon}{\partial \alpha}\right)} \qquad\qquad (6.5)$$

where V_{H_n} = value of V_H for the cg located at x_{np}. The difference $\dfrac{x_{np}}{\overline{c}} - \dfrac{x_{cg}}{\overline{c}}$ is called the

stick-fixed static margin and expresses the strength of the static stability.

$$\boxed{C_{m_\alpha} = C_{L_\alpha}\left(\frac{x_{cg}}{\overline{c}} - \frac{x_{np}}{\overline{c}}\right) = C_{L_\alpha}\left(-Static\ Margin\right)} \qquad\qquad (6.6)$$

6.1.2.2 **Elevator Trim Angle**. Pilots sense static longitudinal stability of an airplane principally through control forces and secondarily through the elevator movement per unit change in angle of attack. Said another way, the magnitude of stick or yoke input required to trim the airplane is the pilot's indication of stick-fixed static margin. Consider how longitudinal control surface deflections affect the pitching moment curves, as sketched in Fig. 6.5. For each elevator setting, trim (equilibrium) is achieved at only one angle of attack. For example, with $\delta_e = 0$, the trim angle of attack occurs at point A. Increments of lift and pitching moment are usually assumed to vary linearly with small changes in α; the C_m-α curves depicted are not strictly straight lines. The pertinent relationships include: $\Delta C_L = C_{L\delta_e}\delta_e$, with $C_{L\delta_e} > 0$ for the standard sign convention (Fig. 6.1a) and $\Delta C_m = C_{m\delta_e}\delta_e$, with $C_{m\delta_e} < 0$, using the same sign convention. Then, we assume linearity in both $C_L = C_{L\alpha}\alpha + C_{L\delta_e}\delta_e$ and $C_m = C_{m0} + C_{m\alpha}\alpha + C_{m\delta_e}\delta_e$. Setting $C_m = 0$ in this last expression gives the elevator angle for trim,

$$\delta_{e_{trim}} = -\frac{C_{m0} + C_{m\alpha}\alpha_{trim}}{C_{m\delta_e}} \tag{6.7}$$

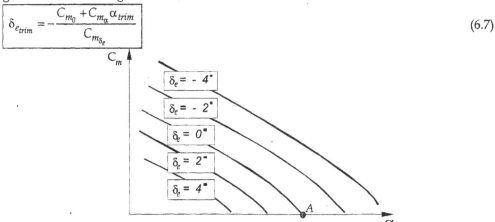

Fig. 6.5 Family of C_m-α Curves for Various δ_e

The trim lift coefficient is: $C_{L_{trim}} = C_{L\alpha}\alpha_{trim} + C_{L\delta_e}\delta_{e_{trim}}$
Eliminating α_{trim} from eqn. 6.7:

$$\delta_{e_{trim}} = \frac{C_{m0}C_{L\alpha} + C_{m\alpha}C_{L_{trim}}}{C_{m\alpha}C_{L\delta_e} - C_{L\alpha}C_{m\delta_e}} \tag{6.8}$$

In eqn. 6.8 we assume that δ_e is measured with respect to a trail position; that is, $\delta_e = 0$ when $\alpha = \alpha_{trim}$. The above expressions are valid approximations for conventional tail-aft airplanes. For tailless aircraft or other unconventional configurations, the equations must be developed assuming that C_{m0} also varies with δ_e.

Equation 6.8 assumes a straight line variation of $\delta_{e_{trim}}$ with angle of attack (Fig. 6.6). This relationship between $\delta_{e_{trim}}$ and cg location (or static margin) suggests a method for determining the stick-fixed neutral point from flight test data. Since the slopes of these curves are functions of cg location, we differentiate equation 6.8 with respect to $C_{L_{trim}}$:

$$\frac{\partial \delta_{e_{trim}}}{\partial C_{L_{trim}}} = -\frac{C_{m\alpha}}{C_{L\alpha}C_{m\delta_e} - C_{m\alpha}C_{L\delta_e}} \tag{6.9}$$

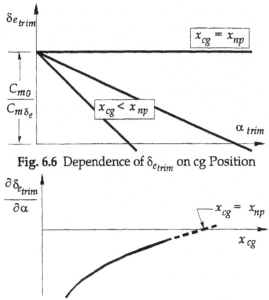

Fig. 6.6 Dependence of $\delta_{e_{trim}}$ on cg Position

Fig. 6.7 Trim-Slope Criterion for Determining the Stick-Fixed Neutral Point

Figure 6.7 illustrates the use of eqn. 6.9 and depicts the "trim-slope" criterion. The derivative is taken with respect to $C_{L_{trim}}$, not α. This change of independent variable means this equation is strictly true only if Mach number effects and speed effects are negligible. Etkin[4] emphasizes this fact and lays out the rationale. Nonetheless, this criterion is often used to estimate the stick-fixed neutral point for low speed airplanes and serves to introduce flight test measurement of the neutral point.

6.1.2.3 **Elevator-Free Considerations**. In section 6.1.2.1 the stick-free neutral point was introduced. We now describe *stick-free* static longitudinal stability. Even with a perfect rigid body airframe, a manual control system allows some freedom of movement for the control surfaces. Cable stretch and pilot inputs alone dictate at least some movement for a reversible system. An irreversible control system closely approximates the stick-fixed assumption. But a manual control system forces the flight test engineer to understand the effects of aerodynamic hinge moments on longitudinal stability. Generally, configurations are less stable when the control surfaces are free to rotate under the influence of these hinge moments. The hinge moments are the result of the force distribution on the control surface. Since friction is always present in a control system, the actual stability perceived by the pilot lies someplace between the two extremes of the stick-fixed (irreversible control systems) and the stick-free (reversible control systems) cases.

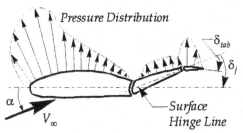

Fig. 6.8 Control Surface Floating Angle

Consider the force distribution illustrated in Fig. 6.8. The surface hinge moment can be written as a linearized function of the local angle of attack at the surface (α_j), the control surface deflection angle (δ_j), the tab setting (δ_{tab}), and a term describing the mass balance of the surface. (The subscript j is generic; it can indicate any control surface attached to the trailing edge of a lifting panel -- elevator, aileron, or rudder.)

$$C_{h_j} = C_{h_0} + C_{h_{\alpha_j}} \alpha_j + C_{h_{\delta_j}} \delta_j + C_{h_{\delta_{tab}}} \delta_{tab} + \frac{W_j x_j}{\bar{q} S \bar{c}} \tag{6.10}$$

where $W_j \equiv$ weight of the j th surface (j can stand for e, a, or r, depending on which control surface is being considered)

$\quad\quad x_j \equiv$ cg position of the jth surface relative to the hinge line (If the surface is perfectly mass balanced, $x_j = 0$.)

$\quad\quad \bar{q} \equiv$ freestream dynamic pressure (to distinguish it from pitch rate)

$\quad\quad C_{h_0} \equiv$ hinge moment coefficient at $\alpha_j = \delta_j = 0$

$\quad\quad C_{h_\alpha} \equiv$ rate of change of hinge moment coefficient with local angle of attack,

$\quad\quad\quad$ evaluated at trim conditions $\left(\dfrac{\partial C_h}{\partial \alpha_j}\right)_{trim}$

$\quad\quad C_{h_{\delta_j}} \equiv$ rate of change of hinge moment coefficient with surface deflection,

$\quad\quad\quad$ evaluated at trim conditions $\left(\dfrac{\partial C_h}{\partial \delta_j}\right)_{trim}$

$\quad\quad C_{h_{\delta_{tab}}} \equiv$ rate of change of hinge moment coefficient with trim tab deflection,

$\quad\quad\quad$ evaluated at trim conditions $\left(\dfrac{\partial C_h}{\partial \delta_{tab}}\right)_{trim}$

The leading term in equation 6.10, C_{h_0}, depends upon several geometric factors like airfoil shape, nose bluntness, and gap seal effectiveness. Oversimplifying for the sake of clarity, we assume a symmetrical airfoil, a surface with perfect mass balance, and a fixed trim tab. Then, with the surface floating freely so $C_h = 0$, equation 6.10 simplifies to:

$$C_{h_{\alpha_j}} \alpha_j + C_{h_{\delta_j}} \delta_j = 0 \text{ or, } \delta_{j_{free}} = -\frac{C_{h_{\alpha_j}} \alpha_j}{C_{h_{\delta_j}}} \tag{6.11}$$

Both $C_{h_{\alpha_j}}$ and $C_{h_{\delta_j}}$ are usually negative, although $C_{h_{\alpha_j}}$ may be positive when a large horn balance is designed into the surface or when the hinge line is set far back from the surface's leading edge. Usually both $C_{h_{\alpha_j}}$ and $C_{h_{\delta_j}}$ are negative, so a positive local angle of attack at the surface produces:

$$C_{L_j} = C_{L_{\alpha_j}} \alpha_j + a_j \delta_{j_{free}} = C_{L_{\alpha_j}} \alpha_j \left(1 - \frac{C_{h_{\alpha_j}} a_j}{C_{h_{\delta_j}} C_{L_{\alpha_j}}}\right), \text{ where } a_j = \left(\frac{\partial C_{L_j}}{\partial \delta_j}\right)_{trim} \text{ and } C_{L_{\delta_j}} = a_j \frac{S_t}{S}$$

If we now focus on the longitudinal axis and define the free elevator factor as:

$$F \equiv 1 - \frac{C_{h_{\alpha_e}} a_e}{C_{h_{\delta_e}} C_{L_{\alpha_t}}}, \text{ where } a_e = \left(\frac{\partial C_{L_t}}{\partial \delta_e}\right)_{trim} \text{ and } C_{L_{\delta e}} = a_e \frac{S_t}{S}, \text{ the coefficient of lift developed}$$

by the horizontal tail is:

$$C_{L_t} = F C_{L_{\alpha_t}} \alpha_t \tag{6.12}$$

If $F < 1$, a freely floating surface is less effective than a fixed one. Of course, if $F > 1$ (as when $C_{h_{\alpha_j}}$ is positive), then the free surface produces more lift than the fixed one. Denoting stability coefficients with primes when the elevator is free to float under the influence of the hinge moment, the aircraft lift coefficient is:

$$C_L' = C_{L_\alpha}'\alpha', \text{ where } C_{L_\alpha} = C_{L_{\alpha wb}}\left[1 + F\frac{C_{L_{\alpha t}}}{C_{L_{\alpha wb}}}\frac{S_t}{S}\left(1 - \frac{\partial \varepsilon}{\partial \alpha}\right)\right] \text{ and } \alpha' = \alpha_{wb} - F\frac{S_t}{S}(\varepsilon_0 + i_t).$$

The aircraft pitching moment coefficient with elevator free is: $C_m' = C_{m0}' + C_{m_\alpha}\alpha'$, where

$$C_{m0}' = C_{m0_{wb}} + FC_{L_{\alpha t}}V_{Hn}'(\varepsilon_0 + i_t) \text{ and } C_{m_\alpha}' = C_{L_\alpha}'\left(\frac{x_{cg}}{\bar{c}} - \frac{x_{np}'}{\bar{c}}\right)$$

Solving eqn. 6.5 for the stick-free neutral point,

$$\frac{x_{np}'}{\bar{c}} = \frac{x_{ac_{wb}}}{\bar{c}} + V_H'\frac{C_{L_{\alpha t}}}{C_{L_\alpha}'}\frac{S_t}{S}\left(1 - \frac{\partial \varepsilon}{\partial \alpha}\right) \text{ or } \frac{x_{np}'}{\bar{c}} = \frac{x_{ac_{wb}}}{\bar{c}} + V_{Hn}'\frac{C_{L_{\alpha t}}}{C_{L_{\alpha wb}}}\frac{S_t}{S}\left(1 - \frac{\partial \varepsilon}{\partial \alpha}\right) \quad (6.13)$$

where V_{H_n}' = tail volume coefficient when the cg is at the stick-free neutral point.

V_H' = tail volume coefficient when the cg is at the wing-body aerodynamic center.

If the variation of tail volume coefficient with cg position can be neglected,

$$\frac{x_{np}}{\bar{c}} - \frac{x_{np}'}{\bar{c}} \approx (1-F)V_{Hn}\frac{C_{L_{\alpha t}}}{C_{L_{\alpha wb}}}\frac{S_t}{S}\left(1 - \frac{\partial \varepsilon}{\partial \alpha}\right) \quad (6.14)$$

Etkin[4] gives exact expressions for the difference between the two types of neutral points, but this approximate expression suffices for our purposes.

Analogous to the trim-slope criterion outlined in section 6.1.2.2, the trim tab angle required to produce various free floating angles gives an estimate of stick-free neutral point.

If δ_{tab} is not zero, equation 6.11 becomes: $\delta_{e_{free}} = -\frac{C_{h_{\alpha t}}\alpha_t + C_{h_{\delta tab}}\delta_{tab}}{C_{h_{\delta e}}}$

Solving for the tab angle necessary to trim and using eqn. 6.7,

$$\delta_{tab_{trim}} = \frac{C_{h_{\delta e}}}{C_{h_{\delta tab}}C_{m_{\delta e}}}\left(C_{m0} + C_{m_\alpha}\alpha - C_{m_{\delta e}}\frac{C_{h_{\alpha t}}}{C_{h_{\delta e}}}\alpha_t\right) \quad (6.15)$$

Substituting $\varepsilon = \varepsilon_0 + \left(\frac{\partial e}{\partial \alpha}\right)_{wb}$ in the expression for α_t,

$$\alpha_t = \alpha\left(1 - \frac{\partial \varepsilon}{\partial \alpha}\right) - (\varepsilon_0 + i_t)\left[1 - \frac{C_{L_{\alpha t}}}{C_{L_\alpha}}\frac{S_t}{S}\left(1 - \frac{\partial \varepsilon}{\partial \alpha}\right)\right] \quad (6.16)$$

Using this expression to eliminate α_t from eqn. 6.15,

$$\delta_{tab_{trim}} = \frac{C_{h_{\delta e}}}{C_{h_{\delta tab}}}\left\{\left[\frac{C_{m_\alpha}}{C_{m_{\delta e}}} - \frac{C_{h_{\alpha t}}}{C_{h_{\delta e}}}\left(1 - \frac{\partial \varepsilon}{\partial \alpha}\right)\right]\alpha + \frac{C_{m0}}{C_{m_{\delta e}}} + (\varepsilon_0 + i_t)\left[1 - \frac{C_{L_{\alpha t}}}{C_{L_\alpha}}\frac{S_t}{S}\left(1 - \frac{\partial \varepsilon}{\partial \alpha}\right)\right]\right\}$$

Differentiating with respect to α and substituting expressions for C_{m_α}, $C_{m_{\delta e}}$, and F:

$$\frac{\partial \delta_{tab_{trim}}}{\partial \alpha} = \frac{C_{h_{\delta e}}}{C_{h_{\delta tab}}}C_{L_\alpha}\left(\frac{x_{cg}}{\bar{c}} - \frac{x_{np}'}{\bar{c}}\right) \quad (6.17)$$

Equation 6.17 is exact only if $V_H = V_{H_n}'$. The parenthetical term resembles the stick-fixed static margin, except it is called the **stick-free static margin**. Equation 6.17 indicates that the slope of the elevator trim tab required to trim versus changes in angle of attack is a measure of stick-free static longitudinal stability. Recalling the difference between V_H and V_{H_n}', and using the approximate difference between the stick-fixed and the stick-free neutral points, eqn. 6.17 quantifies a "tab-slope" criterion for obtaining the stick-free neutral point from measured variations of trim tab with angle of attack (Fig. 6.9).

Fig. 6.9 Tab-Slope Criterion for Stick-Free Neutral Point

6.1.3 Other Concepts of Static Stability

Military specifications[2] do not directly use neutral points to spell out requirements for piloted airplanes. The authors of such standards apparently feel that these concepts are no longer appropriate for high performance aircraft that often operate with relaxed static stability and very complex automatic control systems. It is important that the flight test engineer be prepared for this environment by understanding the terminology.

6.1.3.1 **Speed Stability**. The basic stability criterion set down by the military specification is that of *speed stability*. Paragraph 3.2.1 of the primary document[2] states:

> ...there shall be no tendency for airspeed to diverge aperiodically when the airplane is disturbed from trim with the cockpit controls fixed and with them free. This requirement will be considered satisfied if the variations of pitch control force and pitch control positions are smooth and the local gradients stable...

The specification goes on to say that the speed stability criterion must be met in level flight at constant altitude with no change in throttle setting or trim movements over a range of ± 50 knots or $\pm 15\%$ about the trimmed equivalent airspeed. Figure 6.10 illustrates a stable airplane with respect to stick-fixed speed stability; the elevator trim position to maintain equilibrium meets the requirement.

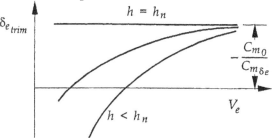

Fig. 6.10 Stick-Fixed Speed Stability

Etkin[4] succinctly relates speed stability to neutral point where compressibility, aeroelasticity, and propulsive effects are negligible, a concept also summarized in Fig. 6.10.

Since $\delta_{e_{trim}}$ is a unique function of C_L with these restrictions and since $C_{L_{trim}} = \dfrac{2W}{\rho_0 V_e^2 S}$, the trim elevator angle is also a unique function of V_{EAS}. As speed increases, $\delta_{e_{trim}}$ increases monotonically for a stable airplane. If $x_{cg} = x_{np}$, the required trim setting is the same for all equivalent airspeeds. Hence, the airplane is neutrally stable, both in the speed sense and under the neutral point concept. However, the speed stability concept is more general in that the trim setting can also be considered a function of propulsive effects, Mach number, and dynamic pressure, as well as angle of attack. Equation 6.8 can be rearranged to give

$$\delta_{e_{trim}} = -\frac{C_{m_0} C_{L_\alpha} + C_{m_\alpha} C_{L_{trim}}}{C_{L_\alpha} C_{m_{\delta_e}} - C_{m_\alpha} C_{L_{\delta_e}}}$$

Since each of these stability coefficients varies with Mach number, then $\delta_{e_{trim}}$ also varies with Mach number. Typical variations with Mach number are shown in Fig. 6.11.

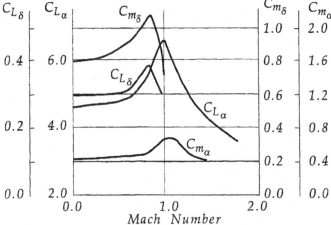

Fig. 6.11 Variation of Longitudinal Stability Coefficients with Mach Number

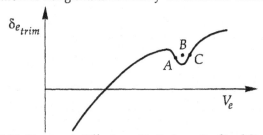

Fig. 6.12 Transonic Effects on Static Longitudinal Stability

In transonic flight Mach number dependence demands modification of the concept of longitudinal speed stability as a measure of static longitudinal stability. MIL-HDBK-1797A relaxes the requirement for an airplane that has a trim curve like that shown in Fig. 6.12. This airplane is not speed stable in the transonic region. Physically, the airplane may start out in equilibrium at point A. If the speed is perturbed to point B by a gust or some other disturbance, $\dfrac{\partial \delta_{e_{trim}}}{\partial M}$ is negative as speed increases, due to the aft shift in the aerodynamic center with increasing Mach number. Thus, the ordinary C_{m_α} criterion for static longitudinal stability loses much its meaning for airplanes operating in the transonic speed regime.

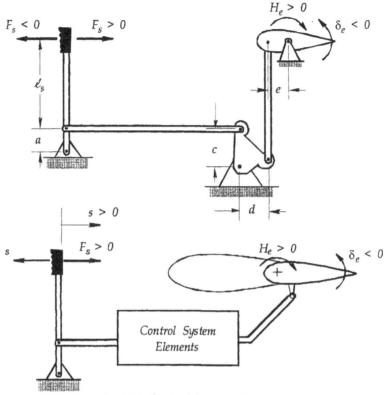

Fig. 6.13 Control System Schematic

6.1.3.2 **Force Gradient for Speed Stability**. Even though most of the airplanes covered by MIL-HDBK-1797A have irreversible flight control systems, the document is more concerned with force the pilot must apply than in the elevator travel itself. At least one proposed revision[7] recommends omitting the constraint on a stable surface displacement, citing the pilot's perception of stability as the more important issue. Consider the control system schematic sketched in Fig. 6.13, noting that a positive stick force is a pull force (in the aft direction). A positive stick force results in a negative elevator deflection, though it produces a positive pitching moment. The gearing ratio (or gain) is a constant relating stick force and hinge moment: $F_s = GH_e$. Applying the principle of virtual work,

$F_s \Delta s + H_e \Delta \delta_e = 0$. Then, $G = -\dfrac{\Delta \delta_e}{\Delta s}$. Writing the stick force in terms of hinge moment coefficient, $F_s = GC_{h_e}S_e c_e \bar{q}$, we assume that V_H = constant and that $C_{h_0} = 0$. Then,

$C_{h_e} = C_{h_{\alpha_e}}\alpha_t + C_{h_{\delta_e}}\delta_{e_{trim}} + C_{h_{\delta_{tab}}}\delta_{tab}$. If $C_{L_{\delta_e}}$ is also small, eqn. 6.8 reduces to:

$$\delta_{e_{trim}} = -\frac{C_{m_0}}{C_{m_{\delta_e}}} - \frac{C_{m_\alpha}C_{L_{trim}}}{C_{L_\alpha}C_{m_{\delta_e}}}$$

Substituting $\delta_{e_{trim}}$ into the hinge moment coefficient expression and eliminating α_t with equation 6.16,

$$C_{h_e} = -\frac{C_{h_{\delta_e}}}{C_{m_{\delta_e}}}\left(\frac{x_{cg}}{\bar{c}} - \frac{x'_{np}}{\bar{c}}\right)C_{L_{trim}} + C_{h_{\delta_{tab}}}\delta_{tab} - C_{h_{\delta_e}}\frac{C_{m_0}}{C_{m_{\delta_e}}} - C_{h_{\alpha_t}}(\varepsilon_0 + i_t)\left[1 - \frac{C_{L_{\alpha_t}}}{C_{L_\alpha}}\frac{S_t}{S}\left(1 - \frac{\partial\varepsilon}{\partial\alpha}\right)\right]$$

For level flight cruising conditions $\left(L = W \quad and \quad C_{L_{trim}} = \frac{W}{\bar{q}S}\right)$, F_s becomes:

$$F_s = A + B\bar{q} \tag{6.18}$$

where

$$A = -GS_e c_e \frac{C_{h_{\delta_e}}}{C_{m_{\delta_e}}}\left(\frac{x_{cg}}{\bar{c}} - \frac{x'_{np}}{\bar{c}}\right)$$

$$B = GS_e c_e C_{h_e} C_{h_{\delta_e}}\left\{\frac{C_{h_{\delta_{tab}}}\delta_{tab}}{C_{h_{\delta_e}}} - \frac{C_{m_0}}{C_{m_{\delta_e}}} - C_{h_{\alpha_t}}(\varepsilon_0 + i_t)\left[1 - \frac{C_{L_{\alpha_t}}}{C_{L_\alpha}}\frac{S_t}{S}\left(1 - \frac{\partial\varepsilon}{\partial\alpha}\right)\right]\right\}$$

Equation 6.18 leads to the following conclusions:

- Stick force is directly proportional to the product of the elevator area and the elevator chord, that is, the size of the elevator.
- Stick force is directly proportional to the gearing ratio.
- Retrimming (altering $\delta_{e_{tab}}$) changes the shape of the parabola as indicated by the dashed lines in Fig. 6.14. Positive $\delta_{e_{tab}}$ reduces the force to be held by the pilot at a given speed.
- The weight affects stick force through the wing loading term $\frac{W}{S}$ such that an increase in wing loading has the same effect as a forward shift in cg.
- Altitude affects only the second term through $\bar{q}$. For a given true airspeed, increasing altitude reduces F_s. Naturally, the second term in the stick force expression varies directly with the square of the true airspeed.
- Shifting the cg location only affects the constant term (A) of equation 6.18. Moving the cg forward translates the curve upward and moving it aft translates the curve downward. Figure 6.14 also illustrates this translation.

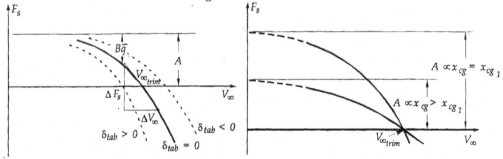

a. Effect of Tab Deflection on Stick Force Gradient   b. Effect of cg Location on Stick Force Gradient

Fig. 6.14 Stick Force Variation with Speed

The slope of the stick force curve is a very important handling qualities parameter. The pilot judges loss of longitudinal stability by the rate of change of stick force with airspeed change. Hoh[7] spells out the recommended maximum allowable size of any unstable gradients in the transonic regime. Equation 6.18 leads to an expression for the stick force gradient. Taking the derivative with respect to V_∞, $\frac{\partial F_s}{\partial V_\infty} = B\rho V_\infty$ or

$$\frac{\partial F_s}{\partial V_\infty} = \rho V_\infty G S_e c_e C_{h_e} C_{h_{\delta_e}} \left\{ \frac{C_{h_{\delta_{tab}}} \delta_{tab}}{C_{h_{\delta_e}}} - \frac{C_{m_0}}{C_{m_{\delta_e}}} - C_{h_{\alpha_t}} (\varepsilon_0 + i_t) \left[1 - \frac{C_{L_{\alpha_t}}}{C_{L_\alpha}} \frac{S_t}{S} \left(1 - \frac{\partial \varepsilon}{\partial \alpha} \right) \right] \right\}$$

At the trim point (where $F_s = 0$), the stick force gradient is:

$$\frac{\partial F_s}{\partial V_\infty} = 2 G S_e c_e \frac{C_{h_{\delta_e}}}{C_{m_{\delta_e}}} \frac{W}{S} \left(\frac{x_{cg}}{\overline{c}} - \frac{x'_{np}}{\overline{c}} \right) = 2 G S_e c_e \frac{C_{h_{\delta_e}}}{C_{m_{\delta_e}}} \frac{W}{S} \left(-SM_{free} \right) \qquad (6.19)$$

6.1.3.3 **Flight-Path Stability**. Paragraph 3.2.1.3 of MIL-HDBK-1797A describes yet another type of longitudinal stability related to "backside-of-the-power-curve" operations:

> **Flight-path stability** is defined in terms of the change in flight-path angle when the airspeed is altered by use of pitch control only (throttle not reset by the pilot).

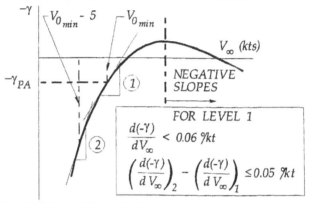

Fig. 6.15 Local Slope Definitions for Flight-Path Stability

This type of stability is especially important for precise control of airspeed, as is essential for carrier approaches or short-field landings. The requirement only applies to airplanes configured for landing. If elevator alone controls airspeed, a pilot-in-the-loop instability can occur at speeds below the minimum drag speed.[7] The requirement is quantified in terms of the local slopes for each level of handling qualities. For level 1 handling qualities, the local slopes must be either negative or less positive than 0.06 °/knot. Figure 6.15 illustrates allowable local slopes. The origin of this requirement is not well understood by many flight test professionals, in part because few are experienced with regularly flying approaches on the back-side of the power curve. Once the airplane is slowed to the back-side of the required power curve, aft stick causes an increase in rate of descent rather than a decrease (the response on the front-side). This reversal in behavior is a physical reality on the back-side. The specification sets an upperbound on the magnitude of the flight path instability. The airplane is allowed to be unstable in flight path, *but not so much so as to result in unpredictable flight path response to stick.*

The specification allows poor flight-path stability to be mitigated by a secondary flight path controller incorporated into the design, such as power or direct lift control. Short takeoff and landing (STOL) aircraft often utilize this means of compensating for poor flight-path stability since their landing approaches are frequently made at speeds well below the minimum drag speed. Naturally, the secondary flight path controller itself must have satisfactory response characteristics if it is to provide acceptable closed-loop (pilot-closure) handling qualities.

6.2 LONGITUDINAL STATIC STABILITY TEST METHODS

Flight test techniques to measure longitudinal stability data are relatively simple and straightforward, although very careful trimming and flying is required. To obtain reliable quantified data, it is practically imperative that the instrumentation include some form of automatic recording and the sensors used are almost always some kind of electronic device. The net effect of both these factors is that stability and control data are harder to obtain than are performance data. The so-called stabilized method and the slow acceleration-deceleration method are the techniques most often used to gather information about the speed stability or neutral points. These methods will be discussed first, followed by a brief discussion of the way that flight path stability tests are conducted. However, before the data procedures are detailed, it is necessary to examine two factors that govern the quality of the data collected whatever the method used.

6.2.1 Stability and Control Flight Test Measurements

Stability and control testing is an exacting process. As suggested previously, virtually all interesting parameters must be measured indirectly and the control surfaces and control tabs are the most common measurements used to back out the desired information. Forces are often measured directly and they are variables of primary interest, but even so, the data must be further manipulated to obtain engineering terms of interest like neutral points and force gradients. For these reasons, data must be taken with as much precision as possible and it is particularly important that flight test engineers understand the uncertainties introduced by the mechanical parts of the control system.

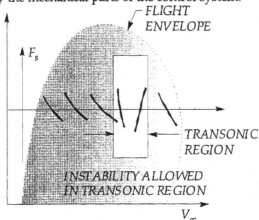

Fig. 6.16 Trim Conditions for a Specified Altitude

6.2.1.1 **Trim**. The first of these uncertainties is introduced because most longitudinal static stability measurements are taken about an equilibrium condition. The requirement quoted in section 6.1.3.1 measures static stability from such a trim condition. Trimming to an absolute equilibrium condition is not trivial, but flight test engineers must insist that the flight crew establish an accurate trim condition. A good rule of thumb is to require the pilot to release all controls for a minimum of ten seconds after trim airspeed is established. If the airplane deviates in either airspeed or altitude, within that period of time, trim should be reset and the check repeated. This process should be repeated until no deviation from the desired conditions can be detected during the specified time interval.

To cover the flight envelope, it is necessary to set up separate trim conditions at convenient airspeed intervals (Fig. 6.16). The increments of airspeed used depend upon data needed and the flight regime. Smaller increments between trim conditions should be used where surface deflection and/or stick force gradients change rapidly. The transonic region is certainly such a region.

6.2.1.2 **Friction and Breakout Forces**. The second uncertainty affecting the precision of stability and control measurements is mechanical friction in the controls. For the pilot to have a feel for the neutral positions of the controls, there is usually an initial force to be overcome in moving the control out of the neutral position. While this kind of force serves a useful purpose in defining the neutral position for the pilot, the control stick will also require some force to overcome the initial resistance to motion at any point in the control throw. This type of force is lumped under the term "breakout force."

> **Breakout force** is defined as that stick force which must be applied to the control system before the control surface begins to move.

It is customary to call the remaining frictional forces simply friction.

> **Friction** is that stick force required to overcome sliding, rolling, or any other form of dynamic frictional forces in the control linkages.

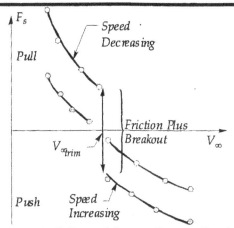

Fig. 6.17 Control System Friction Band

Though friction and breakout have been defined in terms of forces, they both also affect the movement of the pilot's controller. Because of friction and breakout there is no guarantee that resetting the pilot's controller to exactly the same position will set the control surface to the same setting. If either the stick force or the control surface gradients are very small, friction and breakout can introduce large percentage uncertainties into longitudinal stability data. The flight test team must plan and execute the tests in a manner that minimizes these uncertainties to the maximum extent possible. The separation of the two curves resembles the hysteresis loop common in almost any physical system when precise measurements are made (Fig. 6.17). The circles indicate data taken when the pilot moved the controller aft and the squares represent stick movement in the opposite direction. If care had not been taken to keep the controller moving in the same direction at all times, the data points would be scattered between the two curves.

6.2.2 Stabilized Method

One method for obtaining longitudinal static stability is to fly a series of stabilized airspeeds above and below the trim airspeed and measure appropriate control parameters. As in all the techniques, trim conditions must be established carefully and care must be exercised to insure that the stick force, control surface, and control tab measurements are made with the surfaces on one side or the other of the friction band for any points to be joined as a continuous curve. The stabilized method is based on use of the longitudinal control to vary airspeed at constant power setting and most of all at constant trim setting. Once the trim conditions are established and recorded, the longitudinal control alone is used to slow down or speed up to predetermined airspeed points. Altitude is free to vary, but should be controlled within a specified band, usually no more than ±1000 feet from the trim condition. For military requirements, this variation of airspeed about the trim condition should be set to cover a range of ±15% or ±50 KEAS, whichever is less. A good rule of thumb is to plan for at least three points (preferably more) at speeds equally spaced above and below the trim airspeed. As speed is stabilized at each airspeed, care must be exercised to have the stick on one or the other side of the hysteresis loop sketched in Fig. 6.17. Generally, it is easiest for the pilot to accomplish this rather delicate task by attempting to keep the control stick moving forward as speed is increased and aft as the speed is decreased.

Example 6.1: A light twin airplane was tested for static longitudinal stability at two cg locations. The stabilized technique was used, resulting in the data give in the table below.

Stabilized Static Longitudinal Stability Data

x_{cg} = 2.3 feet aft of datum		x_{cg} = 2.75 feet aft of datum	
C_L	δ_e	C_L	δ_e
0.25	-0.5	0.7	0.36
0.61	-2.3	0.6	0.64
0.81	-3.4	0.5	1.07
1.03	-4.5	0.4	1.34
	$\bar{c} = 11.0$ feet	$V_H = 0.42$	

Find the stick-fixed static margin when the cg is 1.98 feet aft of the datum and the elevator angle required for trim with $C_L = 0.63$. Calculate $C_{L_{\delta_e}}$ for the horizontal if $C_{m_0} = 0.04$. What is the position of the stick-fixed neutral point? The data from the table on the previous page are plotted on the right.

A least squares curve it of these two lines gives slopes of -5.14889 and -0.29423. Notice that the intercepts of these two lines will never be identical, simply because no measurements are perfect. A simple average is usually a reasonable approximation. Clearly, it would be preferable to have measurements at more than two cg locations. The desir-

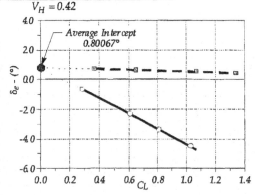

ability of having multiple measurements is illustrated in the plot below of these two straight lines. This plot, using the slopes of the two lines versus x_{cg} (utilizing our assumed linear relationship), illustrates how the neutral point is obtained. Notice that these fictitious data indicate the airplane was flown very near a neutrally stable condition, which is very unlikely! Instead, the flight test engineer usually must extrapolate more than is shown here to find the neutral point. The need for this extrapolation makes it imperative that data be collected for several cg locations, rather than just two.

A straight line is obtained by connecting these two slopes on a plot of elevator angle with change in C_L (could also be elevator angle change with angle of attack) as shown above. Solving this expression when

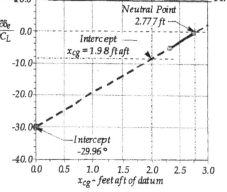

$\dfrac{\partial \delta e}{\partial C_L} = 0$ gives us the neutral point location:

$$\boxed{\dfrac{x_{np}}{\bar{c}} = 0.2525 \quad or \quad x_{np} = 2.777 \text{ feet aft of datum}}$$

For the third cg location, we calculate $\dfrac{\partial \delta e}{\partial C_L} = -8.60109$ from our straight line average of the

intercepts for the tabulated data on the previous page. The average intercept of the two plotted lines is 0.80067, giving

$\delta_e = -8.60109 C_L + 0.80067$ for the given x_{cg}. With $C_L = 0.63$: $\boxed{\delta_e = -7.80° \text{ and } S.M. = 0.0725}$

Stick-fixed static margin is: $\dfrac{x_{np}}{\bar{c}} - \dfrac{x_{cg}}{\bar{c}} = 0.24679 - 0.180$. Recognizing that the intercept in the above calcula-

tion should be a reasonable approximation for $-\dfrac{C_{m_0}}{C_{m_{\delta_e}}}$, we get $C_{m_{\delta_e}} \approx -\dfrac{0.04}{0.80067}$ or $\boxed{C_{m_{\delta_e}} \approx -0.0499}$

6.2.3 Slow Acceleration/Deceleration Method

This test method is perhaps the one most commonly used to collect static longitudinal stability data because it uses test time very efficiently. A large amount of data can be collected in a short time and it is particularly useful for large airspeed envelopes. It is not quite as accurate as the stabilized method, since absolute equilibrium is never attained. Generally though, if the acceleration/deceleration rates are limited to no more than 2 knots/second, the data are adequate for most purposes. An automatic recording scheme is absolutely necessary, preferably one from which the data can be acquired and formatted directly into data files for further reduction on a computer.

As for all stability and control flight tests, the first step in performing a slow acceleration/deceleration is to trim carefully. The importance of this step cannot be overemphasized; the airplane must be trimmed precisely at this equilibrium condition. This point is the only one where a true equilibrium is attained in this method. The pilot or test engineer must activate the data recording system to automatically record the trim conditions.

Leave the data recorder running and mark the point where a smooth acceleration or deceleration is begun. Apply smooth control inputs throughout the acceleration/deceleration. Power (or thrust) for level flight is noted during trimming. Use as small a change as possible from this trim power setting to accomplish the acceleration or deceleration. About 5% change in power usually avoids large changes in pitching moment with power. Longitudinal trim is not changed throughout the maneuver. Continue the acceleration or deceleration to the end of the airspeed range and then reverse the sense of the longitudinal control force. It is important that this reversal occur only at the extremes of the airspeed range; otherwise, hysteresis effects (paragraph 6.2.1.2) inject considerable uncertainty in the data. Continue the acceleration or deceleration to the end of the airspeed range and reverse the force rate of change. The maneuver is completed by returning to the trim condition and recording it. Using an automated data reduction scheme is advantageous because of the large number of data points. Figure 6.18 shows data from a slow acceleration/deceleration after reduction and plotting.

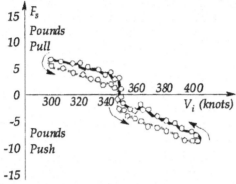

Fig. 6.18 Slow Acceleration/ Deceleration Data

6.2.4 Power Acceleration/Deceleration Method

This technique is identical to the slow acceleration/deceleration method except that larger power changes (idle up to maximum power) are used to accelerate and decelerate and altitude is approximately constant. This procedure can only be used with configurations for which change in pitching moment with power setting is small. Automatic data recording is again essential. Like the previous method, equilibrium is attained only at the initial trim condition and the rate of acceleration or deceleration is constantly changing.

As usual, carefully trim. Smoothly set the throttle, allowing the recorder to run continuously. Mark minimum speed and top speed range. Reset the throttle and reverse the direction of the force change and continue the maneuver to the opposite end of the speed range. Shutting off the recording device while making changes outside the data range and then restarting the recorder is improves efficiency. Care must be taken to avoid reversing control forces, as mentioned before. Upon reaching the end of the speed range, reset the power and reverse the rate of change of stick force until reaching the equilibrium point. Constant pressure altitude should be maintained as nearly as possible by flying a slight climb or descent appropriate for the position error correction of the test airplane.

6.2.5 Flight-Path Stability Method

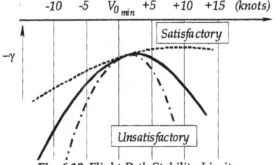

Fig. 6.19 Flight-Path Stability Limits

Flight-path stability tests (applicable to approach configurations only) modify the stabilized method (Fig. 6.19). After setting gear and flaps, the airplane is trimmed in a normal glide path for a power-on approach at $V_{0_{min}}$, the normal final approach speed. Airspeeds for this condition over a range of weights are calculated by the flight test engineer during preflight planning along with anticipated rates of descent for a 3° glide path. Trimming must be precise, even though the configuration and airspeed combination often make trimming difficult. The trim condition should be set at a predetermined nominal altitude. Once the configuration and rate of descent are selected for test weight, the pilot climbs approximately 2000 feet above the nominal altitude and starts the maneuver by setting power to give the desired rate of descent within ±100 fpm. Altitude, airspeed, and rate of descent are recorded as soon as stabilized. The nose of the aircraft is then raised to smoothly reduce the airspeed about 5 knots. Altitude, airspeed, and rate of descent are again recorded with airspeed stabilized 5 knots below $V_{0_{min}}$. Airspeed control within ±1/2 knot is essential for good data. This procedure is repeated for $V_{0_{min}}$ - 10, $V_{0_{min}}$ + 5, and for $V_{0_{min}}$ again. At least four points are required to define the slope at $V_{0_{min}}$ and $V_{0_{min}}$ - 5 knots for MIL-F-8785C. These data must be obtained quickly to minimize altitude loss; more than 4000 feet of change in altitude invalidates the thrust setting. Repeating $V_{0_{min}}$ as the last point provides a reference for correcting hand-recorded data.

Example 6.2: The data in the table below were collected on a standard day to measure the flight path stability of a jet trainer. Does the airplane meet the level 1 criteria of MIL-F-8785C? Carefully plot the curve and show the slopes used to make this determination. $V_{0_{min}}$ = 146 knots (TAS) for the test weight.

Flight Path Stability Example Data

Calibrated Airspeed (knots)	Rate of Descent (fpm)	Pressure Altitude (feet)
130	1000	11,000
126	980	10,700
124	900	10,400
120	800	10,200
136	750	9,550
130	800	9,100

Flight Path Stability Calculated Performance

Calibrated Airspeed (knots)	Pressure Altitude (feet)	Density Ratio	True Airspeed (knots)	Corrected Rate of Descent (fpm)	Flight Path Angle (degrees)
130	11,000	0.7155	153.68	1000.0	-3.6816
126	10,700	0.7224	148.25	1001.2	-3.8610
124	10,400	0.7292	145.21	963.2	-3.7531
120	10,200	0.7338	140.08	884.2	-3.5713
136	9,550	0.7490	157.15	902.6	-3.2494
130	9,100	0.7596	149.16	1000.0	-3.7934

The first step is to find the density ratio for each of the pressure altitudes at which data were hand recorded. Using eqn. 2.7a, we can calculate density ratios for each of the pressure altitudes listed above in the data table. Then, the equivalent airspeed could be calculated using the expression that generated Fig. 2.4 (see page 13). In fact Fig. 2.4 shows clearly that $V_{\infty} \approx V_{cal}$ (or, at least, $\Delta V_{cal} < 1.0$) for the altitudes where the data were taken. The true airspeed becomes $V_{\infty} = \dfrac{V_e}{\sqrt{\sigma}} \approx \dfrac{V_{cal}}{\sqrt{\sigma}}$. This true airspeed estimate allows calculation of the flight path angle from the indicated vertical velocity: $sin\ \gamma = \dfrac{V_{\bar{v}}}{V_{\infty}}$, where both velocities must be in the same units of course. The vertical velocities recorded from the vertical velocity indicator must be corrected for changes in engine thrust over the 1900 feet of altitude spanned in the descents.

That is, $V_{v_{corrected}} \approx V_{vind} + \dfrac{(11,000 - h_{ind})200}{1900}$. Then, the definition of flight path angle (above) is used to calculate the flight path angle for each of the test points. Notice that each of these angles is negative, which is consistent with the typical descent for a normal landing approach. The results of the calculations described above are summarized in the table on the previous page.

Finally, we obtain the curve on the right by plotting the calculated flight path angles versus true airspeed and fitting a second-order curve to the data.

As was discussed in section 6.1.3.2, the slope at point 1 must be less than 0.06 °/knot and the difference between the slopes at points 1 and 2 must be less than or equal to 0.05 °/knot to satisfy Level 1 handling qualities for flight path stability. Using a second-order polynomial curve fit to the data gives:

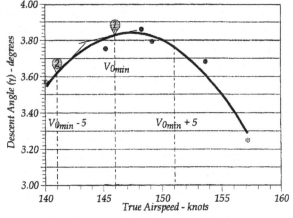

$\gamma = -0.00562286V^2 + 1.65626V - 118.127$. Differentiating with respect to V provides slopes of interest, $\dfrac{d\gamma}{dV} = -0.01124572V + 1.65626$. The slope at the recommended true airspeed for final approach (146 knots) is: 0.014385 °/knot, satisfying the first part of the requirement. The slope at $V_0 - 5$ knots (141 knots) is: 0.076135 °/knot. Subtracting we find the necessary difference in slopes is 0.05623 °/knot, which does not meet the requirement.

6.3 INSTRUMENTATION

Instrumentation for collecting stability and control data are typically found on test aircraft set aside for certification or DT&E by the military. As Lee notes[8], the primary parameters of interest on the longitudinal axis include control force and position (including tab position and/or positions of any automatic retrimming devices), normal load factor, Euler pitch attitude angle, pitch rate, and angle of attack. Time synchronization of these measurements is vital, and is discussed further in conjunction with making dynamic stability measurements in Chapter 9. Individual tank fuel weights, gear and flap positions, and the necessary atmospheric information to correct air data (airspeed, altitude, and dynamic pressure) to standard conditions are also needed. Propulsion systems can profoundly influence static stability. If precise measurements of engine effects on stability are anticipated, engine instrumentation must be available in the time-coded data stream. Most of the static (or near-static) longitudinal stability tests (including those to be discussed in Chapter 7 on longitudinal maneuvering stability) make use of transducers installed for general trajectory reconstruction with the exception of control force transducers and perhaps control surface deflections. These static tests and the attendant measurements should be designed for comparison with computation fluid dynamics (CFD) results, wind tunnel measurements, and basic static parameters (like C_{m_α} and C_{L_α}), along with control effectiveness coefficients (like $C_{m_{\delta e}}$ and $C_{L_{\delta e}}$) for mathematical models. Later, we will notice how these initial verification tests can be extended to system identification techniques that encompass all or at least most of the modeling parameters of interest. Selecting specific transducers, choosing a data recording technique, defining calibration and data quality checks, and assessing the most logical use of signal conditioning are all highly specialized tasks. They are often led by the flight test engineer, but specialists in the analysis of the output and instrumentation engineers knowledgeable in the latest and most efficient, high quality transducers (and associated recording equipment) must be active members of the integrated product and process team (IPPT) that designs, operates, and analyzes the results from this effort. Rarely today does a single individual engineer produce high quality stability and control flight test data; that process almost always entails a team effort.

6.4 SUMMARY

This chapter introduced stability and control flight test techniques used to evaluate the static longitudinal stability of an airplane. The theoretical concepts of stick-fixed and stick-free neutral points were reviewed and this background will be used in succeeding chapters. The importance of the pilot's perception of engineering measurements was emphasized throughout. How elevator control surface deflections and trim tab deflections can be utilized as a measure of stick-fixed and stick-free static longitudinal stability was explained in some detail. Speed stability, defined in MIL-HDBK-1797, was related to the neutral point concept for airplanes not affected by compressibility or Mach number effects. Flight-path stability was introduced as a specialized, but important type of longitudinal stability, to be measured. The importance of trim techniques, friction and breakout forces, and piloting precision for stability and control measurements was emphasized, along with thoughtful use of instrumentation to verify other engineering analysis and testing. Finally, the stabilized, the slow acceleration/deceleration, and the power acceleration/deceleration methods were introduced. With this basic introduction to flight testing for longitudinal stability, the student should be ready to proceed to other tasks.

REFERENCES

1   Perkins, C. D., "Introduction," Chapter 1, Volume II, **AGARD Flight Test Manual**, Pergamon Press, New York, 1959.

2   "Military Standard, Flying Qualities of Piloted Airplanes", MIL-STD-1797A, , Department of Defense, Washington, DC, January 30, 1990 (Notice of Change 1, June 28, 1995; Notice of Change 2, December 19, 1997; Notice of Change 3, August 24, 2004).

3   Electronic Code of Federal Regulations (e-CFR), Part 23, Airworthiness Standards: Normal, Utility, and Acrobatic Category Airplanes, Federal Aviation Administration, Washington, current as of December 23, 2005. (http://ecfr.gpoaccess.gov/)

4   Etkin, B., **Dynamics of Flight-Stability and Control**, (2nd Edition), John Wiley & Sons, New York, 1982.

5   "Stability and Control Flight Test Theory," Vol. I, Chapter 3, AFFTC-TIH-77-1, USAF Test Pilot School, Edwards AFB, California, Revised February 1977.

6   "Fixed Wing Stability and Control: Theory and Flight Test Techniques," USNTPS-FTM-No. 103, Naval Air Test Center, Patuxent River, Maryland, January 1975 (Revised November 1981).

7   Hoh, R. H., et al, "Proposed MIL Standard and Handbook -- Flying Qualities of Air Vehicles," Vol. II: Proposed MIL Handbook, AFWAL-TR-82-3081, Air Force Wright Aeronautical Laboratories, Wright-Patterson AFB, Ohio, November 1982.

8   Lee, R. E., Jr., "Handling Qualities", Chapter 15, Vol. 14, **Introduction to Flight Test Engineering** (Edited by F. N. Stoliker), AGARD Flight Test Techniques Series, AGARDograph 300, 7 Rue Ancelle, 92200 Neuilly-Sur-Seine, France, North Atlantic Treaty Organization, September 1995.

9   Roskam, J., **Airplane Flight Dynamics and Automatic Flight Controls, Part I**, DAR-Corporation, Lawrence, Kansas, 1995, pp. 242-266.

Chapter 7
LONGITUDINAL MANEUVERABILITY TESTS

Chapter 6 discussed longitudinal static stability strictly in terms of unaccelerated, equilibrium conditions. Now we need to consider maneuvering tests in which the flight path is curved by either banking or performing a wings-level pull-up or pushover. In both cases the vehicle's center of gravity is accelerated by a force imbalance. Static longitudinal maneuvering tests are related to turning performance tests, but the objectives techniques are different. Stick-fixed and stick-free maneuver points, which are similar to stick-fixed and stick-free neutral points, are reviewed and flight test techniques for determining maneuvering characteristics are discussed.

7.1 FOUNDATIONS

Longitudinal maneuvering stability is concerned with disturbances in angle of attack and load factor, but not speed. Hence, this chapter concentrates on load factor as the parameter of primary interest. Just as stick-fixed neutral point is set by elevator deflection with airspeed change, stick-fixed maneuvering stability is characterized by elevator deflections with changes in load factor. Similarly, just as stick-free neutral point comes from stick-force variation with airspeed, stick-free maneuvering stability is based on stick-force variation with load factor. These ideas lead to the following figures of merit:

- Elevator angle per g (stick-fixed maneuvering) $\dfrac{\Delta \delta_e}{g}$

- Stick force per g (stick-free maneuvering) $\dfrac{\Delta F_s}{g}$

First, consider one of the simplest cases, a wings-level pull-up.

$$\Delta C_m = C_{m\alpha}\Delta\alpha + C_{m\delta_e}\Delta\delta_e + \frac{\partial C_m}{\partial q}\Delta q \tag{7.1}$$

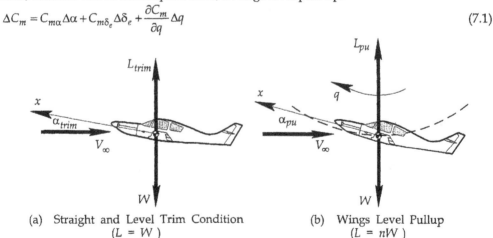

(a) Straight and Level Trim Condition   (b) Wings Level Pullup
$(L = W)$ $(L = nW)$
Fig. 7.1 Differences Between Level, Unaccelerated Flight and a Wings-Level Pull-up

7.1.1   Steady, Wings-Level Pull-up

Consider an airplane that has been trimmed for level flight at a given true airspeed. Assume that it is climbed and then dived without altering the power setting (changing both the altitude and airspeed) and then a pull-up is initiated using the elevator alone. Instantaneously, the airplane will pass through the level flight trimmed (equilibrium) condition during the maneuver and, if precisely flown, this condition can be attained at the original altitude. As suggested in Fig. 7.1, both angle of attack and load factor are greater, resulting in greater lift and a positive pitch rate. These changes in angle of attack and in pitch rate cause a change in pitching moment coefficient compared to the original level flight equilibrium. Hinge moments for the control surface are also affected; that is, both C_m and C_{h_e} are functions of α, δ_e, and q. Notice that q is pitch rate, not dynamic pressure. To avoid confusion, in this book dynamic pressure is denoted by $\bar{q}$.

Considering pitch rate an instantaneous source of centrifugal acceleration (that is, at any instant of time, the flight path can be approximated by a circular arc) and using Newton's second law relates pitch rate to normal load factor and true airspeed as follows:

$$q = \frac{(n-1)g}{V_\infty} \tag{7-2}$$

This pitch rate contributes to the total pitching moment experienced by the airplane by locally increasing the angle of attack at the horizontal tail or the canard. (For simplicity, we will consider only conventional tail-aft configurations.) Figure 7.2 illustrates this local increment in angle of attack at the horizontal tail kinematically produced by the airplane's pitch rate.

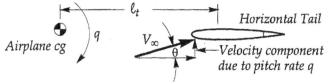

Fig. 7.2 Effective Increase in Horizontal Tail Angle of Attack Due to Pitch Rate

7.1.1.1 Elevator Angle per g. Following Etkin's approach[1] with minor modifications, we derive our first metric. The pitching moment increment due to the pitch rate in curvilinear flight depends on changes in angle of attack, elevator position, and pitch rate. If the total pitching moment coefficient can be considered a linear combination of contributions due to each of these variables (eqn. 7.1) and the increment of C_m due to the pitch rate during a wings-level pull-up gives a negligible angular acceleration (implying a nearly circular path), ΔC_m can be written as:

$$\Delta C_m = C_{m_\alpha}\Delta\alpha + \frac{\partial C_m}{\partial q}\Delta q + C_{m_{\delta_e}}\Delta\delta_e$$

With our assumption of a near circular path, the pitching moment increment due to rotation is 0, just as it is in straight and level flight equilibrium condition. Then,

$$\Delta\delta_e = \frac{C_{m_\alpha}\Delta\alpha + \frac{\partial C_m}{\partial q}\Delta q}{C_{m_{\delta_e}}} \tag{7.3}$$

The increment in angle of attack due to pitch rate is related to the increment in lift coefficient necessary to sustain the maneuver.

$$\Delta C_L = \frac{\Delta L}{\bar{q}S} = \frac{(n-1)W}{\bar{q}S} = (n-1)C_{L_{trim}}$$

where $C_{L_{trim}} \equiv$ the lift coefficient in straight and level flight at a speed and altitude. The change in angle of attack is given by:

$$\Delta\alpha = \frac{\Delta C_L - C_{L_{\delta_e}}\Delta\delta_e}{C_{L_\alpha}}$$

Substituting this expression for $\Delta\alpha$ and eqn. 7.1 for q,

$$\Delta\delta_e = -\frac{\dfrac{C_{m_\alpha}\left(\Delta C_L - C_{L_{\delta_e}}\Delta\delta_e\right)}{C_{L_\alpha}} + \dfrac{\partial C_m}{\partial q}q}{C_{m_{\delta_e}}} = -\frac{\dfrac{C_{m_\alpha}\left[(n-1)C_{L_{trim}} - C_{L_{\delta_e}}\Delta\delta_e\right]}{C_{L_\alpha}} + \dfrac{\partial C_m}{\partial q}\dfrac{(n-1)g}{V_\infty}}{C_{m_{\delta_e}}}$$

which simplifies to:

$$\frac{\Delta\delta_e}{n-1} = -\frac{C_{m_\alpha}C_{L_{trim}} + \dfrac{\partial C_m}{\partial q}\dfrac{(n-1)g}{V_\infty}}{C_{L_\alpha}C_{m_{\delta_e}} - C_{m_\alpha}C_{L_{\delta_e}}} . \quad \text{Using } C_{m_\alpha} = C_{L_\alpha}\left(\frac{x_{cg}}{\overline{c}} - \frac{x_{np}}{\overline{c}}\right), \ C_{m_q} = \frac{\partial C_m}{\partial\left(\dfrac{q\overline{c}}{2V_\infty}\right)} = \frac{\partial C_m}{\partial q}\frac{2V_\infty}{\overline{c}},$$

while recalling that $C_{L_{trim}} = \dfrac{W}{\overline{q}S}$, and defining the relative mass parameter $\mu = \dfrac{2m}{\rho_\infty S\overline{c}}$, the

expression for elevator angle per g becomes:

$$\boxed{\frac{\Delta\delta_e}{n-1} = -\frac{C_{L_\alpha}C_{L_{trim}}\left(\dfrac{x_{cg}}{\overline{c}} - \dfrac{x_{np}}{\overline{c}}\right) + \dfrac{C_{m_q}}{2\mu}}{C_{L_\alpha}C_{m_{\delta_e}} - C_{m_\alpha}C_{L_{\delta_e}}}} \tag{7.4}$$

While it appears that the elevator angle per g is invariant with airspeed, it is not since the trim lift coefficient is inversely proportional to the square of equivalent airspeed.

7.1.1.2 **Stick-Fixed Maneuver Point**. Paralleling our previous definition of stick-fixed neutral point, we now define the **stick-fixed maneuver point** as the airplane center of gravity position for which elevator angle per g vanishes. Mathematically, set eqn. 7.4 to 0 and define x_{mp} as the stick-fixed maneuver point:

$$0 = C_{L_\alpha}C_{L_{trim}}\left(\frac{x_{mp}}{\overline{c}} - \frac{x_{np}}{\overline{c}}\right) + \frac{C_{m_q}}{2\mu}$$

which is solved for $\dfrac{x_{mp}}{\overline{c}}$ to give: $\quad \dfrac{x_{mp}}{\overline{c}} = \dfrac{x_{np}}{\overline{c}} - \dfrac{C_{m_q}}{2\mu}\left(\dfrac{1}{C_{L_\alpha}C_{L_{trim}}}\right) \tag{7.5}$

Of course, $\dfrac{\Delta\delta_e}{n-1}$ can be rewritten with this expression for stick-fixed maneuver point:

$$\frac{\Delta\delta_e}{n-1} = -\frac{C_{L_\alpha}C_{L_{trim}}\left(\dfrac{x_{cg}}{\overline{c}} - \dfrac{x_{mp}}{\overline{c}}\right)}{C_{L_\alpha}C_{m_{\delta_e}} - C_{m_\alpha}C_{L_{\delta_e}}} \tag{7.6}$$

The quantity in parentheses suggests a **stick-fixed maneuver margin** analogous to the stability margin in Chapter 6 as a measure of aircraft maneuvering stability. It is described very much like SM :

$$\boxed{MM \equiv \frac{x_{mp}}{\overline{c}} - \frac{x_{cg}}{\overline{c}}} \tag{7.7}$$

Typically, the stick-fixed maneuver point is about $0.06\overline{c}$ aft of the stick-fixed neutral point for a conventional tail-aft airplane[1]. Considering the definition of the relative mass

parameter $\mu = \dfrac{2m}{\rho_\infty S\overline{c}} = \dfrac{2\left(W/S\right)}{\rho_\infty g\overline{c}}$, $\tag{7.8}$

The relative mass, μ, increases with either altitude or wing loading. Equations 7.5 and 7.8 imply that either of these changes causes the maneuver point to move closer to the neutral point. Consequently, the greatest difference between the stick-fixed neutral point and the stick-fixed maneuver point occurs with large airplanes with a large tail and long tail moment arm, having a low wing loading, and flying at sea level. Said another way, large transport airplanes tend to be more sluggish than fighter airplanes and they are hardest to maneuver at sea level. Figure 7.3 illustrates the relative positions of the two stick-fixed points. Notice also that the elevator angle required to maintain a constant load factor increment in the pull-up does not reverse sign until the cg moves aft of the maneuver point, that is, the airplane can exhibit positive maneuvering stability even though statically unstable. This statement does not take into account the dynamics involved and should not be construed to suggest that one should design for this condition. It does, however, suggest one of the reasons relaxed static stability is attractive for maneuverable airplanes.

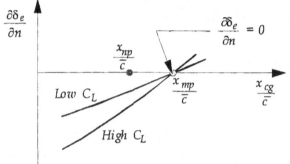

Fig. 7.3 Stick-Fixed Neutral and Maneuver Points

· 7.1.1.3 **Stick Force per g**. In Chapter 6 we learned that stick force is proportional to the elevator hinge moment for a reversible control system. It is natural to infer that the increment of stick force necessary to maintain an increment in load factor in a wings-level pull-up is also proportional to the increment in hinge moment.

$$\Delta F_s = G\bar{q}S_e\bar{c}_e C_{h_e}$$

Still considering conventional tail-aft tail configurations only, the contribution of pitch rate to local angle of attack at the horizontal tail is illustrated in Fig. 7.2. The angle θ is defined by the ratio of the velocity component due to rotation to the velocity component due to translation.

$$\tan \theta = \frac{q\ell_t \cos \alpha_w}{V_\infty} \quad \text{or, for small changes in angle of attack, } \theta \approx \frac{q\ell_t}{V_\infty} \text{ in radians} \tag{7.9}$$

Then the total increment in angle of attack at the horizontal tail is due to both the increment in wing angle of attack required to provide the necessary additional lift and the increment in angle of attack due to pitch rotation at the tail.

$$\Delta\alpha_t = \Delta\alpha_w\left(1 - \frac{\partial\varepsilon}{\partial\alpha}\right) + \theta. \quad \text{However, } \Delta\alpha_w = \frac{\Delta C_L}{C_{L\alpha}}, \ \Delta C_L = \frac{(n-1)W}{\bar{q}S}, \text{ and } q = \frac{(n-1)g}{V_\infty}.$$

Then $\Delta\alpha_t = (n-1)\left[\dfrac{\Delta C_L}{C_{L_\alpha}}\left(1 - \dfrac{\partial\varepsilon}{\partial\alpha}\right) + \dfrac{g\ell_t}{V_\infty^2}\right]$

By assuming that $\Delta\alpha_w = \dfrac{\Delta C_L}{C_{L_\alpha}}$, we neglect any contribution to C_L due to elevator deflection. This assumption is equivalent to taking $C_{L_{\delta_e}} = 0$ for this maneuver. Recalling eqn. 7.4 with this assumption incorporated,

$$\frac{\Delta\delta_e}{n-1} = \frac{C_{L_{trim}}\left(\dfrac{x_{cg}}{\bar{c}} - \dfrac{x_{mp}}{\bar{c}}\right)}{C_{m_{\delta_e}}}$$ and the incremental change in elevator hinge moment is:

$$\Delta C_{h_e} = C_{h_{\alpha_t}}\Delta\alpha_t + C_{h_{\delta_e}}\Delta\delta_e$$

It follows that the change in hinge moment per g is obtained by using the definition of $C_{L_{trim}}$ and the facts that $\dfrac{g}{V_\infty^2} = \dfrac{C_{L_{trim}}\rho_\infty S}{2m}$ and $C_{m_{\delta_e}} = -a_e V_H$ to get

$$\frac{\Delta C_{h_e}}{n-1} = \frac{\Delta C_{h_{\alpha_t}} C_{L_{trim}}\left(1-\dfrac{\partial\varepsilon}{\partial\alpha}\right)}{C_{L_\alpha}} + \frac{C_{h_{\alpha_t}}}{V_\infty^2} - \frac{C_{h_{\delta_e}} C_{L_{trim}}\left(\dfrac{x_{cg}}{\bar{c}} - \dfrac{x_{mp}}{\bar{c}}\right)}{C_{m_{\delta_e}}}$$ or

$$\frac{\Delta C_{h_e}}{n-1} = \frac{C_{h_{\alpha_t}} C_{L_{trim}}}{a_e V_H}\left[\frac{C_{h_{\alpha_t}} a_e V_H}{C_{h_{\delta_e}} C_{L_\alpha}}\left(1-\frac{\partial\varepsilon}{\partial\alpha} + \frac{C_{L_\alpha}\ell_t}{\mu\bar{c}}\right) + \frac{x_{cg}}{\bar{c}} - \frac{x_{mp}}{\bar{c}}\right] \qquad (7.10)$$

Turning our attention to stick-free conditions, we compared the stick-fixed and stick-free neutral points in eqn. 6.14

$$\frac{x_{np}}{\bar{c}} - \frac{x'_{np}}{\bar{c}} = (1-F)V_{H_n}\frac{C_{L_{\alpha_t}}}{C_{L_\alpha}}\left(1-\frac{\partial\varepsilon}{\partial\alpha}\right)$$ where $V_{H_n} \approx V'_{H_n}$

and the free elevator factor is defined as $F \equiv 1 - \dfrac{C_{h_{\alpha_t}} a_e}{C_{L_{\alpha_t}} C_{L_{\delta_e}}}$

Then, $\dfrac{x_{np}}{\bar{c}} - \dfrac{x'_{np}}{\bar{c}} = V_H\dfrac{C_{L_{\alpha_t}}}{C_{L_\alpha}}\left(1-\dfrac{\partial\varepsilon}{\partial\alpha}\right)\dfrac{C_{h_{\alpha_t}} a_e}{C_{L_{\alpha_t}} C_{L_{\delta_e}}}$ and substituting into eqn. 7.10 leads to:

$$\frac{\Delta C_{h_e}}{n-1} = \frac{C_{h_{\delta_e}} C_{L_{trim}}}{a_e V_H}\left[\frac{x_{np}}{\bar{c}} - \frac{x'_{np}}{\bar{c}} + \frac{C_{h_{\alpha_t}} a_e V_H}{C_{h_{\delta_e}} C_{L_\alpha}}\left(\frac{a_e\ell_t}{\mu\bar{c}}\right) + \frac{x_{cg}}{\bar{c}} - \frac{x_{mp}}{\bar{c}}\right] \qquad (7.11)$$

Next, we consider the tail contribution to pitch damping to eliminate the x_{mp} term from eqn. 7.11. This increment in pitching moment is by far the most important contribution to the damping in pitch, usually at least 90% of the total C_{m_q}[1] and is given by:

$$\Delta C_m = -V_H\Delta C_{L_t} = -\frac{V_H C_{L_{\alpha_t}} q\ell_t}{V_\infty}$$ which implies that $\left(\dfrac{\partial C_m}{\partial q}\right)_t = -\dfrac{V_H C_{L_{\alpha_t}}\ell_t}{V_\infty}$ and

$$C_{m_{q_t}} = \left(\frac{2V_\infty}{\bar{c}}\right)\left(\frac{\partial C_m}{\partial q}\right)_t = -\frac{2V_H C_{L_{\alpha_t}}\ell_t}{\bar{c}}$$

Since the tail contribution is such a large part of C_{m_q}, we allow for the wing and body contributions to this damping derivative through K, where K is on the order of 1.1, and write the pitch damping for the complete airplane:

$$C_{m_q} = -\frac{K2V_H C_{L_{\alpha_t}}\ell_t}{\bar{c}} \qquad (7.12)$$

Substituting eqn. 7.12 into eqn. 7.5 and solving: $\dfrac{x_{mp}}{\bar{c}} = \dfrac{x_{np}}{\bar{c}} + \dfrac{K2V_H C_{L_{\alpha_t}} \ell_t}{\mu \bar{c}}$ (7.13)

Returning to equation 7.10, substituting for x_{mp}, and using $\dfrac{C_{h_{\alpha_t}}}{C_{h_{\delta_e}}} = \dfrac{C_{L_{\alpha_t}}}{a_e (F-1)}$,

$$\frac{\Delta C_{h_e}}{n-1} = \frac{C_{h_{\delta_e}} C_{L_{trim}}}{a_e V_H}\left[\frac{x_{cg}}{\bar{c}} - \frac{x'_{np}}{\bar{c}} + (K+F-1)\left(\frac{a_e \ell_t V_H}{\mu \bar{c}}\right)\right]$$ (7.14)

The increment in stick force the pilot applies to generate the wings-level pull-up is related to the required change in hinge moment through the gearing ratio G.
$\Delta F_s = \Delta C_{h_e} G \bar{q} S_e c_e$

Rearranging eqn. 7.12 and substituting ΔC_{h_e} into the expression for stick force

$$\frac{\Delta F_s}{n-1} = G\bar{q}S_e c_e \left(\frac{C_{h_{\delta_e}} C_{L_{trim}}}{a_e V_H}\right)\left[\frac{x_{cg}}{\bar{c}} - \frac{x'_{np}}{\bar{c}} + (K+F-1)\left(\frac{a_e \ell_t V_H}{\mu \bar{c}}\right)\right]$$ (7.15)

This expression is one form of a stick force per g expression. We can simplify by developing the maneuver point concept to include a stick-free case analogous to the neutral point.

Table 7.1 Stick Force per g Limits

	Pilot's Control	Maximum stick force per g (lbs/g)	Minimum stick force per g (lbs/g)
MIL-HDBK-1797A Table XVII, p. 303	Center Stick (Note 1)	$\dfrac{240}{n/\alpha}$, but not more than 28.0 nor less than $\dfrac{56}{n_L -1}$ (Notes 2, 3)	The higher of $\dfrac{21}{n_L -1}$ and 3.0 (Note 2)
MIL-HDBK-1797A Table XVII, p. 303	Yoke or Wheel (Note 1)	$\dfrac{500}{n/\alpha}$, but not more than 120.0 nor less than $\dfrac{120}{n_L -1}$ (Notes 2, 3)	The higher of $\dfrac{35}{n_L -1}$ and 6.0 (Note 2)
FAR 23, §155 (c) AC 23-8B, §51(c)[7] §51(c)CS-23, Book 1, §155(c) and Book 2, §51(c)[9]	Center Stick	Sufficient magnitude to prevent the pilot from inadvertently overstressing the airplane during maneuvering flight	3 lbs/g (local gradient)
FAR 23, §155 (c) AC 23-8B, §51(c)[7] CS-23, Book 1, §155(c) and Book 2, §51(c)[9]	Yoke or Wheel	Sufficient magnitude to prevent the pilot from inadvertently overstressing the airplane during maneuvering flight	4 lbs/g (local gradient)
FAR 25, §143 (f) AC 25-7A, §51(c)[8] CS-25, Book 1, §143(c) and Book 2, §51(c)[10]	Yoke or Wheel	Average stick force per g does not exceed 120 lb/g	No minimum limit specified (Note 4)

Notes 1. The values in this table for military requirements are for Level 1 Flying Qualities only. The source document gives values for Levels 2 and 3 also.
2. The load factor n_L is the symmetrical flight limit load factor for a given Aircraft Normal State, based on structural considerations.
3. The ratio n/α is the steady-state normal acceleration change per unit change in angle of attack for an incremental pitch control deflection at constant speed (airspeed and Mach number).
4. FAR Part 25 and CS-25 do not directly address minimum stick force per g with regard to maneuvering capability (§143), though the do spell out a minimum stick for of 50 pounds to reach

limit strength in steady maneuvers in the absence of deterrent buffet. These two documents (and the associated Advisory Circular for Part 25) provide additional guidance with regard to control forces at high speeds and with mistrim conditions (§255). A plot of stick force versus load factor is suggested as an appropriate way to show compliance with §255. (Figure 7.8 is a plot similar to ones suggested[7,8] in the FAR guidance on data presentation to fulfill these requirements.)

Stick force per g is important in pilot perceptions of handling qualities and both the military specifications[6] and civil certification documents[7,8] set limits on the range of acceptable values (Table 7.1). If this metric is too low, the pilot perceives the airplane as too sensitive in pitch; pitch pointing accuracy is degraded and the airplane may be susceptible to structural overstress. If stick force per g is too high, pilot fatigue is a factor when aggressively maneuvering. The standards also impose requirements on the linearity of stick force per g to ensure predictable longitudinal control forces while maneuvering.

7.1.1.4 **Stick-Free Maneuver Point**. The **stick-free maneuver point** is defined as the airplane center of gravity position for which the stick force per g vanishes. In pilot terms, it is that cg position at which zero stick force is required to pull up at any normal acceleration. Using the definition of $C_{L_{trim}}$ again, eqn. 7.15 reduces to

$$\frac{\Delta F_s}{n-1} = G S_e c_e \left(\frac{W C_{h_{\delta_e}}}{a_e S V_H} \right) \left[\frac{x_{cg}}{\overline{c}} - \frac{x_{np}}{\overline{c}} + (K+F-1) \left(\frac{a_e \ell_t V_H}{\mu \overline{c}} \right) \right]$$

Then, the stick-free maneuver point x'_{mp} comes from

$$\frac{x'_{mp}}{\overline{c}} = \frac{x_{np}}{\overline{c}} + (K+F-1) \left(\frac{a_e \ell_t V_H}{\mu \overline{c}} \right) \qquad (7.16)$$

Equation 7.16 lets us write stick force per g in terms of the stick-free maneuver point:

$$\frac{\Delta F_s}{n-1} = G(W/S) S_e c_e \left(\frac{C_{h_{\delta_e}}}{a_e V_H} \right) \left(\frac{x_{cg}}{\overline{c}} - \frac{x'_{mp}}{\overline{c}} \right) \qquad (7.17)$$

Recognizing that $\dfrac{\Delta F_s}{n-1}$ is an approximate form of stick force per g (strictly speaking, stick force per g is the gradient $\dfrac{\partial F_s}{\partial n}$); thus, in the limit:

$$\frac{\partial F_s}{\partial n} = G(W/S) S_e c_e \left(\frac{C_{h_{\delta_e}}}{a_e V_H} \right) \left(\frac{x_{cg}}{\overline{c}} - \frac{x'_{mp}}{\overline{c}} \right) \qquad (7.18)$$

As we did with the stick-fixed maneuver point, let us close this section with a summary of the physical meaning of these results. First, the preceding analysis is based entirely on a steady state load factor being maintained throughout a wings-level pull-up. The equations shed no light on transient conditions between the initiation of the pull-up and the time that the steady state trajectory is reached. Furthermore, if stick force per g or elevator angle per g is measured in turning flight, the equations must be altered as we will see in the next section. Given these limitations, we note:

◆ Stick force per g varies linearly with cg position and is negative for xcg > xmp'. While stick travel per g also varies linearly with cg location, stick travel per g is related to stick-fixed maneuver point rather than stick-free maneuver point.

◆ Stick force per g varies directly with wing loading and directly as the "volume" ($S\bar{c}$) of the airplane. High wing loading airplanes require more force to move the controls and necessitating an irreversible control system. Large transport or cargo airplanes with large control surfaces also require a mechanical advantage of some type to achieve manageable pilot forces while maneuvering.

◆ Stick force per g is invariant with speed in the absence of Mach number and Reynolds number effects. While the coefficients in eqn. 7.18 depend on Mach number, there are no explicit speed dependent terms.

◆ The relative mass parameter affects the relative distance between the stick-free neutral and maneuver points in just the same ways (altitude, size, and wing loading) as it did the difference between the stick-fixed neutral and maneuver points (see section 7.1.2).

7.1.2 Turns

Consider the forces acting during a constant altitude, constant airspeed turn (Fig. 7.4). The theory developed so far does not properly account for the pitch rate contribution to either elevator angle per g or stick force per g in turning flight. Collecting maneuvering stability data in a turn can be a much less time-consuming process than with wings-level pull-ups. Since flight test time costs money, the flight test engineer must understand the differences in measurements taken with each test method. To types of turns are used to collect maneuvering stability information: (1) steady level turns and (2) windup turns. A steady level turn implies a constant load factor, constant altitude, and constant true airspeed. A windup turn is a dynamic maneuver in which constant load factor is maintained as airspeed is allowed to decrease until some limiting condition is reached. (Note: This definition varies across the test community. Some organizations consider a "wind up turn" to be flown at constant Mach number and increasing load factor, varying bank and altitude to maintain speed.)

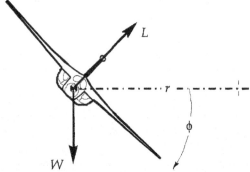

Fig. 7.4. Load Factor in a Turn

Dividing the vertical component of lift by its horizontal component:

$$\frac{L\cos\Phi}{L\sin\Phi} = \frac{gr}{V_\infty^2} \quad \text{or} \quad \frac{V_\infty}{r} = \frac{g\tan\Phi}{V_\infty} = \Omega \quad \text{where } \Omega \text{ is the angular velocity about the local vertical}$$

axis. The components of Ω can be resolved as shown in Fig. 7.4. In a steady level turn, there is a component of Ω about the y body-axis and a component about the z body axis. We are interested primarily in the pitch rate q, the component about the y-axis.

$$q = \Omega \sin \Phi = \frac{g \sin^2 \Phi}{V_\infty \cos \Phi} = \frac{g\left(1 - \cos^2 \Phi\right)}{V_\infty \cos \Phi} = \frac{g}{V_\infty}\left(\frac{1}{\cos \Phi} - \cos \Phi\right) = \frac{g}{V_\infty}\left(n - \frac{1}{n}\right)$$

Taking equilibrium (trim) in a steady level turn at n_0: $q - q_0 = \frac{g}{V_\infty}\left(n - \frac{1}{n}\right) - \frac{g}{V_\infty}\left(n_0 - \frac{1}{n_0}\right)$

Simplifying, $q = \frac{g}{V_\infty}(n - n_0)(1 + nn_0)$. Recalling eqn. 7.3 and modifying it slightly to fit

level turn dynamics, $\Delta \delta_e = -\dfrac{C_{m_\alpha}\Delta\alpha + \dfrac{\partial C_m}{\partial q} q}{C_{m_{\delta_e}}}$, and also modifying the expression for the

incremental angle of attack in a similar fashion for the change in load factor to include

pitch rate in the turn, $\Delta\alpha = \dfrac{(n - n_0)C_{L_{trim}} - C_{L_{\delta_e}}\Delta\delta_e}{C_{L_\alpha}}$

The incremental elevator deflection to maintain the pitch rate in a level turn is:

$$\Delta\delta_e = -\frac{\dfrac{C_{m_\alpha}}{C_{L_\alpha}}\left((n - n_0)C_{L_{trim}} - C_{L_{\delta_e}}\Delta\delta_e\right)\Delta\alpha + \dfrac{\partial C_m}{\partial q}\dfrac{g}{V_\infty}(n - n_0)(1 + nn_0)}{C_{m_{\delta_e}}}$$

Collecting terms not containing $(n - n_0)$ to the left side and solving for $\dfrac{\Delta\delta_e}{n - n_0}$:

$$\frac{\Delta\delta_e}{n - n_0} = \frac{C_{m_\alpha}C_{L_{trim}} + C_{L_\alpha}C_{m_{\delta_e}}\dfrac{\bar{c}g}{2V_\infty^2}(1 + nn_0)}{C_{m_\alpha}C_{L_{\delta_e}} - C_{L_\alpha}C_{m_{\delta_e}}}. \quad \text{Taking the limit as } n \to n_0, \quad \frac{\Delta\delta_e}{n - n_0} \to \frac{\partial\delta_e}{\partial n} \text{ and}$$

inserting μ and $C_{L_{trim}}$, $\dfrac{\partial\delta_e}{\partial n} = \dfrac{C_{m_\alpha}C_{L_{trim}} + C_{L_\alpha}C_{m_q}\dfrac{\bar{c}g\rho_\infty SC_{L_{trim}}}{4W}\left(1 + \dfrac{1}{n^2}\right)}{C_{m_\alpha}C_{L_{\delta_e}} - C_{L_\alpha}C_{m_{\delta_e}}}$. Then, using

$C_{m_\alpha} = C_{L_\alpha}\left(\dfrac{x_{cg}}{\bar{c}} - \dfrac{x_{np}}{\bar{c}}\right)$ to simplify the expression,

$$\frac{\partial\delta_e}{\partial n} = \frac{C_{L_\alpha}C_{L_{trim}}\left[\dfrac{x_{cg}}{\bar{c}} - \dfrac{x_{np}}{\bar{c}} + \dfrac{C_{m_q}\left(1 + \dfrac{1}{n^2}\right)}{2\mu}\right]}{C_{m_\alpha}C_{L_{\delta_e}} - C_{L_\alpha}C_{m_{\delta_e}}} \tag{7.19}$$

Setting eqn. 7.19 to zero to solve for the stick-fixed maneuver point gives

$$\frac{x_{mp}}{\bar{c}} = \left[\frac{x_{np}}{\bar{c}} - \frac{C_{m_q}\left(1 + \dfrac{1}{n^2}\right)}{2\mu}\right] \tag{7.20}$$

Equation 7.20 shows that the difference between measuring maneuver points in a turn and in a wings-level pull-up is a factor of $1+\dfrac{1}{n^2}$. This difference affects each maneuver point with no change in the form for the rest of the equations. As n increases, each pair of measurements is approximately equal. Johnson[3] compares data for the two types of maneuvers (Fig. 7.5). As n becomes large, the slopes of the two curves become nearly identical, consistent with the theory.

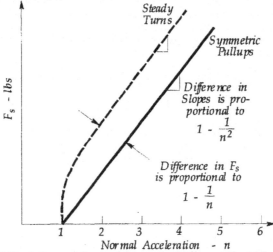

Fig. 7.5 Variation of Control Forces in Different Test Maneuvers

7.2 LONGITUDINAL MANEUVERABILITY TEST METHODS

It is the flight test engineer's responsibility to prepare a matrix of test conditions (airspeeds, airplane configurations, power settings, altitudes, and the like) the test team will use to collect maneuvering flight data. A primary concern is reducing the size of the matrix while still adequately defining the handling characteristics of the airplane. The contractual and the FAR demonstration requirements guide this planning process. Understanding the techniques used to fly each maneuver assists in test planning.

As in all stability and control testing, careful trimming of the airplane to specified speed and altitude is essential for data quality. The pilot is held to very close trim tolerances if precise measurements of angular position and control forces are to be obtained.

7.2.1 Symmetric Pull-up Method

The objective in this maneuver is to establish a steady load factor early in the maneuver and maintain it as the airplane pitches up through the horizontal. The data recorded includes indicated airspeed, altitude, normal acceleration, elevator position, and applied stick force. Automatic recording is almost essential because the pilot achieve the nominal test conditions (airspeed, altitude, and constant acceleration) with the longitudinal reference axis as nearly horizontal as possible. Figure 7.6 illustrates good and bad data runs for a wings-level pull-up.

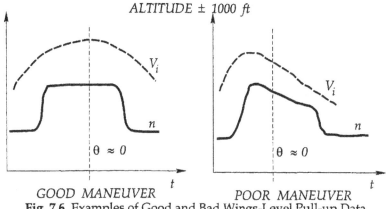

Fig. 7.6 Examples of Good and Bad Wings-Level Pull-up Data

This test method is very time-consuming and the piloting technique requires practice, skill at estimating speed decay, and aggressive maneuvering to arrive at the required test conditions without delay. After trimming the airplane in level flight at the desired conditions and recording these trim conditions on the data record, a climb is made to start the maneuver 200 to 500 feet above the test altitude at some airspeed slower than the trim airspeed. Power is set and a dive angle selected that will accelerate the airplane back to the trim airspeed just before reaching the trim altitude. Ideally the pull-up would be initiated and the normal acceleration established so that the target load factor, airspeed, and altitude all occur just as the nose passes through horizon. The g onset should be smooth and rapid with no overshoot and the load factor should remain constant until the control input is released. A common error is allowing load factor to decrease as the airspeed decays (Fig. 7.6). An ideal data trace may take several practice runs to find the correct starting airspeed, altitude, and dive angle combination. It is helpful to have a real-time data display with at least normal acceleration and indicated airspeed so data points that need to be repeated can be identified before changing trim conditions. In judging quality of a data point, the following conditions are important:

◆ Load factor must be constant (zero slope) at the instant data are read.
◆ Stick forces must be constant.
◆ Trim must be set carefully and recorded to insure that equilibrium stick forces are measured precisely.

The wings-level pull-up is an accurate, though inefficient, method for collecting longitudinal maneuvering stability data. Next, we consider alternative test methods.

7.2.2 **Steady Turn**

7.2.2.1 **Stabilized Load Factor**. A careful trim shot is also vital for this technique. Once trimmed, climb to about 2000 feet above the test altitude and then maintain a fixed angle for the selected load factor, while precisely controlling airspeed. Speed is maintained by carefully adjusting pitch attitude and climbing or descending as necessary. Both airspeed and load factor must be maintained precisely. (Typical limits for acceptable variations during the maneuver are ±1 knot and ±0.1g for bank angles up to 30° and ±2 knots and ±0.1g up to about 60°.) Such precise flying makes sensitive accelerometers and sensitive airspeed indicators mandatory in the cockpit. All data are collected within a maximum band of ±2000 feet from the trim altitude.

When a bank angle of 60° is reached, the usual technique is to maintain a constant bank angle while stepping up through the load factor range in 0.5g increments. Airspeed is again maintained constant by adjusting pitch attitude. Stabilizing at each increasing load factor increment is progressively more difficult because load factor grows exponentially with bank angle. So, this technique is largely applicable for configurations with the limit load factor approximately 2. Transport/cargo airplanes and other airplanes in the power approach configuration allow the use of the stabilized-g, steady turn.

7.2.2.2 **Slowly Varying Load Factor**. This variation of the steady turn is most appropriate for highly maneuverable airplanes with limit load factors greater than 4 and permits a more economical data collection at the high load factors. It is often combined with the stabilized-g method. A careful trim shot is again recorded at the nominal test altitude and airspeed. A band of ±2000 feet is again typical. The airplane is slowly rolled into a continuously increasing bank while load factor is simultaneously increased. The rate of onset of g is held at 0.1g/second or less and indicated airspeed is maintained as closely as possible (±1 knot is desired). Care must be exercised to avoid reversing the stick forces during this dynamic maneuver; otherwise, the friction and breakout force dead band make it difficult to interpret the data. It is usually necessary to "piece together" data segments: it is rare to obtain the complete range of load factors without descending outside the ±2000 feet allowed. Using the stabilized-g method up to about 60° bank angle and then switching to the slowly varying g method is the most common way to collect maneuvering flight test data for fighter and trainer airplanes. (Again, vocabulary varies between organizations, some calling this technique a "Windup Turn".)

7.2.3 Windup Turn

This method is sometimes called the constant-g method since the primary goal of the pilot is to maintain a constant load factor. The trim conditions are chosen close to the maximum speed for the test. Since the maneuver is certainly a dynamic flight condition, it is not necessary to trim exactly on target airspeed. However, the trim state should be recorded before starting the maneuver, with stable equilibrium held for at least 10 seconds with hands off.

After the trim condition is recorded the airplane is placed in a turn at a constant load factor and the data recorder is started. Pitch attitude is adjusted to climb or dive the airplane and maintain a 2 to 5 knots/second deceleration. Typically, a slight climb will be required to maintain this airspeed decay rate at small bank angles and a descent will be needed as the bank angle increases. Data should only be collected within the ±2000 feet specified for maneuvering flight tests. Maintaining the load factor constant (not necessarily exactly at the target load factor) during the maneuver is absolutely essential for repeatable maneuvering flight data. Frequently, it is necessary to discontinue taking data because the altitude tolerance from the trim altitude is exceeded. The pilot should note the airspeed departing the altitude band and the next segment of data should be started at an airspeed slightly above this airspeed once the airplane has been climbed back into the allowable altitude band. This procedure allows the engineer to reduce the data with a check on continuity. Airspeed records should also be marked at the onset of buffet and when the constant load factor can no longer be maintained (the "g-break"). Windup turns can then be repeated at the same trim conditions for increasing increments of load factor. Typically, 0.5g increments are used at higher altitudes and about 1g increments are used at low altitudes. The exact load factor values are not important; it is more important to maintain a constant load factor throughout any given windup turn and to cover the entire range of allowable load factors. As in all flight testing, care must be taken to avoid exceeding established limits, especially when the flight envelope is being explored for the first time. Maneuvering flight tests, especially windup turns, are particularly susceptible to inadvertently overstressing the vehicle. Figures 7.7 and 7.9 illustrate maneuvering flight data for typical military demonstrations[2] and Fig. 7.8 shows windup turn data illustrating how FAR certification data[7] are presented.

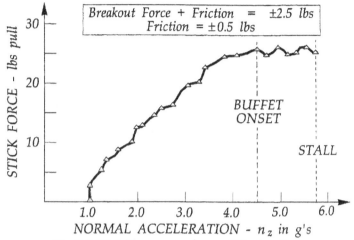

Fig. 7.7 Stick Force per g from a Windup Turn

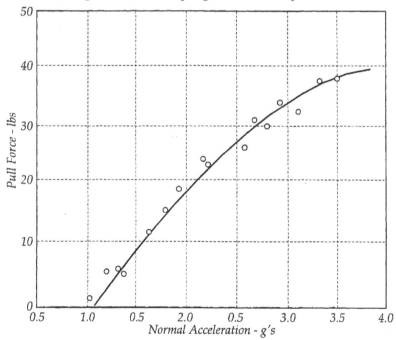

Fig. 7.8 Stick Force per g for FAR Demonstration
(Adapted from AC 23-8B, Figure 51-1[7])

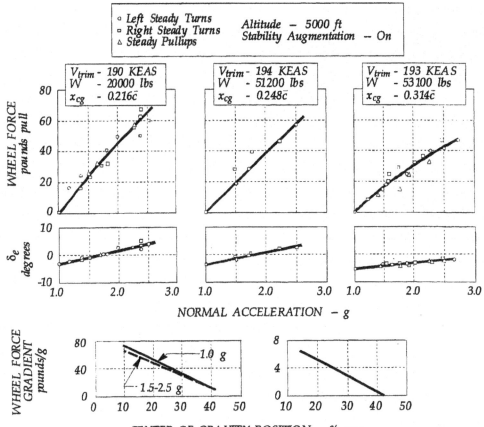

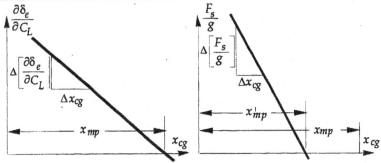

Fig. 7.9 Longitudinal Maneuvering Flight Test Data

7.2.4 Estimation of Control and Hinge Moment Derivatives

Fig. 7.10 Control Surface Gradients

Johnson[3] suggests that maneuvering flight data provides good estimates of $C_{L_{\delta_e}}$, $C_{h_{\delta_e}}$, and $C_{h_{\alpha_t}}$. First, plot the pertinent gradients versus the center of gravity in feet (Fig. 7.10). Elevator effectiveness can then be approximated using the inverse slope of the rate of change of elevator angle with lift coefficient versus cg position.

$$C_{L_{\delta_e}} = \frac{\partial x_{cg}}{\partial\left(\dfrac{\partial \delta_e}{\partial C_N}\right)} \frac{S\bar{q}}{S_t \bar{q}_t \ell_t} \tag{7.21}$$

where C_N is the airplane's normal force coefficient defined as $C_N \equiv \dfrac{n_z W}{qS}$

The elevator hinge moment parameter due to elevator deflection comes from

$$C_{h_{\delta_e}} = \frac{\left(\dfrac{\partial\left(\dfrac{F_s}{g}\right)}{\partial x_{cg}}\right)\tau C_{L_{\alpha_t}} S_t \ell_t}{G b_e c_e^2 W} \tag{7.22}$$

where τ is the ratio of elevator lift effectiveness to stabilizer lift effectiveness and G is elevator gearing in radians/ft.

If τ is set equal to 1 and the elevator dimensions are replaced by the corresponding stabilizer dimensions, eqn. 7.22 applies to an all-moving horizontal tail. Also, both eqns. 7.21 and 7.22 apply without modification to data collected in either steady turns or in wings-level pull-ups. Finally, $C_{h_{\alpha_t}}$ can be calculated from

$$C_{h_{\alpha_t}} = \frac{\left(x_{mp} - x'_{mp}\right)C_{h_{\delta_e}}\bar{q}}{C_{L_{\delta_e}}\bar{q}_t S_t \ell_t \left(\dfrac{1-\dfrac{\partial \varepsilon}{\partial \alpha}}{C_{L_\alpha}S} + \dfrac{180}{\pi S}\left(1+\dfrac{1}{n}\right)\right)} \tag{7.23}$$

if the data were collected in a steady turn. If the data were collected instead in wings-level pull-ups, the term $1+\dfrac{1}{n}$ is left out of the denominator.

Example 7.1: The following maneuvering flight data were collected in a Bell P-63 at 5000 feet on a standard day and a nominal gross weight of 7780 pounds. The aircraft was in its normal cruise configuration (gear and flaps up, cowl flaps closed). Estimate the stick force gradients from each set of data (considering each direction of turn as a separate set of data). Use these estimates to find the predict the average stick-free maneuver point for these conditions.

$\frac{x_{cg}}{\bar{c}} = 0.231$			
Left Windup Turn		Right Windup Turn	
F_s	n	F_s	n
2.5	1.3	6.15	1.95
10.0	2.8	17.5	4.25
16.0	4.1	26.0	5.6
23.5	5.4		

$\frac{x_{cg}}{\bar{c}} = 0.262$			
Left Windup Turn		Right Windup Turn	
F_s	n	F_s	n
2.0	1.4	2.5	1.4
3.5	2.25	13.0	4.3
10.0	4.0	17.5	5.5
14.0	5.2	20.5	6.3

$\frac{x_{cg}}{\bar{c}} = 0.274$			
Left Windup Turn		Right Windup Turn	
F_s	n	F_s	n
3.1	2.2	3.0	1.8
3.6	3.7	3.2	3.5
8.0	4.5	9.5	5.3
10.3	6.0	13.0	6.6

$\frac{x_{cg}}{\bar{c}} = 0.304$			
Left Windup Turn		Right Windup Turn	
F_s	n	F_s	n
1.6	1.95	3.0	3.7
2.0	3.0	5.6	5.7
3.0	4.7		
3.6	6.8		

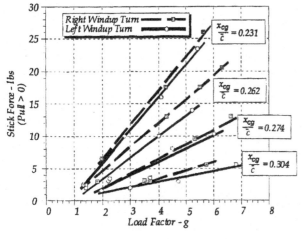

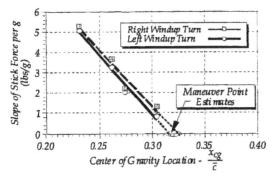

We will estimate the stick-free maneuver point graphically, assuming that all curves are linear (which allows us to use a linear least-squares curve fit to each set of data). Plotting the points shown in the tables above and fitting each set of points with a straight line gives the charts on the next page. Clearly, there is enough data scatter that not all the straight lines have the same intercept (as they theoretically would if the measurements were perfect and if our simplifying assumptions were all absolutely correct). Nonetheless, we can easily extract the slopes of each curve for the given center of gravity locations. Tabulating these slopes and plotting them against cg location, the charts on this page result. As the chart on the lower left shows, the intercepts on the abscissa give estimates of the stick-free maneuver point for each set of turns. Least squares straight-line curve fits give:

$$\frac{\Delta F_s}{\Delta n} = -59.343 \frac{x_{cg}}{\bar{c}} + 18.692$$

for the left turn and

$$\frac{\Delta F_s}{\Delta n} = -56.343 \frac{x_{cg}}{\bar{c}} + 18.205$$

for the right turn. Solving these two equations for the two estimates and averaging, we get:

$$\frac{x_{mp}'}{\bar{c}} = \frac{1}{2}\left(\frac{18.692}{59.343} + \frac{18.205}{56.343}\right) \text{ or } \frac{x_{mp}'}{\bar{c}} \approx \frac{0.315 + 0.323}{2} \text{ and } \qquad \boxed{\frac{x_{mp}'}{\bar{c}} \approx 0.319}$$

Of course, ignoring the difference between the left and right turn data could solve the problem. However, by considering the data as it is naturally grouped the test team is encouraged to explore reasons for the differences in the data. Often this kind of approach leads to better understanding of the underlying physics of the experiment.

7.3 INSTRUMENTATION

Because of the dynamic nature of these tests, automatic recording of measurements is crucial. The minimum instrumentation suggested by Johnson[3] (with details and emphasis added) includes:

- ◆ Normal acceleration must be measured as close to the airplane center of gravity as is feasible, displayed for the pilot, and recorded automatically. As already noted, the pilot's display of load factor must allow him to fly to a resolution of approximately 0.1g if he is to be expected to produce acceptable maneuvering flight test data. A magnetic tape recorder, telemetry, or some other means of high sample rate data collection is a must for obtaining accurate samples of time-varying data like these.

- ◆ Airspeed must be displayed on a sensitive indicator for the pilot, especially for those methods that require constant airspeed. Automatic recording is also essential to alleviate the pilot's workload and to insure precision.

◆ Altitude can be recorded from a standard altimeter, set to 29.92 inches of Hg to provide pressure altitude. It is not always necessary to automatically record altitude, though it often is desirable.

◆ The forces applied by the pilot must be recorded, but no display of them is required. It is desirable to have a near real-time display for the flight test engineer to quickly ascertain data quality. It is much more efficient to immediately repeat a point than to reestablish the test condition later. Quick-look capability pays for itself in short order through savings in test time.

◆ Positions of control surfaces, the pilot's controller (stick, wheel, or hand), and longitudinal trim should also be recorded and displayed. It is possible to omit the last two of these position measurements, but they are highly desirable and data interpretation may be difficult without them..

◆ Angle of attack should be recorded continuously during longitudinal maneuvering. Again, pilot display of angle of attack is not essential but it is desirable. The angle of attack data record helps the engineer reduce the data and compare it to wind tunnel tests or computed predictions.

◆ Accurate accounting for center of gravity movement is imperative. Often, this tracking can be done by hand-recording the fuel counter readings or even fuel gage readings. (Warning: production fuel gages are notoriously inaccurate and should only be used as a last resort.)

◆ The recording device should capture time to synchronize all data channels to the same time base. For digital systems, the flight test engineer must be very careful in comparing continuously varying data that has been sampled at different times. Even small time differences can introduce artificial phase shifts between important variables. This synchronization of the data is particularly important for control surfaces moving at near their maximum rates. Of course, this factor is more important for the dynamic data to be discussed in Chapter 9, but it can also be important in determining stick force per g variation when the inputs are made rapidly.

7.4 SUMMARY

This chapter reviewed the basic principles governing maneuvering flight stability and described concisely how to collect flight test data to measure the necessary stick forces, control surface deflections, pilot input forces, and normal load factor that typically are used as measures of merit for this kind of stability. The feel of the airplane (and therefore the pilot's opinion) depend rather strongly on these maneuverability measurements. We say more about the pilot's subjective opinion in Chapter 9 when dynamic stability measurements are introduced. Typical flight test measurements for maneuverability may be made either using wings-level pull-ups or in a turn. In either case the dynamical system is not truly in static equilibrium, but a pseudo-equilibrium (constant non-zero acceleration is assumed to simplify the techniques). Corrections between wings-level pull-ups or turns are necessary if data taken using the two different maneuvers are compared; corrections are particularly important for maneuvering load factors just slightly in excess of one.

REFERENCES

[1] Etkin, B., **Dynamics of Flight - Stability and Control**, (2nd Edition), John Wiley & Sons, New York, 1982.

[2] "Fixed Wing Stability and Control: Theory and Flight Test Techniques," USNTPS-FTM-No. 103, Naval Air Test Center, Patuxent River, Maryland, January 1975 (Revised November 1981).

[3] Johnson, H. I., "Flight Testing Aircraft for Longitudinal Maneuvering Characteristics," Chapter 4, Volume II, **AGARD Flight Test Manual**, Pergamon Press, New York, 1959.

[4] "Stability and Control Flight Test Theory," Vol. I, Chapter 4, AFFTC-TIH-77-1, USAF Test Pilot School, Edwards AFB, California, Revised February 1977.

[5] "Stability and Control Flight Test Techniques," Vol. II, Chapter 5, AFFTC-TIH-77-1, USAF Test Pilot School, Edwards AFB, California, Revised February 1977.

[6] "Department of Defense Interface Standard, Flying Qualities of Piloted Aircraft," MIL-STD-1797A, Department of Defense, Washington, DC, January 30, 1990 (Notice of Change 1, June 28, 1955; Notice of Change 2, December 19, 1997; Notice of Change 3, August 24, 2004).

[7] "Flight Test Guide for Certification of Part 23 Airplanes," Advisory Circular 23-8B, Federal Aviation Administration, Washington, DC, August 14, 2003.

[8] "Flight Test Guide for Certification of Transport Category Airplanes," Advisory Circular 25-7A, Federal Aviation Administration, Washington, DC, March 31, 1998 (Change 1, June 3, 1999).

[9] "Certification Specifications for Normal, Utility, Aerobatic, and Commuter Category Aeroplanes," CS-23, European Aviation Safety Agency, Brussels, Belgium, November 14, 2003.

[10] "Certification Specifications for Large Aeroplanes," CS-25, Amendment 1, European Aviation Safety Agency, Brussels, Belgium, December 12, 2005.

Chapter 8
STATIC LATERAL-DIRECTIONAL STABILITY TESTS

Lateral-directional static stability cannot be as simply presented as it was for longitudinal motion. First, there are two moment equations and one force equation involved and the moment equations are kinematically coupled through the product of inertia, I_{xz}, as well as aerodynamically. Second, rolling motion has no inherent static stability; that is, no aerodynamic restoring moment is generated directly by a bank angle disturbance. A secondary moment is generated through sideslip; and dihedral effect is a dominant factor. Third, controls used to produce moments about either the lateral or the yaw axis produce moments about the other axis; that is, aileron produces a yawing moment and rudder produces a rolling moment. Even with this inevitable cross-coupling, we can measure static directional stability and dihedral effect and quantify control authorities about the x and z axes with steady state maneuvers. These methods are the subject of this chapter. Chapter 9 will treat the subject of lateral-directional dynamic stability.

8.1 FOUNDATIONS

It is sufficient for our purposes to ignore the side force equation and concentrate on the two moment equations. Using Etkin's notation[1] but simplifying the equations slightly:

$$C_\mathcal{L} = C_{\mathcal{L}\beta}\beta + C_{\mathcal{L}p}p + C_{\mathcal{L}r}r + C_{\mathcal{L}\delta_a}\delta_a + C_{\mathcal{L}\delta_r}\delta_r \qquad (8.1)$$

$$C_n = C_{n\beta}\beta + C_{np}p + C_{nr}r + C_{n\delta_a}\delta_a + C_{n\delta_r}\delta_r \qquad (8.2)$$

Of course, for static conditions, $p = r = 0$, and these equations simplify to:

$$C_\mathcal{L} = C_{\mathcal{L}\beta}\beta + C_{\mathcal{L}\delta_a}\delta_a + C_{\mathcal{L}\delta_r}\delta_r \qquad (8.3)$$

$$C_n = C_{n\beta}\beta + C_{n\delta_a}\delta_a + C_{n\delta_r}\delta_r \qquad (8.4)$$

In eqns. 8.3 and 8.4 $C_{\mathcal{L}\beta}$ and $C_{n\beta}$ are the dominant aerodynamic terms. For static directional stability ("weathercock" stability), $C_{n\beta} > 0$; and for the airplane to have "wing leveling" tendencies, $C_{\mathcal{L}\beta} < 0$. Note that with two equations and three unknowns, the problem is indeterminant, another striking difference from the static longitudinal problem. Longitudinally, a given flight condition (1-g at some altitude, airspeed, and c.g. location) has a unique trim angle of attack and a unique elevator angle. But in the lateral-directional problem there are a number of trim sideslip angles where equilibrium can occur.

8.1.1 Directional Stability and Control

Directional stability depends primarily on $C_{n\beta}$ and the vertical tail is the primary contributor to this derivative. The fuselage, nacelles, and external stores produce an effect secondary to that of the vertical tail. Directional control is exercised primarily through the rudder, but ailerons contribute a significant yawing moment. This control coupling is another reason lateral stability and directional stability are interrelated problems. These two axes cannot be separated for any meaningful stability and control analyses.

8.1.1.1 **Weathercock Stability.** *Weathercock stability* refers to the tendency of a vehicle to turn into the relative wind with sideslip. For directional stability, sideslip must produce an aerodynamic yawing moment that tends to restore zero sideslip (Fig. 8.1). The relevant stability derivative, $C_{n\beta}$, must be positive with the usual sign conventions for sideslip and yawing moment. $C_{n\beta}$ is proportional to the slope of the curve in Fig. 8.2. Although $C_{n\beta}$ is akin to $C_{m\alpha}$ (both are dominant terms for static stability), the wing configuration and the center of gravity position have relatively minor effects on $C_{n\beta}$. For a more complete discussion of the contributions of vertical tail, fuselage and nacelles, and wing, see Etkin[1], Roskam[2], or the notes from one of the Test Pilot Schools[3,4,5].

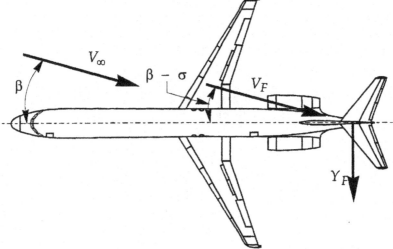

Fig. 8.1 Yawing Moment Produced by Sideslip

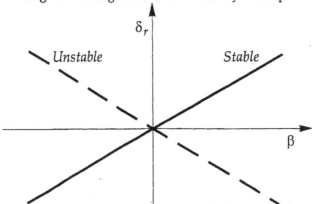

Fig. 8.2 Rudder Deflection versus Sideslip ("Standard" Sign Convention)

8.1.1.2 **Directional Control**. Aircraft and missiles are typically, symmetric vehicles. If a symmetric vehicle has positive directional stability, it tends to fly at zero sideslip. Airplanes are rarely flown with non-zero sideslip for long periods of time. However, when engine failure occurs or when some other asymmetric flow field occurs (like slipstream rotation from a propeller or simply turning flight), sideslip must be controlled. In conventional airplanes the rudder serves this purpose. The stability derivative, $C_{n_{\delta_r}}$, characterizes this control authority is called "rudder power". Rudder deflections maintain constant sideslip whenever asymmetric power is applied, hold steady sideslips, and coordinate turns when aileron deflections produce unwanted sideslip. This derivative is one of those that have different algebraic signs, depending on how positive control surface deflections are defined. The most common approach, the one used in most NASA publications and many textbooks, is not always convenient in flight test. Left rudder, under this convention, leads to a negative yawing moment. Hence, $C_{n_{\delta_r}}$ is negative. The other approach[3], preferred in flight test, makes $C_{n_{\delta_r}}$ positive since positive control deflections are defined as those which produce a positive moment about the axis in question.

The reader is cautioned to take careful note of the method used to assign positive signs to the control deflections in any literature studied.

Steady sideslips are used to measure rudder power. During any steady sideslip the rudder deflection itself is proportional to the ratio of C_{n_β} to $C_{n_{\delta_r}}$, as eqn. 8.3 shows when it is solved for δ_r and the partial derivative with respect to β is taken.

$$\frac{\partial \delta_r}{\partial \beta} = -\frac{C_{n_\beta \text{ fixed}}}{C_{n_{\delta_r}}} \tag{8.5}$$

where the "$_{fixed}$" subscript simply emphasizes that the rudder is not free to float.

The signs for C_{n_β} and $C_{n_{\delta_r}}$ are, respectively, positive and negative, using the "standard" sign convention. So, the slope of the rudder deflection versus sideslip must be positive to have static directional stability (eqn. 8.5 and Fig. 8.2).

Example 8.1: A small business jet with a conventional (reversible) control system has the following lateral-directional control derivatives: $C_{\mathcal{L}_{\delta_a}} = -.065/\text{rad}$; $C_{n_{\delta_a}} = 0.00005/\text{rad}$; $C_{\mathcal{L}_{\delta_r}} = -0.00001/\text{rad}$; $C_{n_{\delta_r}} = 0.005/\text{rad}$.

Sideslip (°)	Aileron (°)	Rudder (°)
-4.50	3.12	34.98
-4.02	2.78	31.21
-2.03	1.41	15.82
0.01	0.04	-0.02
2.04	-1.40	-15.48
3.99	-2.77	-31.22
4.51	-3.11	-35.02

For a series of steady, straight sideslips at 30,000 feet and a Mach number of 0.55, the aileron and rudder deflections at the left were measured. Assuming $C_{\mathcal{L}_{\delta_a}}$ and $C_{n_{\delta_r}}$ are much larger than $C_{\mathcal{L}_{\delta_r}}$ and $C_{n_{\delta_a}}$, calculate approximate values of the stick-fixed directional stability and the dihedral effect at these flight conditions.

From the data given, approximate slopes are:

$$\frac{\partial \delta_r}{\partial \beta} = -7.8 /\text{rad} \quad \text{and} \quad \frac{\partial \delta_a}{\partial \beta} = 0.69 /\text{rad}.$$

Using equation 8.5 and its counterpart for dihedral effect:

$$\boxed{C_{\mathcal{L}_\beta} = -0.045 /\text{rad}} \quad \text{and} \quad \boxed{C_{n_\beta} = 0.039 /\text{rad}}$$

8.1.1.3 **Effect of a Freely Floating Rudder.** The rudder hinge moment coefficient is approximated by specializing eqn. 6.10 (for a symmetric airfoil and no tab deflection).

$$C_h = C_{h_{\alpha_F}} \alpha_F + C_{h_{\delta_r}} \delta_r \tag{8.6}$$

The rudder float angle is obtained by setting C_h to zero and solving eqn. 8.6 for $\delta_{r_{free}}$.

$$\delta_{r_{free}} = -\frac{C_{h_{\alpha_F}} \alpha_F}{C_{h_{\delta_r}}} \tag{8.7}$$

Defining a_r like a_e in section 6.1.2.3; that is, $a_r = \left(\frac{\partial C_Y}{\partial \delta_r}\right)_{trim}$ and $C_{Y_{\delta_r}} = a_r \frac{S_V}{S}$. The vertical tail side force coefficient is given by

$$C_{Y_F} = C_{Y_{\alpha_F}} (-\beta + \sigma) + a_r \delta_r; \tag{8.8}$$

So, eqn. 8.7 and the definition $\alpha_F \equiv -\beta + \sigma$ are used to eliminate δ_r for rudder free conditions (again using a prime to denote a floating surface).

$$C'_{Y_F} = C_{L_{\alpha_F}} \alpha_F - a_r \frac{C_{h_{\alpha_F}}}{C_{h_{\delta_r}}} \alpha_F = C_{L_{\alpha_F}} \alpha_F \left(1 - \frac{a_r C_{h_{\alpha_F}}}{C_{L_{\alpha_F}} C_{h_{\delta_r}}}\right) \tag{8.9}$$

8.1.1.4 **Yawing Moment Due to Lateral Control.** The yawing moment due to aileron is a *cross-coupling* derivative because it produces a moment about an axis other than the lateral axis (input axis). Aileron deflection rolls the airplane, but it also produces yawing moment too. Lateral control devices generally cause a rolling moment by creating an unbalanced lift about the plane of symmetry. The half of the wing with higher lift also has higher induced drag, producing a yawing couple about the z axis. Deflecting a surface like an aileron also produces a change in profile drag. For conventional ailerons in subsonic flight, induced drag usually dominates and the yawing moment produced by deflecting ailerons opposes the desired direction of roll. This effect is called *adverse yaw*; $C_{n_{\delta_a}}$ is negative. If profile drag dominates, as it does at supersonic speeds, $C_{n_{\delta_a}}$ is positive. The effect is called *proverse* or *complementary yaw*. It is desirable for $C_{n_{\delta_a}}$ to be zero or even slightly positive; designers may go to considerable lengths to achieve this goal. Airplanes that use spoilers for roll control exhibit proverse yaw.

8.1.2 Lateral Stability and Control

The rolling moment equation does not lead to stability in the usual sense. An angular displacement in bank angle produces no tendency to return to an equilibrium bank angle. This fact contrasts with the airplane's restorative response to disturbance angle of attack or in sideslip. The natural tendency about the x axis is to slow to zero roll rate, but not to an equilibrium bank angle. It is, however, desirable to return to wings level flight after a small bank disturbance for most purposes; this characteristic is the only sense in which we can speak of lateral "stability." The dominant term producing this effect (eqn. 8.2) is C_{ℓ_β}.

8.1.2.1 **Dihedral Effect**. Dihedral effect, C_{ℓ_β}, is affected most by the geometric dihedral and/or by the wing sweep angle. Both Etkin[1] and Roskam[2] (and many other texts) give excellent discussions of the physical mechanisms that cause this "wing-leveling" phenomenon. Wing-body aerodynamic interference also increases or decreases dihedral effect, depending on the vertical placement of the lifting surfaces on the fuselage. A high wing produces an increment of rolling moment that returns the airplane to wings level when sideslip occurs and a low wing gives the opposite effect. The vertical tail also contributes an increment in C_{ℓ_β} that depends primarily on vertical tail size and moment arm. This moment arm changes with angle of attack and, for large angles of attack, can reverse the sign of this increment. Secondary factors affecting C_{ℓ_β} include aspect ratio, taper ratio, external tanks, and wing flaps. Roskam's discussion of component contributions to C_{ℓ_β} and his illustrations of variations with Mach number[2] are pertinent.

8.1.2.2 **Lateral Control Power**. Ailerons, spoilers, and differential horizontal tail deflections are the most common lateral control devices. Differential elevons, seen frequently on tailless designs, behave as ailerons. Unlike the angular displacements commanded by elevators or rudders (angle of attack and sideslip, respectively), lateral control devices are roll rate controllers. Lateral control power, $C_{\ell_{\delta_a}}$, is negative using either sign convention; a positive aileron deflection (right aileron up) produces a positive rolling moment because of the decreased lift on the right wing and the increased lift for the left wing. The exact value of the lateral control power (or "aileron effectiveness") is difficult to estimate accurately and wind tunnel testing is usually in order. Because lateral controls are typically rate command devices, different sensors are needed to measure the effectiveness of such controls and the effectiveness of the lateral control cannot be measured by static means. A dynamic test (Chapter 9) must be used to confirm estimates of this control derivative. An expression[3] relating aileron control power to the airfoil section (after aileron deflection), the ratio of the control surface area to wing area, and the location of the wing center of pressure along the span is sometimes used to approximate $C_{\ell_{\delta_a}}$:

$$C_{\ell_{\delta_a}} = \frac{C_{L_{\alpha_a}} S_a y}{S b} \qquad (8.10)$$

where $C_{L_{\alpha_a}}$ is the average wing lift curve slope with ailerons deflected and y is the distance from the airplane x axis to the wing center of pressure, again with ailerons deflected. This approximate approach is rather crude and must be verified.

8.1.2.3 **Rolling Moment Due to Directional Control.** $C_{\mathscr{L}_{\delta_r}}$, the rolling moment coefficient due to rudder deflection is another cross-coupling derivative. This derivative is the non-dimensional rolling moment resulting from side force generated by rudder deflection multiplied by the non-dimensional moment arm measured from the reference body axis up to the resultant force on the vertical tail. Because it is measured from the x axis (trim condition), this length is a function of trim angle of attack causing $C_{\mathscr{L}_{\delta_r}}$ to decrease with increasing α or C_L.

$$C_{\mathscr{L}_{\delta_r}} = \frac{C_{Y_{\delta_r}} z_V(\alpha)}{b} \tag{8.11}$$

8.1.3 Lateral-Directional Matrix Equations

The static lateral-directional equations are often written in matrix form. Of all control derivatives in eqn. 8.12, only the side force derivative, $C_{Y_{\delta_a}}$, is typically negligible.

$$\begin{Bmatrix} C_Y \\ C_{\mathscr{L}} \\ C_n \end{Bmatrix} = \begin{bmatrix} C_{Y_\beta} & C_{Y_{\delta_a}} & C_{Y_{\delta_r}} & C_L \\ C_{\mathscr{L}_\beta} & C_{\mathscr{L}_{\delta_a}} & C_{\mathscr{L}_{\delta_r}} & 0 \\ C_{n_\beta} & C_{n_{\delta_a}} & C_{n_{\delta_r}} & 0 \end{bmatrix} \begin{Bmatrix} \beta \\ \delta_a \\ \delta_r \\ \Phi \end{Bmatrix} \tag{8.12}$$

Static lateral-directional flight tests are slightly more difficult to conduct than longitudinal ones. With at least twice as many parameters recorded simultaneously for these tests (compared to longitudinal ones), automated data collection is strongly preferred.

8.2 STEADY STATE FLIGHT TEST METHODS

Requirements for lateral-directional static stability handling qualities vary considerably from civil to military specifications. The prudent flight test engineer is more concerned that the design is safe to fly and easily controlled by the pilot than with just meeting a requirement. Requirements provide guidance aimed at insuring minimum standards are met. Any design is a compromise between improving handling qualities and the need to produce a cost-effective airplane. Every stability and control flight test evaluates this compromise, but lateral-directional requirements reflect considerable subjectivity. FAR requirements[9,10] illustrate:

(1) *The static directional stability, as shown by the tendency to recover from a skid with the rudder free, must be positive for any landing gear and flap position appropriate to the takeoff, climb, cruise, and approach configurations. This must be shown with symmetrical power up to a maximum continuous power, and at speeds from $1.2V_{s_1}$ up to the maximum allowable speed for the condition being investigated. The angle of skid for these tests must be appropriate to the type of airplane. At larger skid angles up to that at which full rudder is used or a control force limit in Part 23.143 is reached, whichever occurs first, and at speeds from $1.2V_{s_1}$ to V_A, the rudder pedal force must not reverse.*

(2) *The static lateral stability, as shown by the tendency to raise the low wing in a slip, must be positive for any landing gear and flap positions. This must be shown with symmetrical power up to 75% of the maximum continuous power at speeds*

above 1.2V_{s_1}, up to the maximum allowable speed for the configuration being investigated. The static lateral stability may not be negative at 1.2V_{s_1}. The angle of slip for these tests must be appropriate to the type of airplane, but in no case may the slip angle be less than that obtainable with 10° of bank.

(3) *In straight, steady slips at 1.2V_{s_1} for any landing gear and flap positions, and for any symmetrical power conditions up to 50% maximum continuous power, the aileron and rudder control movements and forces must increase steadily (but not necessarily in constant proportion) as the angle of sideslip is increased up to a maximum appropriate to the type of airplane. At larger sideslip angles up the angle at which the full rudder or aileron is used or a control force limit contained in Part 23.143 is obtained, the rudder pedal force may not reverse. Enough bank must accompany slipping to hold constant heading. Rapid entry into, or recovery from, a maximum slip may not result in uncontrollable flight characteristics.*

FAR Part 23.177a

Static lateral stability must be positive ($C_{\ell_\beta} < 0$). There must be a wing-leveling tendency when sideslip is generated. These requirements cover virtually the entire flight envelope, including the speed range just above stall up to maximum allowable speed, as well as all reasonable configurations. Demonstrating compliance with these requirements can take an enormous amount of flight test time! Notice also the vague adjectives and the latitude allowed individual FAA inspectors.

The requirements for transport category airplanes are similar:

(a) *The static directional stability (as shown by the tendency to recover from a skid with the rudder free) must be positive for any landing gear and flap position and symmetrical power condition, at speeds from V_{s_1} up to V_{FE}, V_{LE}, or V_{FC}/V_{MC} (as appropriate).*

(b) *The static lateral stability (as shown by the tendency to raise the low wing in a sideslip with the aileron controls free and for any landing gear and flap position and symmetrical power condition) must be positive at V_{FE}, V_{LE}, or V_{FC}/V_{MC} (as appropriate).*

(c) *In straight, steady sideslips (unaccelerated forward slips) the aileron and rudder control movements and forces must be substantially proportional to the angle of sideslip, and the factor of proportionality must lie between limits found necessary for safe operation throughout the range of sideslip angles appropriate to the operation of the airplane. At greater angles, up to the angle at which full rudder control is used or a pedal force of 180 pounds is obtained, the rudder pedal forces may not reverse and increased rudder deflection must produce increased angles of sideslip. Unless the airplane has a yaw indicator, there must be enough bank accompanying sideslipping to clearly indicate any departure from unyawed flight.*

FAR Part 25. 177

The military specification[11] is a bit more specific for static lateral-directional requirements. Rudder deflection or force must produce sideslip opposite to the direction of applied directional control to meet the military specification. In addition rudder forces and rudder deflections must remain linear for ±10° and ±15° sideslip, respectively. The document also limits maximum allowable rudder pedal force to 250 pounds for maximum rudder deflection at any point in the envelope. Furthermore, in a steady sideslip, aileron deflection in the same direction as sideslip must accompany the rudder requirements. The wing-leveling tendencies due to dihedral effect shall not be so strong that more than 75% of roll control power nor more than 10 pounds (stick) or 20 pounds (wheel) of force are required in normal use. The military specification includes a great deal more detail and responsible flight test engineers must carefully study and analyze all current applicable requirements documents for complete details during the test planning phase. Do not depend on textbooks (including this one) to be up-to-date; check the current source regulation and supporting documents.

From the above discussion we see that control forces and surface deflections constitute the principle sources of data for evaluating the lateral-directional stability. Van der Maas[7] calls this approach *control position* stability. Qualitatively, Figs. 8.2 and 8.3 indicate the relationship between control surface deflections and sideslip expected for a subsonic airplane with acceptable controls-fixed lateral-directional characteristics. Similar sketches could be drawn for aileron and rudder forces as a function of sideslip with the controls-free (assuming reversible flight controls). Controls-free stability is irrelevant for fully powered (irreversible) control systems such as the ones on most high performance fighters and many commercial airliners.

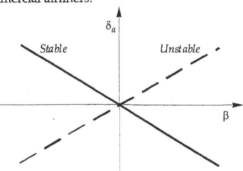

Fig. 8.3 Aileron Deflection versus Sideslip ("Standard" Sign Convention)

8.2.1 Test Methods to Determine Dominant Stability Derivatives

The basic test method is a steady, straight sideslip -- a classical, proven way to determine static directional stability and dihedral effect. It depends, though, on prior knowledge of control derivatives like $C_{\ell_{\delta_a}}$ and Cn_{δ_r}. Like any other stability and control testing, the method also demands appropriate instrumentation, careful attention to trim, and precise control of airspeed and altitude. Because data are collected point by stabilized point in this technique, it takes a lot of flying time to completely explore the flight envelope for all configurations of a given airplane. So, *slowly varying* methods are also used. Both methods are discussed in the following paragraphs.

8.2.1.1 Steady, Straight Sideslips. The steady-state test method is commonly used to measure $C_{\ell_{\delta_a}}$ and $C_{n_{\delta_r}}$ for all classes of airplanes. The standard technique is fairly inefficient for many airplanes and flight conditions; therefore, it is often modified.

Setting up for this maneuver is similar to other stability tests. The test pilot must trim with the care at the nominal test altitude. Once trimmed, he should release the controls and the airplane's airspeed and altitude should not change for at least 10 seconds to guarantee a reliable trim condition. Control surface positions and forces at trim are recorded just before starting the maneuver. Sideslip limits must be meticulously observed; they should be reviewed in the preflight briefing and, if the instrumentation and ground support include real-time support, this parameter should be monitored as a flight safety parameter. Exceeding sideslip limits has caused loss of control and even structural damage in the past. Though steady, straight sideslips usually are not considered hazardous tests, prudence should be exercised with a full understanding of $g*\beta$ limits.

Data are collected at constant, stabilized headings. The pilot chooses a reference point on the distant horizon and flies a stabilized heading (sideslip angle) for each individual point (sideslip angle). Rudder and aileron are applied, essentially simultaneously, to establish a stabilized sideslip, with zero heading rate. This *cross-controlled* condition is an unnatural piloting technique; rudder maintains zero sideslip in normal flight maneuvers. Using rudder and aileron in opposite directions, particularly at large sideslip angles, gives a sensation of "sliding sideways in the seat" due to the lateral forces. These unusual sensations and unnatural control applications force the pilot to concentrate on setting up the conditions and maintaining them. Crosschecking the point chosen on the visual horizon along with the cockpit instruments for constant heading and bank angle should allow the pilot to determine when he has achieved a steady, stabilized sideslip. When equilibrium conditions are established, record altitude, airspeed, sideslip angle, bank angle, control surface deflections (aileron, rudder, and elevator), and control forces for all three axes. Plots like Figs. 8.2 and 8.3 can be constructed and, if the dominant derivatives, C_{ℓ_β} and C_{n_β} are known from wind tunnel tests, $C_{\ell_{\delta_a}}$ and $C_{n_{\delta_r}}$ can be calculated from the slopes $\dfrac{\partial \delta_a}{\partial \beta}$ and $\dfrac{\partial \delta_r}{\partial \beta}$ of the curves. Alternatively, if $C_{\ell_{\delta_a}}$ and $C_{n_{\delta_r}}$ are known, C_{ℓ_β} and C_{n_β} can be calculated.

8.2.1.2 **Slowly Varying Sideslips**. The steady, straight sideslip method can be time-consuming and is often modified to speed up data collection. Time saving is achieved by changing the sideslip conditions continuously rather than stabilizing on each point. Trimming and flying techniques are the similar to the stabilized method. The change in technique is that rudder and opposite aileron are blended in slowly while a constant track is maintained. To acquire the data, automatic recording of some form must be used. The slowly varying method saves time if β does not change too rapidly (no more than ~ 1 °/second) and if the test pilot properly coordinates the rate of change of rudder and aileron to maintain constant track. This dynamic maneuver is slightly harder to fly than the stabilized one; points occasionally must be repeated. Repetitions negate the advantage of the method, but the potential time saving favors the slowly varying technique. It is probably the most used technique for collecting static lateral-directional data.

8.2.1.3 **Steady Turns with Rudder Fixed**. This flight test technique, no longer widely used since parameter estimation techniques (Volume 2) became popular, is simple and little instrumentation is needed. It is a useful way to teach measurement fundamentals.

The airplane must be carefully trimmed at the desired altitude and airspeed conditions. The pilot then holds the rudder at the trim position and banks the airplane using the lateral control alone. This bank should be entered slowly since a steady sideslip and bank angle is sought and too abrupt a lateral control input may induce a Dutch roll oscillation (Chapter 9) that hinders data collection. Once equilibrium has been attained, δ_a, δ_r, F_a, F_r, ϕ, β, and r are recorded, preferably with some form of automatic recording instrumentation. The procedure is repeated at several increments in bank angle and the same parameters are recorded at each test point. Sideslip limits must be observed and it may become increasingly difficult to maintain airspeed and remain within 1000 feet of the nominal test altitude at larger bank angles. Elevator is used to control airspeed but care must be taken to avoid spurious lateral control movements while making corrections with the elevator. Measurements are made during turns in either direction.

Data from are plotted to obtain trim curves of δ_a and F_a versus bank angle and plots of β and ϕ as functions of nondimensional yaw rate $\frac{rb}{2V}$. These plots can then be used to estimate the damping derivative, C_{n_r}, though we will not describe this data reduction.

8.2.1.4 **Steady Turns with Ailerons Fixed**. This test method is essentially identical to the one discussed in the preceding section, except that the turns are commanded by rudder alone and information is measured to estimate C_{ℓ_r} rather than C_{n_r}. Again, we will not pursue the computational details for this damping cross derivative.

8.2.1.5 **Use of Steady Sideslip Data**. The basic steady sideslip flight test technique provides a quick, accurate assessment of the static lateral-directional stability. Steady sideslip data is also used to measure the rudder control power derivative $C_{n_{\delta_r}}$ and the aileron control power derivative $C_{\ell_{\delta_a}}$, as illustrated in the next section. To obtain additional information, like these control derivatives, the flight test planner must often add equipment or devise means of applying known external moments. But, the usefulness of this simple test is remarkable.

8.2.2 **Test Methods to Determine Control Effectiveness**

Measuring the control effectiveness is an important purpose of static lateral-directional flight tests. Since rolling and yawing moment equations are tightly coupled, these tests are difficult to conduct. There are methods that utilize movement of the vertical position of the cg to measure aileron effectiveness but they are not very accurate and, consequently are not generally used[8]. However, steady, straight sideslips at differing longitudinal c.g. locations can produce plausible rudder control effectiveness data. A second approach for measuring $C_{n_{\delta_r}}$ involves deploying a parachute from a fixed wing location. If the parachute's drag coefficient is also known, the resulting drag force can be calculated. The rudder deflection necessary to overcome this known external yawing moment is a direct measure of the rudder's effectiveness. Similarly, an asymmetric moment can be applied about the roll axis by positioning a weight at a known spanwise location and measuring the aileron deflection necessary to balance the load in equilibrium flight. This latter method is straightforward and accurate since it involves no change in drag other than the induced drag due to deflection of the aileron.

8.2.2.1 **Steady, Straight Sideslips at Different C.G. Locations**. In eqns. 8.12 we can usually ignore the effect of aileron (or other lateral controls) on the side force. If the rudder side force term can be neglected and ϕ is small, the equations simplify to:

$$\begin{Bmatrix} C_Y \\ C_\ell \\ C_n \end{Bmatrix} \approx \begin{bmatrix} C_{Y_\beta} & 0 & C_{Y_{\delta_r}} & C_L \\ C_{\ell_\beta} & C_{\ell_{\delta_a}} & C_{\ell_{\delta_r}} & 0 \\ C_{n_\beta} & C_{n_{\delta_a}} & C_{n_{\delta_r}} & 0 \end{bmatrix} \begin{Bmatrix} \beta \\ \delta_a \\ \delta_r \\ \Phi \end{Bmatrix} \qquad (8.13)$$

Flying a series of steady, straight sideslips for a range of β, eqns. 8.13 can be solved at each of the stabilized flight conditions. If the c.g. is relocated between two such sets of steady, straight sideslips, the only aerodynamic coefficients that change significantly are C_{n_β} and $C_{n_{\delta_r}}$. As long as the tail moment arm is large compared to the shift in c.g. location, $C_{n_{\delta_r}}$ is also essentially independent of c.g. position. Changes in C_{n_β} can be calculated from (using the geometry of Fig. 8.4):

$$C_{n_{\beta_2}} = C_{n_{\beta_1}} + C_{Y_\beta} \frac{\Delta x_{cg}}{b} \qquad (8.14)$$

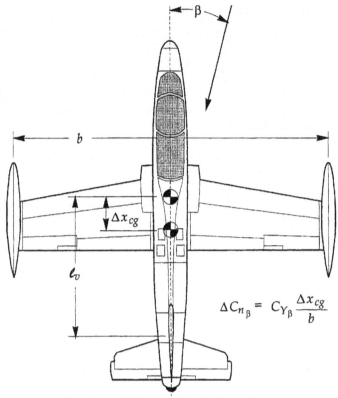

Fig. 8.4 Effect of C.G. Shift on C_{n_β}

Using equations 8.13 and the slopes $\dfrac{\partial \phi}{\partial \beta}$ and $\dfrac{\partial \delta_r}{\partial \beta}$ from a series of steady, straight sideslips, C_{Y_β} can be calculated:

$$C_{Y_\beta} = -C_L \frac{\partial \phi}{\partial \beta} \qquad (8.15)$$

The slopes $\dfrac{\partial \phi}{\partial \beta}$ and $\dfrac{\partial \delta_r}{\partial \beta}$ are usually independent of cg location, but it is good practice to check this assumption by taking sideslip data at several cg positions. Eliminating the side force equation, any two sideslip conditions can be evaluated using

$$C_{n_{\beta_2}} = C_{n_{\delta_a}} \left(\frac{\partial \delta_a}{\partial \beta} \right)_2 + C_{n_{\delta_r}} \left(\frac{\partial \delta_r}{\partial \beta} \right)_2 = 0 \quad \text{and} \quad C_{n_{\beta_1}} = C_{n_{\delta_a}} \left(\frac{\partial \delta_a}{\partial \beta} \right)_1 + C_{n_{\delta_r}} \left(\frac{\partial \delta_r}{\partial \beta} \right)_1 = 0$$

Defining $\Delta C_{n_\beta} = C_{n_{\beta_2}} - C_{n_{\beta_1}}$ and observing that the aileron slope change with sideslip is usually quite small,

$$\Delta C_{n_\beta} + C_{n_{\delta_r}} \left[\left(\frac{\partial \delta_r}{\partial \beta} \right)_2 - \left(\frac{\partial \delta_r}{\partial \beta} \right)_1 \right] \approx 0 \qquad (8.16)$$

If the moment arm for the vertical tail (distance the center of pressure of the vertical tail is above the c.g. for an aft tail airplane) is established, $C_{Y_{\delta_r}}$ can be estimated from $C_{n_{\delta_r}}$, which is calculated from eqn. 8.16:

$$C_{Y_{\delta_r}} = -C_{n_{\delta_r}} \frac{b}{\ell_V} \tag{8.17}$$

Data reduction is straightforward, though flying can be tedious because it is often hard to alter longitudinal c.g. location in flight. Rudder deflection and bank angle are plotted as functions of sideslip angle. At $\beta = 0$ the slopes of these curves for each cg location are obtained and C_{ℓ} is calculated for test conditions and test weight. Then, C_{Y_β}, $C_{n_{\delta_r}}$, and $C_{Y_{\delta_r}}$ are computed from eqns. 8.15, 8.16, and 8.17.

This technique is rather cumbersome and only moderately accurate. A large number of sideslip points are required to credibly establish the small differences that determine the slopes of the measured variables. These differences come from two relatively large numbers so the information is uncertain. The technique is not often used because of the test time needed to acquire the data.

8.2.2.2 **Yawing Moment Produced by a Wing Parachute**. The second method of directly measuring rudder effectiveness is even more cumbersome. It is imperative that the parachute be deployed in flight and jettisoned after data are taken. If care is not taken to ensure that parachute deployment and jettison are completely reliable, the risk to safety is often unacceptable. Uncertainty is added to the process because few parachutes are completely stable after deployment.

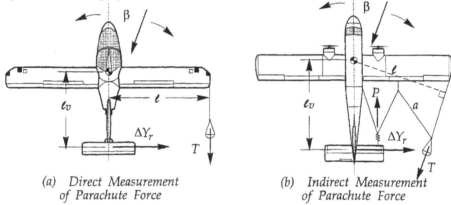

(a)   *Direct Measurement*
of Parachute Force

(b)   *Indirect Measurement*
of Parachute Force

Fig. 8.5 Wing Parachute Installations

Typical installations for a wing parachute are sketched in Fig. 8.5. Figure 8.5b shows one way to provide some stability for the parachute, if the wing tip vortex excites oscillations. A simpler (and less practical) hardware configuration is shown in Fig. 8.5a. It gives the incremental yawing moment created by the parachute:

$$\Delta N = T\ell \tag{8.18}$$

The measurements can be made and the results expressed in terms of x_{cg}, a, and the force P rather than direct measurements like T and ℓ. Van der Maas suggests taking data at several different tether cable lengths with such an arrangement[7].

Equilibrium at zero sideslip (eqns. 8.13) implies that $\Delta C_n = C_{n_{\delta_r}} \Delta \delta_r$, where ΔC_n is the incremental yawing moment coefficient. A known ΔC_n is provided by the parachute since it can be calculated from the parachute's drag coefficient and the moment arm (Fig. 8.5a). The parachute force can be measured directly with either a force gage in the parachute riser or in the tether cable (further complicating the instrumentation). But by definition

ΔC_n is also $\Delta C_n = \dfrac{\Delta N}{\bar{q}Sb}$ and a direct calculation of rudder effectiveness is then possible. The rudder side force coefficient follows from eqn. 8.17 with the required rudder control effectiveness given by $C_{n_{\delta_r}} \approx \dfrac{\Delta C_n}{\Delta \delta_r}$.

Piloting technique for these tests is that described for the steady, straight sideslip method. Care must be taken to avoid oscillations and, if the Dutch roll oscillation is not well damped for the airplane, it may be difficult to stabilize the parachute. Safety procedures must be carefully rehearsed in advance.

8.2.2.3 **Measurements with Weights at Known Spanwise Locations**. A technique similar to the one described above to measure rudder power is used to measure lateral control effectiveness. Moreover, this method is often used to check more sophisticated approaches. Like most other static lateral-directional tests, this one also involves flying a series of steady, straight sideslips. An unbalanced rolling moment is generated by positioning a known weight at a known spanwise location. If the airplane can carry fuel (or other liquids) in tanks that provide an adjustable and precisely known lateral imbalance, there is no need to install special stores or to add weights that can alter the flutter characteristics of the vehicle. The test planner must ensure that safe handling during takeoff and landing is guaranteed for all conceivable contingencies. Aileron and rudder deflections (and the corresponding control forces) required to balance the asymmetric rolling moment are measured over a range of sideslips.

At zero sideslip the equilibrium condition (eqns. 8.13) reduces to: $\Delta C_{\mathcal{L}} = C_{\mathcal{L}_{\delta_a}} \Delta \delta_a$, giving an expression that allows direct calculation of the aileron control effectiveness from measurement of $\Delta C_{\mathcal{L}}$ and $\Delta \delta_a$:

$$C_{\mathcal{L}_{\delta_a}} \approx \frac{\Delta C_{\mathcal{L}}}{\Delta \delta_a} \tag{8.19}$$

At the same time the aileron deflection produces an increment in yawing moment that must be counteracted by the rudder.

$$C_{n_{\delta_a}} \Delta \delta_a + C_{n_{\delta_r}} \Delta \delta_r = 0$$

From this equilibrium expression it follows that

$$C_{n_{\delta_a}} \approx -C_{n_{\delta_r}} \frac{\Delta \delta_r}{\Delta \delta_a} \tag{8.20}$$

Pilot procedures for this test are the same as those for other steady, straight sideslip tests. Considerable care must be exercised when fuel transfer or stores jettison is employed to attain the desired lateral imbalance. While at least two different lateral cg positions are essential for a rough estimate, more cg locations are recommended to check for nonlinearities.

Data reduction for this test is similar to previous tests. First, measured δ_a values are plotted against β to obtain the slope of this curve at $\beta = 0°$. Several measurements at other sideslips allow fairing of the δ_a - β curves and give a better estimate of the slope at zero sideslip. Then, with the rolling moment increment known and $C_{n_{\delta_r}}$ known, eqns. 8.19 and 8.20 allow direct calculation of the two aileron control derivatives $C_{\mathcal{L}_{\delta_a}}$ and $C_{n_{\delta_a}}$.

8.2.3 **Estimation of Stability Derivatives from Steady Lateral-Directional Tests**

Flight test estimates of control effectiveness derivatives have been suggested in the previous paragraphs; we now summarize how static lateral-directional measurements are used to confirm wind tunnel data and analytical estimates of these same derivatives.

First, the control effectiveness derivatives $C_{n_{\delta_a}}$, $C_{n_{\delta_r}}$, $C_{Y_{\delta_a}}$, and $C_{y_{\delta_r}}$ are determined from one or more of the control effectiveness tests described in section 8.2.2. With these values in hand, the dominant lateral-directional stability derivatives, $C_{\mathscr{L}_\beta}$ and C_{n_β}, (along with the less important C_{Y_β}) are obtained from plots of control surface deflections and forces at each of the sideslip angles. The resulting functional relationships are experimentally determined in steady, straight sideslip tests or using the slowly varying sideslip technique. Yaw rate derivatives, $C_{\mathscr{L}_r}$ and C_{n_r}, are calculated from data recorded in steady turns initiated with aileron or rudder alone. This approach provides estimates of nine of the most important lateral-directional parameters with reasonable accuracy from essentially static tests.

8.3 INSTRUMENTATION

Much of what was written about instrumentation in Sections 6.3 and 7.3 applies to collecting static lateral-directional data. However, for most of the test methods discussed in this chapter, data can be recorded by hand; but automated data recording can speed up test events, especially the slowly varying techniques, and make the test time more productive. Lee[11] suggests that the lateral-directional parameters usually measured for static tests include lateral cockpit control force and surface position, yaw control force and pedal (or other cockpit control) position, both lateral and directional control surface deflections, sideslip angle, bank angle, roll rate, yaw rate, lateral acceleration, and position of both lateral trim devices and yaw trim devices. The usual secondary measurements of fuel weight and location are needed to keep track of mass distribution, moments of inertia, and cg position. For some of the lateral-directional stability and control parameters, it is important to know the vertical migration of cg as fuel is burned. Air data measurements for these tests can be complicated by pitot-static system errors associated with significant sideslip angles, though GPS velocity now provides a standard against which a constant true airspeed can be maintained.. Summing up, the added complication of simultaneously measuring forces and moments for two coupled axes essentially doubles the parameter list that must be measured and puts a premium on the use of automated data collection.

8.4 SUMMARY

Static lateral-directional flight tests are slightly more complicated both in measurement techniques and in data reduction requirements than their longitudinal counterparts. Coupling between the two relevant moment equations accounts for this complication. However, if control effectiveness derivatives are known or can be measured accurately, simple steady, straight sideslip tests can reliably determine the dominant lateral-directional derivatives $C_{\mathscr{L}_\beta}$ and C_{n_β}. While they are not as often conducted since parameter estimation identification algorithms have become so widely used, steady turns using aileron or rudder alone also make it possible to straightforwardly estimate $C_{\mathscr{L}_r}$ and C_{n_r}. All in all, these kinds of flight tests provide a wealth of information for a moderate amount of effort and minimal investment in data reduction. Their most serious drawback is that more flight time is required to collect the data than more modern parameter estimation techniques. Such techniques also need sophisticated instrumentation, require considerable test team expertise, and carry a carry a significant computational burden to extract the same stability derivatives.

REFERENCES

[1] Etkin, B., **Dynamics of Flight: Stability and Control** (2nd Edition), John Wiley & Sons, New York, 1982.

[2] Roskam, J., **Airplane Flight Dynamics and Automatic Controls, Part I**, Roskam Aviation and Engineering Corporation, Lawrence, Kansas, 1979.

[3] "Stability and Control Flight Test Theory," Vol. I, Chapter 5, AFFTC-TIH-77-1, USAF Test Pilot School, Edwards AFB, California, Revised February 1977.

[4] "Stability and Control Flight Test Techniques," Vol. II, Chapter 7, AFFTC-TIH-77-1, USAF Test Pilot School, Edwards AFB, California, Revised February 1977.

[5] "Fixed Wing Stability and Control: Theory and Flight Test Techniques," USNTPS-FTM-No. 103, Naval Air Test Center, Patuxent River, Maryland, January 1975 (Revised November 1981).

[6] Perkins, C. D., "Introduction," Chapter 1, Volume II, **AGARD Flight Test Manual**, Pergamon Press, New York, 1959.

[7] Van der Maas, H. J., "Lateral and Directional Control and the Measurement of Aerodynamic Coefficients in Steady Asymmetric Flight and Flight on Asymmetric Power," Chapter 5, Volume II, **AGARD Flight Test Manual**, Pergamon Press, New York, 1959.

[8] Hunter, P. A., "Flight Techniques Used to Determine Adequacy of Lateral Control," Chapter 6, Volume II, **AGARD Flight Test Manual**, Pergamon Press, New York, 1959.

[9] Electronic Code of Federal Regulations (e-CFR), Part 23, "Airworthiness Standards: Normal, Utility, and Acrobatic Category Airplanes", Federal Aviation Administration, Washington, current as of December 23, 2005. (http://ecfr.gpoaccess.gov/)

[10] Electronic Code of Federal Regulations (e-CFR), Part 25, "Airworthiness Standards: Large Commercial Transport Category Airplanes", Federal Aviation Administration, Washington, current as of December 23, 2005. (http://ecfr.gpoaccess.gov/)

[11] "Military Standard, Flying Qualities of Piloted Airplanes", MIL-STD-1797A, , Department of Defense, Washington, DC, January 30, 1990 (Notice of Change 1, June 28, 1995; Notice of Change 2, December 19, 1997; Notice of Change 3, August 24, 2004).

[12] Lee, R. E., Jr., "Handling Qualities", Chapter 15, Vol. 14, **Introduction to Flight Test Engineering** (Edited by F. N. Stoliker), AGARD Flight Test Techniques Series, AGARDograph 300, 7 Rue Ancelle, 92200 Neuilly-Sur-Seine, France, North Atlantic Treaty Organization, September 1995.

Chapter 9
DYNAMIC STABILITY TESTS

Flight testing to determine the dynamic stability of an airplane is even more complicated than the tests outlined in the previous three chapters for static stability tests. Although is it usually still possible to decouple the equations of motion for the longitudinal and the lateral-directional cases, the analysis is considerably more complicated. Dynamic stability describes both the transient and the steady-state response to disturbances from equilibrium. It requires that we study the time-related behavior of the response of the dynamic system, not just its initial tendency after a disturbance from equilibrium. Anderson[1] has captured the essence of dynamic stability:

> A body is dynamically stable if, out of its own accord, it eventually returns to and remains at its equilibrium position over a period of time.

Static stability measurements are necessarily made with all forces and moments in equilibrium. Conversely, dynamic stability measurements, while they are usually initiated after carefully trimming the vehicle, must be made with the forces and moments not in equilibrium. Furthermore, meaningful measurement of these dynamic quantities requires some form of time correlation in order to have meaning.

Dynamic stability is related to static stability. While an airplane can be statically stable without being dynamically stable, it cannot be dynamically stable without being statically stable. Dynamic stability characterizes the vehicle's ability to change from one equilibrium condition to another. The speed and precision with which these changes can be made is determined by the characteristic modes of motion of the airplane.

Dynamic stability is not the only concern of the flight test team engaged in this facet of flight testing. The handling qualities (sometimes called controllability) of a manned airplane are also of prime importance and many of the requirements that drive dynamic stability spring from their impact on the handling qualities. Again, both static and dynamic stability, along with the characteristics of the control system, the airplane's missions or intended use, and the task to be accomplished, determine the handling qualities of the airplane. Controllability has been defined in terms of what the pilot is tasked to do:

> **Controllability** may be defined as the capability of the airplane to perform, at the pilot's wish, any maneuvering required in total mission accomplishment[2].

However, controllability means something quite different to the controls engineer and the term handling qualities is preferred because of this ambiguity. From this discussion it should be clear that the handling qualities of any manned aircraft depend heavily on subjective assessments. Certainly most handling qualities requirements are based on pilot opinion[3].

Before the test team can measure the characteristics of such dynamic motions, it is essential that they have a thorough understanding of these and other terms, the modes of motion, and how to quantitatively define them. Let us turn now to laying the foundation for the measurement of these dynamic properties.

9.1 FOUNDATIONS

To properly understand the dynamics of aerospace vehicles requires a brief return to the six degree-of-freedom equations of motion that have been developed in many textbooks[4,5,6] and to the definitions used to quantify the modes of motion. First, we need to fix the definition of certain terms used in dynamic flight analysis.

9.1.1 Definition of Terms and Assumptions

As stated in the introductory paragraphs, dynamic stability requires that the motion of a body ultimately return to its equilibrium position. There are at least two ways in which physical systems return to (or diverge from) equilibrium as shown in Fig. 9.1. The exponential decay (or divergence) is associated with a linear factor in the governing characteristic equation, while the damped (or divergent) oscillation is associated with a quadratic term in the characteristic equation. Of course it is also possible for oscillatory motion to be undamped and this condition implies neutral dynamic stability. Fortunately, all linear systems can be represented mathematically represented by a combination of either linear terms or quadratic terms in the characteristic equation; that is, the time-dependent solutions are linear combinations of either exponential decays or divergences and damped, neutrally damped, or divergent oscillations.

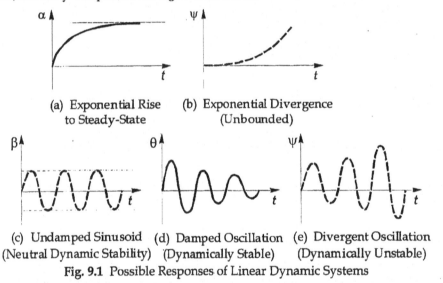

(a) Exponential Rise   (b) Exponential Divergence
to Steady-State   (Unbounded)

(c) Undamped Sinusoid   (d) Damped Oscillation   (e) Divergent Oscillation
(Neutral Dynamic Stability)   (Dynamically Stable)   (Dynamically Unstable)

Fig. 9.1 Possible Responses of Linear Dynamic Systems

Since any linear dynamic system can be represented by a combination of no more than second-order factors, it is instructive to review the definitions used to describe the dynamic behavior of an airplane. Figure 9.2 depicts a spring-mass-damper system that we will use in making these definitions.

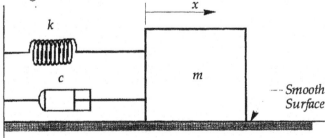

Fig. 9.2 Spring-Mass-Damper Analog

Mathematically the solution to the second-order spring-mass-damper system is identical to solution of the airplane's longitudinal equations of motion. Only the constants change. The equation describing the spring-mass-damper system with no external forcing function is:

$$m\ddot{x} + c\dot{x} + kx = 0 \quad \text{and the characteristic equation is:} \quad \lambda^2 + \frac{c}{m}\lambda + \frac{k}{m} = 0 \tag{9.1}$$

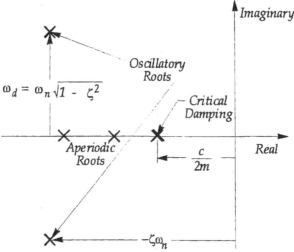

Fig. 9.3 Characteristic Roots in the Complex Plane

For the airplane's longitudinal analog of this motion we need only to define the aerodynamic "spring" that corresponds to k and the damping terms that correspond to c. Typically, the stability derivative C_{m_α} adequately describes the aerodynamic "spring" and the pitch damping C_{m_q} relates to the damping coefficient c in the analogous aerodynamic system. The aircraft moment of inertia is the analog to the mass m in the simpler mechanical system.

To introduce additional definitions of interest in an airplane's dynamic behavior, let us now consider the roots of eqn. 9.1 and how they are affected by changes in $\frac{c}{m}$ and $\frac{k}{m}$. The roots are:

$$\lambda_{1,2} = -\frac{c}{2m} \pm \sqrt{\left(\frac{c}{2m}\right)^2 - \frac{k}{m}} \tag{9.2}$$

If $\left(\frac{c}{2m}\right)^2 > \frac{k}{m}$, the roots lie along the real axis in the complex plane (Fig. 9.3). This situation results in an exponential decay if a root is negative or an exponential divergence if the root is positive. The time-domain behavior of such a root is illustrated in Fig. 9.1a. Other terms used to describe this type of dynamic behavior are *aperiodic* motion or deadbeat subsidence (for a negative root). A system that has a decaying exponential mode of motion is often referred to as *overdamped*. If the damping is reduced or if the spring constant is increased until $\left(\frac{c}{2m}\right)^2 = \frac{k}{m}$, the system is said to be *critically damped*. Critical damping is indicated on Fig. 9.3 by the point on the real axis where both real roots coincide: $\lambda_{1,2} = -\dfrac{c}{2m}$ at point C. The motion is still aperiodic at this point, but it is on a

boundary. Any increase in $\dfrac{k}{m}$ or decrease in $\dfrac{c}{m}$ will produce a complex conjugate solu-

tion to the characteristic equation because $\left(\dfrac{c}{2m}\right)^2 - \dfrac{k}{m} < 0$. Physically, an oscillation will

result. The characteristic equation can also be written in terms used to define oscillatory behavior and compared to eqn. 9.2, $\lambda_{1,2}^2 + 2\zeta\omega_n + \omega_n^2 = 0$, which has the solution

$$\lambda_{1,2} = -\zeta\omega_n \pm \omega_n\sqrt{1-\zeta^2} \qquad\qquad (9.3)$$

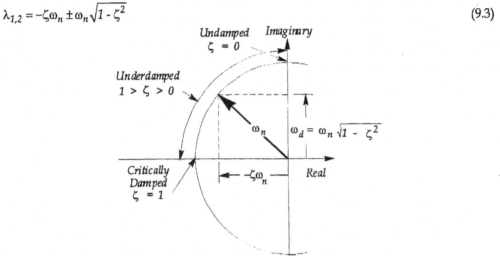

Fig. 9.4 Motion Parameters on the Complex Plane

The *damping ratio*, ζ, which compares the actual damping to critical damping (Fig. 9.4), is a measure of how rapidly an oscillation decays or of how rapidly an exponential decay or divergence occurs. For critical damping, $\zeta = 1$. The system is said to be *underdamped* if $0 < \zeta < 1$ and *undamped* (or neutrally damped) if $\zeta = 0$. The *undamped natural frequency*, ω_n is a measure of how often the peak amplitudes occur. The *damped frequency* of the oscillation (which, strictly speaking, is not a frequency) is simply $\omega_d = \omega_n\sqrt{1-\zeta^2}$. (The time response is not purely periodic unless $\zeta = 0$. Consequently, ω is sometimes called a conditional frequency[7], indicating that it has the units and many of the properties of a frequency.) The *period* of the oscillation is $T = \dfrac{2\pi}{\omega_d}$. Each of these parameters is used to quantify the characteristics of oscillatory roots. The angle θ is measured from the negative real axis to a line drawn from the origin in the complex plane to the characteristic root (or eigenvalue) in question. Therefore, this angle defines a vertical line of constant damping ratio. Clearly, a number of important parameters associated with the modes of motion can be represented on the complex plane.

The transient response of the dynamic system to inputs also must be characterized in terms of "quickness" parameters and there are terms used that indicate both the speed with which the system responds and whether or not it reaches the ultimate value commanded by the input without exceeding or "overshooting" that value. The *steady-state* (or new equilibrium) response of the system to an input is that value which the output will eventually reach. Typical steady-state output responses to a step input are shown in Fig. 9.5. Generally, second-order systems show some oscillatory behavior as suggested by Fig. 9.5a. The *damping factor*, $\zeta\omega$, is the real component of the characteristic root that controls the rate of rise or the rate of decay of the system response after an input. It appears as the constant in the exponential term of the time-domain solution of the system equations. As sketched in Fig. 9.5a, this constant defines the shape of the envelope bounding the peak amplitudes of the oscillation typical of second-order dynamic system. The *time-to-half-amplitude* (or *time-to-double-amplitude* in the case of an oscillatory divergence) is the time required for the amplitude of the motion variable under consideration to change by a factor of two. The *time-to-peak-amplitude*, t_p, is the time required to reach the maximum amplitude of the output.

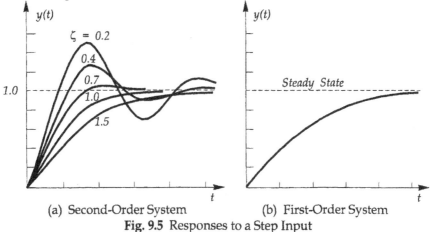

(a) Second-Order System   (b) First-Order System

Fig. 9.5 Responses to a Step Input

Maximum overshoot (or *peak overshoot*) is the largest deviation of the output response to a step input during the transient motion and this amplitude is a strong indicator of the relative stability of the system. It indicates how precisely the system can move from one equilibrium state to another. It follows that the *percentage maximum overshoot* is given by:

$$Percent\ Maximum\ Overshoot = \frac{max\,imum\ overshoot}{steady\ state}x100\%.$$

Settling time, t_s, is another parameter used to measure the transient behavior of a stable linear system. It is defined as the time required for the response to a step input to decrease and stay within a specified percentage of its steady-state value. *Rise time*, t_r, is defined as the time required for the output to increase from 10% of its steady-state value to 90% of its steady-state value when the system is excited by step response. (An alternative approach sometimes used is to give the rise time the value of the reciprocal of the slope of the step response at the instant when the output is at 50% of its final value.) *Delay time*, t_d, is the time required for the output response to a step input to reach 50% of its final value.

All of these time measures of merit are related to the *time constant*, τ. This characteristic is defined as the time to reach 63.2 per cent of the steady-state value for this first order response (as shown in Fig. 9.5b) or for the envelope of the oscillatory peaks to reach the same value. This latter fact means we can still use our definition of the time constant for a second-order response; it is still the real part of the root (and that is the only part for a first-order system) that sets the rate of convergence or divergence. An instability or divergence implies a positive root. Note, though, that the damping factor as shown on the complex plane is a negative number for stable systems. Since ω is always positive, the damping ratio ζ is described as being negative when a positive real eigenvalue exists. Heuristically, this "negative" damping is an appealing way to describe a diverging system. (Again, strictly speaking, damping cannot be negative; but the terminology is widely accepted and understood.)

9.1.2 Equations of Motion

There are two approaches commonly used in the United States to approximately model the linear dynamic motions of an aircraft. Both are based on Bryan's approach to linearizing the equations by assuming that the aerodynamic forces and moments can be adequately represented with a first order Taylor series expansion. (Etkin[4] correctly points out that this approach is mathematically flawed. Specifically, the first order approximation is inadequate, for cases where the aerodynamic forces and moments change abruptly or when the control surfaces are rapidly displaced. However, the transfer function approximation that Etkin suggests to replace Bryan's method has not been widely accepted and it depends on convergence of an infinite series that is not always mathematically well-behaved.) We will restrict our comments to the two formulations that use Bryan's approach, simply because it fits our purposes in this introductory text better than any other approach for two reasons: (1) the flight test engineer is more likely to be provided data based on Bryan's approach from wind tunnel and/or computational estimates and (2) the bulk of the experimental measurements he must make can be readily verified with this relatively simple linear model. These reasons are quite pragmatic, rather than scientifically satisfying. Nonetheless, they are appropriate for introducing the flight test engineer to dynamic stability tests.

The first formulation utilizes dimensional equations developed in most textbooks on the subject of aircraft stability and control[4, 5, 6, 17]. Table 9.1 below summarizes the results, using dimensional stability parameters.

Table 9.1 Linearized, Small Perturbation Equations Using Dimensional Parameters

Longitudinal Equations

$$su + W_0 q + g\theta\cos\Theta_0 = X_u + X_w w + X_{\dot{w}} sw + X_q q + X_{\delta_e}\delta_e$$

$$sw + U_0 q + g\theta\sin\Theta_0 = Z_u u + Z_w w + Z_{\dot{w}} ww + Z_q q + Z_{\delta_e}\delta_e \qquad (9.4)$$

$$sq = M_u u + M_w w + M_{\dot{w}} sw + M_q q + M_{\delta_e}\delta_e$$

Lateral-Directional Equations

$$sv + U_0 r - W_0 p - g\phi\cos\Theta_0 = Y_v v + Y_{\dot{v}} sv + Y_p p + Y_r r + Y_{\delta_a}\delta_a + Y_{\delta_r}\delta_r$$

$$sp - \frac{I_{xz}}{I_x} sr = \mathcal{L}_v v + \mathcal{L}_{\dot{v}} sv + \mathcal{L}_p p + \mathcal{L}_r r + \mathcal{L}_{\delta_a}\delta_a + \mathcal{L}_{\delta_r}\delta_r \qquad (9.5)$$

$$sr - \frac{I_{xz}}{I_x} sp = N_v v + N_{\dot{v}} sv + N_p p + N_r r + N_{\delta_a}\delta_a + N_{\delta_r}\delta_r$$

In Table 9.1 lower case letters (except for s, the Laplace operator) represent perturbed quantities; for example, $U = U_0 + u$, where the upper case symbols with the 0 subscripts are equilibrium (or trim) values for the parameter in question. It is assumed in the equations presented that $P_0 = Q_0 = R_0 = V_0 = 0$ and that all control surfaces are initially in the trail position ($\delta_{e_0} = \delta_{a_0} = \delta_{r_0} = 0°$) in the trim condition. There is by no means consensus about the use of these symbols; Etkin uses ξ, η, and ζ to denote perturbed control surface deflections, while Nelson uses $\Delta\delta_e$, $\Delta\delta_a$, and $\Delta\delta_r$ to identify the same deflections. McRuer[6] and his co-authors point out that the terminology most commonly used ("dimensional stability derivatives") is more properly "dimensional stability parameters". Most authors include either mass or moment of inertia terms in the definitions; that is, $X_u \equiv \dfrac{1}{m}\dfrac{\partial X}{\partial u}$ is the form used for force derivative parameters and $M_q \equiv \dfrac{1}{I_y}\dfrac{\partial M}{\partial q}$ is the form used for moment derivative parameters. Nelson[17] calls these parameters "derivatives divided by mass (or inertia)". Each of these parameters is evaluated at trim conditions in the Bryan linearization and is therefore a constant in eqns. 9.4 and 9.5. Note that this nondimensional formulation is concerned with direct measurements, while a second approach that still uses Bryan's linearization is concerned with force and moment coefficients and nondimensional velocities. Most aerodynamic stability derivative data from wind tunnel measurements is presented in this nondimensional form. Table 9.2 lists a common set of equations using this approach. Typically, when the analysis is concerned with the data base itself, the flight test engineer uses nondimensional forms. However, when he calculates transfer functions, time histories, or complicated time domain simulations that are best illuminated with physical engineering units, the flight test engineer usually prefers the dimensional form for the data. In any event, he or she readily recognize and convert between the two forms.

Table 9.2 Linearized, Small Perturbation Equations Using Nondimensional Coefficients

Longitudinal Equations

$$(2\mu D - 2C_{L_0}tan\Theta_0 - C_{X_u})\hat{u} - C_{X_\alpha}\alpha + C_{L_0}\Theta_0 - C_{X_{\delta_e}}\delta_e = 0$$
$$(2C_{L_0} - C_{Z_u})\hat{u} + (2\mu D - C_{Z_{\dot\alpha}}D - C_{Z_\alpha})\alpha - (2\mu + C_{Z_q})\hat{q} + C_{L_0}tan\,\Theta_0\theta - C_{Z_{\delta_e}}\delta_e = 0 \quad (9.6)$$
$$- C_{m_u}\hat{u} - (C_{m_\alpha}D - C_{m_\alpha})\alpha + (i_B D - C_{m_q})\hat{q} + C_{m_{\delta_e}}\delta_e = 0$$
$$\hat{q} - D\theta = 0$$

Lateral-Directional Equations

$$2\mu D - C_{Y_\beta})\beta - C_{Y_p}\hat{p} + (2\mu D - C_{Y_r})\hat{r} - C_{L_0}\phi - C_{Y_{\delta_a}}\delta_a - C_{Y_{\delta_r}}\delta_r = 0$$
$$- C_{\ell_\beta}\beta + (i_A D - C_{\ell_p})\hat{p} - (i_E D + C_{\ell_r})\hat{r} - C_{\ell_{\delta_a}}\delta_a - C_{\ell_{\delta_r}}\delta_r = 0$$
$$- C_{n_\beta}\beta - (i_E D + C_{n_p})\hat{p} + (i_C D - C_{n_r})\hat{r} - C_{n_{\delta_a}}\delta_a - C_{n_{\delta_r}}\delta_r = 0 \quad (9.7)$$
$$\hat{p} + \hat{r}\,tan\,\Theta_0 - D\phi = 0$$
$$\hat{r}\,sec\,\Theta_0 - D\psi = 0$$

$$\alpha \approx \frac{w}{U_0}; \quad \beta \approx \frac{v}{U_0}; \quad \ell = \frac{\overline{c}}{2} \text{ or } \frac{b}{2}; \quad t^* = \frac{\ell}{U_0}; \quad \mu \equiv \frac{m}{\rho S\ell}; \quad \hat{u} = \frac{u}{U_0}; \quad \hat{q} = \frac{q\overline{c}}{2U_0}; \quad i_B = \frac{I_y}{\rho S\ell^3}$$

$$\hat{p} = \frac{p\overline{c}}{2U_0}; \quad \hat{r} = \frac{r\overline{c}}{2U_0}; \quad i_A = \frac{I_x}{\rho S\ell^3}; \quad i_C = \frac{I_z}{\rho S\ell^3}; \quad i_E = \frac{I_{xz}}{\rho S\ell^3}; \quad \hat{t} = \frac{t}{t^*}$$

Derivatives with respect to $\hat{t}$ are indicated by D.

Small angle approximations help simplify these linearized equations. Etkin points out several different forms for these equations. The chief differences lie in how normalized time (t^*, defined below), is defined; the choice of the characteristic length (ℓ is defined differently for the longitudinal and for the lateral-directional equations); and the definitions used for the nondimensional stability coefficients in Table 9.2. Flight test engineers typi-cally uses the data provided in preparatory wind tunnel studies and computational esti-mates, and then reports in concert in the convention adopted by the program.

9.1.2.1 **Longitudinal Modes of Motion**. For a stable vehicle, the longitudinal motion characteristic equation results in two different oscillations; the eigenvalues are two com-plex conjugate pairs. One pair, usually called the *phugoid*, describes a low frequency in-terchange of potential energy and kinetic energy, which is very lightly damped with a pe-riod of 30 seconds or longer. It typically takes place with negligible variation in α. A sec-ond oscillation, the *short period*, occurs with negligible variation in V_∞. Its period is usu-ally an order of magnitude less than that of the phugoid; hence, its name. Fortunately, this oscillation is usually well-damped throughout most of the flight envelope.

9.1.2.2 **Lateral-Directional Modes of Motion**. Solving the quartic lateral-directional characteristic equation typically produces two real roots and a single pair of complex roots for a stable conventional airplane. The real roots correspond to the *roll mode* and to the *spiral mode*. Typically, the roll mode has a time constant much shorter than the spiral mode. The oscillation described by the complex pair is the **Dutch roll** mode of motion and is moderately damped throughout the flight envelope for a conventional vehicle.

9.1.3 Handling Qualities

The parameters defined above are excellent tools for engineers and designers; in fact, these individuals must have a solid grasp of such dynamic measures of merit. Unfortu-nately, few operational pilots are engineers. And it is the pilot alone who has the ultimate responsibility for controlling the airplane. An airplane's usefulness or marketability may depend upon either the ease or difficulty the pilot experiences performing the diverse mission tasks. *Handling qualities* describes the pilot workload entailed to perform a spe-cific mission task. For the design engineer and for the flight test team it then becomes necessary to communicate with the pilot and assess the handling qualities of a design be-fore it can be developed to ensure, not just "good" performance, but also "good" handling qualities. Since "goodness" is a subjective measure, there is a need to relate the engineer-ing parameters defined previously and the pilots' opinions regarding the airplane. The U.S. military's handling qualities specifications[7,18] for manned aircraft and their substan-tiating documents[8] have emerged as the most helpful guidelines for quantifying these de-sirable attributes. These specifications spell out the ranges of characteristics that have his-torically provided acceptable handling qualities. Nonetheless, these documents are his-torical and often there is no information on how a new design innovation might affect handling qualities. For that reason the test pilot and the flight test team must be familiar with pilot rating schemes and how they are used in the evaluation of handling qualities.

Pilot opinion surveys, utilizing pilot rating scales like the Cooper-Harper scale, have been used extensively to quantify this subjective information[8]. A large number of pilots flew specific airplanes performing well-defined tasks. Then, ζ and ω_n were altered over a wide range of values. From this statistical base and the opinions recorded, acceptable and unacceptable values of ζ and ω_n were inferred. The rather simplistic illustration on the following page (Fig. 9.6) does not tell the whole story, however. Adapted from Cooper and Harper[10], it merely illustrates the general principle.

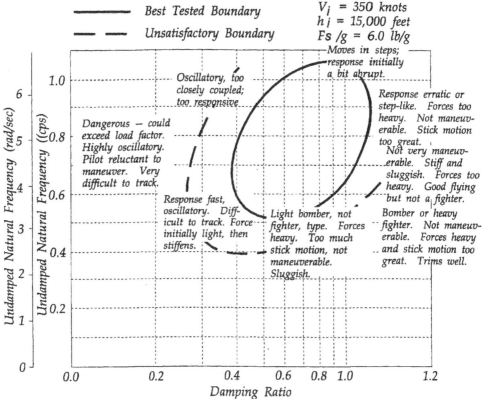

Fig. 9.6. Use of Pilot Opinion Ratings[10]

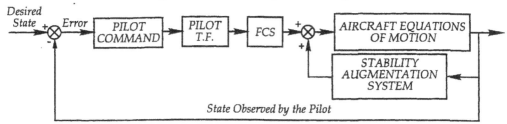

FOR AN OPEN-LOOP SYSTEM, THIS FEEDBACK PATH IS OPEN
Fig. 9.7. Closed- and Open-Loop Block Diagram

9.1.3.1 **Closed-Loop Response versus Open-Loop Response**. The damping ratio and the undamped natural frequency discussed above are properties determined solely by the airplane and its flight control system; that is, they are open-loop parameters. The pilot's inputs close the loop, since he or she acts as an observer (or sensor) and a controller (control law and actuator). The open-loop part of the system is shown in the dashed rectangle in Fig. 9.7, which depicts the closed loop system as well. The component block labeled pilot command is itself a very complex transfer function. A given pilot, performing a particular task at a specific time will have one set of dynamic response characteristics. Change any of these conditions (or even just the pilot's mental and physical state) and the human response is likely to change. This human variability (or, in the best light, adaptability) dictates that flying qualities experiments be carried out under carefully controlled conditions. It also means that the real test of an airplane's handling qualities is in providing satisfactory closed-loop response with a large number of pilots.

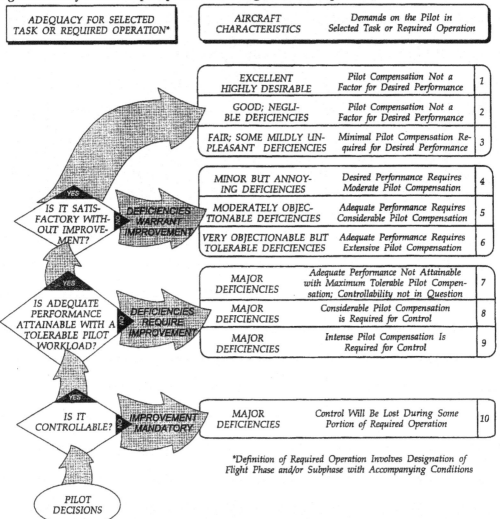

ADEQUACY FOR SELECTED TASK OR REQUIRED OPERATION*	AIRCRAFT CHARACTERISTICS	Demands on the Pilot in Selected Task or Required Operation	
	EXCELLENT HIGHLY DESIRABLE	Pilot Compensation Not a Factor for Desired Performance	1
	GOOD; NEGLI- BLE DEFICIENCIES	Pilot Compensation Not a Factor for Desired Performance	2
	FAIR; SOME MILDLY UN- PLEASANT DEFICIENCIES	Minimal Pilot Compensation Re- quired for Desired Performance	3
	MINOR BUT ANNOY- ING DEFICIENCIES	Desired Performance Requires Moderate Pilot Compensation	4
	MODERATELY OBJEC- TIONABLE DEFICIENCIES	Adequate Performance Requires Considerable Pilot Compensation	5
	VERY OBJECTIONABLE BUT TOLERABLE DEFICIENCIES	Adequate Performance Requires Extensive Pilot Compensation	6
	MAJOR DEFICIENCIES	Adequate Performance Not Attainable with Maximum Tolerable Pilot Compen- sation; Controllability not in Question	7
	MAJOR DEFICIENCIES	Considerable Pilot Compensation is Required for Control	8
	MAJOR DEFICIENCIES	Intense Pilot Compensation Is Required for Control	9
	MAJOR DEFICIENCIES	Control Will Be Lost During Some Portion of Required Operation	10

IS IT SATIS- FACTORY WITH- OUT IMPROVE- MENT?

DEFICIENCIES WARRANT IMPROVEMENT

IS ADEQUATE PERFORMANCE ATTAINABLE WITH A TOLERABLE PILOT WORKLOAD?

DEFICIENCIES REQUIRE IMPROVEMENT

IS IT CONTROLLABLE?

IMPROVEMENT MANDATORY

PILOT DECISIONS

*Definition of Required Operation Involves Designation of Flight Phase and/or Subphase with Accompanying Conditions

Fig. 9.8 Cooper-Harper Pilot Rating Scale

9.1.3.2 Pilot Rating Scales. In the mid-1950s the Society of Experimental Test Pilots (SETP) organized a session of technical papers at an annual meeting of the Institute of Aeronautical Sciences. One of the papers[11] presented was titled "Understanding and Interpreting Pilot Opinion." In 1984 Robert P. Harper, Jr., was invited to give the Wright Brothers Lecture[11] at the 25th AIAA Aircraft Systems Design, Operations, and Test Meeting in San Diego. Much of the background work for this lecture was carried out in variable stability airplanes and in ground simulators but perhaps the most significant result of this lengthy effort is the widely used 10-point Cooper-Harper rating scale (Fig. 9.8). The rating scheme is based on a series of binary decisions in response to these questions:

◆ Is the configuration controllable or uncontrollable?

◆ Is the airplane acceptable or unacceptable?
◆ Is the airplane satisfactory?

Except for a "no" answer to the first question, each of the responses leads to a possibility of three different levels of controllability, acceptability, or satisfaction. If the pilot will lose control of the vehicle during some portion of the mission, then it receives a rating of 10 (the worst qualitative assessment). Now, let's define the governing terms.

Controllability is the ability to command a desired response and is dictated by intended use. In answering the first question, how much attention the pilot must pay to achieve the desired control is not considered. The airplane is *controllable* if he can command the desired response even if he has concentrate all his attention on flying the machine to the exclusion of all else. However, it is not *controllable* in the context of the mission if he cannot maintain control of the airplane with the effort and attention available over and above his other mission duties. Hence, the airplane can be *uncontrollable* for a given mission, even though it does not crash. Cooper-Harper pilot ratings always assess *controllability* for an intended mission. Therefore, the mission and its individual tasks must be clearly and completely defined before pilot ratings have meaning.

Acceptable suggests that the vehicle can accomplish the mission. *Acceptable* does not say how well the required tasks can be performed. It may require an inordinate amount of the pilot's attention to achieve the required level of performance, but it can be done. If the effort, the concentration, and the workload necessary to complete the mission are too high, the pilot may reject the airplane and declare it *unacceptable*.

Satisfactory implies "adequate for the purpose." In pilot ratings, *satisfactory* does not necessarily imply perfection (almost no machine is perfect!). It is good enough that he is not asking that it be fixed; it can meet all the requirements of the assigned mission.

To infuse as much objectivity as possible into the pilot rating process, clear task definition is vital. Not only must the mission be defined, it must be understood alike by both the evaluation pilot and by the test engineer. What the pilot is required to accomplish with the vehicle and the circumstances under which he must perform the mission are two essential elements in this definition. The circumstances may be part of the system being evaluated (like the cockpit displays, the configuration of the airplane, or the weapon controls, for example) or they may come from external influences (like whether turbulence is present or absent, the pilot's level of fatigue, or his proficiency in the task). Since virtually all engineering tests simulate to some degree, this lack of total realism must be clearly understood by both the test engineer conducting the test and the evaluation subject.

No numerical pilot rating totally describes any subject's qualitative assessment. The data must include the subject's narrative comments. The rating itself is merely a summary of all his subjective feelings with regard to the defined task. Any evaluation pilot should be required and encouraged to make qualitative comments over and above the numerical rating. A good flight test engineer will thoughtfully prepare for the debriefing session, seeking to ask questions that will bring out the subtleties that the numerical ratings frequently gloss over. This debriefing session, where such comments are likely to be elicited, should occur immediately after each evaluation. This immediacy suggests that a voice recorder is needed during the flight, especially for complex mission profiles.

Perhaps the most important single element in the subjective rating process is trust between the evaluation pilot and the engineer conducting the experiment. The pilot must be encouraged to believe that the engineer is vitally interested in the qualitative data, and the engineer must be just as assured that the pilot wants to give him accurate, meaningful data. Even when the pilots' comments oppose the engineer's judgment of how the airplane ought to behave based on his knowledge of its characteristics, both parties must strive to communicate and understand each other.

Let us now return to the linearized longitudinal equations of motions succinctly summarized in Table 9.1.

9.1.4 Longitudinal Dynamics

If we define the state vector for the nondimensional equations as $x = [u \quad \alpha \quad \hat{q} \quad \theta]^T$, then the dynamic system can be expressed in conventional state space form.

$$
\begin{aligned}
2\mu D\hat{u} &= (2C_{L_{trim}} \tan\Theta_{trim} + C_{x_u})\hat{u} + C_{x_\alpha}\alpha & & -C_{L_{trim}}\theta & + C_{x_{\delta_e}}\delta_e \\
(2\mu - C_{z_{\dot\alpha}})D\alpha &= (2C_{L_0} + C_{z_u})\hat{u} & + C_{z_\alpha}\alpha + (2\mu + C_{z_q})\hat{q} & & + C_{z_{\delta_e}}\delta_e \\
i_B D\hat{q} - C_{m_{\dot\alpha}}D\alpha &= C_{m_u}\hat{u} & + C_{m_\alpha}\alpha & + C_{m_q}\hat{q} & + C_{m_{\delta_e}}\delta_e \\
D\theta &= \hat{q}
\end{aligned} \tag{9.8}
$$

Equations 9.8 are easily manipulated into matrix form:

$$C_1\dot{x} = A_1 x + B_1 u \tag{9.9}$$

where,

$$
C_1 = \begin{bmatrix} 2\mu & 0 & 0 & 0 \\ 0 & 2\mu - C_{z_{\dot\alpha}} & 0 & 0 \\ 0 & -C_{m_{\dot\alpha}} & i_B & 0 \\ 0 & 0 & 0 & 1 \end{bmatrix}; \quad
A_1 = \begin{bmatrix} 2C_{L_{trim}}\tan\Theta_{trim}+C_{x_u} & C_{x_\alpha} & 0 & -C_{L_{trim}} \\ 0 & C_{z_\alpha} & 2\mu+C_{z_q} & 0 \\ 0 & C_{m_\alpha} & C_{m_q} & 0 \\ 0 & 0 & 1 & 0 \end{bmatrix}
$$

$$
B_1 = \begin{bmatrix} C_{x_{\delta_e}} \\ C_{z_{\delta_e}} \\ C_{m_{\delta_e}} \\ 0 \end{bmatrix}; \quad \text{and, of course,} \quad x = \begin{Bmatrix} \hat{u} \\ \alpha \\ \hat{q} \\ \theta \end{Bmatrix}
$$

In this simplified longitudinal case, where we assume that the elevator is the control (that is, power is not changed and there are no other moveable longitudinal controls), u is a scalar -- not a vector; that is, $u = \delta_e$. If C_1^{-1} exists, eqns. 9.9 can be put into "standard" form by taking $C_1^{-1}A_1 = A$ and $C_1^{-1}B_1 = B$. Then $\dot{x} = Ax + Bu$. A is called the plant matrix and B is called the control matrix.

Operating on eqns. 9.9 with the Laplace operator, they are transformed into algebraic equations which can be solved straightforwardly. If we take Laplace transforms with the usual assumption of zero initial conditions,

$$
\begin{aligned}
(2\mu s - 2C_{L_{trim}}\tan\Theta_{trim} - C_{x_u})\hat{u}(s) - C_{x_\alpha}\alpha(s) & \quad -C_{L_{trim}}\theta(s) &= C_{x_{\delta_e}}\delta_e(s) \\
(2C_{L_0} - C_{z_u})\hat{u}(s) + [(2\mu - C_{z_{\dot\alpha}})s - C_{z_\alpha}]\alpha(s) - (2\mu + C_{z_q})\hat{q}(s) &= C_{z_{\delta_e}}\delta_e(s) \\
-C_{m_u}\hat{u}(s) - (C_{m_{\dot\alpha}}s + C_{m_\alpha})\alpha(s) + (i_B s - C_{m_q}(s))\hat{q}(s) &= C_{m_{\delta_e}}\delta_e(s) \\
s\theta & \quad - \hat{q}(s) &= 0
\end{aligned} \tag{9.10}
$$

The free response comes from solving the equations with the forcing functions (Bu) set to zero. Since the system is linear, the forced response is obtained separately and added to the solution for the free response. The free response can be readily obtained using Cramer's rule or any similar method for solving linear algebraic equations. Symbolically solving for α due to an elevator input, Cramer's rule gives:

$$\frac{\alpha(s)}{\delta_e(s)} = \frac{\det N_\alpha^{\delta_e}(s)}{\det \Delta(s)}$$

where
$$N_\alpha^{\delta_e}(s) = \begin{bmatrix} 2C_{L_{trim}}\,\tan\theta_{trim} + C_{X_u} & C_{X_{\delta_e}} & 0 & -C_{L_{trim}} \\ 0 & C_{Z_{\delta_e}} & 2\mu + C_{Z_q} & 0 \\ 0 & C_{m_{\delta_e}} & C_{m_q} & 0 \\ 0 & 0 & 1 & 0 \end{bmatrix} \text{ and }$$

$$\Delta(s) = \begin{bmatrix} 2C_{L_{trim}}\,\tan\theta_{trim} + C_{X_u} & C_{X_\alpha} & 0 & -C_{L_{trim}} \\ 0 & C_{Z_\alpha} & 2\mu + C_{Z_q} & 0 \\ 0 & C_{m_\alpha} & C_{m_q} & 0 \\ 0 & 0 & 1 & 0 \end{bmatrix}$$

The denominator determinant in the above equation is simply the determinant of the pseudo-plant matrix A_1, which when set to 0, is the characteristic equation of the dynamic system, and its roots are called the eigenvalues. For our simplified longitudinal equations the characteristic equation is a quartic and, for most conventional airplanes, it can be factored into two quadratic terms. These two quadratics describe two oscillations of widely differing frequency; both are illustrated in Fig. 9.9. The lower frequency one is called the phugoid and the higher frequency one is the short period mode of motion.

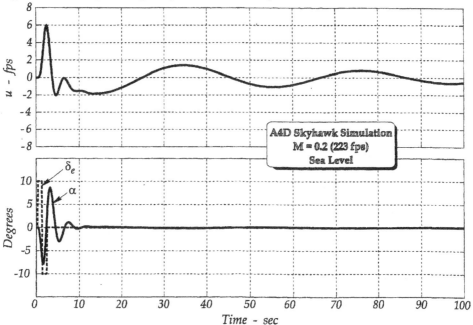

Fig. 9.9 Computed Time Histories after an Elevator Input

The phugoid period ranges from 30 seconds to a minute and a half, while the short period is usually an order of magnitude shorter. The phugoid is also very lightly damped or may be slightly divergent. The pilot's inputs are made often enough that he usually can control a divergent phugoid and not even be aware of a long period instability. Such handling qualities often occur when the airplane is configured for landing (the power approach (PA) configuration in handling qualities requirements[3].) The short period oscillation is consequently of greater importance because the pilot must control it immediately if it is not well-damped. If his reactions are too slow or are phased improperly, his commands may even drive the closed-loop system unstable. Of course, the dynamics of the control system itself may hamper or even preclude the pilot from making appropriate corrections. Such short period motion occurs essentially at constant true airspeed. This fact leads us to an approximation (section 9.1.4.2) for the short period that can be useful in planning flight tests.

9.1.4.1 **Dimensional Form of the Equations**. The linearized longitudinal equations of motions have also been written utilizing dimensional derivatives. McRuer, Ashkenas, and Graham[6] developed these equations with assumptions that essentially parallel the previous development. Taking stability axes that align the x-axis with the relative wind in the trim condition, $W_{trim} = 0$. $X_{\dot{w}} = X_q = 0$ have also proven to be satisfactory assumptions. Then, eqns. 9.4 can be rewritten in matrix form:

$$C_2 \dot{x} = A_2 x + B_2 u \tag{9.11}$$

$$\text{where } C_2 = \begin{bmatrix} 1 & 0 & 0 & 0 \\ 0 & 1-Z_{\dot{w}} & 0 & 0 \\ 0 & -M_{\dot{w}} & 1 & 0 \\ 0 & 0 & 0 & 1 \end{bmatrix}; \quad A_2 = \begin{bmatrix} X_u & X_w & 0 & -g\cos\theta_{trim} \\ Z_u & Z_w & U_{trim}+Z_q & 0 \\ M_u & M_w & M_q & 0 \\ 0 & 0 & 1 & 0 \end{bmatrix}$$

$$\text{and } B_2 = \begin{bmatrix} X_{\delta_e} \\ Z_{\delta_e} \\ M_{\delta_e} \\ 0 \end{bmatrix}; \text{ and, } x = \begin{bmatrix} u \\ \alpha \\ q \\ \theta \end{bmatrix}$$

9.1.4.2 **Short Period Approximation**. Considering eqns. 9.6 with $\hat{u} = 0$ (no perturbation in airspeed), four equations in three unknowns result. Since $\hat{q}$ is simply related to the pitch attitude by taking the derivative with respect to time and since the x force equation represents the momentum change in the direction of u, it is logical to select the z force equation and the pitching moment equation to approximate the two unknowns of interest, α and θ. Sticking to the Laplace operator form and the non-dimensional stability coefficients and assuming that $C_{Z\dot{\alpha}}$ and C_{Z_q} are negligible, eqns. 9.6 reduce to: $\hspace{1cm}$ (9.12)

$$(2\mu s - C_{Z_\alpha})\alpha - (2\mu s + C_{L_{trim}} \tan\Theta_{trim})\theta = C_{Z_{\delta_e}}\delta_e$$

$$-(C_{m\dot{\alpha}}s + C_{m_\alpha})\alpha + (i_B s - C_{m_q})s\theta = C_{m_{\delta_e}}\delta_e$$

For these simplified equations, the characteristic determinant yields a cubic in s that factors readily into a trivial $s = 0$ factor and a quadratic factor if we assume that $\Theta_{trim} = 0$

$$a_2 s^2 + a_1 s + a_0 = 0 \tag{9.13}$$

where $a_2 = 2\mu i_B$, $a_1 = -2\mu(C_{m\dot{\alpha}} + C_{m_q}) - C_{z_\alpha} i_B$, and $a_0 = C_{m_q} C_{z_\alpha} - 2\mu C_{m_\alpha}$

Dividing eqn. 9.13 by a_2 and comparing this result with eqn. 9.3:

$$\omega_{n_{sp}} \approx \sqrt{\frac{C_{m_q} C_{z_\alpha} - 2\mu C_{m_\alpha}}{2\mu i_B}} \quad \text{and} \quad \zeta_{sp} \approx \frac{-2\mu(C_{m\dot{\alpha}} + C_{m_q}) - C_{z_\alpha} i_B}{2\omega_{n_{sp}}} \tag{9.14}$$

These approximations are too complicated to provide ready insight into the important derivatives that affect the short period mode's undamped natural frequency and damping ratio. In the expression above for $\omega_{n_{sp}}$, the product $C_{m_q}C_{z_\alpha}$ is often small relative to the C_{m_α} term. C_{m_α} is the dominant derivative in estimating $\omega_{n_{sp}}$, though physical physical configuration and flight conditions also contribute through μ and i_B. Similarly, in the first term for ζ_{sp}, $C_{m_{\dot\alpha}}$ may be small (more often, it is simply ignored) in comparison to C_{m_q}. Omitting $C_{m_{\dot\alpha}}$ from the expression alters the form of the result not at all and often the value of the damping term changes little. The damping ratio depends primarily on the stability derivative C_{m_q}. The moment of inertia about the y axis is important, as are the flight conditions. With these assumptions, eqns. 9.14 simplify to:

$$\omega_{n_{sp}} \approx \sqrt{\frac{-C_{m_\alpha}}{i_B}} \quad \text{and} \quad \zeta_{sp} \approx \frac{-2\mu C_{m_q} - C_{z_\alpha} i_B}{2\omega_{n_{sp}}} \tag{9.15}$$

Using dimensional derivatives, these approximations take the form:

$$\omega_{n_{sp}} \approx \sqrt{-M_\alpha} \quad \text{and} \quad \zeta_{sp} \approx \frac{-M_q - Z_w}{2\omega_{n_{sp}}} \tag{9.16}$$

If we return to our spring-mass-damper analogy, $-M_\alpha$ is the spring constant in the short period, while the horizontal tail kinematically dominates the damping.

Care must be exercised in applying these approximations. The primary reason for introducing them is to clarify which stability derivatives most influence the dynamic figures of merit. Do not use eqns. 9.15 or 9.16 when precise values for $\omega_{n_{sp}}$ and ζ_{sp} are needed. Too many assumptions are involved. Moreover, numerical methods for calculating eigenvalues of high-order systems are readily available on personal computers.

9.1.4.3 **Phugoid Approximation**. As Fig. 9.9 suggests, the phugoid oscillation occurs at essentially constant angle of attack (remember α is the perturbation in angle of attack from the trim condition). Thus, the equations of motion can be reduced from 4 to 2 with a line of reasoning similar to that used for the short period approximation. In this case the moment equation is the logical candidate for elimination since the rotational motion has little effect on exchange of kinetic and potential energy. Neglect C_{z_q}, take $\Theta_{trim} = 0$, and recall that $\alpha \approx 0$ during the phugoid oscillation, the x and z force equations reduce to:

$$(2\mu s - C_{x_u})\hat{u} + C_{L_{trim}}\theta - C_{x_{\delta_e}}\delta_e = 0$$
$$(2C_{L_{trim}} - C_{z_u})\hat{u} - 2\mu s\theta - C_{z_{\delta_e}}\delta_e = 0 \tag{9.17}$$

The characteristic equation for these approximate equations is simpler than for the full set. Since lift is little different from weight if the vehicle is not perturbed far from equilibrium conditions, a quadratic equation again results with coefficients: $a_2 = 4\mu^2$, $a_1 = -2\mu C_{x_u}$, and $a_0 = 2C_{L_{trim}}^2 - C_{L_{trim}}C_{z_u}$. Then,

$$\omega_{n_p} \approx \frac{\sqrt{C_{L_{trim}}(2C_{L_{trim}} - C_{z_u})}}{2\mu} \quad \text{and} \quad \zeta_p \approx -\frac{C_{x_u}}{2\sqrt{C_{L_{trim}}(2C_{L_{trim}} - C_{z_u})}} \tag{9.18}$$

However, except for transonic flight, C_{z_u} is usually small compared to $2C_{L_{trim}}$; so,

$$\omega_{n_p} \approx \frac{C_{L_{trim}}}{\mu\sqrt{2}} \quad \text{and} \quad \zeta_p \approx -\frac{C_{x_u}}{2\sqrt{2}C_{L_{trim}}} \tag{9.19}$$

To interpret eqns. 9.19 physically, recall that ω_{n_p} is expressed in nondimensional time units; that is, radians/airsec, where, as noted under Table 9.2, $t^* = \dfrac{\ell}{u_0}$. So to put ω_{n_p} into physical time units, we must divide eqn. 9.17a by this parameter. Carrying out this division and noting that $C_{L_{trim}} = \dfrac{2W}{\rho u_{trim}^2 S}$ and that $\mu = \dfrac{W}{\rho g S \ell}$,

$$\omega_{n_p} \approx \frac{2W}{\rho u_{trim}^2 S} \frac{\rho g S \ell}{\sqrt{2W}} \frac{u_{trim}}{\ell} \approx \frac{\sqrt{2}g}{u_{trim}} \tag{9.20}$$

In trimmed level flight, still ignoring transonic effects, $C_{x_u} = -2C_{D_0}$. Thus,

$$\zeta_p \approx \frac{C_{D_0}}{\sqrt{2}C_{L_{trim}}} \approx \frac{D_0}{\sqrt{2}L_{trim}} \tag{9.21}$$

The phugoid damping ratio can also be approximated with dimensional derivatives:

$$\zeta_p \approx -\frac{X_u}{2\omega_{n_p}} \tag{9.22}$$

Equations 9.20 through 9.22 must be used carefully, but they show that the phugoid natural frequency is inversely proportional to true airspeed. This approximation suggests that the phugoid time constant $\tau_p \approx 0.138u_0$. It also indicates ω_{n_p} and τ_p are roughly independent of altitude and gross weight of the airplane. Blakelock[12] shows that both these frequency parameters do depend on variations in density, evidently because of the effects of terms neglected in this analysis. For equilibrium flight eqn. 9.21 implies that ζ_p is directly proportional to total vehicle drag. As trim airspeed increases at constant altitude, phugoid damping ratio increases as the square of the airspeed. Similarly, if true airspeed is held constant, ζ_p decreases in direct proportion to the change in density with altitude. While these approximate equations do not give accurate answers, they do offer insight into the most important stability derivatives affecting the phugoid.

Employing the spring-mass-damper analogy again, the phugoid's spring constant is the lift-weight surplus or deficit as the airplane exchanges altitude and airspeed. At the bottom of an oscillation, the airplane has surplus lift; at the top it has a lift deficit. Aerodynamic drag provides damping.

Example 9.1: Several examples of typical aircraft dimensional stability derivative data are given by McRuer, Ashkenas, and Graham[6]. The data in Table 9.3 summarize such stability derivatives for an attack airplane flying at low subsonic speeds. Solving the characteristic equation that results from equations 9.11 with the data in Table 9.3 we get: $\omega_{n_{sp}} = 1.5611$ rad/sec and $\zeta_{sp} = 0.3588$. Using approximations like eqns. 9.20 and 9.22: $\omega_{n_{sp}} \approx 1.5082$ and $\zeta_{sp} \approx 0.2609$

Table 9.3 Longitudinal Data for a Subsonic Fighter ($M = 0.2$, h = sea level)

X_u	-0.0813 (sec^{-1})	M_u	-0.0029 (ft-sec)$^{-1}$
X_w	-0.0312 (sec^{-1})	M_w	-0.0102 (ft-sec)$^{-1}$
X_{δ_h}	0.00432 (ft/sec^2/rad)	$M_{\dot{w}}$	-0.000646 (ft^{-1})
Z_u	-0.026 (sec^{-1})	M_q	-0.48 (sec^{-2})
Z_w	-0.307 (sec^{-1})	M_{δ_e}	-2.21 (sec^{-2})
$Z_{\dot{w}}$	-0.001681	M_{δ_h}	0.000152 (sec^{-2})
Z_{δ_e}	-7.07 (ft/sec^2/rad)		

<u>Note:</u> This airplane has both a trimmable horizontal tail and an elevator (denoted by subscripts δ_h and δ_e, respectively, above). Elevator deflection does not affect the X force equation.

The approximate undamped natural frequency differs from that calculated from the full characteristic equation by approximately 3.4% while the estimated damping ratio is about 17% higher. A similar calculation for the phugoid mode yields considerably less satisfactory results, with the approximation giving an error of approximately 34% in ω_{n_p} and over 200% in ζ_p. These approximations are useful for quick estimates of the short period but the phugoid estimates are extremely crude.

Table 9.4 Stability Derivatives Significantly Affecting Longitudinal Oscillations[12]

Aerodynamic Parameter	Motion Parameter Affected Most	Effect on Motion Parameter
C_{m_q}	Short period damping ratio, ζ_{sp}	ζ_{sp} increases with increasing C_{m_q}
C_{m_α}	Short period undamped natural frequency, $\omega_{n_{sp}}$	$\omega_{n_{sp}}$ increases with increasing C_{m_α}
C_{x_u} or D_0	Phugoid damping ratio, ζ_p	ζ_p increases with increasing C_{x_u} or D_0
C_{z_u} or $\left(\dfrac{1}{V_\infty}\right)$	Phugoid undamped natural frequency, ω_{n_p}	ω_{n_p} increases with increasing C_{z_u} or $\left(\dfrac{1}{V_\infty}\right)$

9.1.4.4 Sensitivity to Longitudinal Stability Derivatives. Blakelock[12] has also examined the sensitivity of the damping and natural frequency of the longitudinal modes of motion to variations in C_{x_u}, C_{x_α}, C_{z_u}, $C_{x_{\dot\alpha}}$, C_{m_α}, $C_{m_{\dot\alpha}}$, and C_{m_q}. Table 9.4 summarizes his findings for a four engine jet transport.

9.1.4.5 Summary of Linear Longitudinal Dynamics. The linearized longitudinal equations of motion used to analyze airplane pitch dynamics illustrate the complexity of dynamic flight tests. Approximate equations of motion, obtained to help the flight test engineer anticipate trends in dynamic figures of merit, must be used with good judgment. They give insight to help plan dynamic flight tests more efficiently and to identify trends in data collected that indicate undesirable longitudinal dynamic characteristics.

9.1.5 Lateral-Directional Dynamics

The linearized lateral-directional equations (see Tables 9.1 and 9.2) are separated from the longitudinal ones by assuming that the product of inertia I_{xz} is negligible and that there are no other significant aerodynamic or control surface coupling terms. With these decoupled equations we study the asymmetric dynamic response of an airplane or a missile. Choosing the state vector $x = \begin{bmatrix} \beta & \hat{p} & \hat{r} & \phi \end{bmatrix}^T$, we put eqns. 9.7 in matrix form:

$$
\begin{aligned}
2\mu D\beta &= C_{y_\beta}\beta + C_{y_p}\hat{p} - (2\mu - C_{y_r})\hat{r} + C_{L_{trim}}\phi + \quad C_{y_{\delta_a}}\delta_a + C_{y_{\delta_r}}\delta_r \\
i_A D\hat{p} - i_E D\hat{r} &= C_{\ell_\beta}\beta + C_{\ell_p}\hat{p} \quad + C_{\ell_r}\hat{r} \quad\quad\quad + \quad C_{\ell_{\delta_a}}\delta_a + C_{\ell_{\delta_r}}\delta_r \\
-i_E D\hat{p} + i_C D\hat{r} &= C_{n_\beta}\beta + C_{n_p}\hat{p} \quad + C_{n_r}\hat{r} \quad\quad\quad + \quad C_{n_{\delta_a}}\delta_a + C_{n_{\delta_r}}\delta_r \\
D\phi &= \quad\quad\quad\quad\quad \hat{p}
\end{aligned}
\tag{9.23}
$$

These equations can be rearranged into the matrix form of eqn. 9.9

$$C_3 = \begin{bmatrix} 2\mu & 0 & 0 & 0 \\ 0 & i_A & -i_E & 0 \\ 0 & -i_E & i_C & 0 \\ 0 & 0 & 0 & 1 \end{bmatrix}; \quad A_3 = \begin{bmatrix} C_{Y_\beta} & C_{Y_p} & C_{Y_r} - 2\mu & C_{L_{trim}} \\ C_{\mathcal{L}_\beta} & C_{\mathcal{L}_p} & C_{\mathcal{L}_r} & 0 \\ C_{n_\beta} & C_{n_p} & C_{n_r} & 0 \\ 0 & 0 & 0 & 1 \end{bmatrix}$$

$$B_3 = \begin{bmatrix} C_{y_{\delta_a}} & C_{y_{\delta_r}} \\ C_{\mathcal{L}_{\delta_a}} & C_{\mathcal{L}_{\delta_r}} \\ C_{n_{\delta_a}} & C_{n_{\delta_r}} \\ 0 & 0 \end{bmatrix}; \quad \text{and} \quad x = \begin{Bmatrix} \beta \\ \hat{p} \\ \hat{r} \\ \phi \end{Bmatrix}$$

Again, if C_3^{-1} exists, this control equation can be put into "standard" form by premultiplying the plant and the control matrices by C_3^{-1}: $C_3^{-1}A_3 = A$ and $C_3^{-1}B_3 = B$.

9.1.5.1 **Dimensional Form of the Equations**. The linearized lateral-directional equations of motions can also be written using dimensional derivatives. McRuer, Ashkenas, and Graham[6] give the full development and the complete set of assumptions.

$$C_4\dot{x} = A_4 x + B_4 u \qquad (9.24)$$

$$\text{where } C_4 = \begin{bmatrix} 1 & 0 & 0 & 0 \\ 0 & I_x & -I_{xz} & 0 \\ 0 & -I_{xz} & I_z & 0 \\ 0 & 0 & 0 & 1 \end{bmatrix}; \quad A_4 = \begin{bmatrix} Y_v & Y_p & Y_r - V_\infty & -g\cos\theta_{trim} \\ \mathcal{L}_v & \mathcal{L}_p & \mathcal{L}_r & 0 \\ N_v & N_p & N_r & 0 \\ 0 & 0 & 0 & 1 \end{bmatrix}$$

$$B_4 = \begin{bmatrix} Y_{\delta_a} & Y_{\delta_r} \\ \mathcal{L}_{\delta_a} & \mathcal{L}_{\delta_r} \\ N_{\delta_a} & N_{\delta_a} \\ 0 & 0 \end{bmatrix} \quad \text{and} \quad x = \begin{bmatrix} v \\ \hat{p} \\ \hat{r} \\ \phi \end{bmatrix}$$

For either set of lateral-directional equations the control vector includes at least two elements. For conventional aircraft, $u^T = [\delta_a \ \delta_r]$. The plant matrix sets the free response of the system; its eigenvalues describe transient behavior. Typical characteristic roots include two aperiodic and one oscillatory modes (two linear factors and one quadratic factor). These three modes of motion comprise the asymmetric dynamics for a conventional airplane. All three modes are superimposed after an aileron excitation, making it difficult to identify the roll mode (Fig. 9.10, next page). Dutch roll dominates the time history.

9.1.5.2 **Roll Mode**. The roll mode describes the response of the airplane to a lateral or roll command. For a conventional airplane, the control surface input would be the aileron. The expected response is a decaying exponential in roll rate with a small time constant, usually on the order of 1 or 2 seconds. Military specifications establish upper limits on the time constant depending upon airplane category and mission phase[3,8,18]. This mode is illustrated later in Fig. 9.17.

9.1.5.3 **Roll Mode Approximation**. Etkin[4], Blakelock[12], and Roskam[5] retain only the rolling moment equation for an approximate expression that shows which of the stability derivatives most influences the roll mode time constant. The rolling moment alone is assumed to contain all needed information. Moreover, the β and $\hat{r}$ terms are neglected.

$$I_x\dot{\hat{p}} - \mathcal{L}_p\hat{p} = 0 \qquad (9.24)$$

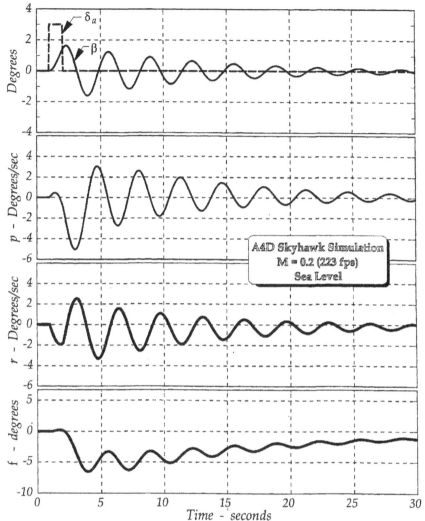

Fig. 9.10 Lateral-Directional Dynamic Response

9.1.5.4 Spiral Mode. The other first order lateral-directional mode of motion has a much longer time constant, typically about 10 times that of the roll mode. This spiral mode relates time to the airplane's tendency to roll and descend if no control action is taken. Bank angle is the most logical dynamic flight test measurement used to describe the spiral mode. Like the phugoid mode discussed under the longitudinal response, the spiral mode can be controlled easily by the pilot under normal circumstances even if the bank angle is divergent. The time-to-double-amplitude must, however, be long enough so that the pilot does not have to devote an excessive amount of his attention to this correction. Figure 9.11 illustrates both a divergent and a convergent spiral mode, from simulations for the A-4 Skyhawk aircraft model given by McRuer, Ashkenas, and Graham[6]. The spiral mode is typical of many aircraft; at high altitude and high α the spiral diverges. The divergent time constant long, suggesting the instability is likely be a nuisance to the pilot. Both military and civilian requirements allow some spiral mode instability, because of the relative ease with which such divergences can be controlled by the pilot.

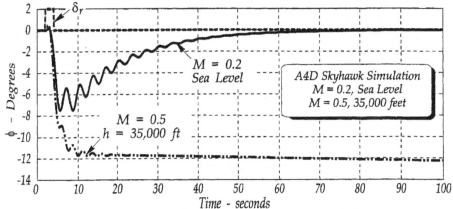

Fig. 9.11 Stable and Unstable Spiral Modes of Motion

9.1.5.5 Spiral Mode Approximation. Roskam[5] suggests an approximate expression for the spiral mode, generated using the same general approach as above. However, this approximation is often quite inaccurate. The highly coupled nature of lateral and directional modes of motion often makes such estimates unacceptably crude. Part of the difficulty lies in deciding which of the four equations best represents this mode of motion. We note that β changes little in a spiral, suggesting that elimination of the side force equation may work; further, in the spiral transient, roll rates are usually low. Following Roskam, we take $p = 0$ and ignore the side force equation. Simplifying eqns. 9.7 with these assumptions, extracting the simplified characteristic equation, and solving for λ_s yields:

$$\lambda_s = \frac{C_{\mathcal{L}_\beta} C_{n_r} - C_{n_\beta} C_{\mathcal{L}_r}}{\dfrac{I_z C_{\mathcal{L}_\beta}}{S\bar{q}b} + \dfrac{I_{xz} C_{n_\beta}}{S\bar{q}b}} \tag{9.26}$$

For conventional airplanes and stability axes, $I_{xz}C_{n_\beta} \ll I_z C_{\mathcal{L}_\beta}$ because of the relative sizes of I_z and I_{xz}. Then, eqn. 9.26 simplifies further

$$\lambda_s \approx \frac{C_{\mathcal{L}_\beta} C_{n_r} - C_{n_\beta} C_{\mathcal{L}_r}}{\dfrac{I_z C_{\mathcal{L}_\beta}}{S\bar{q}b}} \tag{9.27}$$

The inaccuracy of this approximation is underscored using Blakelock's jet transport example and calculating the spiral mode eigenvalue and its associated time constant from the full set of equations. The results are: $\lambda_s = 0.004/\text{sec}$ and $T_s = 250$ sec. By way of comparison, eqn. 9.27 gives: $\lambda_s \approx 0.099/\text{sec}$ and $T_s \approx 10.1$ sec. Clearly, the approximation leaves much to be desired. It did show the spiral to be unstable; but it does a poor job of predicting the transient metrics of the mode. Roskam points out that the asymmetric aerodynamic forces depend on β, $\dot{\phi}$, and $\dot{\psi}$, rather than on β, ϕ, and ψ. The damping terms associated with $\dot{\phi}$ and $\dot{\psi}$ are often of the same magnitude as those due to β. Consequently, they cannot be neglected safely. The approximation exercise is not futile, for we can pick out the significant stability derivatives from eqn. 9.27. The numerator term on the right, coupled with knowledge that dihedral effect is negative for a conventional airplane, leads to the following condition for a stable spiral mode.

$$C_{\mathcal{L}_\beta} C_{n_r} > C_{n_\beta} C_{\mathcal{L}_r} \tag{9.28}$$

Because the spiral mode has a relatively long time constant, it is not absolutely essential that it be stable. As Blakelock shows, many airplanes exhibit divergent spiral modes at low speeds and convergent spiral modes at high speed. The spiral mode and the Dutch roll mode are both strongly affected by dihedral effect (eqn. 9.28); increasing dihedral effect (making $C_{\mathcal{L}_\beta}$ more negative) to stabilize the spiral mode can reduce Dutch roll damping. Often a slight spiral instability is accepted to improve Dutch roll damping, a mode that has a much larger effect on lateral-directional handling qualities. So, except during the performance of certain tasks (instrument approaches, for example) requiring virtually all of the pilot's attention, handling qualities perceived by the pilot may be largely unaffected by an unstable spiral mode. Moreover, the spiral mode can be controlled fairly easily with stability augmentation; yaw dampers, even in their simplest forms, can be designed to improve spiral stability in a closed-loop automatic control system.

9.1.5.6 **Dutch Roll Mode**. This lateral-directional oscillation is a tightly coupled rolling and yawing motions usually occurring at medium to high frequency and having moderate to light damping with no yaw damper installed. Typically, at cruise conditions the period of the oscillation is about 3 seconds. The bank angle to sideslip angle ratio, $\frac{\phi}{\beta}$, is a key parameter, often indicating how pilots react to such an oscillation. Usually, a low $\frac{\phi}{\beta}$ ratio (yaw dominates the Dutch roll) is more acceptable to pilots than an oscillation with relatively large bank angle excursions. If the Dutch roll is lightly damped and/or the frequency is high, it may be necessary to add a yaw damper or similar automatic flight control system component to augment the natural characteristics of the aircraft.

9.1.5.7 **Dutch Roll Approximation**. Roskam[5], Blakelock[12], and Nelson[19] approximate the Dutch roll oscillation by simplifying the equations of motion, each with a slightly different approach. Blakelock suggests that the rudder input transfer function $\frac{\beta(s)}{\delta_r(s)}$ shows that there is a pole-zero cancellation effectively negating the roll subsidence in the lateral-directional characteristic equation. This cancellation allows the rolling moment equation to be ignored in Blakelock's Dutch roll approximation and assumes that Dutch roll consists of only sideslip and yaw. Pure sideslip ($\beta = -\psi$) and zero change in V_∞ during the maneuver are also postulated. Then $r = \dot{\Psi}$. The side force equation does not contribute to the free yawing motion with these assumptions; that is, $-Y_\beta \beta = Y_{\delta_r}\delta_r$. So, Blakelock's approximation is based entirely on the yawing moment equation.

$$\left(N_\beta + s^2 - N_r s\right)\psi \approx 0 \text{ or } \left(s^2 - N_r s + N_\beta\right)\Psi \approx 0 \tag{9.29}$$

If we compare eqn. 9.29 to the standard form for a damped quadratic,

$$\omega_{n_{Dr}} \approx \sqrt{N_\beta} \tag{9.30}$$

This equation shows the dependence of $\omega_{n_{Dr}}$ on N_β. Also, $N_\beta = \frac{C_{n_\beta}\bar{q}Sb}{I_z}$, emphasizing the direct link of $\omega_{n_{Dr}}$ to altitude (through $\bar{q}$). Like the short period, $\omega_{n_{Dr}}$ is directly proportional to V_∞. Increasing airspeed increases $\omega_{n_{Dr}}$ and increasing altitude decreases $\omega_{n_{Dr}}$.

Alternatively, we could improve our approximation by solving the reduced order set (side force and yawing moment equations only) as both Roskam[5] and Nelson[19] do. This approach is useful for airplanes with low dihedral effect. The characteristic equation is:

$$s\left[s^2 - s\left(N_r + \frac{Y_\beta}{V_\infty}\right) + \left(\frac{Y_\beta N_r}{V_\infty} + N_\beta - \frac{N_\beta Y_r}{V_\infty}\right)\right] = 0$$

Now, the approximate expression for $\omega_{n_{Dr}}$ is slightly more complicated.

$$\omega_{n_{Dr}} \approx \sqrt{\frac{Y_\beta N_r + N_\beta V_\infty - N_\beta Y_r}{V_\infty}} \tag{9.31}$$

The middle term in eqn. 9.31 usually dominates the lateral-directional oscillation; so, this approximation is in effect adding smaller terms to the approximation of eqn. 9.30. From this characteristic equation the damping ratio ζ_{Dr} is approximated by:

$$\zeta_{Dr} = -\frac{Y_\beta + V_\infty N_r}{2\omega_{n_{Dr}} V_\infty} \tag{9.32}$$

Damping ratio is dominated by the second term, set by the ratio $-\dfrac{N_r}{\sqrt{N_\beta}}$, and it is related to $\bar{q}$, using similar reasoning as we did for $\omega_{n_{Dr}}$.

Example 9.2: Returning to the airplane considered earlier to illustrate longitudinal dynamics to provide additional insight into lateral-dynamics and our approximations. The data[6] are summarized in Table 9.5.

Table 9.5 Lateral-Directional Data for an Attack Airplane ($M = 0.2$, h = sea level)

Y_β	- 22.9 (ft/sec²/rad)	$\angle_{\delta_a}$	1.875 (sec⁻²)
Y_{δ_a}	- 0.606 (ft/sec²/rad)	$\angle_{\delta_r}$	0.1284 (sec⁻²)
Y_{δ_r}	- 0.00272 (ft/sec²/rad)	N_β	2.8 (sec⁻²)
$\angle_\beta$	- 3.21 (sec⁻²)	N_p	- 0.111 (sec⁻¹)
$\angle_p$	- 0.412 (sec⁻¹)	N_r	- 0.296 (sec⁻¹)
$\angle_r$	- 0.0317 (sec⁻¹)	N_{δ_a}	- 0.0242 (sec⁻²)
		N_{δ_r}	- 1.272 (sec⁻²)

Substituting the derivatives from Table 9.5 into the approximate relations and comparing to the solution of the complete small perturbation lateral-directional equations gives an approximate $\omega_{n_{Dr}}$ that is about 8.5% smaller than comes from the complete equations: $\omega_{n_{Dr}}$ is 1.894 rad/sec from the complete set of equations, while the approximation gives 1.6823 rad/sec. The same comparison for ζ_{Dr} shows that Dutch roll damping ratio is overpredicted significantly; ζ_{Dr} is approximated as 0.1185, compared to 0.0502 for the complete equations result. This error is over 100%. For this example at least, this Dutch roll approximation gives a fairly reasonable estimate of Dutch roll frequency, but the damping ratio is unreliable. The approximation typically gives such results. Roskam applies a similar approximation to a small business jet and finds that the Dutch roll frequency is predicted quite well (1.62 rad/sec from the approximation compared to 1.618 rad/sec from the approximation). Again, the damping ratio is not predicted well (0.058 from the approximate solution vis-à-vis 0.036 for the complete equations).

Table 9.6 Effect of Altitude and Airspeed on the Roll Mode of an Attack Airplane

Flight Conditions		Time Constant (seconds)	
Altitude (feet)	Airspeed (fps)	Approximation (eqn. 9.25)	Full Equations (eqns. 9.7)
Sea Level	223	2.42	1.78
Sea Level	950	0.26	0.26
35,000	487	1.87	1.78
35,000	681	1.23	1.19

Table 9.7 Effect of Altitude and Airspeed on the Dutch Roll Mode of an Attack Airplane

| Flight Conditions | | Damping Ratio | | ω_n (rad/sec) | |
Altitude (feet)	Airspeed (fps)	Approximations (eqns. 9.31/ 9.32)	Full Equations (eqns. 9.24)	Approximations (eqns. 9.31/ 9.32)	Full Equations (eqns. 9.24)
Sea Level	223	0.1185	0.0502	1.68	1.89
Sea Level	950	0.1180	0.1203	8.58	8.29
35,000	487	0.06980	0.0734	2.34	2.55
35,000	681	0.06580	0.0625	3.37	3.47

Table 9.6 summarizes the effects of airspeed and altitude on the roll mode and Table 9.7 illustrates the effect of these variables on the Dutch roll mode. Each tabulation shows the errors introduced in using our approximations. Clearly, the complete equations are preferable. These complete equations generated the time histories in Fig. 9.12 (next page), showing the character of the Dutch roll. The time histories show the strong damping that develops at high dynamic pressure; there is a stark contrast between the first two time histories in Fig. 9.12 that illustrate this effect. Also, the decrease in $\omega_{n_{Dr}}$ as altitude increases is clearly seen. Finally, notice the large increase in $\omega_{n_{Dr}}$ as airspeed increases at either altitude

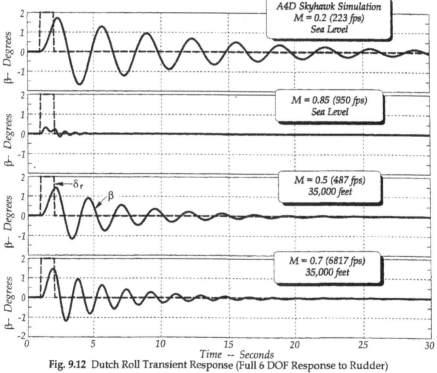

Fig. 9.12 Dutch Roll Transient Response (Full 6 DOF Response to Rudder)

9.1.5.8 **Sensitivity to Lateral-Directional Stability Derivatives**. Blakelock[12] also cites the sensitivity of the lateral-directional modes to variations in asymmetric derivatives. Table 9.8 summarizes the effects of the most significant derivatives on this type of motion, as we previously did for the longitudinal modes of motion. Notice that our example, using the mathematical model of a rather different airplane, leads to the same conclusions.

Table 9.8 Effects of Stability Derivatives on Asymmetric Modes of Motion[12]

Stability Derivative	Motion Parameter Affected Most	Effect on Motion Parameter
C_{n_r}	ζ_{Dr}	Increase $\left|C_{n_r}\right|$ to increase damping
C_{n_β}	$\omega_{n_{Dr}}$	Increase C_{n_β} to increase natural frequency
C_{ℓ_p}	Roll Subsidence	Increase $\left|C_{\ell_p}\right|$ to increase roll mode time constant
C_{ℓ_β}	Spiral Divergence	Increase $\left|C_{\ell_\beta}\right|$ to improve spiral stability

9.1.5.9 **Summary of Linear Lateral-Directional Dynamics.** The linearized lateral-directional equations of motion illustrate how complex asymmetric motions are. Approximate equations are more inaccurate than for symmetric motions. Though these approximations are helpful in planning flight tests, they must be used with discretion.

9.2 DYNAMIC FLIGHT TEST METHODS

Flight tests to determine dynamic characteristics of airplanes are some of the most challenging. Flying precision and care in data reduction require are responsible for this challenge. Moreover, the subjective character of closed-loop handling qualities is tied closely to open-loop dynamic characteristics of the vehicle and its control system. So, cooperation and understanding between pilot and flight test engineer are essential to obtaining meaningful results. First, consider how open-loop dynamics can best be excited.

9.2.1 Types of Control Inputs

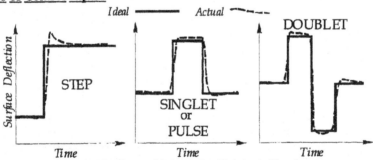

Fig. 9.13 Control Inputs for Dynamic Testing

An infinite number of inputs could be used; indeed, random excitations from atmospheric disturbances excite the dynamics when encountered. However, most linear dynamic theory is built around three ideal inputs -- step inputs, pulse inputs, and doublets (Fig. 9.13). Except for the phugoid and the spiral modes, dynamic motions are usually excited by rapid pilot inputs to the control surfaces. No control system provides an infinite surface rate; so, ideal inputs cannot be achieved. Even if the control system could provide such rates, pilots cannot perfectly return the surface to its trim position. Pilot inputs are not repeatable from test point to test point, much less from pilot to pilot. Some flight test programs use automatic flight control system inputs to excite dynamic modes. Repeatability is improved when electromechanical inputs are programmed into the flight profile. The Shuttle Orbiter and the X-29 are two test programs where such programmed inputs were used to advantage.

9.2.1.1 **Step Input**. An ideal step input moves the control surface to the desired position in zero time. The surface then remains in that position, either because the pilot restrains it or because the surface has no tendency to float with hinge moments (as in an irreversible control system). If the stick or rudder is freed and the trim mechanism moves the stick or rudder back to the original position, the input is no longer a step. The final level is not maintained. So, as Fig. 9.13 shows, there is a finite slope to an actual step input. A step input has the effect of setting the control surface to a new trim position, which causes the vehicle to take on a new equilibrium state. An elevator step input will cause an airplane to stabilize in a new attitude, a new trim airspeed and a new trim α, some time after the input. Any oscillation excited by the input does not return to the original equilibrium, complicating analysis of the time history.

9.2.1.2 **Singlet**. As Fig. 9.13 also shows, a singlet (often called a pulse) is merely a step input, followed a short time later by a negative step input of the same size but opposite sense. The surface deflections occur instantaneously in an ideal singlet. Remember, infinite rates of movement of any physical mechanism are not possible.

9.2.1.3 **Doublet**. A doublet, merely a singlet followed immediately by a second singlet opposite in sense to the first one, is a common technique used to excite dynamic modes of motion. A doublet is ordinarily used when an oscillation about the original equilibrium point is sought. For quick evaluation of dynamic characteristics without mathematical analysis, such a time history is easy to interpret. The doublet is a periodic function if performed perfectly (Fig. 9.13). This sketch makes it easy to visualize the frequency content of such an excitation. As expected, the nature of the response depends on the frequency of this input, a feature to be discussed more fully when we focus on the longitudinal modes of motion. The phugoid, with little dependence on the input nature, allows the pilot to use controls other than the primary surfaces for excitation.

9.2.2 Phugoid Test Methods

The first step in setting up any of the dynamic tests is to carefully trim the airplane at the desired test conditions. The engineer should insist that equilibrium conditions are attained before any excitation is applied. A good rule of thumb is that, if airspeed and airspeed can be maintained within 0.5 KIAS and 20 feet for 10-15 seconds, trim is satisfactorily established. The pilot must make no control inputs during this time. The phugoid test is one of the tests for which a careful trim point is essential.

Typically, a singlet of fairly long duration is used to excite the phugoid. The actual duration of the singlet is not critical, if the initial step is held long enough to reduce (or increase) the indicated airspeed by some set amount (approximately 5% of the trim indicated airspeed is a good starting estimate). Care should be taken to return the control surface as nearly as possible to the original trim position; otherwise, the oscillation will have a climb or dive superimposed on it and data analysis is a bit more difficult. Depending on what measurements are sought, the pilot may fix the stick after returning it to the neutral position (stick-fixed oscillations) or he may release it after returning it to the neutral position (stick-free oscillations). Both types of oscillations should be examined if the control system is reversible. The airplane's free response is sought; the pilot must make no longitudinal inputs after returning the stick to the neutral position. Small lateral control inputs to keep the wings level are allowed while the phugoid characteristics are recorded. Bank angles as small as 5°-10° may affect phugoid damping ratio, ζ_p, and its undamped natural frequency, ω_{n_p}. For some configurations, it is more convenient to change the airspeed using speed brakes or power rather than by elevator or horizontal tail inputs. Any method that starts the exchange between potential and kinetic energy is satisfactory. Calculated phugoid time histories are shown in Fig. 9.14, with a doublet used to excite the motion.

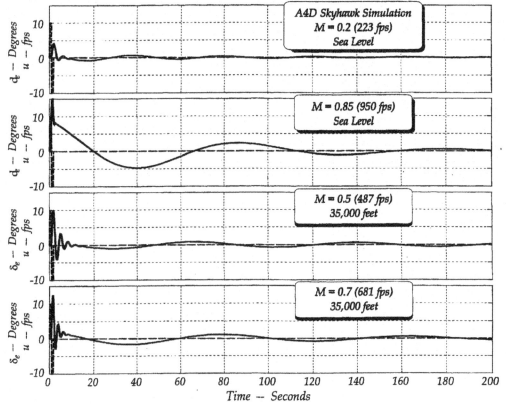

Fig. 9.14 Phugoid Oscillation

As with all dynamic parameters, it is best to record phugoid characteristics with an automatic recording device, though the oscillation is usually of low enough frequency for timing a period with a stop watch. Airspeed, altitude, or pitch attitude all give accurate phugoid oscillation parameters with their response histories. Lacking instrumentation, a video or motion picture footage of the panel instruments provides an accurate record of the phugoid parameters. Repeatable periods for the phugoid can be obtained by noting the time when the vertical velocity indicator passes through zero rate of climb or descent. The period of the oscillation is between adjacent times for zero rate of climb when the indicator is moving in the same direction. Do not start timing for the phugoid period until after the short period damps out; a half cycle of the phugoid is typically adequate for short period motion to be negligible. Timing should start at least one phugoid half-cycle after the input excitation is removed. We defer discussing how to extract phugoid damping ratios and frequencies until after reviewing lateral-directional dynamic modes. The phugoid oscillation is lightly damped and ω_{n_p} increases as altitude increases.

9.2.3 **Short** **Period** **Test** **Methods**

The pilot is quite sensitive to short period frequency and damping; these parameters strongly influence pilot ratings for virtually any flying task requiring pitch precision. The pilot senses dynamic characteristics through both visual and tactile perceptions. He observes pitch attitude variations, feels the normal accelerations, and visually records information from all available indicators (angle of attack indicator, accelerometer, or pitch rate indicator). All of these cues are integrated in the human brain as frequency response information defining the airplane's dynamic behavior. The stability and control manuals[2,9] from the test pilot schools have more complete discussions of how each of the dynamic parameters affects pilot opinion of an airplane. Perhaps the most complete document discussing this important aspect of airplane dynamics is Chalk's work[8]. This document is "required" reading for those regularly engaged in flying qualities tests.

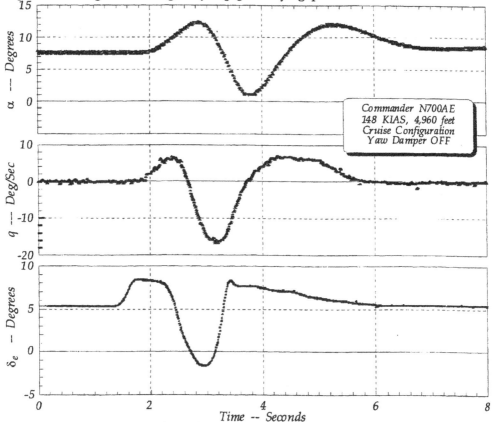

Fig. 9.15 Short Period Response to a Doublet for a Light Twin

A typical measured short period oscillation for a light twin is shown in Fig. 9.15. The most common input used to excite the short period is the doublet. It is usually adequate for exciting the short period while suppressing the phugoid, simply because, if performed correctly, the input begins and ends at the trim pitch attitude at very nearly the trim airspeed. Starting the doublet with a nose down pitch rate is slightly more comfortable for most pilots, but satisfactory data is obtained with either sequence. The doublet causes transient deviations in pitch rate, normal acceleration, angle of attack, and pitch attitude that are all associated with short period motion.

Airplane response must be measured after the control inputs have ceased; but, unlike the phugoid measurements, the important part of the time history is immediately after the doublet is completed. It is important to record control inputs simultaneously with the other dynamic parameters. Recording devices are essential for quantifying characteristics like short period damping ratio, undamped natural frequency, and damped natural frequency (ζ_{sp}, $\omega_{n_{sp}}$, and $\omega_{d_{sp}}$, respectively). The pilot can obtain a rough estimate of ζ_{sp} by counting the number of peaks of the oscillation in pitch attitude until he can no longer discern an oscillation. If the damping ratio is $0.1 < \zeta_{sp} < 0.7$, as it is for most aircraft,

$$\zeta_{sp} \approx \frac{7 - number\ of\ peaks\ counted}{10}.$$

The singlet can also be used to excite the short period mode of motion. Unfortunately, especially for slow-responding airplanes like most commercial airliners and most bombers and tankers, this input also excites the phugoid and separating the two quadratic factors complicates data analysis. The singlet is useful for quick-responding airplanes that also have adequate pitch damping to cause the short period to subside before the phugoid develops.

Finally, a form of the step input can also be used to excite the short period when the airplane has a low frequency short period and/or heavy damping. It is especially appropriate for airplanes requiring a larger amplitude motion for accurate data reduction. The disadvantages of this excitation method are that it requires more test time and maneuvering by the pilot. It is usually not as repeatable as the doublet excitation. This technique is sometimes called the "2g pull-up" method, though any normal acceleration level consistent with airplane limitations and the pilot's skill can be used. After carefully trimming, airspeed is traded for altitude and then the pilot pushes over to establish a shallow dive. The dive angle must be adjusted for each configuration and for different points in the operating envelope. This adjustment is often an iterative process and adds to the required test time. Trim altitude should be approached in a steep enough nose-down attitude so that the pilot can pull up sharply to the desired normal acceleration and establish a constant pitch rate. As the airplane approaches the initial trim attitude in this rotation, the pitch rate should be constant, normal acceleration should be constant at approximately the desired value, and the altitude should be very close to the initial trim altitude. At that point the longitudinal controller should be smartly neutralized and either fixed in the neutral trim position or freed at that position.

The use of traditional second-order metrics (damping ratio and undamped natural frequency) alone has led to some inexplicable discrepancies between pilot opinion ratings and these measures of merit. Military specifications[3,8,18] state requirements in terms of another parameter, $\frac{n}{\alpha}$. The ratio of maximum pitching acceleration to steady-state normal acceleration during maneuvers is roughly equal to the ratio $\frac{\omega_{n_{sp}}^2}{n/\alpha} \frac{\omega_{n_{sp}}^2}{n/\alpha}$, which is called the *control anticipation parameter* or *CAP*. This parameter seems to better describe the initial response than ζ_{sp} and $\omega_{n_{sp}}$ alone. Obtaining this parameter for each test condition is often a simple task with automated data acquisition. If the normal acceleration and the angle of attack at any desired flight condition can be recorded, obtaining $\frac{n}{\alpha}$ is a simple division.

One technique for obtaining $\frac{n}{\alpha}$ is a is a near-sinusoidal pumping of the longitudinal controller while recording normal acceleration and angle of attack. The frequency of the periodic input is varied to cover the range of frequencies of interest; these data are also used to determine the minimum transient stick force per g ratio. This ratio is usually obtained when the stick is pumped at a frequency close to $\omega_{n_{sp}}$. Care must be exercised by the test pilot in making such inputs; they must be small enough to avoid overstressing the airplane as the input frequencies approach $\omega_{n_{sp}}$. Aggressive input may excite a resonance or lead to pilot-induced oscillations. When conducting such a test, use very low amplitude inputs and build up to larger ones only if needed for data analysis.

9.2.4 Dutch Roll Test Methods

The Dutch roll is the only remaining oscillatory motion normally encountered in dynamic stability testing. This coupled lateral-directional oscillation can be quite uncomfortable to both crew and passengers and may seriously affect the utility of the airplane. Swept-wing commercial airliners often need yaw dampers to augment natural damping of the aircraft in order to achieve either good ride qualities or good handling. Implications of inadequate damping include passenger discomfort or nausea from Dutch roll oscillations excited by atmospheric turbulence. Military ground attack aircraft may not allow precise tracking of targets at low altitudes if Dutch roll is not adequately damped.

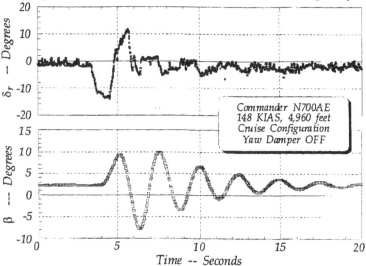

Fig. 9.16 Dutch Roll Oscillation Excited by a Rudder Doublet

A typical Dutch roll oscillation is depicted in Fig. 9.16. This particular test sequence was initiated by a rudder doublet (and a rather poor one at that). Notice that the aperiodic lateral-directional modes affect this oscillation. It is virtually impossible to excite the Dutch roll without exciting the other two modes of motion.

Dutch roll, like the short period, is most commonly excited by a doublet, though other forms of inputs can be used. The rudder pedals are usually the pilot's choice to input this doublet. If the pilot input is not symmetric, it is easy to excite the roll mode and/or the spiral mode and complicate data analysis. Dynamic sideslip limitations must be observed when exciting the Dutch roll. At high dynamic pressures, deliberately inducing large magnitude Dutch rolls can easily overload the vertical surfaces. Several test aircraft have lost parts of the vertical tail or the rudder due to such aerodynamic loads during dynamic overshoots. Care must be exercised; loads should be monitored in real time if the aircraft is well-instrumented with telemetry capability.

An aileron singlet also may be used to excite the Dutch roll. Ordinarily, this maneuver is started with the airplane at a steady bank angle. Aileron is applied as rapidly as possible (near a step input) to roll out of the turn. Opposite aileron is abruptly applied as the level flight is approached. For aircraft with high inertias, this technique often provides more realistic amplitudes than rudder doublets. This input may also end with the rudders fixed or free in the neutral position.

The Dutch roll can also be excited by another form of the singlet, though this input involves the use of two controls simultaneously. The controls are abruptly released from a steady, straight sideslip by simultaneously neutralizing the rudder and the ailerons (and then either fixing or freeing both at zero deflection). This technique is useful for airplanes for which a single control input (either rudder doublet or aileron singlet) does not adequately excite the Dutch roll oscillation. Ordinarily, this method works better if the Dutch roll is highly damped. Releasing the controls abruptly from a large sideslip can produce unexpected results, from dynamic overshoots of maximum allowable sideslip angle to structural overloads on the vertical tail. Such safety considerations dictate that the pilot should build up cautiously by starting with small values of β and then increasing β incrementally until an oscillation with satisfactory characteristics is achieved. Do not attempt this form of excitation from maximum static sideslip angles without such a preliminary buildup.

Whatever input is used, quantitatively analyzing Dutch roll oscillations requires automated data recording. High frequency data recording is not essential; frequencies of interest are usually on the order of 10-25 Hz. Digital recording is feasible at relatively low cost. Remember, though, that discrete sampling rates must be at least twice that of the highest frequency of interest, according to the sampling theorem. Most flight test agencies target a sampling rate ten times greater than the highest frequency studied.

9.2.5 Spiral Mode Test Methods

The spiral mode is a slow divergence or convergence in heading when the airplane is banked away from wings-level equilibrium. Exciting this mode requires very little control input. After trimming carefully at the desired test conditions, roll the aircraft to a bank angle of approximately 10° and stabilize in the ensuing turn. Either fix or free the ailerons and the rudder (the elevator may be used to maintain constant airspeed). If the airplane rolls out of the turn, the spiral mode is stable (convergent). Time-to-half-amplitude is how long it takes to reach 20° bank from 10° bank. Conversely, if the bank angle increases, the mode is unstable. Time-to-double-amplitude is the time to proceed from the original 10° bank condition to 20° bank. Bank angles greater than 20° are to be avoided; if ϕ is large, the linearizing assumptions used in small perturbation equations are no longer valid. For multiengine airplanes, all engines must produce the same thrust; asymmetric moment produced by the engines may overpower spiral mode behavior.

The spiral mode usually has such a long time constant that it has little effect on the handling qualities of a conventional airplane, even if it is unstable (Table 9.9[8]). Notice that the minimum times-to-double-amplitude are significantly longer than the typical Dutch roll period; if they are shorter than indicated, pilots object because the spiral mode interferes with precise maneuvering, increasing pilot workload. Such additional workload is particularly unwelcome during precision maneuvers that occur over a long time period, like instrument approaches or takeoffs and landings.

Table 9.9 Typical Spiral Stability Requirements: Time-to-Double-Amplitude (seconds)

Class	Flight Phase Category	Level 1	Level 2	Level 3
I and IV	A	12	12	4
	B and C	20	12	4
II and III	All	20	12	4

--Adapted from Chalk[8]

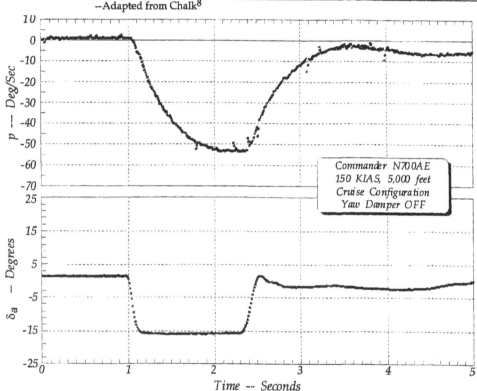

Fig. 9.17 Roll Mode Tests: 45°-45° Bank Change for a Light Twin

9.2.6 **Roll Mode Test Methods**

The roll mode is most often excited by a step or a singlet aileron input. Figure 9.17 illustrates the results of a roll mode test excited by a step input for a general aviation light twin. Procedurally, the most efficient way to collect roll rate measurements is to roll from a chosen bank angle to the same bank angle of the opposite sign; once stabilized at this opposite bank angle, roll back in the other direction with an identical step aileron input of the same magnitude. Temporary stops are often used to keep the aileron inputs to approximately the same size and to make them precise and repeatable. The usual necessity for trimming precisely at the desired flight conditions applies to this test. The choice of the initial bank angle to use largely depends on the type of aircraft being tested. Typically, fighters, trainers, and other smaller airplanes are more maneuverable and 45° is used. This bank angle change was used for the light twin in the maneuver depicted in Fig. 9.17. For larger aircraft, 30° is more appropriate. Some requirements documents specify times to roll through 60° or 90°; if these data are also sought, be sure the pilot carries the roll slightly beyond the bank angle of opposite sign before stopping the roll. Otherwise, the times are likely to be inaccurate. Recording bank angle and surface position time histories is highly desirable, though stop watch timing of such rolls gives approximate information if instrumentation is meager. Record the complete time history to extract the dynamic information; the roll mode time constant is almost always too short to be observed manually. Record variations in airspeed during roll mode testing, especially as you build up to maximum aileron deflections. It is permissible to use the longitudinal control to help maintain airspeed during rapid rolls. Roll tests are carried out in both directions, since there are often factors (like propellers or turbine rotations) that produce different roll dynamics in each direction.

9.2.7 **Basic Data Reduction Methods**

We now turn our attention to data reduction techniques. In this introductory text we confine our study to simple methods, techniques that could be called "hand-calculations". These basic tools may be implemented on a computer, but before automating a process, you need to understand it. We describe data manipulations in graphical terms to make the material easy to understand. Most of the calculations can be readily automated; in fact, homework exercises used by the author in formal classes often ask students to write simple programs to obtain pertinent dynamic parameters from response data. Much of the material in this section is adapted from Appendices III and VB of Chalk's report[8].

Table 9.10 Applicability of Basic Graphical Techniques for Determining ζ and ω_n

Name of Method	Range of Applicable Damping Ratio
Transient Peak Ratio (TPR)	$-0.5 < \zeta < 0.5$
Modified TPR (MTPR)	$-0.5 < \zeta < 0.5$
Time-Ratio (TR)	$0.5 < \zeta < 1.2$
Maximum Slope (MS)	$0.5 < \zeta < 1.2$
Separated-Real-Roots (SRR)	$\zeta > 1.1$

Adapted from Chalk[8]

While it is useful to apply more advanced tools like parameter estimation to response data collected in flight, these more advanced topics simply cannot be adequately covered in this first volume. We defer discussing them to Volume 2, where we elaborate on the work of Iliff[13], Ljung[14] , and others to give a broader view of parameter estimation methods. Even if you already use parameter identification extensively, the simpler techniques discussed in this chapter should be helpful in evaluating computational results.

There are four basic data reduction techniques (plus variations) to be discussed and each of them is best suited for analysis of specific problems. Table 9.10 summarizes the applicability of these four methods for extracting ζ and ω_n from measured oscillations. All of them give ζ and ω_n for a second-order system and, of course, our usual quartic characteristic equations readily break down to no higher than second-order components. The choice of method is tied rather closely to the damping ratio of the motion mode being analyzed. The most important method to be discussed is the transient peak ratio (TPR) method. It is the most usable of the reduction schemes if $-0.5 < \zeta < 0.5$, the most common range for ζ_{ph}, ζ_{sp}, and ζ_{Dr}. The time-ratio (TR) method and the maximum slope (MS) methods both fit a slightly higher range of ζ, $0.5 < \zeta < 1.0$, though both of them may be helpful for ζ up to 1.4. The separated-real-roots (SRR) is useful for the real roots common with the lateral-directional quartic. All methods assume the time history being analyzed starts with zero slope at the initial time, t_0. It is also assumed that this timing starts with $t_0 = 0$. A basic assumption is that any of the oscillations associated with aircraft dynamics can be analyzed as either a first- or second-order response. With these applicabilities and assumptions established, we next describe each method.

9.2.7.1 **Transient Peak Ratio Method**. First, we determine the transient peak ratio

(TPR) from: $\dfrac{\Delta x_1}{\Delta x_0} = \dfrac{\Delta x_2}{\Delta x_1} = \dfrac{\Delta x_3}{\Delta x_2} = \ldots$ or, if the modified TPR method is used:

$\dfrac{\Delta x_3}{\Delta x_2} = \dfrac{\Delta x_2}{\Delta x_1} = \cdots$. If the ratios are not identical (and they typically are not, for actual

flight test measurements), an average of the measurements is often used. If the TPR technique is selected, damping ratio can be read from a chart like Fig. 9.19 (next page). Finally, ω_n comes from the measurements, since the damped period, T, is scaled as the time between the local maxima or minima or is the measured time between the steady

state crossings (Fig. 9.18a). Then, ω_n is $\dfrac{2\pi}{T\sqrt{1-\zeta^2}}$. Figure 9.18a shows the TPR method,

while Fig. 9.18b illustrates a modification that does not require a steady-state system response.

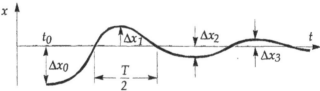

a. Transient Peak Ratio Measurements

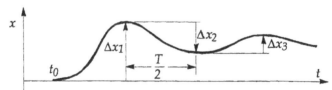

b. Modified Transient Peak Ratio Measurements

Fig. 9.18 Measurements for TPR and MTPR Methods

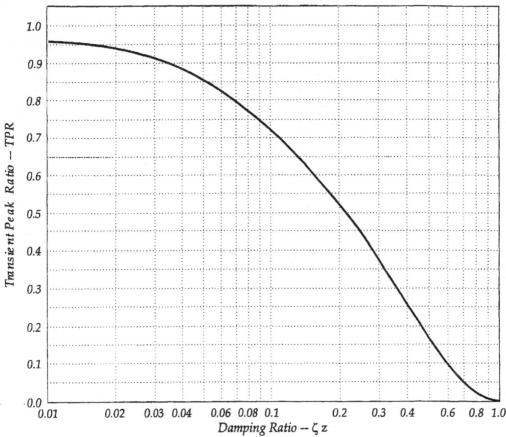

Fig. 9.19 Transient Peak Ratio Versus Damping Ratio

9.2.7.2. **Time-Ratio** **Method**. To use the time-ratio (TR) method, you must be able to ascertain steady-state equilibrium after the excitation has subsided. This method, described by Dolbin[15], utilizes the three specific values along the output response curve to calculate three estimates of ζ, at specific fractions of the change in the output variable. As

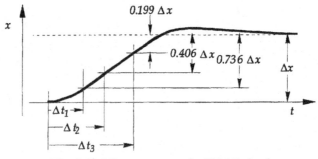

Fig. 9.20 Measurements for TR Method

is shown in Fig. 9.20, these times are measured where x, the output response, is $0.736\Delta x$, $0.406\Delta x$, and $0.199\Delta x$ below the final steady-state value, respectively, for Δt_1, Δt_2, and Δt_3.

Then the ratios $\Delta t_2/\Delta t_1$, $\Delta t_3/\Delta t_1$, and $(\Delta t_3 - \Delta t_2)/(\Delta t_2 - \Delta t_1)$ are calculated and used to enter the chart (Fig. 9.21). This chart then yields three values for ζ. We can average these three

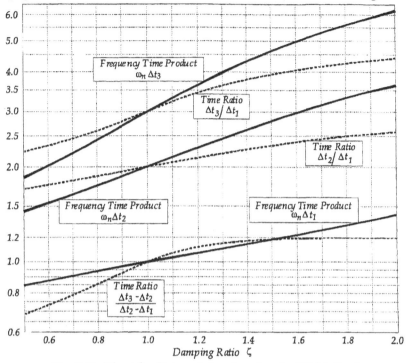

Fig. 9.21 Chart for Determining ζ and ω_n by TR Method

numbers, though it is prudent to weight each estimate of ζ according to how much the oscillation measurements are distorted from a pure second-order system. Generally, Δt_1 is the least accurate of the time measurements because it is quite sensitive to choice of t_0. The response is often affected significantly in this region by control system dynamics, which introduce higher order responses. But, Δt_3 can also be in error due to errors in determining the final steady-state value. These factors suggest using sound engineering judgment in deciding which damping ratio to weight. The TR method does provide three checks. Undamped natural frequency is read from the Fig. 9.21, just as the values for ζ are obtained. The only difference is that $\omega_n t_1$, $\omega_n t_2$, and $\omega_n t_3$ are read from the ordinate of the chart and then divided by the appropriate time to obtain three estimates of ω_n. Naturally, the remarks about use of engineering judgment in either averaging or choosing the best estimate of ω_n still apply.

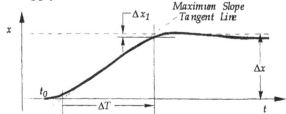

Fig. 9.22 Measurements for the Maximum Slope Method

9.2.7.3 Maximum Slope Method. The maximum slope (MS) method was developed[16] to reduce the inaccuracies in the TR approach associated with steady-state response. Figure 9.22 shows the measurements taken from the response time history for the MS calculation. The peak response amplitude and the maximum slope of the tangent to the transient rise are used instead of intermediate times (TR method). But, the MS technique has an inherent error source: Δx_1 is usually small and difficult to measure accurately. This error effects ζ mostly; ω_n is largely unaffected by this uncertainty.

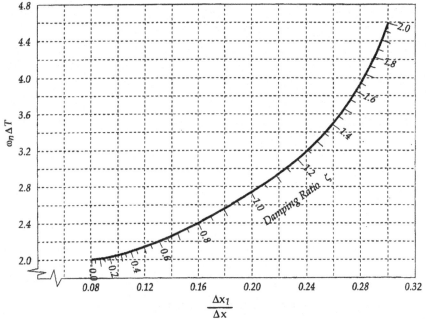

Fig. 9.23 Chart for Determining ζ and ω_n by the Maximum Slope Method

The ratio $\dfrac{\Delta x_1}{\Delta x}$ is then calculated and used to enter Fig. 9.23, where both ζ and $\omega_n \Delta T$ are obtained graphically. Then, $\omega_n = \dfrac{\omega_n \Delta T}{\Delta T}$.

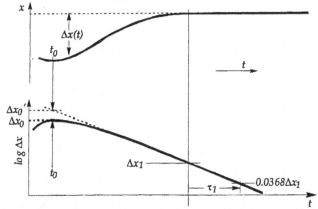

Fig. 9.24 Measurements for the Separated-Real-Roots Method

9.2.7.4 **Separated-Real-Roots** Method. As Table 9.10 indicates, the separated-real-roots (SRR) technique was developed to evaluate responses composed of two unequal real roots. It is useful only if the damping ratio is large enough to ensure strongly convergent aperiodic modes, which typically fits the roll mode behavior from the lateral-directional quartic. It is often analyzed using the SRR technique, especially if the spiral mode is also convergent. Figure 9.24 sketches out the parameters to be taken from the output response. Once again, it is necessary to select the steady-state output and the method is moderately sensitive to how accurately this value is determined. With this approach you must also plot $\Delta x(t)$ on semilog paper. After the faster root (t_2) has decayed, the semilog plot will be a straight line, whose slope determines the smaller root (t_1).

Then, $t_2 = t_1 \dfrac{\Delta x_0}{\Delta x_0}$, where $\Delta x_0{}'$ is the intercept of the straight line on the semilog graph.

Alternatively, t_2 can be determined from the slope of a semilog plot of $\Delta x(t)$ versus t.

Whichever of these two graphical methods is used to obtain t_1 and t_2, the damping ratio and the undamped natural frequency come from:

$$\zeta = \frac{(t_1 + t_2)\omega_n}{2} \quad and \quad \omega_n = \sqrt{\frac{1}{t_1 t_2}}$$

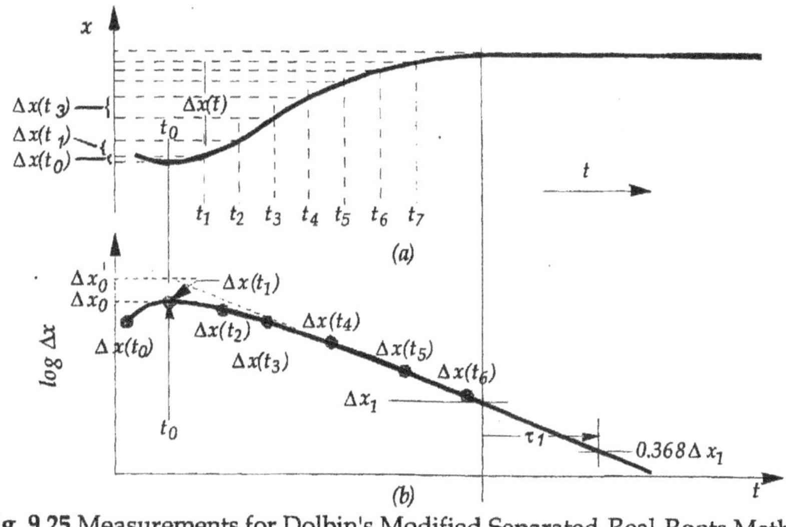

Fig. 9.25 Measurements for Dolbin's Modified Separated-Real-Roots Method

To help reduce the sensitivity of the SRR procedure to errors in graphically estimating the steady-state response, a modification (due to Dolbin[15]) may be helpful. The values of $\Delta x(t)$ are measured so the steady-state value is unnecessary; they are measured at equal time increments (Fig. 9.25). Then, each value of is $\Delta x(t)$ simply: $x(t + \Delta T) - x(t)$, where

$$\Delta T = (t_1 - t_0) = (t_2 - t_1) = \cdots = (t_{n+1} - t_n)$$

Plotting $\Delta x(t)$ on the semilog scale, as in the basic SRR method, leads to the same result as before, except no steady-state value for the response is needed. There is usually more scatter in the data points on the semilog plot with this modified approach, but the slope of the faired line is often more accurate. If you use the unmodified SRR technique and assuming that $\zeta > 1$ when ζ is actually less than 1, you may not find a part of the semilog plot that is adequately fitted with a straight line. With the modified method, this sort of faulty assumption is not as likely to be noticed. You can usually fit a straight line with reasonable scatter to these points. However, the two real roots that you extract from these modified calculations, ζ and ω_n will be grossly in error. If you suspect the damping ratio is greater than 1, check the SRR results using the TR or the MS methods.

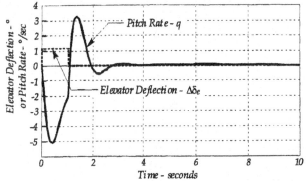

Time - seconds

Example 9.3: The time histories above were generated from a simulation of an F-89 Scorpion flying at 20,000 feet on a standard day at a Mach number of 0.638 (660 fps). The airplane weight was 30,500 pounds. Graphically estimate the short period damping ratio and the undamped natural frequency using the time-ratio method. Then, repeat the estimate using the maximum slope technique. The first plot above shows the overall pitch rate response of the Scorpion for several seconds after a very small step elevator input (just over 1 degree change in elevator position). This small input is removed approximately 1 second after initiation. The free response is heavily damped.

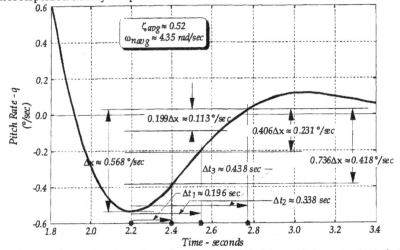

Time - seconds

   To graphically estimate damping ratio and undamped natural frequency, we must greatly expand the scales to have any hope of reasonable accuracy. We choose the region where the response trace just drops into the negative range and analyze the overshoot characteristics. For the time ratio method, we also must know the steady-state value and we notice from the chart above that it is just slightly above the zero grid line, at approximately 0.01 degrees/second. We could even take the statistical average of the readings at 10 seconds beyond to get this value. Next, measure from this steady-state value for pitch rate down to the minimum pitch rate (shown below) to get a Δx of approximately *0.568 °/second.*

   Draw the three horizontal lines that correspond to the three levels of overshoot from the steady-state value of q suggested in Fig. 9.20 (0.199 Δx, 0.406 Δx, and 0.736 Δx). Where these overshoot levels intersect the response curve, drop three vertical lines to the time axis and graphically measure the indicated time increments from the time when the minimum q was achieved (the peak overshoot time). For this example those values are shown on the chart as: $\Delta t_1 \approx 0.196$ seconds, $\Delta t_2 \approx 0.338$ seconds, and $\Delta t_3 \approx 0.438$ seconds. Forming the ratios necessary to enter Fig. 9.21: $\dfrac{\Delta t_2}{\Delta t_1} \approx 1.72$, which gives $\zeta \approx 0.50$ from Fig. 9.21; $\dfrac{\Delta t_3}{\Delta t_1} \approx 2.23$, which gives $\zeta \approx 0.51$ from Fig. 9.21; and $\dfrac{\Delta t_3 - \Delta t_2}{\Delta t_2 - \Delta t_1} \approx 0.70$, which gives $\zeta \approx 0.55$ from Fig. 9.21. Averaging these values,

$$\boxed{\zeta_{avg} \approx 0.52}$$

Read from the other solid lines in Fig. 9.21 (the Frequency-Time Product lines) to obtain the following values for $\omega_n \Delta t$ and then ω_n: $\omega_n \Delta t_1 \approx 0.865$, $\omega_n \Delta t_2 \approx 1.46$, and $\omega_n \Delta t_3 \approx 1.90$. Dividing by the appropriate times and averaging again:

$$\boxed{\omega_{navg} \approx 4.35 \ rad/sec}$$

Now, estimate the same parameters using the maximum slope method. We still need the expanded scale drawing of the response curve, which is repeated below. For this procedure start by drawing a line tangent to the response curve at the point of maximum slope for the response. For this pitch rate response segment of the data, that line is tangent at approximately 2.5 seconds on our time scale. Next, draw two horizontal lines at the minimum q and at the maximum q for the segment of data we have chosen to analyze and extend them right and left, respectively, until they intersect the maximum tangent line. From these points of intersection drop vertical lines to the time axis and measure $\Delta T \approx 0.5$ seconds. Then, measure the approximate value of the second overshoot (the positive overshoot) above the steady-state value of q. Graphically, $\Delta x_1 \approx 0.08$ °/sec. Then, forming the ratio needed to enter Fig. 9.23,

$$\frac{\Delta x_1}{\Delta x} \approx \frac{0.08}{0.65} \approx 0.123$$

$$\boxed{\zeta \approx 0.48}$$

Similarly using the same ratio to obtain $\omega_n \Delta T \approx 2.17$ from Fig. 9.23,

$$\omega_n = \frac{\omega_n \Delta T}{\Delta T} \approx \frac{2.17}{0.50}$$

$$\boxed{\omega_n \approx 4.34 \ rad/sec}$$

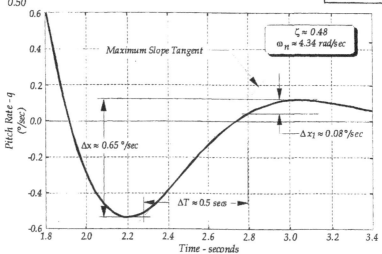

The values obtained from these two graphical procedures are reasonable. Since the response data were generated mathematically, we know the actual values for ζ and ω_n. These actual values are:

$$\boxed{\zeta = 0.493} \quad \text{and} \quad \boxed{\omega_n = 4.27 \ rad/sec}$$

9.2.8 Calculation of Lateral-Directional Parameters from Response Data

This section illustrates the techniques of the previous paragraphs applied to analysis of the lateral-directional response to a step aileron input to obtain estimates of all the roots of the quartic. The development again closely follows Appendix VB from Chalk[8]. Naturally, we continue to assume that linearity (and, therefore, superposition) holds and that the response represents the usual roll mode, spiral mode, and Dutch roll mode common to most rigid aircraft modes of motion. The complete roll rate response to the hypothesized step aileron input is shown in Fig. 9.26.

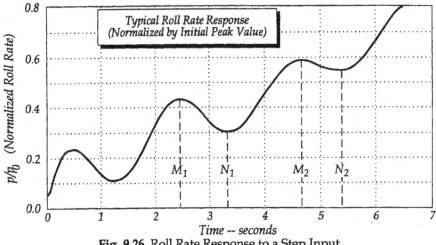

Fig. 9.26 Roll Rate Response to a Step Input

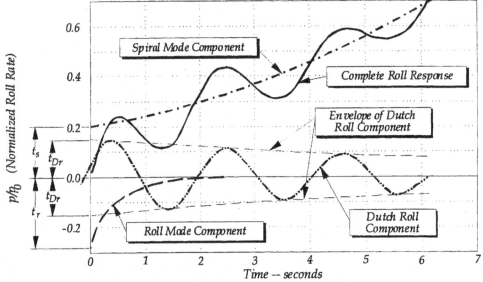

Fig. 9.27 Components of a Roll Rate Response to a Step Input

From such a response, we will learn that typical components which correlate to the eigenvalues of the lateral-directional quartic are of the form shown in Fig. 9.27. We postulate a convergent roll mode, a divergent spiral mode and a moderately damped, medium frequency Dutch roll oscillation. It is easy to synthesize the output response by adding up each of these contributions to the total response. Indeed, the time domain equation of such a total response illustrates this summation process common to linear systems:

$$p(t) = K_s e^{-\frac{t}{\tau_s}} + K_r e^{-\frac{t}{\tau_r}} + K_{Dr} e^{-\zeta_{Dr}\omega_{nDr}t} cos\left(\omega_{nDr}\sqrt{1-\zeta_{Dr}^2} + \Psi_{phase}\right)$$

Our task is not to synthesize from known components; we seek to break down a measured response that contains all the components and identify individual parameters -- K_s, τ_s, K_r, τ_r, K_{Dr}, ζ_{Dr}, and $\omega_{n_{Dr}}$. Chalk presents both a graphical technique and an analog-matching approach, but we restrict our discussion to the graphical method.

This technique produces good results only for a conventional airplane with a Dutch roll damping ratio less than approximately 0.3 and with the spiral and roll modes widely separated in frequency. This latter assumption allows us to expect that the roll mode will have little influence after the first few seconds. Typically, τ_r is about 1 second and such a first order mode has reached approximately 95% of its final value within 3τ after the exci-tation is removed. Consequently, after about 3-4 seconds, we can anticipate that the re-sidual oscillation is composed almost entirely of the spiral mode and the Dutch roll mode. Look first at breaking out the spiral mode from the latter part of the time history data where we can reasonably expect these two modes of motion to dominate.

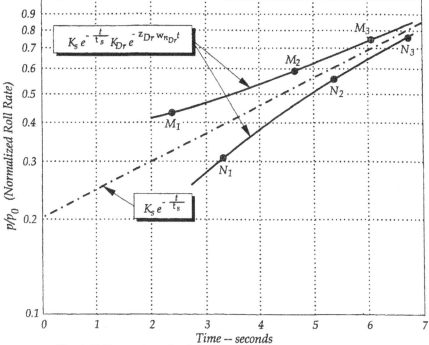

Fig. 9.28 Extracting the Spiral-Dutch Roll Mode Envelopes

Pick out the maximum and minimum points of the response from about 3 seconds onward (to avoid contamination from the roll mode) and plot them on semilog paper as sketched in Fig. 9.28. The points of tangency of the Dutch roll envelope to the total re-sponse should be carefully plotted, but simply taking the peaks is well within any likely graphical accuracy. However, if you decide to numerically implement this technique on a computer, keep this subtle point in mind. Local maxima and minima for times less than 3 times the roll mode time constant (τ_r) should be ignored in this envelope estimation. We must have an oscillatory response measurement that lasts long enough so that these later peak roll rates are well-defined. Smooth curves are then drawn through the upper and lower peaks (maxima and minima, respectively) to define the envelope of the spiral mode and the Dutch roll mode components on the semilog working plot. The numerical average between the envelope boundaries defines the spiral mode component. This average should be a straight line on the semilog plot and K_s is the intersection of this straight line with the zero time axis. (K_s is also called the spiral mode residue.)

The slope of the average straight line defining the spiral mode on the semilog plot yields the time constant for this mode of motion through the following relationship:

$\tau_s = \dfrac{\Delta t}{ln \dfrac{x_2}{x_1}}$. The time-to-double-amplitude (for a divergent spiral mode as has been

sketched) or the time-to-half-amplitude (for a convergent spiral mode) can then be calculated directly using: t_2 or $t_{1/2} = 0.693\tau_s$

The next step in the graphical procedure is plotting the spiral component on the linear time scales and subtracting it from the overall response time history (Fig. 9.29). The resulting plot contains both the roll and the Dutch roll mode components of the original response; the spiral mode has been removed. The only points that must be plotted carefully are those in the first three seconds (so the roll mode can be extracted accurately) and the peaks of the Dutch roll oscillation at later times in the oscillation. Figure 9.29 illustrates this step and the complete curves are shown there for clarity, with illustrative points marked with triangles to show what you must do to obtain an accurate estimate of modal components.

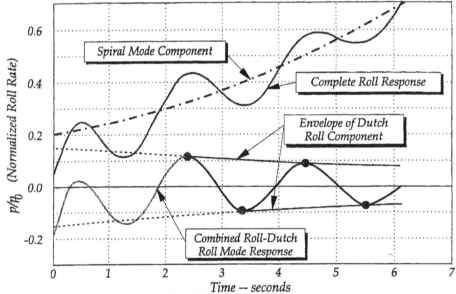

Fig. 9.29 Combined Roll Mode-Dutch Roll Mode Components

Now, we return to semilog paper and plot the peaks (the later ones) from the combined roll mode-Dutch roll mode envelope (Fig. 9.29). This procedure is illustrated in Fig. 9.30. As the sketch shows, this plot usually results in two parallel straight lines, one for the local maxima and one for the local minima. The slope of either of these lines should define ζ_{Dr}. If ζ_{Dr} has been previously estimated, this estimate should be checked against these measured slopes. Strictly speaking, the Dutch roll envelope does not touch the peaks. Rather the tangent points are just to the right of the peaks for the convergent oscillation. This angular displacement is approximately $sin^{-1} \zeta$ (in degrees); the time equiva-

lent of the angle comes from the period of the damped Dutch roll oscillation (T_{Dr}):
$\dfrac{T_{Dr} \sin^{-1} \zeta_{Dr}}{360}$. For low damping ratios ($\zeta_{Dr} < 0.3$), this displacement is small and can be safely ignored.

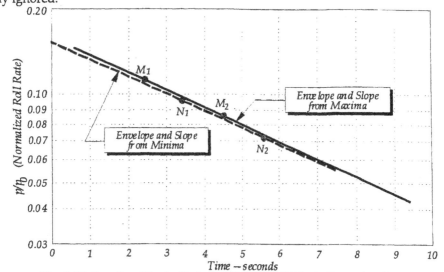

Fig. 9.30 Semilog Plot to Estimate Dutch Roll Mode Damping Ratio

Finally, the estimated Dutch roll envelope is transferred back to the combined roll-mode-Dutch roll mode time history (Fig. 9.29) to estimate the roll mode time constant. Often, it is useful to enlarge the first few seconds of the oscillation, as shown in Fig. 9.31.

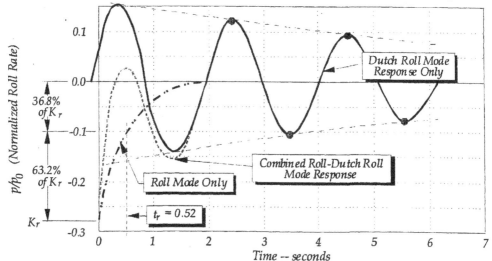

Fig. 9.31 Estimation of the Roll Mode Component

The Dutch roll mode period and damping ratio are now known; they are used to reconstruct the initial part of the Dutch roll component (enlarged scale of Fig. 9.31). This reconstructed oscillation is subtracted graphically from the combined roll-Dutch roll mode component time history to yield the roll mode time history trace. This estimate for the roll mode component of the time history is also illustrated in Fig. 9.31. For the interested student, an alternate method of determining the initial Dutch roll mode that utilizes polar plots is given by Chalk. In the interest of brevity, that alternative is not covered.

The roll mode time constant comes from Fig. 9.31. Calculating $0.368K_r$ and drawing a horizontal line at that value of normalized roll rate, the time where this horizontal line intersects the estimated roll rate time history is τ_r. We could also go back to the semilog plot and find K_r as the intersection of the straight line at $t = 0$ seconds, just as we did for the spiral mode. Another way to obtain τ_r is to simply calculate it from a time increment and the natural logarithm of the corresponding amplitude ratio: $\tau_r = \dfrac{t_{k+1} - t_k}{ln\,(p_{k+1}\,/\,p_k)}$. Both alternative methods are illustrated in Fig.9.32.

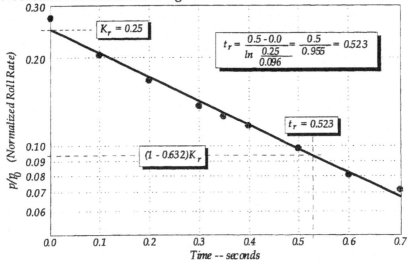

Fig. 9.32 Alternative Calculation of the Roll Mode Time Constant

9.3 INSTRUMENTATION

Instrumentation used to measure dynamic stability parameters varies widely for specific flight test objectives, from subjective assessments made by the test crew on the basis of qualitative observations to complex identification of the most likely multivariable mathematical model for a given aircraft/stores configuration. More often than not, as noted previously, any static measurements needed are more than adequately covered by instrumentation needed to fulfill the requirements for dynamic measurements. Eshelby[19] suggests that the general principles of the measurement approach can best be understood by considering a single measurement channel.

9.3.1 Basic Interrelationships

A measurement channel generally consists of three interdependent sets of characteristics: (1) static characteristics, (2) dynamic characteristics, and (3) installed system characteristics. Static characteristics include range of the measurement, nature of required calibrations, accuracy, and steady-state errors. Dynamic characteristics include all measurements related to natural frequency and damping of the measurement scheme – the transient (short-term) measures of merit. Installation of the measurement system in the aircraft inevitably subjects the sensors, signal conditioning, and recording elements to the flight environment with its several uncontrolled variables. The major elements of a measurement channel (as originally described by Eshelby in his block diagram like Fig. 9.33) are lumped into airborne elements and ground elements. The flight test engineer must pay careful attention to the interfaces (both within these two groupings and across their interface). Compatibility in time coding and in data format is an obvious issue, but more subtle interactions (electromagnetic interferences, isolation of measurements, and the like) are just as important. Perhaps of the utmost importance is devising an efficient scheme to facilitate data reconstruction from whatever media (disk, magnetic recording, etc.) and/or telemetry stream are available is one of the most important preplanning chores for the flight test engineer.

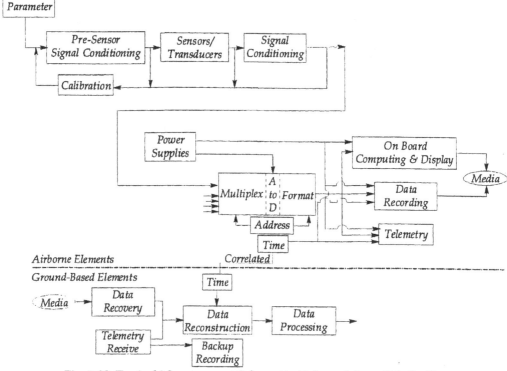

Fig. 9.33 Typical Measurement Schematic (Adapted from Eshelby[19])

9.3.1.1 **Static Characteristics**. Measurement range describes the values of a parameter over which it can be measured within specified accuracy, sensitivity, and linearity limits. Range is usually given in terms of Full Scale Range (FSR) of each measurement channel and is usually spelled out in volts in modern electronic data acquisition systems. Typically, a zero state reference is used for typical FSR of ±5 or ±10 volts. Alternatively, the range may be "single-sided", that is, 0-10 volts. It is often useful to specify an Over-Range to indicate the margin allowed before permanent damage to the system occurs and to make allowance for it in the design of the system. This Over-Range condition may be dictated by sensor limits or by physical limits on the measurand (control system stops, for example). It is quite common to consider the effect of environmental variables (temperature, vibration, shock, current, and pressure) for the sensors, the signal conditioning, power supplies, and all other system elements.

Aside from measurement range, the flight test must be cognizant of calibration definitions (like sensitivity, resolution, and linearity). *Sensitivity* is the ratio of the output change (often in volts) to the input change (physical units like pounds or degrees) or more properly, it is the local tangent to the output-input curve at the operating point. For a linear measurement channel the slope is constant, as depicted in Fig. 9-34. A force transducer might have sensitivity spelled out in volts/pound, for example. *Resolution* refers to the smallest detectable change in measurand that produces a change in output. *Hysteresis*, illustrated on the right side of Fig. 9.34, is a form of nonlinearity that makes an output double-valued, depending upon the direction of change for the input excitation. It produces a lag effect as shown in the cartoon. *Threshold* indicates the maximum incremental input before a change in electrical output takes place; it is tied to both *resolution* and the *hysteresis* characteristics of the measurement channel. Figure 9.34 illustrates these concepts for a digitally sampled measurement channel and for an analog output channel. Not shown in this sketch are the long-term time-dependent errors like *drift* (shifting of the zero point) and gain (or *sensitivity*) changes that may be due to environmental effects like temperature. These latter errors may also be a function of worn components within the transducer or other elements of the measurement channel.

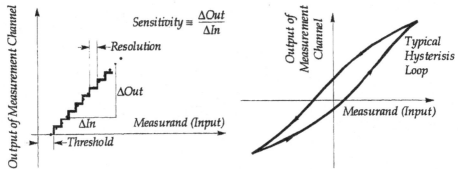

Fig. 9.34 Measurement Terminology

9.3.1.2 Dynamic Characteristics. Dynamic characteristics are extremely important if input excitation varies rapidly or has distinctive frequencies. Linearity is more critical for dynamic measurements since analysis tools for nonlinear systems are limited. Though pure linearity is typically not achievable, it is usually sought to avoid the complicated and frustrating corrections associated with nonlinear dynamics. Dynamic characteristic equations for sensors may be first-order (temperature probes) or second-order (most accelerometers) for most instrumentation applications (Fig. 9.5 illustrates these characteristics, though that sketch is not specific to instrumentation channels). It is also important to represent the phase-amplitude characteristics of a measurement channel accurately as well. Nyquist polar plots are one way to depict such characteristics.

9.3.1.3 System Characteristics. Airborne elements of an instrumentation system are exposed to a rather severe set of environmental conditions not experienced by many measurement environments. The ambient pressures and temperatures vary widely in a typical test mission; pressure at 50,000 feet is less than 15% of its sea level value, for example. Humidity changes drastically when taking off from near sea level and cruising at 35,000 feet. Vibration levels can literally destroy sensitive transducers. Resonance between rotational machinery and aerodynamic excitation induces structural frequencies that can wreak havoc on some measurements. Electromagnetic interference can contaminate and make unusable the signals from sensors. These uncontrollable variables change very rapidly for high performance airplanes and the measurement channels must be reliable in such conditions. Finally, it is imperative that the installed instrumentation have *"finesse"* which is an indication of the effect the sensor and associated equipment have on the measurand. Inevitably, the sensor affects the measurement: a pressure probe alters pressure distribution, a micrometer exerts a force on the object being measured and deforms it slightly; and the mass of an accelerometer affects the mass distribution of the structure to which it is attached. All of these examples illustrate how the measurement system influences the measurement. If these influences are low or negligible, the *finesse* of the system is considered high and desirable.

9.3.2 Transducer Fundamentals

Most modern measurement systems for flight test have transducers responding to physical stimuli and producing some form of electrical output, though mechanical systems (as in the pilot or flight crew's displays are still used to provide visual outputs – mechanical pointers, for example). However, electrical outputs are much more convenient and efficient for automated data reduction and have become the norm for measurement channels in serious flight test data packages. Gregory[20] describes a transducer as having two elements, assuming an electrical output signal: (1) the sensor element normally in direct contact with the physical quantity to be measured and (2) the electronic element directly associated with the sensor that produces a voltage or current output proportional to the change in the physical quantity. Gregory goes on to describe transducer design and applications to flight test measurements in considerably more detail; such descriptions, along with descriptions of newer devices from specific manufacturers, are indispensable to a fuller understanding of instrumentation for dynamic measurements.

9.4 SUMMARY

Dynamic flight tests are one of the most challenging types of tests encountered by a flight test engineer. They require a thorough understanding of stability and control principles, a moderate knowledge of instrumentation to can record the necessary parameters automatically, insight into handling qualities and how pilot ratings were developed, knowledge of the types of standard inputs (pilot-induced or not) that produce responses adequate for analysis, and at least an introductory understanding of how to extract dynamic measures of merit from response data. This chapter has explained each of these fundamentals. The serious student of flight test dynamics should continue his study with more training in experimental instrumentation, sampling theory, and in parameter estimation. Each of these topics offers the flight test engineer more advanced tools.

REFERENCES

1   Anderson, J. D., Jr., **Introduction to Flight** (3rd Edition), McGraw-Hill Book Company, New York, 1989.

2   "Fixed Wing Stability and Control: Theory and Flight Test Techniques," USNTPS-FTM-No. 103, Naval Air Test Center, Patuxent River, Maryland, Jan. 1975 (Revised Nov. 1981).

3   "Military Specification, Flying Qualities of Piloted Airplanes," MIL-F-8785C, Nov. 1980.

4   Etkin, B., **Dynamics of Flight - Stability and Control**, (2nd Edition), John Wiley & Sons, New York, 1982.

5   Roskam, J., **Airplane Flight Dynamics and Automatic Control**, Part 1, Roskam Aviation and Engineering Corporation, Lawrence, Kansas, 1979.

6   McRuer, D., Ashkenas, L., and Graham, D., **Aircraft Dynamics and Automatic Control**, Princeton University Press, Princeton, New Jersey, 1973.

7   Kuo, B. C., **Automatic Control Systems** (6th Edition), Prentice-Hall Inc., Englewood Cliffs, New Jersey, 1991.

8   Chalk, C. R., et al, "Background Information and User Guide for MIL-F-8785B (ASG), Military Specification - Flying Qualities of Piloted Airplanes," AFFDL-TR-60-72, Air Force Flight Dynamics Laboratory, Wright-Patterson AFB, Ohio, Aug. 1969.

9   "Stability and Control Flight Test Theory," Vol. I, Chapter 6, AFFTC-TIH-77-1 USAF Test Pilot School, Edwards AFB, California, Revised Feb. 1977.

10 Cooper, G. E. and Harper, R. P., Jr., "The Use of Pilot Rating in the Evaluation of Aircraft Handling Qualities," NASA TN-D5153, Apr. 1958.

11 Harper, R. P., Jr. and Cooper, G. E., "Handling Qualities and Pilot Evaluation," **Journal of Guidance, Control, and Dynamics**, Vol. 9, Sept.-Oct. 1986, pp. 515-529.

12 Blakelock, J. H., **Automatic Control of Aircraft and Missiles** (2nd Edition), John Wiley & Sons, Inc., New York, 1991.

13 Iliff, K. W, "Parameter Estimation for Flight Vehicles," **Journal of Guidance, Control, and Dynamics**, Vol. 12, Sept.-Oct. 1989, pp. 609-622.

14 Ljung, L., **System Identification: Theory for the User**, Prentice-Hall Inc., Englewood Cliffs, New Jersey, 1987.

15 Dolbin, B.H., "Study of Some Hand-Computing Techniques to Determine the Approximate Short Period Mode from Airplane Responses," FDM No. 371, Cornell Aeronautical Laboratory, Inc., Mar. 1966.

16 Neal, T. P., "Frequency and Damping from Time Histories: Maximum Slope Method," **Journal of Aircraft**, Vol. 4, Jan.-Feb. 1967, pp. 76-78.

17 Nelson, R. C., **Flight Stability and Control and Automatic Control**, McGraw-Hill Book Company, New York, 1989.

18 "Military Standard, Flying Qualities of Piloted Airplanes", MIL-STD-1797A, , Department of Defense, Washington, DC, January 30, 1990 (Notice of Change 1, June 28, 1995; Notice of Change 2, December 19, 1997; Notice of Change 3, August 24, 2004).

19 Eshelby, M. E., "The Metrological Characteristics of a Measuring Channel", Chapter 4, Vol. 1 (Issue 2), **Basic Principles of Flight Test Instrumentation Engineering** (Edited by Borek, R. W. and Pool, A.), AGARD Flight Test Instrumentation Series, AGARDograph 160, 7 Rue Ancelle, 92200 Neuilly-Sur-Seine, France, North Atlantic Treaty Organization, March 1994.

20 Gregory, R., "Transducers", Chapter 5, Vol. 1 (Issue 2), **Basic Principles of Flight Test Instrumentation Engineering** (Edited by Borek, R. W. and Pool, A.), AGARD Flight Test Instrumentation Series, AGARDograph 160, 7 Rue Ancelle, 92200 Neuilly-Sur-Seine, France, North Atlantic Treaty Organization, March 1994.

Index

Chapter **5** Takeoff and Landing Flight Tests (continued)

Chapter 9 Dynamic Stability Tests (continued)

Chapter 9 Dynamic Stability Tests (continued)

Chapter 9 Dynamic Stability Tests (continued)